Bird of Passage

RUDOLF PEIERLS

Bird of Passage

RECOLLECTIONS OF A PHYSICIST

PRINCETON UNIVERSITY PRESS

Copyright © 1985 by Princeton University Press
Published by Princeton University Press, 41 William Street,
Princeton, New Jersey 08540
In the United Kingdom: Princeton University Press, Guildford, Surrey

All Rights Reserved

Library of Congress Cataloging in Publication Data will be
found on the last printed page of this book

ISBN 0-691-08390-8

This book has been composed in Linotron Sabon and Goudy

Clothbound editions of Princeton University Press books
are printed on acid-free paper, and binding materials are
chosen for strength and durability

Printed in the United States of America by Princeton University Press
Princeton, New Jersey

To my teachers and pupils,
and all others with whom I have argued

Contents

Acknowledgments

Numerous friends have read partial or complete drafts of this book, and their criticism has helped me to eliminate some errors of fact, obscure explanations, and awkward phrases. Particular thanks for such help are due to Dick Dalitz, Maureen and Jack Christian, to my brother and sister, and to our children. In checking on old dates and names, the collection of my pre-1974 papers deposited in the Bodleian Library at Oxford, and catalogued by Mrs. Jeannine Alton and Mrs. Harriot Weiskittel of the Contemporary Scientific Archives Centre, proved useful. In fact, most queries could be settled by using the excellent catalogue without going through the cumbersome routine of consulting the papers in the library.

But above all, the standard of the final product owes much to the continuous severe, but constructive, criticism of my wife.

Many of the old photographs reproduced in the book are my own, but I have no record of who took some of the others; my apologies to the unknown photographers. Those taken by known sources have been credited in the figure captions.

I am indebted to the publisher's editor, Mrs. Alice Calaprice, for her efficient help in getting the text tidied up.

Preface

"You are getting very old," said Nino Zichichi, the chairman of the Erice summer school, "you must have known many of the great men of physics that we only read about. Could you not tell us about them?" Well, this is not exactly what he said; he is too polite, but that was the idea. I accepted the invitation to speak, and the lecture proved so popular that I had to give it again and again in different places. Each time, someone would ask why I was not writing my reminiscences, until I began to take the idea seriously. My wife objected strongly at first: "It will not be Literature!" But eventually she conceded that, while perhaps not literature, the result might conceivably turn out to be a readable book.

So I finally decided to try. A title was needed, and I wished I had thought of the title *What Little I Remember* before it was used by Otto Robert Frisch. *Bird of Passage* suggested itself in view of my (and later our) many moves from place to place, except for a somewhat more sedentary period in Birmingham and more recently in Oxford. Some of these moves were imposed by circumstances, but many were by choice. We seem to thrive on the nomadic life.

So here we are. I never kept a diary, and I have lost many of the letters from my early life, so I am writing mostly from memory. This sounds like a very risky undertaking because human memory is frail, and mine is as frail as they come. But it functions more or less like a leaking pot: some of the contents disappear, but what stays is genuine. I am sure I have forgotten many stories that would be worth telling, but what I do remember should be more or less correct.

This book contains many anecdotes and many quite inconsequential episodes. This is mainly so because my memory tends to preserve these incidents above all, but often they also give a vivid picture of a person or a situation.

As I sorted out what to write about I began to realise that my memory, leaky as it is, had preserved too much material. I could not possibly mention every interesting person or place I remembered without letting the book get out of hand. So I looked for rational selection principles. Should I choose the people I liked best, or those I respected most? The most unusual characters, or those with the funniest adventures? Any such rule would have been pedantic. So I decided to take the memories as they came, and present the reader with a random selection from these different types of people and places.

Of course I could not write without mentioning the developments in physics that were such a central part of my life. Yet I wanted this to be intelligible to nonscientists, and I have tried to sketch the nature of the problems in simple language. But this is not meant to be a painless introduction to modern physics. The idea is to give the reader some impression of how it feels to be involved with these problems, and the excitement this process can bring. I hope the reader can get a sense of this thrill even if he or she cannot follow some of the details of scientific explanations.

December, 1984

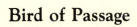

Bird of Passage

1

Origin and Background

Childhood

I was born in 1907. The suburb of Berlin where I was born and grew up was dominated by the cable factory of the Allgemeine Elektrizitäts-Gesellschaft (A.E.G.), of which my father, Heinrich Peierls, was the managing director. He came from a family of Jewish merchants in Breslau (now Wroclaw) and had risen rapidly in the new industrial empire of the A.E.G. He had not been a great success at school; his abilities were not in academics, and the teaching seems to have been very uninspired. So, at the suggestion of the school, he left early. At this time the death of his father had left the family short of money, and he took up a commercial apprenticeship. In his time this involved a very tough regime. Working hours were long. When he asked his employer for permission to leave early on his last day before leaving town on a night train, so that he could have a farewell dinner with his mother, permission was given rather grudgingly: "Your train does not leave until 11." He moved to Berlin to take a junior post in the A.E.G. In approximately twelve years he became the managing director of a large factory.

My father was respected as an outstandingly efficient administrator. He would always anticipate ways in which plans, big or small, could go wrong because of misunderstandings or because people did un-expected things, and he would try to prepare for such mistakes. One of his favourite sayings was, "No man is wise enough to think of all the ideas that can occur to a fool." I am told he was the first to introduce time-and-motion study in German industry.

As a busy man who had to husband his time, he had a device to get rid of visitors who stayed too long. There was a button under his desk that he could press without being noticed, and this would alert a secretary to come in and say he was wanted urgently somewhere in the factory. He once told this to a colleague he visited in his office, who in turn confided his own scheme: when a long-winded visitor would arrive, he would say a code word to his secretary, and she would appear after a reasonable interval to tell him that the deputy director wanted him urgently. At that very moment, the secretary appeared and said just that. My father departed hurriedly in spite of the colleague's protestations that it was all a mistake.

He was good with people because he understood them, and because he respected them with all their frailties. Even now, nearly forty years after his death, I still encounter people who remember his help or kind advice with gratitude. He was not religious and did not like philosophical discussions of ethical principles; but it was obvious to him, and he made it obvious to us, that certain things were just not done.

He was a great raconteur and had an inexhaustible stock of jokes and anecdotes. Many of these were Jewish jokes of the kind that Jewish people liked to tell about each other but did not like to hear from Gentiles. The jokes often poked fun at the stereotypical characteristics of Jews, as in the one about the difference between Jews and Gentiles: "If a Gentile has had a glass of beer and is still thirsty he will say 'Waiter, another glass!' If a Jew has had a glass of beer and is still thirsty, he will go to his doctor and ask 'Have I got diabetes?' " Then, there was the question of what every Jewish housewife possessed: "The best husband, the sweetest children, one room too few, and nothing to wear." He was also not above a rather more primitive kind of humour, as in the riddle: "What is this: You eat with it, you drink from it, you write with it, and you sleep in it?" The answer: "A spoon, a glass, a pen, and a bed."

He also had a great stock of amusing happenings. One of his favourites was the story about the factory director's wife in a small suburb of Dresden, who returned from town on the last suburban train at night, and went to the toilet at the station. She found that the door lock was faulty and could not be opened from the inside. She called for help, but the station staff had gone home, and she was trapped inside. Hours later she heard steps and again shouted for help. The night watchman heard her and opened the door: "But Frau Direktor, what are you doing here?" She explained that the door would not open from the inside. "Nonsense," he said, "I will show you," and before she could stop him, he was inside, and of course the door did not open for him either. So there they both remained until the station staff came on duty in the morning and released them. They promised each other, and also made the station people promise, not to talk about this incident; but because the watchman had not clocked in on his rounds, he had to appear at a disciplinary hearing. The lady had to testify where the watchman had spent the period from midnight to 6 A.M. The result was such embarrassing ridicule that her husband had to move to another town and another job.

Father claimed that people from Breslau were afraid of appearing ostentatious. He used to tell us how, in a train on holiday abroad, some passengers had ticket booklets whose coupons indicated, by their colour, that the travellers had left home, and were returning home, by second class, while all intermediate travel was by first class. Evidently they did not wish to be seen travelling in luxury. He then said, "These people must be from Breslau." And so they were.

He also delighted in teasing my grandmother, his mother-in-law, about the story of the partridge. She was in charge of the household when my mother was away, and the canteen manager, who had been shooting partridge, offered some to us, as was his practice. But my grandmother told him we could not use them. When Father remonstrated, she replied; "You men don't understand these things, but I have checked: they will not keep till Sunday!" The thought of eating partridge on a weekday evidently had not occurred to her.

Father was not very good with his hands, and, for example, he never learned to tie a knot. He had his boots fitted with special hooks on which he could anchor the laces without tying them. He also could not shave himself, and the barber came daily to shave him.

My mother, his cousin, née Elisabeth Weigert, was eleven years younger. She was a gentle person and very attractive. I do not remember her very clearly because from the beginning of the First World War, when I was seven, she was very busy with charitable and other volunteer work, and we did not see much of her. Later she suffered from depression, from which she had barely recovered when she developed Hodgkin's disease and died in 1921.

I was the youngest in the family, being eight and six years junior to my brother and sister, respectively. I was looked after by an adoring nanny, who complied somewhat reluctantly with the injunction not to spoil me. She had originally come into the family to look after the two older children, and when a third child was due she wanted to leave. But she was persuaded to stay. Eventually I became her favourite, for which I can claim little credit. As a small boy I must have been rather spoiled. It was the custom in the household to give two rings on the bell to summon the maid, in order to avoid confusion with the doorbell, and, being a logical child, I decided to extend the principle to using three rings for calling the nanny. She put up with this until the family stopped the practice.

She was a Roman Catholic, and another injunction was not to indoctrinate me, which she observed quite fairly. We children were

5

actually baptised as Protestants. Although our parents were not religious, my father thought this would allow us to make our own choices when we grew up. (I did make my choice when I came of age by leaving the Church.)

We attended Scripture lessons at school, and only gradually became aware of our Jewish origins. In pre-Hitler Germany, being Jewish was a bearable handicap. There was no official discrimination, and discrimination by "private enterprise" was sporadic and could usually be avoided. But one learned to be on one's guard in social encounters. Any new acquaintance might be an anti-Semite, and if one's name and appearance were not too obviously Jewish, one always had to gauge the point at which it would be wise to explain the position, to forestall embarrassment. In some way this was a good education.

Our flat was in a house owned by the factory and was adjacent to it. The address was Kunheimstrasse 1, but the street itself ceased to exist once it was bought by the A.E.G., and we felt distinctly superior living in a nonexistent street. Our suburb Oberschöneweide ("upper beautiful pasture"; its colloquial name, expressing typical Berlin humour, was Oberschweineöde, "upper swine desert") was close enough to the city by train and tram for visits to theatres and concerts, and to entertain guests from the city and other suburbs. My parents entertained a good deal. Many of their friends were musical, some professionally, and both parents had good voices. My mother played the piano a little, and my brother became a good accompanist on the piano, so we had music on most of these social occasions. We had guests on most weekends, and enjoyed games with them in the garden in the summer and indoors in the winter.

Life changed, of course, when the war broke out in 1914. My father became much busier than before and had less time for the family. He also took less time for lunch, which he usually had at home; but he retained the habit of a brief siesta, during which he slept in an armchair for fifteen minutes and awakened rested.

In his attitude toward the war he was a realist and was not caught up by the war fever. Rather, he cursed the inefficiency and stupidity of the government that had involved the country in an unnecessary war. He realised quite early that Germany was going to lose; but he fulfilled his duty in converting the factory to wartime needs, and he worked on committees that organised the use of scarce materials and substitutes. I was too young in 1914 to comprehend the gravity of the situation. For example, one day a guest gave me a little rubber stamp which printed "Gott strafe England" (God punish England), and I delightedly stamped the message onto any object within reach, until my horrified parents noticed and confiscated the stamp.

The wartime shortages made no deep impression on me. There was enough to eat, and if the food was simpler and less interesting than before, I hardly noticed. I do remember that we were not allowed to have both butter and jam on our bread, and even today I feel slightly wicked in taking both.

One day, about a year after the outbreak of war, we were visiting friends, who said they had a special treat for me. They presented me with a bread roll. Rolls had not been baked since the start of the war, and I was specially fond of them, so I bit into this one with great delight. It seemed delicious, if a little dry. Our hosts were amazed. The roll was left over from prewar days, and served as a joke; it was so hard that other visitors had been unable to make an impression on it. A change brought on by the war that pleased me particularly was that the car that was at my father's disposal for official journeys could no longer be used for private purposes, and we used a carriage and horse instead—a much more interesting mode of transportation from the point of view of an eight-year-old.

No close relations were fighting in the war. My brother was called up in 1918, and after completing basic training was sent to France; but the war ended before he had to go to the front. An uncle did serve in the medical corps, and he brought back some interesting stories of his adventures.

In our suburb, my father was an important person, but my parents were insistent that this should not make us feel important. One episode left an impression on me. A cleaner from the factory, called Lehmann, would come to our house to empty the dustbins and perform other small jobs, and by some members of the family he was referred to as "the little dustbin-Lehmann." So I also adopted this usage when talking about him. This brought a sharp rebuke from my parents: "Who are you to talk in this tone about a man who does an honest day's work?" I saw the point of this remark, and took it to heart. Ever after, I tried hard not to presume.

But sometimes my effort at humility became a little pedantic. My morning walk to school took me past the factory gate, where the uniformed porter would salute me. Now, in the German etiquette of the time, there was a firm rule that the socially inferior person must greet the more respected person first. I therefore felt it intolerable that the porter should salute me before I would greet him, so I doffed my school cap before he had time to salute me. But then he started saluting earlier, forcing me to take my cap off at a greater distance, until the exchange of greetings took place as soon as I was visible. No doubt he and his colleagues found this an amusing game. But stripped of the exaggeration, I always remembered the lesson of the little Lehmann.

I recall another episode that illustrates my concern not to exploit my father's status. Our school required its pupils to wear a cap of a different colour, or with different stripes, for each form (grade). One year I had left it too late to order the new cap, and went to the local hatter's shop only a few days before the beginning of the new school year. The hatter was cross and made sarcastic remarks about young gentlemen who could not bring their orders in time and then wanted the work done in a hurry, and he would not promise to have the cap ready in time. When he took down the particulars and heard my name, his attitude suddenly changed: "Oh, the son of Herr Direktor Peierls? We shall certainly have the cap ready." I went home distressed by this flagrant social discrimination. I discovered only much later that this hatter had arrived many years before as a penniless Jewish immigrant, and that my father had helped set him up in business and sent him customers. So the apparent class discrimination was only one kindness done in return for another.

School

I started school a year late. I had to wear glasses for reading, and my parents felt that I could not be trusted to handle this problem at school without losing or breaking my glasses. They were probably right. So for the first year I was taught at home by my mother. I considered this a great deprivation, of course, and counted the days until I could get to school. Within a week, however, I felt school was rather boring. I continued to feel that way for the next two years in preparatory school and for the following nine years in the local Gymnasium in our suburb. The standards in the latter were not high, and I could get good marks without exerting myself, and I was usually at the top of my form. So I never really learned to work hard while I was at school, and that became a handicap later, because learning to work when you are older is much more painful.

In subjects such as history or geography, where one has to know facts, I often failed to know the answers to the teachers' questions. My remedy was to raise my hand enthusiastically, when the teacher would say, "I know that you know it; I want to hear it from the others." On the rare occasions when he could not get an answer from

8

the others and called on me, he would not believe that I knew nothing. "You obviously are not in good form today," he would say.

But I had no such problems with languages. The emphasis was on translating from a foreign language, and I soon discovered that you can understand and translate a text if you know only about half the words in each sentence; it is usually easy to guess the rest. This was a rather unorthodox education in languages, but it was useful, and I have enjoyed translating ever since.

Speaking foreign languages was another matter. In our school the principal foreign language was French, which we were taught for nine years. The teacher was, for most of this time, a man whose command of spoken French was very poor. He explained, "Our object is not to teach you to speak French fluently; any waiter can learn that. We teach you to appreciate the grammar." Our principal was a specialist in French and had written a textbook. So when my parents had some French guests, they invited the principal to dinner, thinking he would enjoy the opportunity to converse in his specialty. But the poor man was afraid to open his mouth the whole evening. After having been taught this way for nine years, I am not surprised that I am fairly good at French grammar, but quite inadequate in conversation. Fortunately I fared better with English, which was taught only for the last four years. We had two young teachers who had been to England and who managed to convey to us their feeling for English as a live language.

Mathematics was easy; it was enjoyable for me. The school had an excellent teacher of mathematics who also had the reputation of being a very strict disciplinarian. Before you got to the forms that he taught, you would hear horror stories about his strict regime and the terrible things he would do to transgressors. One approached his class with apprehension. Yet I never saw him punish anybody, or even speak a sharp word—his reputation was enough to guarantee obedience! He taught us well, and included some unusual but very useful material, such as abridged multiplication, in his course. This kind of multiplication allowed one to do arithmetic without generating more decimals than are significant. For example, when multiplying two numbers of five digits, the normal multiplication would generate a result of ten digits, of which only the first five are significant. It is therefore useful to be able to write down only five figures (or six, for safety) in the first place. The same can be done for division and even for computing square roots. Of course, with the availability of pocket calculators today there is not much interest in how to do arithmetic, but it is still a valuable aid in developing a feeling for numbers.

I was a failure at sports. This was partly because I was usually one of the smallest in stature in my form, but probably it was more due to my innate lack of athletic ability. I tried dutifully to do my best in the gymnastics lessons, but when teams were chosen for games (there were no official competitive games) I was always the last to be picked. I did enjoy swimming, however, but loathed skating, which made me feel clumsy and miserably cold.

I was somewhat clumsy, in general. It was said that my shoelaces were perpetually undone: legend had it that on my way to school, a fifteen-minute walk, I had to stop when nearly there because someone had slammed the front door of our house and trapped my shoelaces. I was also absent-minded enough for a future professor. To illustrate, I recall that I was very proud when I was sent by myself for the first time to make an important purchase: I was to go into town and buy some shirts. I completed this transaction to my satisfaction, but when I got home I found I had left my package in the suburban train.

Much of my time was spent reading rather indiscriminately whatever was at hand, but especially popular science. I enjoyed mechanical toys and started at an early age to play with simple electric circuits; I also tried my hand at small domestic repairs. I was therefore particularly interested in the physics lessons at school, but our physics teacher was not very good. I could often prove him wrong, to his great embarrassment, and I ceased to believe what he said, even when he was right.

I was eleven when the war ended and when the "revolution" led to the Weimar Republic. For the school the immediate result was that its name, Hindenburg-Schule, which had been adopted in the patriotic fervour of the war, gave way to Humboldt-Schule. There were also spontaneous attempts to set up pupil committees, and on a few occasions we even took part in marches to support some not very clear objectives; but all this did not last long.

A typical sign of the times was an article in a suburban paper of April 1920, which we treasured for many years. It said, approximately: "A May Day celebration will be held in the town hall, to which all residents of the area, particularly those with revolutionary-socialist views, are cordially invited. The address will be given by the teacher, Mr. X, who, on previous occasions, such as the Kaiser's birthday, also found moving words."

Most of the teachers at my school soon saw that it was not necessary to be revolutionaries, and they returned to the old ways. In particular, at all assemblies the principal subjected us to subtle reactionary propaganda—for example, by persuading us to support an organisation called "Verein für das Deutschtum im Auslande" (Society for the German Spirit Abroad), which claimed to support cultural ties with Germans overseas, but in fact was an organisation for pan-German propaganda. I did not see many of the political struggles that took place before the Weimar Republic, however shaky, become established. My brother Alfred, then an engineering student, joined a group of volunteers who were to maintain essential services during strikes. I was very envious, because it seemed enormous fun to drive trains or look after electric power stations. No doubt this was also the attraction for the young volunteers. I realised only much later that it was by no means obvious that strike breaking was a desirable activity.

In 1921, when I was fourteen, my mother died. After a short time, a lady came to look after the household, and before long my father married her. She was the daughter of a famous actor, and she had to give up her own career on the stage because of frail health. The position of a stepmother in a family is always difficult, but she tried hard to gain our confidence and affection. I had no more resentment than is usual for a teenage boy against any authority, though things were not made easier by the fact that I soon decided she was not very intelligent. Life was harder for my sister Annie, who had been very close to our mother, and for whom, as a girl of nineteen, the other woman aroused much deeper emotions.

Else, our stepmother (this term was never used in the family), was the sister-in-law of Ludwig Fulda, a well-known poet and playwright. Her family was an interesting addition to our circle. Ludwig's son Carl was about my age, and we saw a good deal of each other. The Fuldas had a house in the Italian Alps, and I spent several summer vacations as their guest. Carl and I spent much time hiking the Dolomites, and we also did some mild climbing.

During this time the economic situation in Germany was worsening, and inflation was rampant. The value of the mark fell at an ever-accelerating rate, until it was finally replaced by a new stable currency at a conversion rate of one to one million millions! This turn of events was a calamity for many, but life remained bearable for those in salaried positions. Wages were paid frequently—sometimes daily—and the money was spent at once, on anything obtainable, because it would have lost much of its value by the next day. But people living on fixed incomes or on their savings were thrust into abject poverty.

I recall many anecdotes, told in a kind of gallows humour, about this runaway inflation. My favourite story is the one about a patient who is discharged from a lunatic asylum and takes a taxi home. When he asks for the fare, the driver says, "4,500 million." When the bewildered passenger says he does not have that kind of money, the driver asks him how much he has. Fishing around in his pocket, he produces a gold 10-mark coin. "Wonderful," says the driver, "you get 8,200 million change." —"Keep the change, and take me back to the asylum!"

The rapid change of the value of the money was confusing to everybody, including Carl Fulda and me. One evening we obtained, through the theatrical connections of Carl's father, some tickets to a very important "first night". When we got to the theatre, we saw a notice that posted the charge for leaving overcoats in the cloakroom (which was compulsory), and we were horrified to find that the charge was beyond our means. We did not want to miss the performance because of our overcoats, so we tried desperately to find someone in the theatre who would allow us to take our coats with us, or lend us some money, or something; but we had no success. Feeling disheartened, we looked at the notice again and discovered that we had misread the number of zeroes! The charge was in fact ten times less than we had thought, and that much money we had.

Among my friends at school I was rather close to Wolfram Schoembs, the son of the principal of the girls' school. This was an interesting friendship, because we were very different. He was artistically talented and wrote poetry, and he tended to regard me as rather a Philistine; but he enjoyed our arguments and discussions. I was very shaken when, at the age of sixteen or so, he committed suicide, and I never understood why.

I met, at intervals, with a group of my school friends for serious discussions about contemporary topics. I do not recall much about those who took part in this discourse except for Heinz Rudolph, who was then my closest friend; he was a rather quiet boy, but we seemed to have similar views on many topics. I do remember, however, many of the subjects we discussed, which included psychoanalysis and Marxism. I shall never regret sitting down with the books of Freud and Karl Marx and making a serious effort to understand their thought. Freud left me rather sceptical, and the economic theories of Marx seemed to me quite ludicrous and illogical, notwithstanding his great insight in recognising some basic social truths. I later found it an advantage, when arguing with convinced Marxists, to have read *Das Kapital*, which most of them had not.

In 1924 the family moved into town. My father had become a member of the board of the company, and had given up his special connection with the cable works, so his work was now mainly in the city. I had one more year at school, and in order not to change schools

I commuted to Oberschöneweide for the last year. I passed the school-leaving examination (*Abiturium*) easily.

The school years also saw the beginning of my friendship with Franz Jacobsohn, a distant cousin, who lived in the city. We enjoyed going for long country walks together. I remember in particular a long tour in which we explored the old towns of southern Germany and talked about big and small problems on the way. He was unusually well informed for someone his age, and had a rational answer for everything, expressed usually with a pungent Berlin humour. I learned much from him, and he seemed to me the essence of an unemotional, no-nonsense person. We kept in touch when we were university students. He studied medicine, preparing to become an eye doctor, like his father.

As a medical student, Franz became acquainted with a woman writer several years his senior. The father of her two children had deserted her, and, being an unpractical person, she did not seem to cope with life very well. Franz made it his business to look after her. Neither of them had much money. His parents objected strongly to this relationship, and under parental pressure he gave up seeing her for a time. He met her again later by accident and found that once again she had got into trouble. He was convinced she needed him in her life, and he disobeyed his parents from then on.

About this time I left Berlin and did not see him again for a long time. I heard the rest of his story only much later. When the Nazis came into power, Franz and his wife (I believe she was his wife by this time) decided to leave the country, leaving the children in a convent school. When their train, on its way to Italy, I believe, stopped somewhere in Germany, they and a number of other passengers were arrested by the police under some pretext. Franz realised that they were in danger. He saw that the inspector in charge of the station was a policeman of the old school, obviously not too fond of the young officers who were bullying people around. So Franz went up to the inspector and said, "I want to complain; we have been robbed. Our property has been taken away without receipt and without being recorded!" He showed the inspector where their confiscated money, and that of other prisoners, had been hidden. The inspector was upset by this evident breach of rules, and, instead of arguing with his younger colleagues, he chose to discharge the couple. Franz's fearlessness and quick thinking certainly avoided much unpleasantness, and very probably saved their lives.

They tried to settle in Egypt, where his medical credentials were recognised. However, one of the local doctors warned him that the other doctors would do everything in their power to obstruct his practice of medicine, as they did not like foreign competition. So they went to Eritrea, but things did not work out much better there. Finally they departed for Ethiopia, where they arrived very ill with malaria. The hotel personnel expected them to die and lodged them in the worst rooms, which were part of a stable, and Franz had difficulty getting someone to call a doctor. Soon thereafter he saw an apparition, a man in a black suit, who said, "I am Dr. Jacobsohn from Berlin."—"Excuse me," said Franz. "*I* am Dr. Jacobsohn from Berlin, and I know you are only a hallucination—you are not really there!" The next day the visitor was back. He was real; it was a pharmacist who managed to get a doctor. After recovering, Franz did settle in Ethiopia and started a practice, and he became personal eye doctor to the emperor. This made him such an important person that people had to step off the pavement to let him pass.

But this state of affairs did not last, because Ethiopia was invaded by Mussolini's troops, and the Jacobsohns had to leave again. They tried to settle in India, but this did not work out, either, and they moved on to Bangkok. Here Franz was able to start a practice, and to found an eye hospital and a school for the blind. The latter project was particularly satisfying because the local tradition was not to care for blind children at all.

When the Japanese occupied Bangkok he continued to practice, but with many difficulties and hardships. By this time he had a son in addition to the stepchildren, but the boy died during that difficult time. They had no electricity, and because Franz needed light for his operations, the boys would take turns pedalling a bicycle whose generator provided a modicum of light. Eventually he managed to acquire a petrol-driven generator, which, however, broke down almost at once. Finally, after Franz's frantic efforts to repair it, it started up again. He promptly used the new source of electricity to turn on the radio and listen to the BBC—just in time to hear the speech in which Churchill announced the dropping of the first atom bomb on Japan and mentioned my name among those who had contributed to the bomb's development. Then the generator broke down again, forever. Franz said it was the most expensive broadcast he ever heard, but it was worth it. They knew that the Japanese had planned to intern all Europeans, and the news meant that they were now safe.

I saw the Jacobsohns in 1953, on my way back from a conference in Japan. They seemed well settled, although I was surprised to find that Franz had never learned to speak Thai. He communicated with his patients via the nurse, and that seemed to function well. He worked very hard, as he never took a partner. He was afraid that the Thai laws were strongly biased against foreigners, so that he would have been entirely at the mercy of any Thai partner. He had hoped that perhaps one of the sons would join his practice, but the boys, who were educated in America, preferred to stay there.

I heard about the sons as a result of a coincidence. In 1975 I was in Seattle and had lost my reading glasses. Needing a prescription to order another pair, I went to the eye doctor closest to the university, and found she was a German refugee who had studied in Berlin. I asked if she knew Franz; she turned out to be one of his friends and had kept an eye on the boys when they were at school in Oregon.

But let us return to the Berlin of 1925.

2

The Student Years

Berlin

I had to make a decision about what subject to study. I wanted to become an engineer because I was fascinated by machinery, by railways, motorcars and airplanes, and by the radio, which was just coming into general use. This was more than a boy's normal interest in mechanical toys; I had read a good deal on these subjects, and sometimes I could explain to my brother and his friends details which they did not know—for example, of the signalling system on the railways. But the family was convinced that I would not make a good engineer because I had to wear glasses, and "an engineer has to have good eyesight". Also, I was rather clumsy with my hands, and "an engineer must be able to make things". At the time, and also now, I did not think that these were good reasons, but I was obedient and accepted the advice of experienced people. So I chose what seemed to be the next best thing, namely physics. In spite of my somewhat irrational method of entering into a physics career, I have no regrets. But I think I could also have been quite happy as an engineer.

Next was the question of whether it was to be experimental or theoretical physics. In the German universities it was useful to decide between these options quite early. For advice on this decision I visited Fritz Haber, the famous chemist, whom my father knew. He asked me what I had read recently and what problems had attracted me particularly, and after listening patiently he said he thought I would be best at doing experimental work. I took note of this advice, but was a little sceptical and decided to keep an open mind.

The normal time for university entry was October, and courses lasting more than a semester were usually started with the winter semester. My school was unusual in having a school year that terminated at Easter, so that I could have entered the university for the summer semester. But this would have meant starting in the middle

16

of some courses, so I put off my entry until the autumn, and as a result had some six months to spare.

If I had studied engineering, I would have, at some stage, spent time in industry to gain practical experience, and I was anxious to do this, anyway. Because I was not going to be an engineer, I could not enter industry through the scheme for engineering students; but I was accepted in the research department of the telephone factory of Mix & Genest (Berlin nickname, *Murks und geht nicht*: "mess and does not work"), a subsidiary of the A.E.G., as an unpaid trainee.

I thoroughly enjoyed that summer. I was taught the proper use of various tools, including a power drill and a lathe, and with these tools produced a number of pieces that were required in the laboratory. This I found very satisfying. But I also took part in some simple experiments, and designed some automatic circuits with relays (this was long before the days of the transistor, and we could not use valves because they used too much power for our purposes). This part of the job was great fun: after we had designed a circuit and put it together, we would call in a colleague who would try to make the circuit malfunction by pressing buttons in the wrong order, or pressing several at the same time, and so forth. Similarly, we would try to pick holes in our colleagues' designs. If I were that age today, I would no doubt enjoy playing with computer programmes.

But now I had to choose a university. I was anxious to see the world and would have liked to go to a university in another town, but according to parental opinion I was too young to leave home. So at the beginning of the winter semester of 1925 I turned up at the offices of the University of Berlin, signed the forms, paid a nominal fee, and became a student of physics.

Before I go on, I had better sketch the system then obtaining in the German universities, because it was very different from that in England or the United States, and, I believe, it was also different from the present German system. There was great emphasis on academic freedom. Anyone who had passed the *Abiturium* had the right to enter the university. Attendance at lectures was not compulsory, and there was not a set syllabus of lecture courses required, for example, for a degree in physics. Practical classes were a requirement, and some universities also had compulsory problem classes in theoretical subjects. In physics there was no equivalent of the bachelor's degree, and unless one wanted to become a schoolteacher, the first examination one would pass was the Ph.D. (called Dr.phil.). There was no fixed duration of study, only a minimum period, usually three years. In physics it

17

was impossible to get to the Ph.D. in three years, but in some other subjects, such as economics, this could be done.

There were no tutorials, and there was no other organised contact between teachers and students. The practical classes were, of course, supervised, usually by assistants. Professors would give their lectures and then disappear. There were exceptions, but these depended on the personal initiative of the professor. This lack of contact changed when the student began to participate in research, that is, when he became what elsewhere would be a graduate student.

There were practically no scholarships. Some competitive grants were available, but they paid only for the very modest fees and carried no subsistence stipend. In partial compensation, students were regarded as "deserving poor". Shops allowed substantial discounts on presentation of a student card; there were student tickets at reduced prices for theatres and cinemas; and there was usually a university canteen (*Mensa*) where simple food was obtainable at a very low price. Nevertheless, students from working-class homes found it a very hard life. The fact that the course of study did not have to be completed in a fixed time made it possible, in principle, to earn one's living while studying, but during the recession finding a job was difficult.

Many students, particularly those in law and economics, the subjects that traditionally served as preparation for careers in business or in government service, were interested only in the credentials they would receive, and not in the subjects. They would therefore spend the first years of their studies having a good time—or what they considered a good time—and attend lectures mainly for amusement (lectures on forensic medicine were popular). In their last year they would go to a tutor to cram only what was needed to pass their exams. A large number belonged to the student "Korps", societies whose tradition went back to the mid-nineteenth century, when student activists took an important part in the fight for democracy. But by now most had degenerated into drinking and duelling clubs. Fortunately that type of student was not common in physics.

On starting in the university, I had to decide for what courses to register. First-year students were not allowed to take the practical physics class, because it was overcrowded, and we were told to postpone this to the second year. Meanwhile we were to dispose of as many of our mathematical and theoretical subjects as possible. Because of this accidental circumstance, I concentrated on theory and mathematics in my first year and have stuck with it ever since. This was not a deliberate decision to ignore Haber's advice, but it suited me.

In my first semester I was registered for thirty-six hours of lectures a week. Of course I did not attend all of these all the time, but I did go to most of them most of the time. Two courses that I abandoned quite soon were in philosophy. By Berlin regulations you could not qualify for the Ph.D., which, after all, was a doctorate of philosophy, without making philosophy one of your subjects, and it seemed wise to get this out of the way. However, I found these lectures unattractive, being reminded of the definition, "Philosophy is the consistent misuse of a terminology specially invented for the purpose."

In physics, I attended the big lecture series on theoretical physics given by Max Planck. It was arranged in a three-year cycle, and in my first semester it had reached the course on optics. Planck's lectures were, I think, the worst I have ever attended. He would read verbatim from one of his books, and if you had a copy of the book you could follow it line by line. I knew that he was a very famous man, but I had no idea what he was famous for. In my school physics, and in what books I had read, there was no mention of the quantum theory. The first indication that there were exciting new things happening in physics came in a lecture course called "X-ray Physics", given by Walther Bothe, later famous as a nuclear physicist. A wise friend had advised me to go to these lectures. Here I heard terms such as the "quantum of action", the "Bohr orbits", and other expressions I had never heard before. These were the first intimations of the new physics.

The main introductory lecture course on physics was given by Walther Nernst. It was customary for the most senior professors to give the elementary lectures that had big audiences. The reason for this was that the lecturer was entitled to a small fee for every student who attended, and by teaching a large class one could augment one's salary. The result was usually good, because it meant that the important introductory courses were given by the most experienced teachers, though, as in the case of Planck, the method was not infallible.

Nernst was a great physicist of rather small stature and an even smaller sense of humility. He had been president of the Physikalisch-Technische Reichsanstalt, the equivalent of the National Physical Laboratory in England or the Bureau of Standards in the United States, and liked to be addressed as "Präsident". Once, when a student came to his office and did not use the correct form of address, Nernst picked up the phone to call his house, and asked for the Frau Präsident. When told she was out, he left a message that the Herr Präsident would be home for lunch at a certain hour. The student took the hint.

He was the inventor of the Nernst lamp, a not-very-successful alternative to Edison's carbon filament bulb. When, in his lectures, he talked about electric light, he would preface the description of the

19

Nernst lamp with the words, "Gentlemen, when Bunsen had to mention the Bunsen burner in his lectures, he always referred to the 'nonluminous burner'. In the same spirit I shall now talk about the 'electrolytic lamp'."

The University of Berlin had a very unique setup in mathematics and physics. The regulations had a provision for students in each subject to organise a *Fachschaft*, a sort of club, which was nonexistent for most subjects or operated in only a very perfunctory way. But a different spirit had developed among the mathematics students. In the period after the First World War, the mathematicians became concerned about the lack of foreign books, which the library could not afford to buy. So student volunteers sat down in relays to copy the essential books in longhand. After that it was only fair that students should be allowed to use the library, but because of the great value of the books, including the handwritten ones, this required supervision. So again, volunteers would take turns guarding the mathematics library.

In my time the need for copying books had passed, but the volunteer librarian service continued, and in this I also took my turn. There was a remarkable spirit of cooperation and it generated many other activities. For example, the "MAPHA" (Mathematisch-Physikalische Fachschaft) organised discussion groups in which the more senior students would help junior ones who had difficulties with their lectures. Since there were no official tutorial classes, and too few problem sessions, this was extremely useful. As the name indicated, the society covered physics as well as mathematics, and many physicists belonged to it; but the centre of gravity was clearly in mathematics, where the need for obscure foreign books and for tutorials was greatest.

The society also had the usual social functions of a student organisation, and one of the highlights was the Christmas party, which one year took the form of a sit-down dinner and was held in one of the university drawing offices. The tables were arranged in the shape of the Hebrew letter Aleph, which was used in the topical set theory of the time. Table linens, plates, and cutlery were brought by members from their homes. The room had to be cleared after the dinner for use the next morning. The chairman of the society, Alfred Brauer (he later made a name as a mathematician in America), ended up staying very late to clear up, and left with a large amount of silver cutlery, elegant tablecloths, and so on, which he had borrowed from his parents. He missed his last train home, but caught one on another line, which, however, required that he walk across a forest. Here he encountered some policemen, who wanted to know where he was coming from at this time of night. When he answered that he had just come from the university, they said, "Then, please, can we see what you are carrying in your suitcase?" He spent the rest of the night in the police station.

Although the initiative in all these activities came from the students, the professors approved, of course, and relations between staff and students were very friendly and informal. Among their courses I remember an excellent one in algebra by Professor Schur, a distinguished algebraist. The lectures were a bit too difficult for a beginner, but I was fascinated nevertheless, and was given a taste of what modern algebra was all about. Another course, simply called "Introduction to Higher Mathematics", covered, in an exercise class, many of the tools of the trade, such as vectors, matrices, and orthogonal sets of functions. I later regretted that other universities did not offer similar courses.

But even with all these lectures, I did not feel that I was pressed for time. Berlin in 1925 was an exciting place, full of intellectual life, theatres, cabarets, lectures on any topic imaginable, and I had time for all of this. I even joined a physical education class run by the university, as I was getting worried about my lack of physical prowess and my poor posture. This class took place at about 7:30 a.m. at a place reached by bus or suburban train, and there was just enough time to get to the university for a 9 o'clock lecture. I do not believe this physical education did much for me.

I was very fond of sailing. My brother had a sailboat, and I had often accompanied him on excursions to the many lakes in the environs of Berlin. During this time he was in America for a few years, and I had the exclusive use of his boat. Of course, this privilege also meant spending much time in the winter scraping and painting the wooden hull and the deck. But sailing in the summer was a just reward. Here again my parents did not have much confidence in my reliability, and I was allowed to sail only under the supervision of an older man, who was appointed for this purpose. I have always remained fond of sailing, but, with the exception of Zurich, I have tended to live in places with no suitable body of water.

I made many friends among the students, including the Sperling sisters: Käte, dark and attractive, who studied mathematics; and Lotte, fair and placid, who studied physics. One day Professor Schur, the mathematician, was ill and asked his wife to phone a message to the mathematics library that he would be unable to lecture. She reported to her husband that Miss Sperling had answered the phone. "Which one?" he asked, wanting to be sure that the message would reach the mathematicians. "Käte or Lotte?" She did not know. "Was she fair or dark?"

In 1933 Käte left Germany and came to stay with us in England for awhile. She later moved on to Copenhagen and married Werner Fenchel, who had been a more senior student in our circle, and who became a lecturer and later a professor in Copenhagen. They were there when Denmark was invaded by the Germans. Although at first Denmark was not subject to much pressure from the Nazis, the day came when they decided to intern all Jews. But the news of the plan leaked out, and practically all Jews, including the Fenchels, were smuggled in fishing boats across the sound to Sweden. Käte and Werner remained there until the end of the war, with the help of generous and kind Swedish friends.

Another student friend, Hans Lehnsen, now lives near Princeton, New Jersey, where I encountered him at a meeting some fifty years later. Then there were the Russian sisters Polyanowski, Esther and Fanya. Esther was a student of physics, while Fanya studied literature and philosophy. In the 1930s Fanya lived in Cambridge, where she married Roy Pascal, a scholar of German, and we became very close to both of them. This friendship continued when all of us lived in Birmingham.

There was Kurt Hirsch, a pure mathematician with a lively mind, who was much involved in the intellectual life of Berlin. His sister, Annemarie Haase, was quite successful as a performer in highbrow cabarets, and his brother-in-law was perhaps the most classical example of an intellectual bohemian I have ever encountered.

There were also the Zarniko sisters. Barbara was a physics student, lively and with very strong opinions on any subject, and I found this characteristic very interesting. She later married Martin Ruhemann, an experimental physicist. When the Nazis came into power, they went to the Soviet Union and worked at the research institute in Kharkov. By this time her strong opinions had crystallised into orthodox Marxism: she could say nothing negative about the Soviet regime, even after they had to leave the Soviet Union in the xenophobia of the late thirties. Of her sisters, one married the science writer J. G. Crowther, the other married Kurt Mendelssohn, a distinguished low-temperature physicist, who settled in Oxford.

As I write this account of my Berlin contacts, it strikes me that all the people I mentioned are Jews, with the exception of the Zarniko sisters, and even two of them married Jews. Perhaps I was subconsciously attracted to Jews because of our similar backgrounds and a similar sense of humour; or perhaps I remember only those who emigrated, while I lost contact with those who stayed in Germany. I do not know the answer.

22

Munich

After two semesters I was convinced that I was old enough to leave home, and my parents no longer resisted the idea. It was known that the greatest teacher in theoretical physics was then Arnold Sommerfeld in Munich, and I enrolled as a student there. There was no difficulty in changing universities, since in any case there was no set syllabus. Of course one had to risk getting into the middle of a two or three-year cycle in theoretical physics again, but I was lucky in that the lecture cycle in my first semester at Munich was just starting with mechanics, the most basic part of physics.

Sommerfeld undoubtedly deserved his reputation as a great teacher. His introductory lectures were a model of clarity. He never let you forget that physics was an empirical subject, and that, although in doing theoretical work you were concerned with laws that could be expressed in mathematical terms, you always had to be clear about their empirical basis. He was also a master at mathematical techniques, and managed to make very sophisticated methods transparent. But his greatest strength lay in the way he could guide research students. He always managed to find problems that were interesting and difficult enough to be worth a serious effort, yet not too difficult for the student.

On first acquaintance he seemed a little formal, even pompous. He, like Nernst, had a favourite title, which was "Geheimrat", a courtesy title given to distinguished academics. An American visitor had at first addressed him as "Herr Professor". Later the situation was explained to the visitor, so at his next call he changed to "Herr Geheimrat". Sommerfeld beamed and said, "Your German is making very rapid progress." (The title was never used, or expected, within the department.)

But this was only superficial. Once you got to know him, you found a human warmth and interest in his students. He owned a cabin in the mountains jointly with the chief mechanic of the institute (although it was an Institute of Theoretical Physics, there was an experimental section, in which Max von Laue had earlier discovered X-ray diffraction). During winter weekends he would often invite parties of students for skiing.

The accommodation available to theoreticians in Sommerfeld's department consisted of two rooms: one was the professor's, and the other was a large room in which his assistant and research students could work and in which seminars were held. For me the most important of the other students was undoubtedly Hans Bethe. He was one year my senior, which meant that he was employed to mark the students' work for the problem classes, including my work. So at first he appeared to be my teacher rather than a fellow student. He was tall and heavily built, and spoke very slowly with a deep and sonorous voice. All this tended to give his statements the air of great authority. This was fair enough, because he did speak on most subjects with great authority.

After a while our differences in age and in seniority seemed to matter less, and we formed a close friendship, which has lasted until now, in spite of many geographical separations. When, during our student days, either or both of us were on vacation, we would correspond and exchange news about physics and other matters. At the time he had the habit of numbering all his letters consecutively, starting with the first ones he had written when leaving home. He also numbered the pages consecutively. I still have his letter No. 710, starting with page 1,055. I do not know how long he kept this up.

Our letters and our conversations were spiced with jargon and with allusions to familiar jokes and anecdotes, so an outsider would find them difficult to understand. For example, we always referred to any excursion in the mountains as "valiantly climbing the rough mountains" because once, when Hans and some friends had set out from a holiday resort in walking clothes, they heard a little boy say admiringly to his mother, "Das sind richtige Männer, die wacker auf die rauhen Berge steigen" (These are real men, who valiantly climb the rough mountains). Another phrase we used frequently was based on a well-known anecdote: In explaining that binocular vision is essential for judging distances, a schoolteacher told the story of Ulysses and how he had put out one eye of the Cyclops, enabling him to escape because the Cyclops could not judge the distance to catch him. When one of the pupils pointed out that the Cyclops had only one eye to start with, the teacher says, "Und das kommt noch dazu" (And that, too). This became our standard phrase for a situation in which someone has missed the main point. Hans was long remembered in my parents' house for a lunchtime visit when my father, who liked to dispose of lunch quickly, apologised for leaving and asked the visitor to continue eating at his leisure. Hans replied, "I always eat slowly and generously."

The image of Bethe dominates my recollection of the Munich period, so that I do not remember much about the others in Sommerfeld's group. There was Bechert, who was Sommerfeld's assistant, and there was Unsöld, who later became a distinguished astrophysicist and whose strong south-German accent I found charming. There were also two Americans, Houston and Eckart, who worked with Sommerfeld on his electron theory of metals. Houston later taught at the California Institute of Technology and then became the president of Rice University in Houston, Texas (the coincidence in names was purely accidental). He was very approachable, and liked to discuss the differences between life in Germany and in the United States. Eckart seemed to me more reserved. Another student was Brück, who later switched to astronomy and became Astronomer Royal for Scotland.

It was an exciting time in physics, and during my Munich days I learned enough to appreciate just how exciting it was. The old physics, based on Newton's mechanics, Maxwell's electrodynamics, and the statistical mechanics of Gibbs and Boltzmann, failed in the atomic domain. It could not account for the stability of atoms, or for the nature of the light they could absorb or emit, and it could not explain why radiation that fills an enclosure would reach a definite equilibrium at any given temperature. Planck had succeeded in explaining the latter phenomenon by introducing the "quantum of action", and his idea was made more precise by Einstein, who introduced the light quantum—or "photon", as we now like to call it—which helped to explain a number of other phenomena. According to this idea light consists of indivisible units, the light quanta, each containing an amount of energy that depends on the frequency, or colour, of the light ($E = h\nu$, where ν is the light frequency, and h is Planck's constant). This idea was almost directly confirmed by the photo-electric effect, in which light striking a metal surface ejects electrons, and particularly in the Compton effect, discovered in 1923, which is really a collision between a light quantum and an electron. But all this seemed to contradict the established fact that light consisted of waves.

Similar ideas were used by Niels Bohr, inspired by Planck and Einstein, to propose an explanation of the behaviour of atoms. In this theory an electron orbiting around the nucleus of an atom can move only in certain selected orbits, defined by a rule in which Planck's constant again appears. This model had an immediate success by explaining the spectrum of hydrogen, the simplest atom, and describing, at least qualitatively, the properties of all atoms. But again there was a contradiction between the old and the new. Newton's mechanics was assumed valid while the electron was moving in one of the "allowed" orbits, but not valid when the electron moved from one orbit to another, causing it to lose energy by emitting light. Sommerfeld elaborated the Bohr rules, and the Bohr-Sommerfeld quantum theory served to explain many phenomena. But it failed with others, and above all it contained a number of internal contradictions.

That was the situation when Werner Heisenberg wrote his famous paper in the summer of 1925, in which he no longer tried to describe the actual orbits of electrons in the atom. Instead, he introduced new rules that would predict the possible energies, but that would also— for sufficiently large systems or for sufficiently high energy—approach the laws of the old mechanics. Heisenberg's ideas were accepted at once by all who could understand the rather abstract new methods. Foremost among those who responded to Heisenberg's idea was Paul Dirac, a young theoretical physicist in Cambridge. After hearing of Heisenberg's first paper, he developed the rest of the theory in parallel with Heisenberg and added many original results of his own.

At the beginning of 1926 Erwin Schrödinger came up with a quite different approach, which assumed that not only light, but also electrons, consisted of waves. What is more, his results agreed with Heisenberg's, and he was able to show that his theory and Heisenberg's were merely different ways of expressing the same thing.

Sommerfeld was particularly enthusiastic about Schrödinger's version. Waves were something one could visualise, and from his earlier work with electromagnetic waves he was familiar with all the necessary mathematical methods. So when I arrived in Munich in the autumn of 1926, everybody was studying Schrödinger's work. I had never learned much about the Bohr-Sommerfeld quantum theory, which I got to know only later. I went straight into Schrödinger's wave mechanics, while also continuing the study of classical physics. Sommerfeld and Schrödinger hoped for a time that the new waves would turn out to be real objects, such as water waves or sound waves. But this view was not tenable because it could not be reconciled with the fact that the electron is indivisible and shows itself as a corpuscle in many other ways.

With both light and electrons, one was faced with the so-called "wave-particle duality": both could be regarded as waves for some purposes and as particles for others. An important step in resolving this paradox was a paper by Max Born in July 1926, in which he suggested that the waves determine the probability of finding the particle in a particular place. This idea was already considered much earlier by Einstein, but it was rejected by him. This interpretation of the theory was further developed in the spring of 1927 by Heisenberg, who formulated his "uncertainty principle", which said that we could not talk about the motion of atomic particles in the same way as we are accustomed to think of the motion of larger bodies, because if we measured some quantities relating to their motion, this would change others in unpredictable ways. So, for example, it was impossible to know both the position and the velocity of a particle to more than a limited accuracy. The more accurately we measure the one, the more uncertain the other must become. As a result we can never speak of the orbit of an electron in the atom, because an observation that would determine one point on the orbit would cause enough of a disturbance to throw it off the rest of the orbit. These thoughts are difficult to get used to because they seem to contradict what our intuition tells us. But our intuition has developed from our experience on the everyday scale, where the same uncertainties exist in principle but are so minute that they escape detection.

At about this same time Dirac wrote a paper that proposed a general theory of how measurements should be described in quantum mechanics. Similar work was also done by P. Jordan in Göttingen. These two papers constitute what is called transformation theory, because they show how one can transform information gained by measuring one quantity into predicting information about another. One day Sommerfeld said to me, "There are these two papers on transformation theory, which none of us has understood yet. Would you like to try to read them and report to our weekly seminar?" Our seminars were usually meetings at which members of the group gave reports on published papers, covering in a semester some section of the subject. Sometimes people would report on their own work, as is now common, but at that time it was the exception.

My task was quite an assignment for a beginner, but after struggling with the two papers I understood the problem and gave my talk. I certainly learned a lot from this exercise; whether the audience learned much, I do not know. Nobody complained; the only person evidently unconvinced was Wilhelm Wien, the professor of experimental physics, who did not believe any part of the quantum theory (although his work had made an important contribution to the early foundations) and therefore was not convinced by my exposition, either.

At this time Sommerfeld was making progress with the electron theory of metals. Until then the understanding of the conduction of electricity in metals had been a very frustrating subject, full of contradictions. From certain experiments one was able to estimate the number of electrons, which was about the same as the number of atoms. The fact that they could carry electricity along a wire showed that they were moving fairly freely. The kinetic theory of heat therefore predicted that they should contribute as much as atoms to the specific heat, and that seemed in accord with the temperature change when a current passed from a hotter to a colder part of the metal. But the measured specific heat showed no sign of a contribution from the electrons.

27

The clue to this and other difficulties came from a suggestion made by Wolfgang Pauli, a former pupil of Sommerfeld's. He had resolved problems in atomic physics, which had worried physicists for a long time, by postulating a new law that applied to electrons, the "exclusion principle". This law stated that no two electrons in an atom could be in exactly the same state of motion. Enrico Fermi in Rome and Dirac in Cambridge had independently concluded that the same must be true for any two electrons, whether or not they are in the same atom, and that this fact would make a profound difference to a substance containing a lot of electrons. Pauli in turn showed how this could explain the magnetic behaviour of metals, which had been a puzzle, and now Sommerfeld was applying the same ideas to the question of specific heat. Even at the absolute zero of temperature, the electrons cannot be at rest, because rest is a definite state of motion, allowed only to one electron. The remaining electrons have to be distributed over other states of motion, and as a result most of them move about quite fast. Upon raising the temperature, they should move a little faster, but most of them are incapable of doing so because that would bring them into states already taken up by other electrons, and as a result there is not much change in their motion with temperature.

The papers containing these findings were being written during my Munich days, and Sommerfeld gave a series of lectures on this subject. It was very exciting to hear about the results as they developed. In these lectures, addressed to people with some background in the subject, Sommerfeld explained the principles very clearly without being pedantic about details. Once, in doing a calculation on the blackboard, he made a mistake by omitting a factor 2. When he approached the final result, which happened to be a formula in which the numerical factor was well known, he realised this would come out wrong, and, without a moment's hesitation, he said, "And then we must remember that there are as many electrons going from right to left as from left to right," and doubled what he had on the board.

Besides the theoretical work, I also did the beginners' physics laboratory, which was not inspiring, and took the lectures in physical chemistry by Fajans, who managed to make the subject exciting. I also attended lectures in mathematics. I remember particularly those by Carathéodory, a charming Greek, whose lectures were not very well organised. On one occasion he came into the lecture room and said, "Yesterday I thought of a proof for the theorem I want to prove today, but on the way to the university I realised that it was wrong." So for the whole hour he tried devising another proof, but got nowhere. As the bell rang, he said, "Oh, I see now that my proof of yesterday is all right!" I found that I gained much more from this kind of lecture, in which you see the mental processes of the lecturer, than from perfectly organised ones, which tend to hide the difficulties and pitfalls.

But it was not all work in Munich. It was a cheerful town, with many young artists and writers. I used to go to a café which was reputed to be their meeting place, but I soon discovered that most of the people were outsiders, like myself, who watched each other under the illusion they were watching artists enjoying themselves. Yet occasionally the right people turned up. I recall the celebration of some anniversary, when Joachim Ringelnatz spoke in honour of the proprietress. He wrote witty and sarcastic verse and is still known to many. On this occasion he claimed to be describing how the owner concocted her pineapple cup, then a popular drink in the place: she filled a bowl with water, took it outside in the sunshine, and let the shadow of a pineapple fall on the water. This irreverent exaggeration was characteristic of his style.

Practically no work was done in Munich during the carnival, or *Fasching*, as it is locally known. There were balls and dances almost every night. At the peak of the celebrations there were processions, perhaps not of the same standard as those in Rio, but they were taken very seriously. The overhead wires of the trams in Munich were fixed well above standard height to allow more freedom for the floats in the carnival procession. I attended some of these balls, of course. On one occasion I was dancing with a local girl, who learned from our conversation that I was from Berlin and thus a Prussian. At first she was shocked by this discovery, but then said, "Well, never mind, they are also humans." This was my first experience with such regional prejudice. I learned later that an expression of regional animosities can be found in the names used for cockroaches: in Berlin we called them *Schwaben* (south Germans), whereas in Bavaria they are *Preussen* (Prussians), which is also the name used in Russia.

I think I only once achieved what was regarded as the ultimate in fast living: to dance until the early hours, then change and catch an early train to the mountains to go skiing. I had learned to ski in Munich and liked it. Skiing is an activity that, unlike skating, you can enjoy even if you do not do it well. At least this was true of the kind of skiing done at the time. There were no ski lifts, and anything that wanted to come down first had to go up, which was accomplished by use of a special climbing wax or seal skins on the skis. This provided a healthy exercise, and gave one the freedom to explore the mountains without depending on organised routes.

I spent many weekends and vacations skiing. We would have occasional adventures, since mountains like to be taken seriously, but fortunately we avoided any major disasters. I recall an incident occurring on a Monday, when Hans Bethe and I were peacefully working in the seminar room after a skiing weekend. Evidently he had got frostbite when skiing and complained about pains in his foot. We took him by taxi to hospital, where a young doctor was very unsympathetic. He not only poked the foot more violently than necessary, causing severe pain, but he also expressed the opinion that Hans would never walk again. In any case, it was clear that the patient should go home to his family. The only problem was that he had to change trains to do this, and it took some organising skills to make this arrangement. We put him on the train after having sent a telegram warning the station master at the intermediate station. He had a porter with a wheelchair meet the train, and the patient was safely conveyed to the connecting train. And fortunately, Hans soon regained use of his foot.

Another Munich friend was Hans Thorner, a medical student. He made a serious, almost gloomy first impression and talked slowly, with a sonorous voice that showed interest and concern—in fact, he had a good bedside manner; he ended up becoming a psychoanalyst, and I suppose the perfect couchside manner is not so different. He had an excellent sense of humour. One Christmas season I went for a week's skiing with him in the Austrian Alps, trusting, as many still do today, that you can be sure of snow at Christmas. But that year the weather was warm, and there was no chance of skiing. We decided instead to walk to the top of a nearby mountain. The path went up the southern slope most of the way, but the last part was on the northern side, which still had some hard, crusty snow. After a while we became uncomfortable and decided to turn back. Then, at a place we had already passed safely going up, the crust broke and started to slide down, taking me along with it, while Thorner managed to jump clear. The snow and I started rolling downhill, causing a minor avalanche— a very unpleasant experience. Fortunately we hit something hard, which made the snow scatter, and I found myself sliding along on my own and eventually stopped. The snow continued its descent into the valley, leaving me with a deep respect for traversing steep, snowy mountain slopes.

We often spent summer weekends walking in the mountains. On one occasion a party including Hans Bethe and Hans Thorner decided to go up the Zugspitze, the highest mountain in Germany. This is normally a very easy walk, but while we were on the way up, a blizzard started. As it was June, we carried no warm clothes and got miserably cold. We did have a first-aid kit, and wrapped bandages around our

hands to make it easier to hold our sticks. We reached our destination—the alpine refuge—but after a while, as the storm showed no
signs of abating, we made our way across to a big hotel, from where
there was a cabin lift down the mountain. Many people were waiting
to make the trip, but after an hour or two it was announced that the
storm was too strong and the lift would stop running. This left us
marooned at the top, with all the other people who had come up in
the lift. All of us had lectures or other engagements the next morning,
and the cost of spending the night in the hotel was out of our range.
So we decided to leave. By now it was dark, and the descent in the
storm looked difficult, so we hired two guides with a rope. With one
guide at each end of the rope, and everybody else in between, we ran
down the mountain. All went well, and the only unpleasantness I
remember was being stuck underneath a little waterfall without being
able to move forward or back because the person behind me had
stumbled, and the one ahead wanted to move on, so they held the
rope taut.

Other companions on our walks were two Greeks, one an experimental physicist and the other a mathematician, very appropriately
named Embirikos and Kritikos. Embirikos was with us when we went
on a walk that crossed into Austria, and he was worried because
foreigners were not allowed to cross the border without papers. As
German citizens did not have to show any papers, we said, "Don't
worry, who will know that you are not German?" But when we came
to the border post, the guard said very politely, "Excuse me, you are
from the Balkans, aren't you?" At the time I was most impressed, but
now, with more experience, I could probably have done the same.

In Berlin I had been very impressed by the student organisation
MAPHA, and decided such a group would also be useful in Munich.
I discovered the university made provisions for such societies in the
rules, and they could even claim a modest amount of money for expenses. So I set about organising a group, and succeeded in getting a
reasonable number of students to come to meetings. I was elected
chairman, and the other officer elected was one of the Korps students.
He was a serious student of mathematics, but socially there were
complications. He explained to me that I should not be offended if
he did not greet me when I met him in the uniform of his Korps—the
rules of his organisation did not allow him to be seen in contact with
non-Korps students outside the classroom. The rules of these societies
made a class distinction between people who were *satisfaktionsfähig*,
i.e., with whom it was de rigeur to have a duel (mostly students of
other Korps), and others. In one university this led to a memorable

resolution about women students: on social occasions outside the university, they were to be treated as ladies; but a woman student in the classroom, or clearly on the way to or from the university, was nothing but "ein nicht satisfaktionsfähiger Kommilitone". But between the two of us we managed the MAPHA activities with reasonable success. Unfortunately, nobody else came forward willing to share in the responsibility or to show some initiative. The society folded up soon after I left Munich. This taught me that it takes more than good intentions and a reasonable objective to run an organisation.

Leipzig

In the spring of 1928 Sommerfeld left to spend a year in the United States, and on his advice I went to Leipzig, where Heisenberg had started a school of theoretical physics. I arrived there in the summer semester of 1928. Heisenberg was a very different personality from Sommerfeld, with not a trace of the "Geheimrat" about him. In fact, he was very modest in manner, and if you met him casually you might not have guessed that here was a great scientist, at least until you noticed his eyes, whose sparkle expressed enthusiasm and intelligence. Before the weekly seminar, there was tea, and for that purpose the professor would go out to a nearby pastry shop to select a suitable collection of cakes for the participants. At least this was my recollection; however, it has been challenged by Guido Beck, then Heisenberg's assistant, who told me that it was *his* job to get the cakes. I accept this correction; he should know, and also, as a Viennese, he was certainly a most suitable person to be entrusted with the job. I must have remembered some occasion when Beck was out of town. In any case, even if not true, the story is consistent with Heisenberg's informal attitude.

Heisenberg was appointed to the Leipzig chair at a very young age. He had been very active in the Youth Movement, and the story goes that, when he was visiting his parents' house in Munich shortly after his appointment, a journalist who wanted to speak to the new professor was told by the maid, "No, the professor is out with the Wandervögel" (which was something like the Boy Scouts).

In moments of leisure, our group would adjourn to the basement of the institute for a game of table tennis. Heisenberg was very good, and his ambition to excel at the game was more obvious than his ambition to be a great scientist. It was therefore a sensation when a Chinese visitor arrived and beat Heisenberg. I have been told that on a tour around the world shortly afterwards, he spent most of the voyage across the Pacific practising table tennis, to prevent a repetition of this disaster.

Where Sommerfeld enjoyed doing mathematics, for Heisenberg it was just a necessary tool. When he was faced with a problem, he would almost always intuitively know what the answer would be, and then look for a mathematical method likely to give him that answer. This is a very good aproach for someone with as powerful an intuition as Heisenberg, but rather risky for others to imitate.

When I arrived in Leipzig, Heisenberg was working on the theory of ferromagnetism. It was known that the magnetism of such substances as iron was due to the "spin" of the electrons inside the substance. Each electron spins like a little top, and in the iron there is a "molecular field", a force that tends to align the spin of each electron with that of its neighbours. But the nature of this field was unknown. It could not be a magnetic effect because magnetic forces are much too weak to account for the observed behaviour. Heisenberg saw that the answer lay in the Pauli exclusion principle, which says that no two electrons can be in exactly the same state. Thus two electrons with the same spin orientation keep out of each other's way; while this repulsion may increase their energy of motion, it diminishes their mutual repulsion, and can therefore lead to a decrease in total energy, making the parallel alignment of the electron spins energetically favourable. He had encountered this mechanism in the theory of atomic spectra and concluded that it was also responsible for ferromagnetism.

However, calculating the energies of all possible configurations of electron spins was a prohibitively difficult task. So he used a rather crude approximation that predicted that ferromagnetism required each atom in the solid to have at least eight neighbours. It also predicted that ferromagnetism should disappear not only at very high temperatures, which is true, but also at very low temperatures, which is false. Heisenberg's explanation of the nature of ferromagnetism remains valid; his calculation has been forgotten.

My first task in Leipzig was to follow up one of Heisenberg's ideas about an experimental result. An observation had been made that the spectral lines in light emitted by canal rays were wider than expected. Canal rays consist of fast-moving atoms that have lost an electron, so they are positively charged and are accelerated in the electric field of a discharge tube. They are drawn into the cathode, and can be made to appear behind it if there are holes or "canals" through the metal (hence the name). Heisenberg suspected that the extra width was due to their quick passage past the spectrometer slit, so that they could be observed for only a short time. This would have been a nice illustration of that form of the uncertainty principle that links the length of time of an observation with the uncertainty of the energy, or frequency, so that the greater uncertainty in the light frequency would broaden the spectral lines.

I set to work with enthusiasm. Because of my lack of experience, I had to sort out many aspects of the problem. For example, I had to decide whether the motion of the atoms should be described by quantum mechanics, or whether it would be enough to use Newton's mechanics. Finally, after a week or two, I had sorted out my approach and started to make it quantitative. It became clear immediately that the explanation would not work. The time during which the atoms were visible was much too long for the uncertainty principle to be of any importance. I went back to Heisenberg, fearful of having missed the point, but he agreed at once that the explanation was unsuitable, and that he must have misunderstood what the experimentalists had told him. The time taken by this little abortive calculation was not wasted, however. It gave me some experience in setting up an approach to an unfamiliar situation, and, better still, it got me into the habit of never starting an analysis without first working out the orders of magnitude of the relevant effects on the back of an envelope.

My next assignment concerned a much deeper problem. It related to the work of Felix Bloch, who was Heisenberg's first research student. He carried the electron theory of metals a step beyond the work of Sommerfeld, which I had watched in Munich. While this had explained some previously paradoxical features in the behaviour of metals, it could not explain the great ease with which electrons appeared to move through the structure of the metal. The magnitude of the electric conductivity of a reasonably pure metal showed that an electron could travel many times the distance between atoms with only a small chance of hitting something on the way. This average distance travelled before making a collision, the "mean free path", became even larger at lower temperatures, and this, too, seemed incomprehensible.

Bloch's explanation was based on the wave nature of the electron. In a perfectly regular periodic structure, such as the lattice network formed by the atoms in a metal, waves can progress indefinitely without being deflected. The motion of the waves—and hence of the electrons—is impeded only by the irregularities caused by the heat motion of the atoms, and by impurities and other imperfections of the structure. He could explain the effect of temperature and of impurities on the conductivity of metals.

Bloch was still in Leipzig, finishing his thesis, when I arrived there, and I benefited greatly from my discussions with him. One's first impression of him was that of a solid Swiss citizen, but his slow and deliberate speech hid a nimble mind and a warm sense of humour. He was a keen mountaineer, and a few years later nearly lost his life in a climbing accident. He was on a climb with the Swiss physicist Egon Bretscher and his wife when, walking along a ledge, he slipped, and Bretscher, behind him on the rope, was able to hold on to a rock. In falling, Bloch broke his leg, which got caught in a crack, but this probably broke his fall and allowed Bretscher to take the strain. He was hauled back to the ledge, which had enough room for him to lie, Mrs. Bretscher to sit, and Egon Bretscher to stand. They spent the night that way, and in the morning Bretscher went down to get help. Though completely exhausted he wanted to go up again to guide the stretcher party to the scene of the accident, but they did not let him. Eventually Bloch was brought down and taken to a hospital.

In the thirties Bloch moved to Stanford, where he remained until his recent death. He produced many important ideas there, including work on magnetic resonance, for which he was awarded the Nobel Prize.

But to return to Bloch's Leipzig thesis. His method of describing the electrons in a metal disregards the fact that, having like electric charges, the electrons repel each other. In other words, his theory treats an electron as equally likely to find itself near an atom that already has its full complement of electrons, and is electrically neutral, as near one that has an electron missing and is thus positively charged. Heisenberg suggested that I try to see what one could do with the opposite extreme, assuming that each atom always had its correct complement of electrons, so that the electrons could only change places. This approach had been applied successfully to the theory of molecules by Heitler and London. After struggling with the problem for some time, I concluded that this model would not give any conductivity at all. To get any current through the system, it would be necessary for all the electrons in a row to jump at the same time, and the chance of this was entirely negligible.

At about this time I spent a summer vacation in England, in the course of which I briefly visited Cambridge. I plucked up my courage to call on Dirac, whom I had already met when he visited Leipzig to give a talk. He was extremely kind, and introduced me to R. H. Fowler, then the senior theoretical physicist in Cambridge. Fowler was delighted to hear that I came from Leipzig and said, "You must tell us about the work of Bloch. It happens that we have no speaker for this week's meeting of the Kapitza Club, so you can talk there." It did not occur to me to refuse, though neither my English nor my recollection of the details of Bloch's work was really adequate.

The meeting of the Kapitza Club, which was then the main forum for discussing physics in Cambridge, went off without disaster. I was conscious of the fact that I would not have been asked to speak if Fowler had realised how raw a beginner I was. This experience was typical of what happens when you visit new places—people are not too clear about your status and qualifications, and you get a chance to show what you can do. This is one benefit of being a "bird of passage".

I had told Fowler about my attempt to treat electric conductivity by the Heitler-London model, and he told me that his student, W. H. McCrea, was trying to do the same. He tried to get us together, but McCrea was not around. By a curious coincidence, I met him the following weekend at a student gathering that had nothing to do with physics. It turned out that his project was not similar to my abortive one, after all. When I encountered him again years later, he had become a distinguished astrophysicist. To add to the improbabilities, I also met a young girl, Netta Koutane, at this gathering, and I saw her again some ten years later in Bristol as the wife of the physicist Ronald Gurney.

When I was back in Leipzig, Heisenberg suggested a new assignment, which proved fruitful. The problem concerned what was then called the anomalous Hall effect. If an electric conductor carrying a current is also exposed to a magnetic field, it develops an electric potential difference at right angles to the current. This is explained by the magnetic deflection of the electrons carrying the current. But some metals showed an effect of the opposite sign, and this had been one of the great puzzles of the classical electron theory of metals.

My job was to see whether the new mechanics could throw any light on this riddle. At last I had a problem to sink my teeth into. Bloch had shown that the possible states of motion of electrons in the periodic crystal lattice of the metal grouped themselves into bands, and within each band the state of motion was characterised by a wave vector k, which is inversely proportional to the wavelength. For tightly bound electrons, these states could be worked out explicitly. This showed that if an electron started from rest and an electric field was applied, the wave vector of the electron would grow until it reached the maximum possible in the band, and would then appear at the opposite edge of the band. The velocity with which the electron moved, increased at first, then reached a maximum and finally decreased again to zero at the band edge, growing in the opposite direction when the electron passed from the opposite band edge toward the centre.

This meant that the electron was, at some stage, being accelerated in a direction opposed to the force of the field, and this looked promising for explaining the odd behaviour. But first one had to make sure that all these deductions were right, which meant finding a simple proof for the dependence of the velocity on the wave vector, and for the way the wave vector changed as a result of the applied field.

One worry was that this odd behaviour might in some circumstances lead to a negative conductivity, i.e., to a current flowing in the opposite direction to the field, which would have indicated that the theory must be wrong. But I found this worry was unfounded. Because of the Pauli exclusion principle, the electrons must be spread over the available states; but they settle down to the states of lowest energy, so that as more electrons are added, the energy levels in the band fill up like a bucket fills with water. The states lowest in energy behave normally in the field, and so at any level of filling there are more states in which the electrons accelerate in the right direction than in the wrong direction. The current caused by the field thus always flows in the right direction. When all the states in the band are filled, the "right" and "wrong" accelerating electrons just cancel out.

Indeed, when the band is full, the Pauli principle allows each electron to move only into a state vacated by another. The result is only a game of musical chairs, and as the electrons are indistinguishable, this is the same as no change, so no current is produced. If the band is almost full, it is easier to think of the few empty places moving, rather than counting up what happens to each of the many electrons. Each empty place, or absence of an electron, carries a positive electric charge, and in this sense the almost full band is like a system in which the carriers of electricity are positive. No wonder their acceleration is in the "wrong" direction.

I still had to find what the magnetic field did to the electrons, but this turned out to be fairly straightforward. It showed that once again the behaviour near the top of the band was like that of a positively charged particle. So now I had my explanation: if the band containing the conduction electrons was nearly full, the Hall effect would be positive, i.e., anomalous; if it was nearly empty, it would be negative, i.e., normal; and in between, it changed sign somewhere. Heisenberg, who had kept an eye on my work and had given constructive advice when I ran into difficulties, was pleased and told me to write up my results for publication. He also arranged for me to report to a regional meeting of the German Physical Society.

I remember a significant conversation with Heisenberg, but unfortunately I cannot remember when it took place. He told me, "This situation looks very similar to one I have encountered in atomic spectra, where the spectrum of an atom with one or two electrons in the last shell is very similar to that of an atom that has one or two electrons missing from the complete shell." I wish I could remember when he said this. If it was when I presented my results, it simply meant that he appreciated their significance immediately. If it was said when he introduced me to the problem, then he knew the answer from the beginning (which is quite believable, considering his powerful intuition) and left me just to work out the mathematical details.

While I was a student at Leipzig I chose to take part in the advanced practical laboratory, though this was not usual for theoretical students. I had not found the elementary laboratory classes in Munich very useful, since they consisted of prepared experiments; they were probably useful for students who had never wired up an electric circuit or read a galvanometer. Perhaps they should have provided training in keeping notes on experiments, for which I certainly had little talent; but in Munich such note keeping was not considered important.

The advanced laboratory in Leipzig was much different from the elementary lab in Munich. We were required to build up our experiments from the beginning. One of my tasks was to measure the fine structure of one of the mercury lines by using a simple spectrometer and a parallel-plate interferometer. For the latter I was given a good optically flat glass plate and told to put on a partly transparent silver coating. The books in the library stressed the importance of cleaning the glass and suggested immersing the plate for a certain length of time in a caustic-soda solution of a certain strength. I wanted to make quite sure of getting a good silver coating so I used twice the recommended strength and left the plate in for twice the recommended time. As a result I got a beautiful coating, but when I tried to look for the interference fringes, there were none. "Nonsense," said the supervisor, "I'll show you." But he could see no fringes, either, and went away shrugging his shoulders. After some time it dawned on me that by my fierce cleaning I had ruined the flatness of the plate. I guessed it would still be flat enough over small areas, so I covered it with black paper with only a small pinhole in it—and there were the fringes. Of course, this wasted a lot of light intensity, so I had to make a long exposure to get my photographs, but I did complete the experiment.

This laboratory was done in the experimental part of the institute headed by Peter Debye. He was famous for inventing a method of X-ray crystallography together with Paul Scherrer of Zurich, and was a master at finding simple approximate models for apparently complex physical situations. He looked like a prosperous businessman and was rarely seen without a cigar. Rumour had it that he was very good at negotiating a high salary for himself by exploiting competing offers from other universities.

There was also a second chair of theoretical physics (I believe it was actually called mathematical physics), which at first was held by Gregor Wentzel. He had helped in the early stages of the development of quantum mechanics, and had an excellent instinct for what was important. He was very even-tempered; I believe I have never seen him excited or ruffled. After my first semester in Leipzig, he moved to Zurich and was succeeded by Friedrich Hund. Hund came from Göttingen, where he had worked with Max Born, and looked much younger than his years—more like a boy scout than a professor. His very modest manner concealed the fact that he was the greatest expert on atomic spectra.

Heisenberg's assistant was Guido Beck, whom I already mentioned in connection with the cakes for the weekly tea. He was an extremely sociable person with an incredibly wide acquaintance among physicists and an encyclopaedic knowledge of many branches of physics. When Hitler came to power he left Germany for a professorship in Odessa, where he stayed until the xenophobia of the Soviet Union in the late thirties forced him to leave. He went to Paris and managed to get away from the German-occupied part of France, only to be interned in Vichy France. Eventually he slipped out over the Pyrenees to Portugal, and from there went to Latin America, where he still lives. He spent periods living in Brazil and in Argentina, moving from one to the other according to where the dictatorial regime was less unbearable at the time. He has now settled in Brazil, but one can still encounter him almost anywhere between Vienna and Copenhagen, Odessa or Africa, visiting his many former students and friends or seeking new adventures.

Through Beck I met George Placzek, who was a frequent visitor to Leipzig. He was a young man of unusual charm. In spite of his great ability, erudition, and savoir faire, he managed to be quite disorganised in small things. He was born in what is now Czechoslovakia, so he was a Bohemian in both senses of the word. He travelled a great deal but never managed to pack his things in time. When we met his train, it was not uncommon for us to discover that he was almost carried on to the next station while frantically stowing some of his belongings into an overstuffed suitcase. He would emerge at the last second, probably leaving some items behind, and trying to keep things from falling out of his bag.

Placzek liked a good argument. Close to the Physics Department in Leipzig was a swimming pool with a restaurant, where we used to go for lunch and a quick swim. Once, Placzek appeared in swimming trunks, and the attendant wanted to send him back to the changing room because the rules required that men wear full swimsuits. George pointed to several bathers who had one shoulder strap undone and half their chests uncovered. "That is all right," he was told by the attendant, "as long as one side is covered."—"What other requirements are there?"—"That is all. One side must be covered." The next day he appeared in a swimsuit he had bisected vertically, so that it covered his right side completely, and the left side was held up with string. Of course he was not surprised that the attendant turned him back again, in spite of his insistence that he had meticulously met the conditions as stated.

We became friends and his name will appear again many times in my narrative.

Zurich

In the spring of 1929, when I had been in Leipzig for two semesters, Heisenberg went to the United States for a time, so I moved again. On his recommendation I joined Pauli at the E.T.H. (Eidgenössische Technische Hochschule, the Federal Institute of Technology in Zurich). The fact that Switzerland was a different country had no significance for me at the time. I had visited Switzerland before on vacations; the differences in accent and customs did not seem greater than variations within Germany, and the E.T.H. was a German-speaking institution with many, if not all, of the German academic traditions. But I looked forward to meeting Pauli with some apprehension; his sharp tongue and witty but merciless comments had a formidable reputation.

In fact I did not, in these early days, find any cause for alarm. Pauli received me in the most friendly manner, his well-rounded body radiating good will. His daily routine involved appearing in the institute just before lunch, looking through his mail, and then going off to lunch in the company of anyone who was around and willing to join him. Not everyone would join him every time, as his favourite eating places tended to be beyond our means, and he would not descend to our level of dining.

At the beginning of the Zurich period, I had another project, besides settling down in the institute. Before leaving Leipzig, a publisher had invited me to translate a new book on wave mechanics by de Broglie from French into German. The situation was that no French publisher had the courage to publish a book on what seemed a very esoteric subject. (It was published in French only years later, when the Nobel award to de Broglie seemed to create sufficient demand.) But it was to be published in German and in English, and it was clearly a commercial advantage to be first. So I was asked to do the translation as fast as possible, which was a challenge I liked. The publishers paid for a typist, to whom I dictated the translation, and we got the job done within a few weeks.

I found the contents of the book very interesting. De Broglie was unhappy about the probability interpretation of wave mechanics, and tried, in the book, to establish an alternative in which the waves would have some physical reality. In a serious analysis he came to the conclusion that no such alternative interpretation was feasible, and that one had to accept the standard interpretation of Born, Heisenberg, and Bohr. He later changed his views again.

My translation turned out to be very satisfactory, in spite of the speed with which it was done; but this could not be said for my proofreading. I have never been very good at reading proofs, and this was my first experience, apart from the few papers in journals, where the publisher's proofreading standards were high. In particular, the equations, which were copied directly from the French manuscript, looked very beautiful to me, but I missed seeing the many little errors in them. My negligence was not discovered until the book was already printed, so a substantial errata sheet had to accompany it, to the publisher's great annoyance.

Soon afterwards Pauli suggested a new problem for me to work on. This related to the vibrations of atoms in a crystal lattice. To a good approximation the equations for these vibrations are linear and therefore relatively easy to handle. They had therefore formed one of the earliest important applications of quantum theory, pioneered in a famous paper by Einstein, which showed that quantum theory could explain the low specific heat of solids at low temperatures. This was followed by the more accurate calculations of Born and von Kármán, and the elegant simplified approximation of Debye, the master of simplified models.

But it was also known that for some purposes the small corrections due to the deviations from linear behavior, the so-called anharmonic terms, were important. These terms cause a coupling between the otherwise independent waves of different length and direction. They are responsible for the absorption of sound waves, which, in the linear approximation, could travel indefinite distances without damping, and for the heat conductivity. Without damping, the waves would carry energy freely and would give infinite heat conductivity, as in a perfect gas whose molecules did not collide with each other.

Pauli had looked briefly at the problem of sound absorption and reported his results at a conference. An abstract of this talk was published, but he never wrote a full paper because he had some doubts about his calculation. He showed me his notes (about four handwritten pages) and suggested I look at the effect of the anharmonic terms, particularly for the conduction of heat. Debye had already written a paper on thermal conductivity; but it was a classical treatment, expected to be valid only at high temperatures, at which quantum effects are negligible. It evidently needed generalising to include quantum effects.

It turned out that the discussion in terms of the quanta of vibration, or, as they are now called, the "phonons", becomes much easier to visualise, so that it pays to use this description even when quantum effects are unimportant. If we keep track of the numbers of quanta in each possible wave, the most important processes caused by the anharmonic terms are "three-phonon processes", in which two phonons combine into one, or, conversely, one splits into two. If two phonons of frequencies ω_1 and ω_2 combine into one of frequency ω_3, the condition $\omega_1 + \omega_2 = \omega_3$ must be satisifed. This rule expresses the conservation of energy, since the energy of a phonon by the basic rule of quantum theory is Planck's constant times its frequency. The same rule follows in a classical description from the way frequencies combine in "combination tones" or beats.

In addition, spatial interference leads to a similar rule about the wave vectors, which, in a continuous medium, would have the form

$$\vec{k}_1 + \vec{k}_2 = \vec{k}_3.$$

Here the k are directed quantities, in the direction in which the wave is travelling, and of the magnitude of the inverse wavelength. The " + " sign indicates a composition by the parallelogram rule.

In the crystal, its atomic structure allows more general combinations, in which, together with the change of two phonons into one, there is a diffraction by the crystal lattice. This results in the addition of a fixed amount, of the order of the inverse of the atomic spacing, to the equation. This is evident from the fact that there is only a limited range of the wave vectors k, because in a wave consisting of the motion of atoms, a wavelength shorter than the distance between atoms makes no sense. If, for example, k_1 and k_2 are in the same direction and near the maximum permissible, their sum would lead to an excessively large wave vector, i.e., too short a wavelength. The diffraction, which just straddles the whole range of permissible wave vectors, brings us back to a permissible point, a wave travelling in the opposite direction. For this process I used the German term *Umklapp* (flip-over) and this rather ugly word has remained in use.

The important point about these Umklapp processes is that they become extremely rare at low temperatures, because they require the presence of very short-wave phonons, which, at low temperatures, are in short supply. Without them, the phonon system could not come into equilibrium, because the sum of the wave vectors of all the phonons could not change, so any forward drift could not be stopped. As a result, thermal conductivity becomes infinite in the absence of such Umklapp processes, and it becomes very large at low temperatures, when the Umklapp processes are rare.

All this is true for perfectly pure crystals. Impurities or imperfections can also result in deflecting phonons from their initial direction, without the intervention of Umklapp processes. I did not appreciate at the time that, to be perfect for this purpose, a crystal must not contain different isotopes, i.e., atoms of different weight, since these respond differently to the vibrations, and therefore act as impurities. Because of this oversight, the experimental discovery of the rapid rise of thermal conductivity at low tempertures, which I had predicted, was delayed, and it was not until 1951 that Berman in Oxford found the effect in some substances and noticed that these happened to be the ones that did not contain different isotopes.

I also saw that my results disagreed with Debye's, because he had treated the crystal as a continuum and had neglected the Umklapp processes. Yet he had found a finite thermal conductivity. It took me some time to discover what had gone wrong in his simple treatment: he had based his argument on the analogy between the scattering of lattice vibrations, i.e., phonons, and the scattering of light, for which there existed a well-known treatment. In both cases the phonons caused variations in the local density that were responsible for the scattering of light and of the phonons themselves. He had, however, overlooked the fact that in the case of light, one could regard these changes in density as standing still, because the speed of light is so fast that they move little while the light is passing over them. But for the scattering of phonons they must not be regarded as standing still, because the speed with which they move is just the speed of phonons.

Pauli's result was wrong, too, because he had found a damping of sound in a linear chain of atoms, whereas there are no three-phonon processes possible in this one-dimensional case. He made the error only because he used some confusing notations. By going into the specific form of the dependence of frequency on wavelength too early, he arrived at rather complicated equations, so one could not see the wood for the trees.

I reached these conclusions in the summer of 1929, and wrote them up for my thesis. For my birthday in June my parents had given me a portable typewriter, and I decided to type the thesis myself. The result was a typescript that was not beautiful but acceptable. One semester's residence in Zurich was not sufficient to qualify for a Ph.D., so I submitted the thesis to Leipzig, where two semesters were sufficient. For this purpose I returned to Leipzig in July.

In retrospect, the period from April to July appears rather short for all that seems to have happened. I have no recollection of being pressed for time (except in the first few weeks when I was doing the translation). There was plenty of time for concerts and cinema, and for sailing. It was then easy to rent a sailboat for a few hours, and I liked to take friends out on the lake. I even persuaded Pauli to come sailing— I cherish a photo showing him, Robert Oppenheimer, and I. I. Rabi on the boat. There was also a conference, the *Röntgenwoche* (X-ray week), held in Zurich during that time, and one could meet many famous physicists in the lecture room or on the swimming beach of the lake. There must have been more hours in the day then!

In Leipzig, I had to arrange my Ph.D. examination. The custom was that one could express a preference for certain examiners, and the preference was usually honoured. For physics the obvious choice was Hund, the second professor of theoretical physics, since Heisenberg was abroad. For mathematics I chose Liebermann, whose lectures on differential equations I had attended; and for chemistry I chose the physical chemist, LeBlanc. Custom required one to call on the examiners a few weeks before the examination to introduce oneself, and I took the occasion to explain to LeBlanc that I had learned only physical chemistry, which in other universities was a separate subject. He said, "But here chemistry is a single subject and I shall have to ask you about everything."—"But I know no organic chemistry at all."— "I shall not expect very much, but I am sure you will be familiar with X, Y, and Z." This was a blow, because these were all topics of which I had never heard.

I spent a most unhappy two weeks swotting up organic chemistry. Guido Beck tried to comfort me by betting me a bottle of wine that I would pass. I am a born optimist, and did not really expect to fail;

but I accepted the bet, reasoning that if I passed I would be happy to stand him a bottle of wine, and if I failed I would at least have the wine to comfort me.

In fact, the chemistry examination went off tolerably well, and the mathematics examination was so ridiculously easy that I was horrified to think about the professor's experience with other physics candidates. The physics exam proved more gruelling than I expected. I thought I would be asked questions relating to my thesis, or at least about quantum mechanics. In fact, Hund asked mainly about the classical equations of a spinning top, a rather complicated subject for which most students have little affection but a healthy respect. After I had struggled through this material somehow, Hund smiled and said, "I asked you these questions only so you should not think you know everything!" I was now a full-fledged Herr Doktor and happily paid off my debt to Guido Beck with a bottle of wine, which we of course consumed together.

3

Assistant to Pauli

Living with Pauli

Before I left Zurich, Pauli had offered me the job of *Assistent* for the following year, and I had accepted with pleasure. The duties of the appointment were not onerous; the main requirement was to do research, which was of course what I wanted to do anyway. In theory there was some obligation to do the research that the professor wanted done, but this took care of itself—for the most part, Pauli let me get on with what I wanted to do. If our conversations brought out some problem worth looking at, I was only too delighted to pick it up. There were a few minor chores; for example, he asked me to sort his collection of offprints of other people's papers, and occasionally he had some bits of paperwork to be done. The post was really what we would today call a postdoctoral fellowship.

By now I had got to know Pauli and his famous biting remarks. The earliest on record (which of course I know only from hearsay) goes back to his student days under Sommerfeld. He was still unknown but was writing his thesis on the hydrogen-molecule ion using the old quantum theory, while also preparing his big article on relativity, which remains one of the best treatments of the subject. Einstein was visiting, and after a colloquium talk he made some comments, which moved young Pauli to get up at the back of the room and declare, "You know, what Mr. Einstein said is not so stupid!"

His remarks acquired a different flavour when, in later years, he was an established authority himself and was addressing his equals or his juniors. He made one of his typical remarks during a visit to another university, when he got directions from one of the locals for finding a good cinema; he usually liked to spend the evening on such entertainment before settling down to work at 11 or so. When the man asked Pauli next morning whether he had found the place, he replied, "Oh yes, easily. You express yourself quite intelligibly when you don't happen to talk about physics!" I was a witness to that occasion, but

46

not when he met one of his former women students at a conference and greeted her with "Hello, Miss X!" When told she was now Mrs. Y, he said, "Oh, so you did succeed, after all?" He had the suspicion that, with few exceptions, women were in physics only to find husbands. But perhaps the most beautiful rudeness was his comment in a discussion with a colleague, who asked him to slow down because he could not think as fast as Pauli: "I do not mind if you think slowly, but I do object when you publish more quickly than you can think." The surprising thing is that the victims of such remarks never bore him a grudge. Perhaps the reason was that they knew he applied the same high standards and the same sharp criticism to himself and his own ideas.

What impelled him to make these stinging comments? Perhaps he enjoyed his facility in scoring a bull's eye. He once told me, "Some people have very sensitive corns, and the only way to live with them is to step on these corns until they are used to it." But I think he was rationalising.

Working with him naturally exposed one to this kind of treatment, but I did not fare too badly. Shortly after I started as his assistant, he invited me to his flat, and gave me a lot to drink, until he decided I was drunk (I don't think I was). Then he looked at me and said, "No, you don't get any more interesting when you are drunk", and sent me home. He used to say about me, "He talks so fast that by the time you understand what he is saying, he is already asserting the opposite." My corns do not seem to be sensitive—I found these remarks easy to bear.

Then there was the legend of the so-called "Pauli effect": whenever Pauli entered a laboratory some disaster would strike—a glass apparatus would break, there would be a short-circuit, and so on. But, the legend said, no harm would ever come to Pauli as a result of these accidents. Once, at a big conference, some young physicists planned a practical joke of this legend. At a big reception they suspended the chandelier in the big hall by a rope running over a pulley so that, when Pauli entered the room, they would release the rope and the chandelier would crash down. As Pauli arrived the signal was given and the rope was released, but it jammed in the pulley and nothing happened. So a real Pauli effect had spoiled their joke!

But most of my time with Pauli was spent not on personal remarks, but on arguments about physics. He knew what was going on, not only from the journals, but also from his very intensive correspondence. He had a tendency to write long letters about physics to his friends or in reply to people who asked for his opinion. His letters were usually written by hand; he used a secretary only for the most official of communications. He kept no copies, of course, and many of these letters are lost. This is a pity, because they were certainly full of pungent and witty remarks and contained much wisdom about physics. Those that survived are now being published.

Pauli liked to discuss problems he found interesting, which was a rather restricted category. Visitors who came to present him with problems that he considered uninteresting were not left in any doubt about this fact. Similarly, in seminar meetings a boring subject would cause him to shake his head continuously. This was not so much a protest against what the speaker was saying, but an expression of his own unwillingness to concentrate on the subject. From time to time he would say in a loud aside, "That is not interesting", or words to that effect. But when the topic interested him, he would follow carefully, and his concentration would find expression in rocking his rotund body backward and forward. A poem composed for some celebration contained the lines: "Und wenn er mit Problemen kämpft, dann ist die Schwingung ungedämpft" (when he struggles with problems, the oscillations are not damped).

Whether in a seminar or in private discussion, once he was interested he would insist on getting to the bottom of the problem, and would not stand for any sloppy or half-baked argument. To explain to him a point you had understood, or thought you had, was very good discipline. He could occasionally be wrong in condemning a promising speculation, but usually could be convinced if the proposer of the argument stood his ground. The most famous occasion when this went wrong was when R. Kronig suggested the idea of the electron spin before it was put forward by Uhlenbeck and Goudsmit, and Pauli talked him out of it. Pauli did not like to be reminded of this story.

He did not care much about priority. He used to say, "I do not know why people get into arguments about who was first with an idea. If the idea is so near the surface that it occurs to several people about the same time, it does not really matter who is first. What really gives one pleasure is to think of something that otherwise would not occur to anybody for a long time!"

He had wide interests. His friends included the pianist Arthur Schnabel and the psychoanalyst Carl Jung. As a young man, he had not touched alcohol, but when he worked in Hamburg his colleagues persuaded him to try. He got to like it perhaps a little too much and tended to drink rather more than was good for him, though he was by no means an alcoholic. In Zurich he liked to go out with Paul Scherrer, the professor of experimental physics, who frequented bars of all sorts, from elegant hotels to small bars in rather disreputable districts. The story was told that Scherrer got into an argument with a man in one of the latter places, and threw him into a fountain. When Scherrer was taken to court, he defended himself by arguing that there was no sign on the fountain that prohibited throwing people in, but this did not prevent him from being fined. Scherrer was also an enthusiastic teacher, and took great trouble with the demonstration experiments in his lectures. The introductory course (or the professor) was so attractive that one usually found some elegant ladies from town in the front row.

Landau

One of the first visitors in the autumn of 1929 was Lev Landau, and we became friends almost immediately. He was a few months younger than I, but his command of physics was much more mature than mine. He had had his research training in Leningrad under V. A. Fock, but had learned much on his own from the literature. His method of understanding a theoretical physics paper was to glance at it to see what the problem was, and what assumptions the author had made. He would then sit down and solve the problem on his own, and if his answer agreed with that given in the paper he was satisfied.

He had come with a Soviet government fellowship, and this caused some trouble, because there were then no diplomatic relations between Switzerland and the Soviet Union. So he was given a permit to stay for only a very short time. This was extended after urgent appeals by Pauli and Scherrer, but for an even shorter period, and after a further renewal he had to leave. He was amused by all this trouble and thought it was rather flattering: "Lenin stayed in Switzerland for years and was not able to start a revolution, but they evidently think I could!" He came back the following year with a Rockefeller Fellowship, and had no trouble with his stay.

Any problem he tackled was pursued systematically to its conclusion, and that applied not only to problems in physics, but to everything. He graded physicists into classes. The first class contained people like Niels Bohr and Rutherford (Einstein was in a class by himself), and he hoped he himself might qualify for the second class. He was sure that theoreticians could be productive only when young. When a name he did not know came up in conversation, and it was explained this was a theoretician aged twenty-seven or so, he exclaimed: "What, so young, and already so unknown?" I have heard this remark attributed to Pauli, but I am sure it was Landau's; this was not Pauli's style.

The same systematic approach was applied to human problems, including "situations". A situation was a relationship between a man and a woman, and it could be satisfactory or otherwise. When he found that a situation among his friends was unsatisfactory, he felt it was his duty to let the couple know, which was not always welcome.

He also strongly disapproved of beards, particularly when worn by young men. He regarded these as an outmoded Victorian relic and a symbol of a reactionary attitude. One experimentalist in the institute sported gigantic sideburns, which were also not to Landau's liking. He phoned the man's wife, whom he had not met, to ask when she would get her husband to shave off such ridiculous sideburns. He claimed more beards were to be seen in the streets of the West than in a Russian town, and made a bet to that effect. We jointly counted a sample in Zurich, and I later made a count when visiting Russia. I won the bet by a handsome margin, which he claimed was due to the changed economic situation. My visit took place during the period of great hunger in the USSR due to the policy of collectivisation. As a result, Landau said, many village people migrated to the towns, and he knew that it was common for villagers to have beards.

Landau was extremely thin at that time, and remained so all his life. This hungry look aroused motherly instincts in all housewives he met, and they felt the urge to feed him, in spite of his outspoken views, of which they often disapproved. But he was really quite tough. He joined us on skiing trips during weekends, and although his athletic ability was not outstanding, he persevered gallantly and untiringly.

When he arrived in Zurich, he had just completed his work on the diamagnetism of metals. It had been easy to get wrong results on this problem until Niels Bohr showed that in classical physics a magnetic field does not produce any magnetisation in a system of moving charges. Because of the many wrong solutions in the literature, many physicists were wary of the problem and regarded it as very intricate. When Landau produced a very simple solution in quantum mechanics, it was regarded with a good deal of suspicion. But Pauli saw the point at once. He had come up with a theory of paramagnetism due to electron spins and was therefore very interested. He knew the work of Bohr and understood how one should look at the situation, and was very impressed with Landau's work. On other matters, there were arguments. This led to Pauli's memorable comment at the end of an afternoon of hot debate, when Landau asked Pauli if he thought that all he had been saying was nonsense: "Oh no, far from it, far from it. What you said was so confused, one could not tell if it was non-sense!"

The most debated subject at that time was quantum electrodynamics. Evidently quantum theory had to be applied not only to mechanics—i.e., the motion of electrons and other particles—but also to electromagnetic fields and radiation; indeed, it was here, in the hands of Planck and Einstein, where it had started. The classical theory had a difficulty that concerned the electric field of the electron. If one assumed it to be a point charge, then the field strength, which goes with the inverse square of the distance, would become infinitely strong at points immediately adjacent to the charge (zero distance), and in fact the total energy content of the field would be infinite. By the relativistic equivalence of mass and energy, this would give the electron an infinite mass, which is obvious nonsense. H. A. Lorentz was aware of this and tried the idea that the electron was not a point, but had a finite extension. But this approach also leads to trouble, because in relativity a rigid body is impossible, and one would have to consider the possibility that the electron is deformable and introduce the forces that kept it in shape. There seemed to be no way to make all this into a simple workable theory.

The advent of quantum mechanics resolved so many of the paradoxes of classical physics that it was hoped this paradox would go away, too. After all, the precise position of an electron was a more complicated concept now than in classical physics, so perhaps its point nature would not show up in the same way. However, when Heisenberg and Pauli looked into this problem it became clear that the trouble persisted.

This work was fresh in 1929; in fact, Heisenberg and Pauli were still working on a second paper, and there was much discussion on how the difficulty might be resolved. (Indeed, the solution was not found until some sixteen years later.) Landau and I tried to see if we could get any new insight by looking at the behaviour of light quanta, or "photons", in space, and wrote a wave equation for photons in a manner similar to the Schrödinger equation for electrons. One obstacle was that the number of photons is always changing, since the effect of electrons or other charges is to emit or absorb them. This requires, then, not one wave equation but a whole sequence of them—one describing the state of affairs with no photon, one with one photon, the next with two, etc. This could be done, and we wrote a paper deriving these equations. It did not give any new insights, however, and the equations turned out to be uncomfortably complicated. I understood the reason for this only later: while it is possible, in principle, to observe the position of an electron with unlimited accuracy, even to within a fraction of the wavelength of the associated wave—though according to the uncertainty principle this will give it a strong recoil of unpredictable amount—no such experiment is possible for a photon. The observation of the photon position would contradict general principles, and therefore a description based on the positions of photons is physically not sensible.

More about Metals

I returned from time to time to the problem of the infinite field energy of the electron, but made no progress. Meanwhile, I continued thinking about solids and particularly about metals.

I was worried about the fact that in my paper on the Hall effect I had used facts about the Bloch bands which I knew to be true only in the limiting case of very tightly bound electrons. What happens in the general case, in particular for nearly free electrons, when the force due to the lattice of atoms is very weak? I brooded over these questions, and then suddenly saw the answer: free electrons running through a periodic structure, such as the atomic lattice in a metal, are diffracted. For certain wave vectors they are completely reflected, and at these wave vectors their speed of progress is zero. So if we increase the wave vector of an electron—for example, in an electric field—its velocity will increase, like that of an electron in free space, until it hits one of the wave vectors that can be diffracted by the lattice, and there its velocity drops to zero. This happens only on the boundary of the Bloch band. So the feature I invoked in my Hall effect paper shows up even if the electrons are almost free, except that then the phenomenon is confined to a very narrow neighbourhood of the boundary. Having recognised that very tightly bound and nearly free electrons behave qualitatively in the same way, one sees that this also goes for the intermediate case.

This insight gave me great pleasure: the idea is suddenly there, and it takes only a few lines of calculations to verify it. The pleasure of this short moment makes up for many months of seemingly fruitless search. I wrote a paper in which I worked out the new result only for the case of one dimension, which seemed enough to make the principle clear. The paper would probably have been more effective if it had concentrated on this single point; but I put into it a number of other considerations about the electric and thermal conductivity of metals, in which I disagreed with some details of Bloch's treatment. I thought I could show that at low temperatures the electric resistivity of a pure metal went as the fourth power of the absolute temperature, instead of the fifth power found by Bloch, but this turned out to be due to an incorrect approximation. In a later paper I corrected this to the fifth power, in agreement with Bloch's result. One person who saw the point of my treatment of nearly free electrons was Léon Brillouin, who worked out the consequences for the general case of three dimensions and developed the theory of what is now known as Brillouin zones.

Besides doing my own research, which included also some other, more detailed, papers on the electron theory of metals, I attended seminars in physics and in mathematics. The mathematics professor was Herman Weyl, who was not only a great authority on group theory, but also had a great interest in the borderland between mathematics and theoretical physics. The seminar he conducted was very stimulating. One of the mathematics students who took a very active part in the discussions was a very bright local girl, Hanna Greminger, who later married Egon Bretscher, one of Scherrer's senior collaborators; I got to know both of them very well.

One of my more memorable activities was to talk with Professor Stodola—a famous professor of engineering, a wizard with turbines—who had an amateur interest in physics, particularly in relativity and quantum theory, which he wanted to understand in detail. He was a very systematic person. He would buy two copies of the important textbooks, so that he could mark one up by underlining passages in different colours and writing comments in the margins. He liked to find quotations from famous people that contradicted each other, and he was delighted when I had to admit that what Einstein, or Bohr, or Pauli had said on one occasion could not be quite correct. I came to him once a week or so for a session after lunch. He would offer me a cup of coffee with an air of conferring a princely remuneration for my services. But I enjoyed the experience; it was fun to argue about physics with someone of such a different background. Our conversations took place in a room with a big organ. He was very musical, and took music as seriously as everything else: when he heard a piece of music at a concert, he could not listen to any other music for a day or two until he had finished digesting the one piece.

Travels. Ehrenfest, Bohr, and Others

During Easter vacation of 1930 I decided to visit some more of the other places where good physics was going on, and I followed Pauli's example and spent some time in Holland and in Copenhagen. Holland was then a strong centre for theoretical physics—with Paul Ehrenfest in Leiden and Hendrik Kramers in Utrecht—and was still under the influence of H. A. Lorentz, though he had died recently. I first visited Utrecht, where George Placzek was spending some time. I stayed in his lodgings, and, as always happened in his company, the conversation covered everything under the sun, from physics to politics and literature. I remember one evening when he had a bottle of Advocaat, the Dutch liqueur of a custardlike consistency, which was unfamiliar to both of us. We were experimenting to find the most palatable way of consuming this drink, and after extensive trial and error we decided that it was best spread on rusks. This continued and our discussions went on until the landlady appeared with breakfast, and the bottle was empty.

In the Physics Institute I was hospitably received by Kramers, a tall, fair man, whose round face and unruly lock of hair made one think of a schoolboy, in spite of his size. His understanding of physics was impressive.

One of the days I was in Utrecht happened to fall on the day when all of Kramers's group went across to Leiden for the weekly colloquium. The train from Utrecht to Leiden stopped at Woerden, and at the time there were particularly cheap fares for short journeys, so that the fare from Utrecht to Woerden plus that from Woerden to Leiden was cheaper than the fare for the whole trip. So while the train stopped for a few minutes at Woerden, the whole contingent of theoreticians raced through the underpass to the ticket office to buy tickets for the second part of the journey, under the frowning glance of the train conductor. I cannot remember whether Kramers took part in this exercise; I certainly did. When in Rome. . . .

The colloquium was run by Ehrenfest, who had started the practice. Today the colloquium in Leiden is still known as the "Ehrenfest Colloquium". He was a lively man, very given to arguments in which he tended to insist modestly that he was just a schoolmaster trying to teach his students, and for this he had to understand the material clearly; in fact, the points he claimed he did not understand and wanted to have explained by the younger people were usually very basic and deep queries.

He made all visitors sign their names on the plastered wall behind the sliding blackboard. This custom has been kept up by his successors, and when the institute moved into a new building, the plaster layer was carefully transferred to the new place, where I had occasion a few years ago to check that my 1930 signature was still there. There was almost a break in the continuity, because while the new building was going up, the institute was in temporary quarters, and signatures were collected on a temporary wall. Then one day the cleaner came to the professor and said, "Terrible how the students always scribble on walls. But fortunately I was able to wash it all off!" Luck would have it that all the lost signatures were from people in the neighbourhood and could be restored.

After Utrecht I visited Haarlem, where Felix Bloch was then working with Fokker, a worthy and upright citizen. Shortly before this, Landau had visited Haarlem. A little later Bloch was having a meal in the Fokker house, when Mrs. Fokker asked him politely whether his Russian friend was still staying with him. No, said Bloch, he had left, whereupon Fokker's little daughter, who had not met Landau, but evidently had overheard her parents' comments, said, with a sigh of relief, "Thank God!"

Bloch took me to Amsterdam to look at the museums, and there we caught up with Pauli who was visiting. We had dinner in some restaurant with him and Fokker. During the meal Pauli incessantly teased Bloch about a paper in which, he claimed, Bloch had made a mistake by a factor of ten thousand. This was not a fair comment on Bloch's paper—he had merely tried to see whether a certain mechanism could be invoked to explain an observed effect, and found it was ten thousand times too little. But Pauli went on and on about the "mistake". Finally he turned to Fokker and said, "I am sure this could not happen to you." Fokker looked pleased. "I am sure in your papers all the factors are correct." Fokker still looked pleased. "You could well write a paper which does not have the slightest physical significance, but the factors would all be correct." Fokker no longer looked pleased.

I left Holland and continued on to Copenhagen. Our Easter vacation was very long, and as Pauli spent much of the time away from Zurich, there was no obligation for me to be there, as long as I stayed in contact with physics. In Copenhagen, Niels Bohr's institute was a focus of attraction for physicists. Small, informal, but very intense conferences were held there most years, and at any time one could find a number of visitors from all over the world who wanted to learn the new physics or bring themselves up to date.

Bohr had enormous charm. He was one of the most famous scientists of his time, but was completely lacking in arrogance or pomposity. His inclination was to treat everybody with respect and courtesy, no matter what their status. But he would press with absolute insistence what he saw as the truth, and what he felt was the right way of expressing it. These two trends could produce odd results, such as the famous remark: "I am not saying this in order to criticise, but this is sheer nonsense!" He had his own way of using words, in any language, and this was infectious. One could usually recognise people who had spent some time in Copenhagen by their use of some of Bohr's phrases, such as "It is not the meaning to . . ." in the sense of "It is not my intention to. . . ."

He was not always easy to follow when he spoke or wrote. He said himself that truth and clarity are complementry. This means that if you try to say something in clear and simple language it will not be quite correct, and if you express the precise truth it will be complicated. In this conflict he tended strongly toward the absolute truth, and his papers were not easy to read. They invariably went through many stages of drafting. First would come a handwritten text, usually written at his dictation by whoever was around, enabling Bohr to walk around and think. When the text began to take shape it was typed. In this form one could get a better view of what it would read like; then it would be further amended, often after consultation with others about the finer points of style or expression. When there were enough amendments to make the text illegible it would be retyped, and there were usually many typed versions before the text was finally sent off for publication. In proof one could still see weaknesses in the wording that had escaped notice in the typescript, and this led to further corrections in the proofs. It is said that some of his papers went through twelve sets of proofs. This was possible because the Proceedings of the Royal Danish Academy, in which many of his papers appeared, considered it a great privilege to publish his papers, and it was easy enough to send a boy across with another set of proofs.

The inclination to keep improving things up to the last possible stage does not seem to have been confined to papers, as shown in the following anecdote. Bohr was visiting the site of an extension to the institute when the old builder's foreman, who knew him well, pointed to a wall and said, "Professor Bohr, if you want to move that wall again, you had better be quick, because in a few hours the concrete will have set!" In discussion, too, he was not always easy to understand. He spoke in a soft voice with imprecise pronunciation and long sentences, but he was always worth listening to. He was better at talking than at listening, and in discussion with him one had to be very energetic and persistent to be heard.

That spring was the first of many, mostly short, visits I made to the institute. In preparation I tried to learn a little Danish. Although the language is very easy to read if one knows German and English, spoken Danish is extremely difficult. When I returned to Copenhagen for a longer stay in 1979, I was surprised to find that I remembered completely what little Danish I had managed to learn in the thirties. Perhaps this was because these visits were so exciting to me that their importance was out of proportion to their duration.

On that first visit I had arrived during the Easter holiday while Bohr was in his country house in Tisvilde, north of Copenhagen. Several of us, including George Placzek, stayed in a small inn nearby and spent much time with the Bohr family, mixing physics with football. Bohr was an accomplished football player, though not of the same standard as his brother, the distinguished mathematician Harald Bohr, who was practically a professional. The story goes that Harald was once travelling in a tram car with his mother; they did not speak with one another, so it was not obvious that they belonged together. When he got off first, another passenger said to the mother, "Do you know who was sitting next to you? That was the famous footballer Harald Bohr!"

After the Easter holidays everybody moved back into town, and the discussions continued at the institute. I cannot recall precisely what subjects were discussed because in my recollection I cannot keep the different visits to Copenhagen separate. Bohr usually preferred to discuss physics in a descriptive way, using words rather than mathematics. He understood the language of mathematics, and the importance of using it in the right places, but he was at his best on questions of principle and interpretation. By 1930 the interpretation of quantum mechanics was fairly well settled. Everyone understood Heisenberg's uncertainty principle and Bohr's way of expressing the same idea in terms of "complementarity". But he still liked to come back to these general principles, to make their expression more precise, and to find new examples. These questions of the interpretation of the theory, of the nature of measurement in the atomic domain, of the relation of the observer and the object he observes, are sometimes called philosophy. There is nothing wrong with using this name, as long as it is understood that these philosophical problems are intimately connected with the content of the basic laws of physics, and can be discussed only by someone with a deep understanding of physics.

Bohr's care in looking for a precise formulation of the principles made him reluctant to accept new hypotheses readily, until he felt sure they could be brought into an acceptable framework. I remember how (probably during my first visit in 1930) he expressed grave misgivings about Dirac's way of avoiding the difficulties associated with the possible negative-energy states of electrons. This was the so-called "hole theory". In Dirac's relativistic theory of electrons, there are states of negative energy to which an electron could jump from its normal state and emit radiation. This would lead to bizarre consequences. Dirac suggested that all states of negative energy were already filled with electrons, but that these would give no observable effects. Because of the Pauli principle, no further electrons could then go into these states, so that the normal electrons would be perfectly stable. An unoccupied state of negative energy would then amount to the absence of a negative charge and of negative energy, so it would carry positive charge and positive energy.

Bohr was reluctant to accept this as a sensible hypothesis. I tried hard to persuade him that it could be made into a consistent picture, but I did not succeed. Even after the discovery of the positron, which behaved exactly as Dirac had predicted a hole would behave, Bohr was cautious and urged that it should not be taken for granted that this was the right interpretation of the new particle.

He thought deeply about many subjects besides physics, and could discuss very seriously the details of the latest detective story or adventure film. I found many of his words and stories worth remembering. He was strongly opposed to nationalism in any form, but said that if there had to be nationalism he preferred the Anglo-Saxon variety, expressed in the slogan "My country, right or wrong". He did not approve of this sentiment, but a German or French nationalist would never admit that his country could be wrong. He liked to illustrate excessive patriotism with one of his favourite stories about a young girl in Ecuador whose bicycle brakes failed as she rode down a steep hill. The cycle went faster and faster, and she almost gave up and fell off when she said to herself, "I am an Ecuadorian." This thought gave her the strength to hang on and control the cycle until the road levelled off. As Bohr pointed out, if instead of "Ecuadorian" you say "German" or "Briton" or "American", the story is no longer funny.

About the attitude of physicists or similar scientists toward political or general problems, he used to say that we were no less prejudiced than other people, but as physicists we had necessarily gone through the experience of asserting something and then being proved wrong. He pointed out that this is a very wholesome lesson, one a philosopher or sociologist might never experience.

He was also opposed to superficial views about heredity. He questioned whether there was sound evidence for believing that genius was inherited. In the case of a number of famous families in which fame continued for many generations, and which were often quoted as evidence in the "nature versus nurture" debates, he felt it was not easy to distinguish heredity from education, tradition, and opportunity. He was delighted to hear that in one of these famous families the chain of heredity had been broken somewhere by an adoption, and this case gave evidence for the importance of environment rather than heredity.

A Red Face at a Conference. More Colleagues

Back in Zurich for the summer semester, I returned to some further problems in the theory of metals. One of the intriguing puzzles at that time was magnetoresistance, i.e., the increase of the electric resistivity of metals caused by a magnetic field. There were interesting experiments, particularly by Kapitza in Cambridge, in which the resistivity, after an initial gradual rise, became proportional to the strength of the magnetic field. All theories gave the additional resistance as proportional to the square of the field. Furthermore, the theory by Sommerfeld predicted an effect thousands of times smaller than the one observed. Bloch had tried to invoke the action of the magnetic field on the electron spins, which, by the Pauli exclusion principle, would force them to alter their state of motion, and this would affect their contribution to the conduction. He found that this effect also was about ten thousand times too small. This was, in fact, the "error" about which Pauli complained in Amsterdam.

I saw a reason why the quadratic law would cease to hold when the field became so strong that the electrons, which follow spiral orbits in the magnetic field, would complete several turns, on the average, before making a collision. I had not shown that after that a linear law would follow, but at least the deviation from the quadratic law was in the right direction. I decided to present my argument in a talk at a conference in Leipzig to which I had been invited. But a few days before my talk I realised that, on the assumptions I had made, one could predict not only how the effect would vary with the field, but also its magnitude, and when I did that, the different parts cancelled out and there was no effect. So my mechanism, like that of Sommerfeld and Bloch, could not explain the phenomenon. This discovery, on the eve of my talk, came as a great shock. I could not very well cancel the talk, and the best I could do was to review the situation and discuss what was needed to put it right. I felt most embarrassed.

I found the answer shortly after the conference. It was also found by others, including Hans Bethe, with whom I was in correspondence. My memory is hazy on the question of how much he actually explained to me and how much I had known before I got his letter. The point is that the simple model that both Sommerfeld and I had used assumed that all electrons had the same "mobility", i.e., reached the same speed under the influence of a given electric field. In that case, it turned out, there is no magnetoresistance. Sommerfeld's approach actually included a slight variation of mobility with speed. In a more realistic description, the mobility of an electron depends on its direction of motion relative to the crystal lattice. If this is allowed for, the phenomenon can be understood. In writing up the text of my talk I was able to insert a note about the correct explanation, and later I wrote a detailed paper about it.

The conference talks were later also published in English, and the publishers sent me proofs of the translation of my talk. This became an occasion for a lesson in the pitfalls of the English language. By this time I knew the language quite well, and I had no problem dealing with the proofs. When I had returned them, I received a printed postcard from the publishers, reading "Messrs. Macmillan & Co. beg to acknowledge the receipt of the proofs of. . . ." All the words in this sentence were familiar, and I interpreted them to mean that they requested me to acknowledge the receipt of the proofs. I was puzzled, particularly by this being a printed card, which suggested that this happened frequently. But the wording was quite clear, and I wrote a reply saying I was sorry not to have acknowledged the proofs, but I did not know this was expected, and in any case I had already returned them. This probably amused the publishers, but I heard no more.

There were new faces in Zurich. Léon Rosenfeld arrived from Belgium, a stubby young man with a serious round face. He was given to philosophical contemplation. He had a powerful command of mathematics without losing sight of the physical facts. Pauli liked to discuss the finer points of field theory and relativity with him. I recall one occasion when Rosenfeld and I had coffee together, and I offered him cream and sugar. "No, thank you," he said, "I drink my coffee black and without sugar." He then reflected a little and said, "I got this habit during the war" (the First World War, of course), "when we had no cream and no sugar in Belgium." He reflected a little more. "It is true we had no coffee, either."

Another visitor was George Gamow—like Landau, a Russian from Leningrad. He was already famous for his explanation of alpha decay, one of the early successes of quantum mechanics, and perhaps he was even more famous for his funny drawings and his jokes. He was absolutely uninhibited when speaking or writing in any language. After he spent a few weeks in Copenhagen, he started to correspond with Bohr in Danish—or at least a kind of Danish, full of grammatical errors and atrocious spelling, but very expressive. That was his way with all languages. In Russian his grammar was rather stronger, but his spelling was equally dubious. He had a talent for drawing Mickey Mouse, then at the height of his fame, and this caricature adorned many of his letters. It also appeared in many of the pictures he drew as illustrations for comic journals and other entertainments at the Copenhagen conferences.

In the summer, he, Rosenfeld and I went on a walking tour in the mountains of the Engadin. As we got to the top of a mountain with a picturesque name—Piz da Daint—Gamow pulled a few sheets of paper from his pocket. These were an unfinished letter to the journal *Nature* about some question in nuclear physics. He had left out the closing sentence, so he could add it now and date the letter from the mountain. He even added an acknowledgment to Rosenfeld and me "for the opportunity to work here". To prove it was all genuine, I had to take a photograph of him sitting in the snow and writing.

Some time during that summer we had a *Kernwoche* (nuclear week) in Zurich. As yet little was known about the nucleus, and I cannot recall what aspects of nuclear physics we discussed. I do recall that one of the members of the conference was Patrick Blackett, a Cambridge experimentalist of enormous charm. I also remember that I was asked to give a talk on the Swiss radio to describe the conference in layman's terms. This was my first experience in broadcasting, and my first attempt at popularisation.

Odessa Conference. A New Friend

The main attraction and adventure of the summer of 1930 turned out to be a conference in Odessa. In those days, no kindhearted organisations were willing to pay the expenses of poor young physicists travelling to conferences, and we normally had to get there under our own steam, usually sitting up all night in a third-class railway carriage (fourth-class was not available on long-distance trains). So it was a special pleasure to receive an invitation to a conference in which the hosts would be paying at least all the expenses in the Soviet Union. This was a national conference, with only a small number of foreign visitors, so it was an honour to be invited. I probably owed the invitation to Ya. I. Frenkel, the Leningrad theoretician who had seen some of my papers and was interested in my work, and perhaps to a recommendation by Pauli, who was also invited. The trip promised to be an adventure, because one knew very little about life in the Soviet Union. Those who had been there usually found their prejudices confirmed: it was either a paradise or it was hell, depending on what they had expected to find.

I set out by train for Odessa via Poland (of course by third class and of course overnight) and arranged to meet Pauli at the border. We had about an hour's wait and decided to have dinner. The manager of the station restaurant urged us to have a big meal, because, he assured us, this was going to be our last decent meal for some time. Then our train pulled slowly across the border, with one carriage and three passengers: Pauli and I and a Polish physicist who was bound for the same conference. The train was supposed to reach Odessa in the morning, but it did not arrive until the afternoon. There was no dining car and we became very hungry, thus partly confirming the prediction of the Polish restaurateur. I was worried that because of our late arrival we would get no food until dinner time, but when we arrived at our hotel, we found, to our relief, a large group of physicists having a meal. I made a mental note: "In Russia one eats at 3:30 P.M." But I was proved wrong the next day when, at the end of the morning session at about noon, people suggested, "Let's go and eat." The answer clearly was that there was no habitual time for meals there; one ate when one was hungry and when circumstances allowed.

This was the first of many adjustments we had to make. There was the pervasive impression of things being run down—overcrowded trams running on worn-out rails, houses badly needing a coat of paint, shops having nothing to sell. The shortages did not affect us as visitors; hotel meals were good and, for us, interesting.

When one gained the confidence of some of the Russian scientists they would express resentment at living under the political pressure, and at the lack of freedom of speech, more than at the economic hardships and the shortages. On the other hand, science was being encouraged, there was no shortage of jobs, and all students were supported by the state, though in rather primitive conditions. Not everyone who wanted to get to a university could get a place. The chance of admission depended on ability and on social background; working-class origin was a decided advantage.

The conference was lively and interesting, and I made the acquaintance of many of the Soviet physicists. I met Frenkel, who had made contributions to many branches of modern theory, and was a very important influence on the younger people, including Landau and Gamow. I also met Igor Tamm, one of the most charming personalities in physics. He had an agile mind, and an equally agile body, and the first impression he gave was of never standing still. I tried to take his picture during a talk at the conference, but my camera and film were not fast enough to capture him motionless. While everybody else in the room came out perfectly sharp, Tamm is represented by a great blur in the middle of the picture. This photograph has remained for me a symbol of his temperament.

Tamm was modesty incarnate. He would not ask for any of the privileges to which a Soviet academician is entitled. Even during his last illness in the late 1960s he refused to claim such comforts, which would have given relief. He was a keen mountaineer, and insisted on strenuous climbs even when his friends felt that at his age it was a risky thing. On one of these excursions he was persuaded to take a horse, but he felt that riding it would be an admission of weakness; instead, he led, or practically dragged, the horse up the mountain.

A good deal of our time was spent at Lusanovka, the beach in Odessa.There I met, among others, a girl from Leningrad, Eugenia (Genia) Nikolaevna Kannegiser, who had recently graduated in physics. She seemed to know everybody, was known to everybody, and was more cheerful than everybody. After the conference, all participants were taken by boat across the Black Sea. This included Genia, with whom I talked a good deal during the voyage. She did not speak German, and I knew no Russian, so our only common language was English, which Genia could speak reasonably but not fluently. If I was asked why I did not seek the company of the many other young people, who included many accomplished linguists, I could say only that the thought had never occurred to me. As a guest, I was travelling in first class, while Genia, as a junior member of the conference, had a berth in third class, which was so uninviting that she preferred to sleep on deck under a lifeboat. I felt uncomfortable about this, and would have liked to change places with the lady; but as I was sharing a cabin with Pauli, there was nothing I could do!

During the voyage, Sommerfeld insisted on giving a talk about some new results of his, for which there had been no time at the conference. Everybody was in a holiday mood and did not feel like hearing another lecture, so we were delighted when Sommerfeld said he could not talk without a blackboard. Surely there would be no such thing on a Black Sea steamer. But we had not reckoned with the Soviet system, in which the crew on such a boat receive regular instruction in political philosophy, and in due course a blackboard was brought from the crew quarters. The lecture turned out to be amusing and did not last too long.

The boat called at two ports in the Crimea. With a small group of other young people I decided to go by taxi from one port to the other, so that we could see some of the country. Our seniors advised against this enterprise, because, they warned, if the taxi broke down, we might miss the boat. They were wise, because the taxi did break down; but fortunately it was so close to Yalta, our destination, that we could walk the rest of the way and still get there in good time for the boat. The risk had been worthwhile. The drive was very beautiful: you drive along a plateau that rises gradually until you come through a natural gateway between the rocks and suddenly have the sea and the fertile coastal strip at your feet.

The boat took us to Batum, and this was my first experience in a subtropical climate with unfamiliar vegetation, at its best in the beautiful botanical gardens, some way out of town, which we visited. But coming back, we had a little adventure. We were just in time to catch the train that was to take us back into town, but there was a long queue at the ticket office, and it was obvious that we would miss the train. I mentioned that at home we would just get on without a ticket and pay on the train, and our Russian friends said, "Let's try that!" But the conductor on the train was not amused. He called the armed guard that accompanied the train. Two soldiers stood over us with fixed bayonets, and in Batum they marched us to the station master's office. After difficult negotiations it was ruled that the Soviet citizens in the party would have to pay a fine; the foreign visitors, who could not be expected to know the rules, were let off. Needless to say, the fine was shared.

We went on by train to Tbilisi (Tiflis) with a diminishing group. It was an old town, beautifully situated among mountains. The Georgian people were not as wild as they looked, with the men's enormous handlebar moustaches and traditional costumes. One heard many tales about the wild temperament and the drinking habits of the Georgians, but our stay was too short to witness any of it.

An even smaller group, but still including my new friend Genia, continued in a hired car to Vladikavkaz beyond the mountains, where there is a railway to the north. Here the group dispersed; Genia and I decided to visit Kislovodsk, a resort in the high mountains. This involved another overnight journey by train. I was anxious to see how the locals travel and wanted to go by the "hard" class, where seats are not reserved. So Genia and I got into a crowded carriage full of wild-looking local types. Genia squeezed into a seat between them. There was no seat left for me, but I spotted some empty space on the wooden luggage rack. I climbed up and tied myself down with my belt so that I would not fall off while asleep. I slept so soundly that Genia had to shake me when we reached our destination. The stay in the mountains passed only too quickly, and when Genia and I parted

I left with the feeling that something new and permanent had entered my life.

From here on I travelled on my own. I suppose someone must have bought my tickets for the rest of the trip, and made the reservations, because my Russian would not have been up to it, but I do not remember how it was done. I had learned a little of the language before coming to the Soviet Union, as I had done before going to Holland and Denmark. I knew that the first thing to learn in a new language are the numbers. They are usually not too difficult to remember, and it is remarkable how much you can do with them.

I arrived in Kharkov one morning, and had no idea how far it was to the research institute I was to visit, or how to get there. I decided to get an estimate of the distance by asking one of the *izvozchiki* (horse-cab drivers) for the fare, for which my knowledge of numbers was adequate, and this would give me an estimate of the distance. The man said 15 roubles (then about £3 or $12-$15). I decided this suggested a distance one could walk, so I thanked him and went on. He shouted after me "10 roubles" but I was not interested. He drove after me, and when the fare had come down to 2 roubles, I got in. I learned from this that you are in the best position for bargaining if you do not really want the article on offer. The institute was new, and its members were very proud to show a visitor around. The equipment seemed sound but not luxurious; the rooms in which the members lived were adequate but very simply furnished, showed poor workmanship, and most doors did not fit properly.

The next night I was on my way again by train to Moscow, where I was met and taken to the university. I met Leonid Mandelstam, the professor of experimental physics who had discovered the Raman effect independently, but published only a little after Raman. He was a very gentle person with a very wide knowledge and understanding of physics. This is illustrated by an anecdote about him and the theoretician Tamm. They were working together during the Revolution, when there was no electricity, by the light of an oil lamp. The lamp was accidently knocked over, and the oil spilled onto a divan, which caught fire. Mandelstam grabbed a bucket of water to throw on the flames, when Tamm tried to stop him. "Don't you know it is wrong to throw water on an oil fire?" Mandelstam poured the water on anyway, and this extinguished the flames. He had realised that normally the oil will float to the top of the water and continue burning over a wider area, but in this case the oil was trapped by capillarity in the padding of the mattress. This kind of instant applied physics takes presence of mind and confidence in your own reasoning.

I did not see much of Moscow on that occasion, nor of the spectacularly beautiful city of Leningrad, the last town I visited on this trip. I went out to the Physico-Technical Institute where Frenkel worked. He invited me to come back to the institute for a longer period next Easter.

Landau Again

Back in Zurich, Landau appeared for another, longer, visit, which enabled him to join Hans Thorner and me for a skiing Christmas at Arosa. In our discussions we came back again and again to the unsolved problems of the quantum theory of fields, of which the infinite self-energy of the electron was a symptom.

We came to the conclusion that the uncertainty relations, stated by Heisenberg for nonrelativistic quantum mechanics, needed extension in the relativistic field. In other words, not every measurement consistent with these relations could in fact be carried out. In particular, a measurement of the momentum of a particle necessarily took time—the more time, the higher the accuracy of the measurement. Further, in measuring the intensity of electric and magnetic fields, there were not only limitations on the accuracy with which two of these quantities could be measured in the same region of space and at the same time, as provided for by Heisenberg's principle, but even one of them by itself could not be measured with unlimited precision. If this was true, it would suggest that the mathematical form of the theory should be changed to take account of these limitations.

When Niels Bohr heard of these ideas, he was violently opposed to them. He felt sure that it must be possible, in principle, to measure electromagnetic fields as accurately as the theory allowed—i.e., up to the limits of the known uncertainty principle. When Landau and I were in Copenhagen again in the early spring of 1931, there were very heated discussions on this subject. Later Bohr and Rosenfeld started an analysis of field measurements, and this eventually resulted in two monumental papers that have become classics. I am still not convinced. The analysis of these papers is undoubtedly correct, but the process of measurement to which they lead involves densely filling the small region of space in which the field is to be measured with positive and negative charges, which cancel each other out, together with other mechanisms. Whether this can still be called a measurement of the field is perhaps debatable. On the other hand, our idea that accepting further limitations would point toward a better theory did not materialise. In this sense, our paper made no constructive contribution to the development of the theory.

During the winter I started taking Russian lessons, since the language intrigued me. I also kept up a correspondence with Genia. It had already been clear from our summer trip that our sense of humour was compatible—the same things made us laugh. Now it transpired that many of our views of more serious matters were also compatible. Our tastes and opinions on many matters might differ, but we agreed on what was important, and also on what one must do and what one ought not do. At least, that seemed the most rational explanation for the attraction I felt, which seemed to become stronger during our six-month correspondence.

At the end of the winter semester I set out on my visit to Leningrad. I first stopped in Copenhagen for a few days to discuss the paper I had written with Landau, and to participate in part of a conference. This was, I think, the first time I met Hendrik Casimir, a young Dutch theoretician and student of Ehrenfest. He is very bright, but as bright theoreticians go, he is exceptionally normal—always cheerful, fluent in many languages, and in every way the antithesis of the absent-minded professor. One very characteristic incident comes to mind. In 1947 we had a little conferencee at Birmingham, and the university gave a dinner for the participants, presided over by the vice-chancellor, who had insisted that this would be a quite informal occasion, with no speeches; he would just briefly welcome us. But his words of welcome developed into a substantial talk. I was sitting next to the secretary of the university, and said I thought this called for a reply by one of our guests. He agreed, but added that it was clearly too late to arrange this. I said, "You will be surprised!" and leaned over to ask Casimir to reply. When the vice-chancellor sat down, Casimir got up and gave a little speech in perfect English that was perfectly appropriate for the occasion.

Lecturer in Leningrad. A Rash Marriage?

From Copenhagen I went on to Leningrad via Stockholm and the Baltic. The boat from Stockholm to Finland ran into thick ice, and although it was built as an icebreaker, it had to turn back and find another route where the ice was not so thick. We eventually reached Finland and I waited for a day in Helsinki for the night train to Leningrad.

In the Physico-Technical Institute I was taken in hand by J. Dorfman, a senior experimentalist, since Frenkel was in America. Dorfman suggested I give a course of lectures on solid-state physics, and he further suggested I should give it in Russian. I agreed, perhaps unwisely. I greatly enjoyed the process, but for the audience it must have been an ordeal. However, I still occasionally meet Russian physicists who say that they learned the beginnings of solid-state physics from my course, so they must have understood something.

But much of my free time was spent with Genia, and after ten days or so we decided we would get married. At that time there was no obstacle to Russians marrying foreigners, but whether Genia would be able to leave the country was another question. Genia had another worry. She was reminded of a short story by Maupassant, in which he meets a friend on a cross-channel steamer, who is radiantly happy. He has just married an English girl. She is pretty and fair and charming, but the most enchanting thing about her is the way she speaks French: it is funny, and absolutely adorable. A few years later he meets his friend again, who looks gloomy and dejected. "What happened? Did she die?"—"No, she learned French." Genia gave me fair warning about this cautionary tale. Perhaps to avoid any such danger in our case, she has managed to retain her Russian accent and her special way of using any language.

Our plan was to marry on Friday, the 13th of March, to mock superstition, but this plan was not realised. At that time, a compulsory smallpox vaccination was in effect, as there had been some cases of the disease, and I had a reaction to the vaccine. On the 13th I was in bed with a high fever, and the marriage was postponed to Sunday the 15th. Sundays had no significance in Russia at the time. The week had been officially replaced by a five-day period, with every fifth day a day of rest.

So on Sunday morning we set out for the register office. But we found it had been moved and had to get directions from a policeman. The procedure was very simple (it has become much more ceremonious by now)—we just signed a form that had been filled in by a clerk. The clerk did spoil two forms, because first she could not spell my name and then she could not spell Genia's. When she finally got it right, and had correctly entered our professions as "scientific workers", she put her pen down and said, "You are both scientific workers? And both so cheerful?"

At that time I felt strongly that getting married was the private affair of two people, and not an occasion for crowds to celebrate, but I consented to our being toasted by Genia's family. I had of course met her family by this time; in fact, I had called on them during my first visit to Leningrad. Her mother, very gentle and feminine, had unbelievable energy when it was required—and bringing up a family during revolution, civil war, and hunger had certainly required it. Genia's father, a famous gynaecologist, had died when she was a baby; her stepfather was a wonderful person, trained as an engineer, but also a talented writer and translator, a great raconteur, and a man of outstanding integrity. Genia's sister, Nina, a biologist, completed the family. Another important member of the household was Nastya, who for many years had been the help and friend of the family. A cousin, who was family photographer, also stayed in the flat. Without an extra person, the flat would have been too large and would have had to be shared with strangers.

The news of our marriage spread rapidly through the theoretical physics community. It aroused interest because I was about the first of my age group to be married, and Genia was famous among the Russian physicists, particularly for her poems, which would mercilessly poke fun at her seniors. Quite recently a visiting theoretician from Moscow told us that these poems are still quoted as folklore, not always with a knowledge of who was the author. Unfortunately they do not translate well.

During the rest of my stay I talked much with the people in the institute about their experiments, and met A. F. Ioffe, the grand old man of Russian physics, who was playing an important part in securing government support for science. He was an expert on semiconductors, and at the time I was there he indulged in grand speculations about a city of the future, which would be totally enclosed and uniformly heated, and would get its power from solar cells. He shocked the local physics world when, in his late forties, which to us seemed a ripe old age, he left his wife and married a graduate student.

I also met a young theoretician, M. P. Bronstein (nicknamed Abbat [abbot] because of his serious demeanour), who was a close friend of Genia's and Landau's. He was a brilliant populariser, as well as a very original researcher, and worked on the relationship between quantum mechanics and gravitation. His papers, which emphasised the importance of "Planck length" and "Planck time", have a very modern ring today. He later perished in a camp.

Another man I met was Iwanenko, a very lively character. He was always well informed about what was going on in physics, and always ready to comment on any subject. He would talk very fast, usually in a mocking tone, which made one feel that what he was saying was not meant seriously or was not seriously thought out. This was indeed true sometimes, but occasionally his casual remarks contained an important insight. He and Landau had been the closest of friends, but they fell out and became implacable enemies. Later still, he found himself at loggerheads with most of the theoretical physics community in the Soviet Union. This had to do with the repressive Stalin period when, it is said, he put his career above consideration for others.

The rest of the time passed very quickly, and I had to return to Zurich. Application had of course been made for Genia's papers, but the whole process would take some time. She applied for permission to change her citizenship. By German law the wife of a German automatically acquires German citizenship; but by Soviet law she was still a Soviet citizen, and could not change without permission. An alternative, which perhaps would have been easier, was to go abroad with a Soviet passport. However, it would have been valid for only a single foreign trip, and she would have had to apply for permission to leave the Soviet Union every time she came to visit her family. When I left we had no assurance that she would ever be able to join me, or that I would ever get a visa to come back. But we were optimistic and hoped to get together again at least in the summer.

The return to Zurich was via Berlin, where my family were very worried, understandably, about my marriage to a girl they knew very little about, and whom I had seen altogether for perhaps three weeks, not counting the long correspondence in between. It took some time before they saw that the result might not be a complete disaster. I have to admit that we took a gamble, but now, after fifty-four years, we may perhaps assert that the gamble has come off.

I have no very clear recollection of the summer semester of 1931—perhaps my heart was not altogether in Zurich. Pauli went to the United States before the end of the semester, and as there were not many people around in Zurich, he suggested I spend the last two weeks in Leipzig. There was no formal conference, but a number of theoreticians happened to be there: besides Heisenberg and Hund there were Felix Bloch and George Placzek. I also met Viktor Weisskopf and Giancarlo Wick for the first time.

Finally the semester was over, and I set off for Leningrad. I had once again obtained a visa, with the help of an invitation from the institute. Genia and I decided to travel to the Caucasus for a holiday, and stopped in Moscow to visit her relatives, who included the physicist Mandelstam. We also called at the office that handled her application to change her citizenship, but there was no news of any progress. We had reservations on a train south, and set off, in the company of a cousin, for the station. We enquired about where to catch our train and were directed to a very distant platform; but there was no sign

70

of our train. Something seemed to be wrong. Leaving the cousin and our luggage, we rushed back to the only people who might help us— the GPU, or political police. Their uniformed branch was not concerned with catching counterrevolutionaries, but to look after routine problems, and were always willing to assist foreign visitors. They used two phones to call all other stations in Moscow and learned that our train was leaving from another station. While I rushed to recover our luggage and cousin from the distant platform, Genia started the search for a taxi. Eventually a taxi turned up and was immediately besieged by several other would-be passengers. The driver did not accept any of them, declaring that he was going off duty. I had not yet experienced Genia's power in a crisis. After a few words with the driver, we were speeding off in the taxi, leaving our amazed competitors behind. At the proper station, we sprinted toward our train and, without much concern for women and children, we got there just in time. It would have been disastrous to miss it, since reservations were very hard to come by.

Travelling on a Russian train has something rather cosy about it. In anticipation of spending several days and nights in the train, you settle in as well as you can. In the "soft car" (which must not be called "first-class" because that would imply that the Soviet Union has class distinctions), you have a comfortable berth, and you brew tea more or less all day, with boiling water sometimes supplied by the conductor, and sometimes collected from a tap at every station.

Few trains had dining cars, but that was no problem. At every station peasants would line up along the train to sell food. As we moved south, the bread, chickens, and hard-boiled eggs gave way to melons and grapes, very delicious and very cheap. We bought an adequate supply but had to dispose of it quickly, for fear of attracting flies. At the next station the fruit looked even more delicious and was even cheaper; so of course we had to sample it. And so it went on. To make a long story short, Genia had to spend the first few days of our holiday in bed.

Our destination was a holiday home for scientific workers in a resort in the mountains, which was reached by bus from the railway line over a narrow dirt road. Our bus driver raced another bus up the mountain and Genia earned the wrath of the other passengers by urging him on.

Our room was in an annex to the men's and women's dormitories, where we could have a room together. While Genia was ill, I got quite good at negotiating the steep hill between the buildings, carrying a plate of rice, a pot of tea, and a thermometer. A slight disadvantage,

71

particularly in view of Genia's condition, was that there was no indoor sanitation, and that the outside toilet had no door. The occupant would generally avoid embarrassment by loudly singing or whistling a tune.

The scenery was beautiful and the long valleys offered enchanting views of the high mountains. There was no public transport, but you could hire horses and a boy to look after them. We had never ridden before, but as the horses were quite docile, we could manage. There was one awkward moment, however, when, in dismounting, one of my hobnailed boots got stuck in the stirrup. The horse was standing very peacefully, so I let go of the reins in order to free my foot, upon which the horse bounded forward. With one foot in the stirrup, I was dragged along, made somewhat more uncomfortable by the fact that, in the hot weather, I was wearing nothing above the belt. The hooves, very close to my face, looked awfully big. Fortunately, a fence was just ahead and forced the horse to stop. The boy came running to free me.

One evening we attended a meeting at which the head of the local collective farm talked about his organisation and its work. The members belonged to one of the numerous ethnic groups in which the Caucasus abounds, and traditionally all the agricultural work was done by women, while the men were hunting or fighting. With this in mind, one of the guests from the north asked how it was with the problem of female labour, and got the reply, "No problem; they work very well."

On the journey back, we lost an attaché case. Thefts were common on trains in those days, so at night the doors at one end of each car were locked, and a conductor was placed at the open doors of two adjacent cars to check who went in and out. But at night some member of the train staff had passed through and had forgotten to lock the connecting doors. A thief evidently had followed him and gone off with various bits of property. The loss of the case was painful because it contained all my film from the Caucasus, which had not even been developed yet. But our neighbour was in worse trouble. His case contained the only trousers he had with him, and worse still, his letter of credit was in two parts, for security. One part was in his trouser pocket, the other in the case, so they were both gone. On the advice of the conductor we went to report the matter to the police at the next station. When we described the circumstances, the policeman said, "I am sorry, I can't help you. You have been honestly robbed." Our neighbour was indignant: "What do you mean, honestly robbed? What would you consider dishonest?"—"Well, maybe if someone hit you over the head. . . ."

We stopped in Moscow and again called at the register office to check on Genia's papers. We were greeted with the announcement, "Good news: your application has been granted; the papers have gone off to Leningrad." This was indeed good news, and we returned to Leningrad to start preparations for our departure. But the weeks passed and there was still no sign of the papers. The end of my vacation was approaching; if the papers did not turn up soon, we would again have to separate. I decided to go to Moscow to check on the situation.

An amusing, and I think instructive, incident occurred on the train. I shared a compartment (this was an "international" car, with two to a compartment) with a uniformed officer of the GPU. I knew that those in uniform were not the ones to be feared, but I was on my guard. In the morning I could tell that he was anxious to start a conversation, and I became even more apprehensive. But soon his purpose became clear: he had forgotten his shaving soap; might he borrow mine? I shall always remember the lesson that one should never exclude harmless explanations when one encounters suspicious situations.

In the Moscow office I was not kindly received: "Your papers have gone off; we have nothing more to do with the matter!" I persisted. To what address had they been sent? To the right one, I was assured. Could I speak to the person who dispatched them? No, but they would check with her, if I insisted. I did insist, and it turned out the papers had been sent to another office in Leningrad. I wanted to communicate this to the family in Leningrad as quickly as possible, and used a new picture telegram service for the purpose. I wrote my message on a form, and the same afternoon the facsimile was delivered in Leningrad. Genia had a cold, so her sister went to the other office, and after some search a clerk found the papers in a drawer, and commented "Oh, that Maria Ivanovna; she always misplaces things!" But at last Genia and I could depart together.

Genia's departure from her family was not easy, and she was in tears for the first part of the journey. (When I travelled by the same train the following year, the conductor recognised me and asked whether Genia had eventually cheered up.) We were seen off by a crowd of relatives and friends, and since it was generally known that both of us were fond of caviar, we were presented with a considerable quantity. We did not know the German customs regulations and decided we best eat our delicacy on the way. The train passed through Lithuania, where we were joined by a cavalry officer in a resplendent uniform; his horse was travelling in a freight car attached to the train. We offered him a good helping of caviar on a large piece of bread, and he accepted it with pleasure. When the train stopped at his station, his mouth was still full and he was quite embarrassed, since it was not proper for officers in uniform to be seen eating bread and caviar in public.

We stopped in Berlin for a few days so my family could make the acquaintance of the new daughter-in-law. By a curious coincidence, my brother had also married a Russian woman a few years earlier. She had been working for the Soviet trade mission in Berlin, and he had met her when they were involved in a near-accident with his car. She was a very charming and attractive woman, warm, impulsive, and likeable.

Married Life in Zurich

When we arrived in Zurich, we soon found accommodation in a house uphill from the institute, with lovely views. Our landlord was a blind masseur, who lived there with his Dutch wife and their 2½-year-old daughter. Genia could never get over the fact that the little girl addressed her as "Frau Doktor Peierls".

Our rooms consisted of a fairly large and pleasant sitting room and an unheated attic bedroom. We had no running water, just a washstand, but we did have use of the bathroom and the kitchen. In the winter our attic was very cold, and we would undress in the sitting room and then rush upstairs to bed. We used a large glass bottle as a hot-water bottle; one day it was knocked over and froze solid, and of course burst with a loud crack. We left the ice on the floor, where it stayed for a month or so.

For lunch I quite often went to the student canteen, and Genia joined me a few times. But, being brought up on her mother's excellent cooking, she soon decided that the food was terrible. She discovered that for much less money she could have a bar of chocolate, an egg, an orange, and a glass of milk, which seemed like luxuries and were far tastier than the mass-produced canteen food. The fact that a woman from hungry Russia would not eat the student food caused a small sensation among our friends.

New people had arrived at the institute, including Max Delbrück. He came from a distinguished German academic family and was lively and full of fun. He was self-confident without being arrogant, but he could be very outspoken. Once, on meeting one of our friends, he exclaimed, when the friend was out of the room, "This man is even more stupid than my brother-in-law!" He had a good understanding of the new physics but published sparingly, though his papers were very good. A few years later he turned to biology, the field in which he became famous.

Another visitor was Giulio Racah, who came from Rome. He was very intense and hard-working, and an enthusiastic car driver. Sometimes he undertook a little too much driving, as when he returned from Italy from his uncle's funeral, and fell asleep at the wheel. He was awakened when his car knocked over three of the stone posts marking the edge of the highway and careened into a field. Still dazed, he saw one of his wheels rolling off into the field, and started running after it. The bystanders, who expected to extricate an injured driver from the collapsed car, must have been surprised to see a man emerge from the wreck and run off into the distance.

As a wedding gift, we had received a cheque from an aunt, and the question of what to do with it almost caused our first disagreement. Genia liked the idea of buying a motorcycle, but I regarded these vehicles as dangerous and undesirable (and still do). Another possibility was buying a carpet, but it would be an encumbrance in moving around. Finally, we solved the problem to our mutual satisfaction by using the gift for a weekend trip to Paris.

It was a very intense weekend. We travelled by night train, sleeping as usual on the hard bench of a third-class carriage. The train arrived at 6 A.M., and that was just the right time to start with a visit to Les Halles, the famous food market. We saw the usual sights and visited Genia's relatives, who advised us on the current attractions in modern cabarets. We were completely exhausted when we took the night train back. We had intended to repack our suitcase before reching the Swiss border, to make our few purchases, which included a bright-red raincoat for Genia, less obvious. But we had fallen asleep and were awakened by the customs official, so we had to declare all our purchases.

Night trains became our favourite means of travel. When we had to travel some distance, as from Berlin to Zurich, we would, if time allowed, select an interesting town somewhere in between, and have a day of sightseeing between two night journeys. We usually slept well without sleeping cars, and this arrangement meant we did not waste any day on travel, or any money on hotel rooms.

On one of these trips we stopped in Ulm and visited the cathedral with the tallest spire in the world. We climbed to the top and admired the view of the old town, then suddenly realised that it was getting late for our next train. The run down the spiral staircase was memorable, but we made our train, if somewhat out of breath.

On another occasion we decided that, on leaving Berlin, we would stop in Freiburg in the Black Forest, a pleasant town we had not seen. My father approved. "Do that, and while you are there, call on Uncle Felix. He is, after all, your grandmother's only surviving brother." The uncle was a retired judge, by then almost blind, but cheerful and hospitable, and we enjoyed the visit.

Swiss officials are very accommodating to tourists; but their attitude can be quite different toward foreigners who try to live there. In our case, the aliens' police were never quite certain that our Soviet marriage was valid. We had a translation of our marriage certificate validated by the German consulate; but this was not enough for the Swiss, and I think the question was still not settled by the time we left. One day Genia had a visit from a detective of the aliens' police. He questioned her on various things, including my morals: "Does he run after girls?" He also asked about my salary, and when he heard I was earning 500 Swiss francs a month (which was not really an enormous sum) he seemed sufficiently impressed, took off his hat, and said, "Adieu, Frau Doktor." We heard no more.

That Christmas we decided to gather people together for a party and rent a chalet in the mountains for skiing. We decided on St. Antönien, a rather isolated village in the mountains east of Zurich. We had a big box of groceries sent up by a local shop, which left us only milk, eggs, and potatoes to be got locally. The Swiss valleys are very isolated because of difficult communication, and many people tend to have the same names. Letters to the owner of our chalet had to be addressed to "Herr Peter Flütsch, jüngerer Lehrer". His full name and the designation as teacher were not enough to identify him: he was the *younger* teacher Peter Flütsch. Our party included Hans Bethe, Max Delbrück, Hans Thorner, his fiancée and her brother, and the Bretschers. Emilio Segré from Rome also joined us for a few days, so our party contained three future Nobel laureates.

Genia had no experience in mountain skiing, but gallantly came along on some small excursions. Once Hans Bethe suggested a longer excursion with a tiring ascent but easy descent. His navigation went wrong, and we ended up descending a fairly steep slope through trees. We managed all right, except when Genia somehow became stuck with her feet and skis in the branches of a tree and her head hanging in soft snow, a position from which we had some difficulty extracting her.

Cooking was collective and sometimes a little confused. One evening we thought we had finished a generous dinner, but then discovered that we had forgotten about a dish of Mont Blanc aux marrons (chestnuts in whipped cream) meant for ten. Nobody felt able to touch it, except Hans Bethe, who, in a performance that has become a legend, sat down and finished the dish, with relish. On leaving, I settled the bill with Peter Flütsch (the young teacher). It was a complicated calculation because of the food and firewood he supplied. When it was all worked out and I paid the amount due, he returned one franc to me, as a token to show that we had been satisfactory tenants. A charming custom.

The carnival, or *Fasching*, was serious business in Zurich, though not to the same degree as in Munich. The most important event was the ball put on by the art school, where the art students, and others, could show their imagination in their costumes. Genia decided to dress up as a Negro girl from the American South, with a few bits of cloth making up a short striped skirt, a white blouse, an apron, and a hat. A generous application of black makeup, which covered all visible parts of her body—and rather beyond—and a cheerful grin completed the picture. She won second prize for her costume and for her spirited dancing; she was very proud. Racah came to the ball, also painted black and also had great success in his own way—next morning his landlady gave him notice.

At Easter we went for a holiday to a small place on Lake Lugano in the Ticino, the Italian-speaking part of Switzerland. We were joined by the Solomons. Jean Solomon was a French theoretician and had recently arrived with his very attractive wife, the daughter of Langevin. At the end of our stay we decided to join an excursion that would take us by steamer along the lake, by bus to the next lake, and on again by steamer. While we were queueing for the tickets, the Solomons saw us and decided to come, too. Just before we reached the ticket booth, he said, "Uh, we have no money with us; do you have enough for four?" A rapid count of our liquid assets and a rapid calculation suggested that it could just be done, if we cut out the optional lunch. It was a glorious trip, and we arrived enchanted, but exhausted and hungry. We had to wait for the late train back to Zurich, and now our resources were minimal. After due discussion a proposal by Genia was accepted: we should buy some bread, as the cheapest way to get bulk, and add some radishes for lasting taste. Arriving in Zurich in the early hours, we had a little money left to pay either for the tram ride home, or for a cup of coffee in the station. The tram won. There were other trips that did not have the surprise addition of extra people, from which we returned with very little cash, but never quite as broke as on that occasion.

Another remarkable excursion was to a meeting of the Swiss Physical Society at Vevey on Lake Geneva. The town of Vevey was honoured by the presence of many learned people, to whom it gave the freedom of the municipal wine cellars. There were rows of enormous casks containing the local wine, labelled by type and vintage, and we took full advantage of the offering, fortified by French-style ham rolls. When we finally emerged, we were rather cheerful. Somehow we ended up at an elegant hotel, where a band was playing. The drummer seemed to be absent, so Pauli and Genia together took his place and had a marvellous time doing it.

I earlier mentioned Pauli's suspicion of female physicists. He had been worried when Genia arrived, and I had to promise him that she would not feel entitled to spend time in the institute. Evidently she had abided by the bargain to his satisfaction (which was very easy, as she had no desire to stay in the institute; life was much too interesting outside). So now, as partners playing drums, they were on the most friendly terms.

Scherrer, who had come by car, offered us a ride back to Zurich the next morning. Rather late that night, he announced that he had changed his mind and was going back right now; anybody who wanted to come along was welcome. So we set out along the road to Zurich. Suddenly, somewhere along the way, the car did not take a curve but went straight ahead into a field, and did not stop until the wire stay of a telegraph pole brought it to a gentle halt. Scherrer, who had probably fallen asleep, murmured something about "fault in the steering". He got the car back on to the road, and we continued home, without the steering giving any further trouble.

When the weather got warmer I persuaded Genia to go sailing with me. We rented a boat and also had two guests on board: Solomon, and Eugene Feenberg, who had recently arrived from America. He had been preceded by a rumour that he was from Texas, and we had visions of a cowboy with high heels and a ten-gallon hat. Instead there appeared a tall but very thin stooped man who resembled a Talmud scholar more than a cowboy. However, for the duration of his stay he was called "the cowboy".

We set out in the boat, and, as it was early in the year, we were alone on the lake, except for a sail visible in the far distance, too far to see any detail. Genia announced, "I don't like that boat; we are going to collide with it." This, of course, produced great hilarity, but collide we did. The other boat, which was a boat used in races and much faster than ours, had two very young boys in charge. They passed us smartly while we were tacking and then, when going about, overdid the turn and ran into our side. For a moment there was a great confusion of sails, sheets, booms, and other rigging, but everything cleared, except that our boat had lost a mast stay. We could continue only by keeping the wind to one side of the boat, which we managed until we got to a village where we could get a piece of wire for first-aid repairs. It was only when this episode had passed satisfactorily that we discovered that Solomon and Feenberg could not swim. Since then Genia has not been keen on sailing.

Once my uncle Adolf spent a few days in Zurich and invited us to lunch. He was my father's brother-in-law and evidently a very able businessman, as he had retired very early and was now just looking after his investments. He had succeeded in keeping his capital intact during the German runaway inflation and other crises; he did lose a little money in the devaluation of the dollar and took this as a personal insult. He was staying in the Baur-en-Ville, one of the best hotels in Zurich, and there we met him for lunch. Before we could indicate our preference, he said, "The table d'hôte is always the best value, don't you think?" So we meekly ordered the table d'hôte. At the end he said, "You don't want any coffee, do you?" I said I was going back to work and would like some. Genia also said she would like coffee. The uncle called the waiter and asked for one coffee (which comes in little jugs) and two cups. The waiter explained they were not allowed to split portions. The uncle got angry and said he was an old customer who had stayed in the hotel many times and surely they ought to oblige him, etc. He lost the argument, and we had a coffee each.

This was not unexpected. I knew that, while he was very well off and liked to eat well, he always kept his wife short of housekeeping money, so that she would sometimes borrow from my father to avoid shortages. For her birthdays he would go to a place that sold items abandoned in railway cars, and he would proudly come home with a used but still usable umbrella or something similar.

It is a strange phenomenon that rich people sometimes lose their sense of proportion over small matters. No doubt they got rich by being careful with money, but presumably in the acquisition of wealth a sense of proportion is essential. My father told similar stories about Emil Rathenau, the founder of the A.E.G., who used to visit my father's factory in Oberschöneweide at intervals. During these sessions he liked to drink lemonade, and would send a messenger for some. Now, this could be obtained at a pub across the road from the office for 10 pfennig, but he insisted that it be brought from the works canteen, which was a long way from the office, because there it was only 5 pfennig. When the messenger returned with the bottle, Rathenau would give him a 10-pfennig piece and hold out his hand for the change.

Meanwhile, I had of course been busy with physics. There still was much to do on electrons in metals. I wrote up the paper on magnetoresistance, the problem that had troubled me at the Leipzig conference, and corrected the wrong statement I had made about the resistance of pure metals at very low temperatures. I was asked to write a review article about the electron theory of metals, and enjoyed doing so. It received complimentary reviews.

Then I started thinking about the absorption of light in solids. In certain cases, in which the effect of the incident light is to excite an atom, the result will be the re-emission of light when the atom returns to its normal state, unless its energy can be converted into atomic vibrations. Without this conversion we would have scattering of light, but no true absorption. Now, the trouble with the conversion is that the excitation energy of the atom is much larger than the energy of the most energetic phonon, so that the process would involve the simultaneous creation of many phonons. In a naive approach one gets the impression that phonons can be created only one at a time, so the simultaneous creation of a large number would be a very rare event. It took some time before I understood that the naive approach is not correct, because the rule that phonons are generated singly applies only to vibrations of small amplitude—i.e., if each atom remains close to its normal position. In fact the distortion of the atomic lattice around an excited atom involves large displacements.

A paper on this subject was submitted for my *Habilitation*. In the German-speaking universities this was a procedure by which you acquired the *venia legendi*, the permission to lecture in your own right. It involved, besides a thesis, also a sample lecture usually attended by many of the professors. My lecture was on the limitations of the analogy between light and matter. Quantum mechanics teaches us that both light and material particles, such as electrons, can behave as waves and as particles, and this gives the impression that it was just an accident of history that we first encountered electrons as particles, and light as waves. It turns out that this is far from accidental, and that there are good reasons why electrons cannot, in a classical limit (i.e., with quantum effects negligibly small), be treated as waves, or light as particles.

Meanwhile, I had many discussions with Pauli on a wide range of subjects. He was then working on a review article on quantum mechanics, which discussed in depth the achievements and the unsolved problems in this field. He had also recently proposed the idea of a neutral particle (later called the neutrino), and of course the difficulties of quantum electrodynamics were a recurring theme. Pauli liked to discuss his thoughts, and to listen to him was probably one of the essential duties of his assistant. This, however, did not exclude his being a very severe critic of my work. A letter that summer, after commenting adversely on things I was doing, ends with "I hope your physics will improve; I am not very satisfied with it."

I was to leave Zurich in 1932, since Pauli liked to change his assistants; in fact, three years was, I believe, a record length of tenure. He advised me to make an application for a fellowship of the Rockefeller Foundation, which he would support. It was then the policy of the Foundation to give fellowships only to scientists who had an academic position to return to, since they did not want the benefit of the fellowship to be wasted on people who would then drop out of academic life. So Pauli confirmed that I was entitled to return to Zurich after the fellowship year, but it was understood that I would not take up this entitlement.

One of the members of the fellowship committee came to Zurich, and it would have been normal for me to be interviewed by him, but just when he arrived, both Genia and I were in bed with the flu. I recall that, as we could not go out shopping or deal with other housekeeping problems, we engaged temporary household help, a spinster called Fräulein Ritterknecht (which literally means "Knight's Serf"). Perhaps it was just as well, because I got the award anyway, so the interview could only have made things worse.

4

Rockefeller Fellow

Rome. Farewell to Germany

I chose to divide the fellowship year between Rome and Cambridge, which was what Hans Bethe had done previously. But he had gone to Cambridge for the winter, and to Rome for the summer, and I improved on that by reversing the order. Most of that summer in Zurich had been cold and wet, and we felt that for our summer holiday we had to be absolutely sure of sunshine. So we consulted the meteorological map of Europe for the place with the lowest rainfall in August, and this turned out to be the Costa Brava, the Spanish coast north of Barcelona. The guide book, the famous Baedeker, had only half a page in small print about the whole region, so we decided this was the place for us.

True to tradition, we made the journey in stages, mostly by night train, and saw Avignon and Arles on the way. We even stopped in Tarascon, a pleasant provincial town made famous by Daudet's book. We could see no traces of Tartarin, but we were amused by the local name for a public convenience: "Chalet de Nécessité."

We found our destination as attractive as we had expected, and as sunny. We stopped in the little port of San Feliú, where one of the waiters in the hotel spoke a little French and was most helpful as an interpreter. When we offered him a good tip on leaving, he refused, assuring us that a service charge was added to the bill. A rare experience! Friends in Zurich, who had been in the region, had described a very nice hotel to us, but they did not remember its name or exact location. During a walk along the coast, we saw, in the distance, a house on a cliff above the sea, and we decided that must be the place they had mentioned. We spent the rest of the holiday there. A French couple left just as we arrived, so we were the only foreigners in the place. We were noticed in the village, and on one occasion a very small boy said, "I know, you are German, and she is Russian."

The weather was as promised: not a drop of rain during our whole stay. We finally left via a small train to Gerona, the provincial capital. The train had only fourth-class carriages, filled with people, chickens, and goats. We meant to stay overnight in Gerona, which is an interesting old town, but discovered that our tickets to Barcelona were valid only for the day on which they were bought, so we had a hurried tour of the town and took the last train to Barcelona. We stayed in an hotel in the old part of town, in a street so narrow that our taxi had to back up to let a cyclist get out. It was a hot night, and we slept without night clothes. In the morning Genia sat up and was surprised to see herself in a mirror. She could not recall seeing a mirror in the room the night before. She then realised that the mirror was in a room in a house across the street.

In Barcelona we went to see a bullfight, expecting to dislike it but to be interested in the reaction of the crowd. In fact we were fascinated by the elegance of the movements of the matadors. As to the crowd, we were puzzled when at one point half the audience booed violently, and the rest applauded with equal vigour. Our neighbours explained that some were booing the matador, the others applauding the bull.

On leaving Barcelona we decided to walk across the Pyrenees into France. We went by bus to Andorra, the small state governed by a Spanish bishop and the president of France, and walked over a mountain pass. We spent the night in a small Andorran village; as the houses did not seem very sanitary, we asked for permission to sleep in a hay barn. Communication was difficult, since the women spoke only Catalan, and the men were out (most likely smuggling tobacco into France). We understood that it was all right to sleep in the barn, but not that others would also be there. At night more people arrived. They banged on the door we had bolted, and I had quite a problem trying to find the right direction to the door in the dark and in all that hay. The night obscured the fact that they had a dog, which ate all our provisions except for a tin of sardines.

The next day we walked for a bit with some of the tobacco smugglers, one of whom remarked, "I wish my wife could walk like that!" Eventually we reached a small French village without having passed a border post, so we had no French entrance stamp in our passports, which caused raised eyebrows when we later left the country. We were tired, hungry, and dirty; when we enquired whether there was an hotel in the village, and found out there were several, we asked for the best. There they had vacant rooms, but when we enquired about the bathroom, they thought we were joking. So we grandly called a taxi to take us to the nearest railway and ended our tour in an hotel in Toulouse, with a four-poster bed.

We later visited my parents in Berlin. The economic situation in Germany was getting worse, unemployment was high, and political life was becoming more violent. Assassinations had been common during the whole period of the Weimar Republic, and now the brown shirts of the National Socialists were increasing in number and in aggressiveness. They were opposed by armed groups of communists and by a not very efficient group of young men supporting the republic. Clashes between the opposing groups were common. Yet few people had any inkling of the disaster that was imminent.

In October we arrived in Rome and settled in a small boarding-house, where we were the only foreigners. The place was an unending source of amusement, but also occasionally of irritation. The flat that comprised the boarding-house was run by an Italian woman from Alexandria in Egypt whose husband's business had failed. He was back in Alexandria learning a new trade, and she was making ends meet by running the boarding-house. When we first arrived we were shown around a spotlessly clean flat by a maid with the face of a Perugini Madonna. Within a few weeks the flat became crowded, Letitia, the maid, moved into the kitchen, and the landlady slept in the dining room to accommodate more guests. As a result the maid became overworked and things started to go wrong. Meals were not ready on time, and once the cook gave all knives in the house to a knife-grinder who had solemnly promised to return them in time for lunch. Needless to say, he didn't, and my penknife was passed around to cut the chicken.

The gas water heater in the only bathroom was padlocked, to make sure guests paid for their baths. But two engineers tried to beat the system by bypassing the padlocked tap. They must have been poor engineers, because the result was a gas leak, and when the maid tried to light the heater there was an explosion, which did no damage but badly frightened her. The landlady was so angry that she stamped her foot, breaking a large flower pot, and hurting her foot so badly that she had to retire to bed for a few days.

In a room next to ours were two students from the Abruzzi, the mountains east of Rome. Men from that region have the reputation of being rather wild, and these two seemed to be no exception. We had a portable gramophone with us and were surprised when, on the morning after our return from a trip, we were woken up by the sound of our records, played on our gramophone next door. Other guests included a *duchessa* and her gigolo, and an elderly gentleman who had lived in Paris for a time, and made himself unpopular with the other guests by insisting that Paris was better than Rome. He wore a monocle, and we were waiting for the moment when it would drop into his soup; when it finally did, it was hard to keep a straight face. Another guest, who did not stay but often came for meals, was the landlady's Sicilian boyfriend. One evening we were invited to a restaurant to celebrate the landlady's wedding anniversary with her and the boyfriend.

In time it became clear that Letitia, the Perugini Madonna, was pregnant. In the middle of one night we were awakened by her screams. The landlady's boyfriend, who unaccountably was around at this hour, phoned for an ambulance, but it did not arrive until it was no longer needed. The landlady and the cook had done their best to assist in the birth, but they were inexperienced, as neither had any children. However, Letitia told them what to do—it turned out to be her second child. She was unlucky, however. Some time earlier, Mussolini had instituted child allowances for unmarried mothers in order to increase the birthrate, and this had been enough for her to place the first child with foster parents. But the scheme worked so well that it became too expensive for the government, and the rules werre changed, giving a much smaller allowance for the second child. This happened while she was pregnant and left her very poor.

She left fairly soon afterwards, and her successor had poor relatives in a village, so that she sent home every few lire she received as a tip. She had a young brother in the village, for whom the landlady found work; but he could not accept the offer, as he could not afford shoes to come into town.

One saw signs of Mussolini's regime not only through these economic symptoms. One Sunday we went for a walk in the Pincio, the park of the Villa Borghese. After a while we were told by the police to walk along a certain path, and at the end we were again pointed in a specific direction until we found ourselves at the edge of the park. Here we ordered a drink at a café. Soon the waiter asked us to pay our bill because, he said, we would shortly have to leave. In answer to our questions, he explained that later in the afternoon Il Duce would be making a speech, so the park had to be cleared. Later, presumably, carefully screened crowds would be admitted to do the cheering.

Near the Palazzo Venezia, where Mussolini worked, two people always waited by the bus stop, but their bus never came. They were security men, recognizable by the umbrellas they carried, rain or shine. The security forces were not short of manpower, because serving them for a period was a prerequisite for a job in the Civil Service.

An aunt of Genia's lived along the route Mussolini took from his residence to his office, and each time he passed, a security man came to stand on her balcony. She asked him one day if this was not a terribly dull job. "Oh, no! It's much better than sitting in a manhole." Apparently for Mussolini's protection a man went down each manhole in the street.

The newsreels in the cinema always featured an item called "Opere del Regime" (achievements of the regime), which showed the latest buildings or bridges and so forth, usually in very poor taste. So when we came across a particularly ugly modern building, we tended to say to each other (but not too loudly), "Opere del Regime!"

Many people in Italy were able to get rail tickets at reduced prices. For example, state employees (this included university professors), and people travelling south for the Sicilian spring or to a trade fair paid a reduced fare. It was said that anyone who paid a full fare would be introduced to the Minister of Transport. Once we came from the north at a time when special tickets were available for visitors attending an exhibition in Rome that extolled the glories of fascism. To validate the return part of the ticket, one had to visit the exhibition. We went through the turnstile, had our tickets stamped and went straight out again. The attendants glowered, but we had satisfied the rules.

The average Roman was (and still is) friendly, talkative, and loud. Fascism did not change his manner. We found that only people who wore uniforms and had someone else to give orders to showed the strutting chin and self-importance fostered by the system.

None of this applied to the scientists, of course. I did not meet one physicist who was sympathetic to the regime, although there were a few, no doubt. The ones I did meet could be divided between those who tried to forget what was going on in the country and get on with their work, and those who were aware of the political atmosphere and felt very unhappy about it, though they would not complain in public. Fermi belonged to the first kind. He accepted an appointment to the Academy that was set up by Mussolini, because this would put him in a better position to get support for his research.

I had met Fermi before, but I came to appreciate his impressive qualities only in Rome. He had a mind of exceptional clarity, and he knew the answers to an incredible range of problems. Indeed, when you asked him about any problem of physics, the chances were that he would take one of a number of black notebooks from his shelf and turn up a page where the solution to your problem was worked out. His methods were always simple, and he did not like complicated techniques. When a problem became complicated he lost interest. But it must be explained that in Fermi's hands, problems that had been terrifyingly complicated for others often became very simple.

At the time I was in Rome, he was preparing to change to experimental work. The discovery of the neutron by Chadwick earlier that year had revolutionised our ideas about atomic nuclei, and presumably Fermi decided that the next exciting progress in nuclear physics would come from experiments. To build up the necessary equipment takes time, so while I was there, there was much discussion about nuclear physics, but the experiments did not start until later.

Meanwhile, the department's main activity centered around the details of atomic spectra, and for this one needed atomic wave functions, which could be obtained only by numerical calculations. Therefore, many members of the department were busy turning the handles of small manual calculators to solve the wave equation. I was familiar with these machines. To multiply a number by, say, 136, you set the number on levers, then turned the handle once, shifted the carriage, turned three times, shifted again and turned six times. It takes less time to do this than to explain it.

But I had no experience in solving differential equations numerically, and asked if I could join the project. So for a while I turned out wave functions myself, and was impressed by the ease with which one can obtain solutions that way. This is often much faster than exact so-called analytic solutions that take the form of a very complicated formula, or a long series, from which it is very laborious to get actual numbers. By playing with the numerical solution, one often gets a much better feeling for the nature of the equation and the behaviour of its solutions. This was a very valuable lesson.

Apart from this I continued working on electrons in metals. The behaviour of diamagnetic metals was not yet understood. Landau had solved the problem of the diamagnetism of free electrons, but it was not clear how this would be modified by the presence of the atoms in the metal. There was also the mystery of bismuth, which showed a much greater diamagnetism than any other substance, and at low temperatures its magnetic behaviour showed curious oscillations as the magnetic field strength was varied. This was discovered by W. J. de Haas and his student P. M. van Alphen in Leiden. I remember that when I visited Leiden, de Haas was completely mystified by what he found in bismuth. As one could not understand the effect, he was studying the influence on it of all possible variables, including time. He kept a sample of bismuth in his cupboard and every few months remeasured its magnetic behaviour to see if it changed.

While working on these problems I suddenly realised that these oscillations were in fact to be expected in the Landau model. Landau himself had pointed this out in his paper but had decided the oscillations would not be observable. I had not paid attention to his remark, nor did anyone else, and it was pointed out to me only many years later. So the explanation of the curious oscillations was now clear. In most metals they could be observed only at very low temperatures and in extremely uniform magnetic fields, but bismuth happens to be an exceptionally favourable case. Later work, particularly by Shoenberg in Cambridge, led to measurements of the effect in all metals, and it became a very powerful method for gaining information about the state of the electrons in each metal.

Other theoreticians working with Fermi included Giancarlo Wick, of whom we saw a good deal. He was one of the people who was intensely unhappy about the Mussolini regime. After the war he left Italy and settled in the United States. It was typical of him that when, during the McCarthy era, the University of California required a loyalty oath of their professors, he resigned from his professorship at Berkeley.

There was also Majorana, a theoretician of outstanding ability. He came from an old Sicilian family, and he himself was extremely modest and shy. He was reluctant to publish his work because he never felt it was good enough. It took great pressure and persuasion to get him to publish papers, many of which have become classics.

I recall a conversation I had with Fermi about Chadwick's discovery of the neutron. It followed Irène Curie's experiments, which, as one can now see by hindsight, were clear evidence that the radiation in question consisted of heavy neutral particles and not gamma rays, as she believed. Fermi expressed sympathy that she missed the discovery, but his tone made me suspect that he had known the result all along. I found out later that, on seeing the report of the Curie experiment, Majorana had immediately said, "How stupid these people are! This is a heavy neutral particle!" A few years later, he mysteriously disappeared from a ferry between Sicily and the mainland, and it is not known whether this was accident or suicide. There were even rumours that he went into hiding in a monastery.

The rest of the senior members of the department were mainly experimentalists, though they all had a good grasp of theory. Franco Rasetti was the oldest among them. His many hobbies included an interest in road building, especially the many Roman roads still in use. On excursions he would disconcert his companions by suddenly lying down in the road to inspect the details of its construction. He eventually went to Canada and taught at the University of Quebec. Emilio Segré was also there. He later went to the United States and worked in Berkeley, where he shared the Nobel Prize for the discovery of the anti-proton. All members of the Rome group had nicknames, and I recall that Fermi was "the Pope," while Segré was "the Basilisk" because of his capacity to annihilate people in debate. Still another member, Edoardo Amaldi, remained in Italy and became the leader of experimental physics after the war; he later played an important role in the European Physical Society.

We used all our available time to see the sights of Rome. Six months is not enough to see everything that is worth seeing, but one can see a good deal. On one occasion we were in Trastevere, the district across the Tiber River, and followed the instructions in our guidebook to go to the top of a park on the side of a steep hill, where we had an impressive panorama. The guidebook further recommended going all the way down through the park to regain the road at the bottom. We did this, but found that the gate at the bottom was locked. We were not enthusiastic about going all the way up again, and Genia suggested climbing over the fence, which was quite low. I did not like the idea, as the police were very strict, and we might get into some trouble; but I gave in. As we started to climb, we heard an enormous bang above our heads, and I exclaimed, "There, I told you!" But we happened to be right below the noon gun, and it was twelve o'clock.

For Christmas we went to Kitzbühel in the Austrian Alps to do some skiing. Genia found that she was pregnant with our first child, so she could ski only with the greatest caution, but nevertheless enjoyed the exhilarating winter mountain scene. David Inglis, an American visitor in Rome, came with us. He had not skied before, but he would heroically go straight down the steepest slope. At the bottom he invariably fell on his nose, and he carried a mark there until after his return to Rome.

Anticipating motherhood, Genia worried about her lack of experience with children, particularly because her family was so far away. She therefore arranged to work as a part-time volunteer in a nursery, which proved to be a valuable experience. The arrangement was made by Laura Fermi, Fermi's wife, with whom we made friends—a very good-looking, very gentle, and very intelligent woman. Her great energy and strength of personality were not immediately apparent, and we learned to appreciate these qualities only much later.

The problem of finding a job after the end of my fellowship was of course in our minds. It seemed natural to return to Germany, so I was pleased to get a letter from Hamburg offering me an appointment. This was only an assistantship, but it was a job held by Pauli at one time, and it seemed a good springboard for an academic career. Besides, Pauli had told me about the atmosphere in the Hamburg Physics

Department, largely due to the presence of Otto Stern, the professor of physics and a great experimentalist—a lively person interested in good physics and in good food and drink. In fact the letter came from him, although the position was under Lenz, the theoretical physicist. They wanted to fill the appointment soon, and asked me to come at Easter 1933, which meant forgoing the second half of my fellowship. But that seemed worthwhile, and I tentatively answered that I would accept the offer.

But at that time the political situation in Germany, which had not looked too good for some time, took a turn for the worse. Hitler and his hordes were becoming more powerful and were gaining the support of some conservative politicians, who thought they could use Hitler to counter communism. They also thought they could keep him under control. The president was Hindenburg, the popular field marshal, who was getting very old and did not seem to understand the political situation. The head of the government, the chancellor, was Schleicher, a conservative but very honest man. When Hindenburg sacked him and put von Papen in his place, we realised that the situation in Germany was heading for disaster.

We discussed this problem, of course, with our friends in Rome, and they said: "We understand your feelings, but you are too pessimistic. We, too, went through a fascist revolution, and while it has its unpleasant aspects, it is still possible to live and work here." But we were not convinced, and when the official invitation came, I turned it down.

I went to see my father and urged him to leave Germany. He agreed with our reading of the situation, but said that he was too old to go to a foreign country: he did not know any languages, and was too old to learn; and though he would be able to take his savings with him, he would lose his pension and be dependent on other people. He had, in fact, a wealthy brother in New York who was always ready to help relatives and would surely have been glad to support his brother if necessary; but my father was reluctant to accept such help and stayed in Germany.

Cambridge

In the spring of 1933 we left Rome and, after our usual stopovers, reached England, where I was to spend the second half of my fellowship. When one comes from the Continent, England seems strange in many ways, and it takes some time to adjust. Our first impression was

90

of a toylike quality: the trains and houses looked so small. The landscape was unfamiliar because of the absence of forests, though the beauty of individual trees was more apparent. ("On the Continent you do not see the trees for the woods," we used to say.)

But more important, we noticed typical differences in the relations among people. We had been told that the English are very reserved and would not easily talk to strangers. This might have been true at some time, perhaps before the First World War, but it was certainly not so in the thirties: it was as easy as anywhere else to get into conversation with complete strangers. Usually one's neighbours, or casual acquaintances, are aware of the possibility that you may want to be left alone and do not press their company on you unless your response is positive. The rules of polite behaviour are much less rigid than they were in Germany, and are mostly directed toward trying to make the other person feel comfortable. For example, if in Germany you visited someone's house and started to leave, it was obligatory for the host to say it was still early, and would you not stay a little longer? The first few times we were invited out in England and the hosts peacefully acquiesced to our departure, we were very shocked, thinking we must have overstayed our welcome. It was even more embarrassing when once we had lunch with friends, and at 2 P.M. the host said, "You will have to excuse me; I have a meeting in the lab." But one soon gets to accept these things as natural. It is polite also in England to let others pass through a door first, and particularly ladies, but one does not fuss about it. The situation gave rise to the beautiful saying, "Nothing will stop a German but an open door."

We had greater problems adjusting to the food, particularly that in restaurants and boarding-houses. Presumably the deplorable standard of English food originated from the puritanical idea that food is something material, and that it is bad form to be interested in it or to talk about it. Indeed, during the Second World War, when the food shortages made it a patriotic virtue to take an interest in food preparation in order to get more out of what was available, there was a marked improvement in the general quality. I even proposed a theory of the typical English boarding-house food: it would be undemocratic for the cook to impose his or her taste on the guests, so things are boiled until only a neutral matrix remains, to which the guest can give any flavour by adding salt, pepper, horseradish, mustard, ketchup, and so on. This may be exaggerated, but I am sure it contains an element of truth. But even in the thirties one could, of course, find excellent food in private homes or in special restaurants. The best English food could be obtained by starting with excellent raw materials and not spoiling them.

When we arrived in Cambridge, we first stayed in the house of C. H. Waddington, the biologist, who had recently been divorced and was abroad. His house had effectively become a boarding-house, with a housekeeper who cleaned the house and fed the guests. The work was apparently too much for her, because both the cleaning and the food suffered. The food, in any case, was very English, in the sense I have already described. So after a while we moved into a tiny furnished house.

When I went to the Cavendish Laboratory to report to R. H. Fowler, the senior theoretician, I knew his room was on the first floor of the laboratory. But there I found a number of unmarked doors, and nobody to ask. (This was, at the time, a general trend in England; trains usually had no signs showing their destination—you just knew.) I finally decided to try the most inconspicuous-looking door to ask for directions. This turned out to be Rutherford's office, but only his secretary was there, who told me where to find Fowler.

I knew Fowler from my previous visit. He was well known for his work on statistical mechanics and on astrophysics, which included many important contributions, but, in true Cambridge tradition, had a rather mathematical flavour. He supervised more theoretical research students than anyone in Cambridge, and because of the high prestige of Cambridge in the mathematical sciences, these students represented the best available in the country. Yet, while a few of them were very successful in their later careers, their number was disappointingly small. Perhaps this was due to the system by which theoretical physics was treated in Cambridge as a branch of mathematics, so that the students never saw the inside of a laboratory. Or perhaps it was due to Fowler's method of putting each student to work on a small corner of a project, whose overall design was clear to Fowler, but not necessarily to the student.

As a person, Fowler was very positive and clear in the use of language. I had written to him from Zurich when A. H. (now Sir Alan) Wilson had attacked Bloch's and my theory of metals, and our correspondence had not led to agreement. I wrote to Fowler asking whether he would communicate my reply to the *Proceedings of the Royal Society*, in which Wilson's paper had appeared. He replied that he would, provided my reply was carefully worded: "You can call someone a fool, but you must not call him a damned fool." Actually Fowler's letter was delayed because he was abroad, and I had already sent my reply to the *Zeitschrift für Physik*. I believe it did not call Wilson a fool, let alone anything worse.

Of course one soon got to know Rutherford, both at meetings in the Cavendish and at some of the parties held regularly at his house. It goes without saying that I found his command of physics and his energy as impressive as his reputation had led me to expect. What one had not been led to expect was his simple directness and his warm interest in people. He loved to tell stories, and I recollect, for example, one of his favourite stories about the new University Library being opened by King George V and Queen Mary. An enthusiastic librarian showed the royal visitors the bookshelves, which were of a new design, and had some advantages. To show interest, the king asked what they were made of. "Of steel, Your Majesty."—"Will they last?" This earned him a poke in the ribs from the Queen's umbrella: "Don't be silly, George, of course they will last!" Another of his stories was of the earlier days in Cambridge, when the social life was so stratified that professors would visit only each other, and the heads of colleges also kept a close circle. The wife of a master of one of the colleges was thus heard to remark, "I wish I knew what they talk about in a professor's house."

It is said that Rutherford did not approve of theoreticians, but I never experienced any lack of courtesy or consideration. He certainly thought highly of Gamow, whose application of quantum mechanics had solved the mystery of alpha radioactivity, and had shown that for splitting nuclei much lower energies were sufficient than expected from classical physics. His warm friendship for Niels Bohr had endured since the old Manchester days, and he was the best of friends with Fowler, who happened to be his son-in-law. So at most he disapproved of *some* theoreticians.

It was an exciting time in nuclear physics. Chadwick's discovery of the neutron the previous year had opened up new approaches, and Cockcroft and Walton had shown how to produce nuclear reactions with artificially accelerated particles. Blackett was developing the Wilson cloud chamber into a sophisticated tool for studying nuclei and cosmic radiation. I tried to learn as much as possible about these new developments, but my own work was still concerned partly with electrons in metals, and partly with the difficulties of relativistic field theory, including Dirac's "hole theory". This showed some new kinds of infinities, which I thought I could do something about. On these problems my main contacts were Dirac, of whom I shall have to say more later, and the younger theoreticians. These included in particular Nevill (now Sir Nevill) Mott, perhaps the friendliest among many kind

93

and friendly people we met then. Very tall and fair, he had a superficial resemblance to Gamow, and the two were sometimes confused when both were in Cambridge. At the time he was working on relativistic electron theory, and his solutions to many problems in that area have become classics. Later, on moving to Bristol, his interests shifted to the theory of solids, in which he became a leader.

V. F. Weisskopf was also on a Rockefeller fellowship. Being from Vienna, he has the proverbial soft charm of the Viennese. He had previously been in Göttingen, and after the end of his fellowship in Cambridge was to go to Zurich as Pauli's assistant; he was a little apprehensive, and asked about my experience in living with Pauli. In fact, when he later arrived in Zurich, Pauli welcomed him with the explanation that he had really tried to get Bethe to come. When Weisskopf had been there a few weeks, a problem came up to which Pauli asked him to find the solution. When Weisskopf did not have it ready the next time they met, Pauli shook his head and said, "I should have got Bethe!"

In Cambridge I was also intrigued by the experiments of Peter Kapitza, which included the phenomenon of magnetoresistance, with which I had struggled in Zurich. Kapitza, who recently died at the age of 89, was a physicist of great initiative and fertile imagination. He decided that very strong magnetic fields could provide important information about the structure of matter, and set about producing stronger magnetic fields than had been used before. In such fields iron would be saturated, and therefore the ordinary magnet with a big iron core would be useless. Instead, he passed a very short but intense burst of current through a coil by short-circuiting a generator through it. All this required heavy equipment, and he managed to convince Rutherford to support this project, although Rutherford's inclination was to do physics without large or expensive apparatus, by the "string-and-sealing-wax" approach. In 1933 the Mond Laboratory, a purpose-built laboratory for Kapitza's experiments, was being completed, to be operated under the auspices of the Royal Society. He was an innovator in other ways. He started the "Kapitza Club", which met once a week, usually in his rooms in Trinity College, where the latest developments in physics were reported. As a club it had a limited membership, due to the limited accommodation in the college room.

Kapitza was a fellow of the Royal Society, although he was a Soviet citizen. Fellowship of the Royal Society was open to British subjects only, and I have never been able to find out how it came about that he was elected. One theory is that the officers of the society took it for granted that he had become a British subject, without checking this.

94

He was also in an unusual position as a Soviet citizen because he had a permanent passport for foreign travel. Normally such a passport is valid only for one journey, and a new application has to be made for each renewal. Permanent passports were only for diplomats and other government representatives, but for some reason Kapitza had one, and he usually went back to Moscow for summer vacations. He enjoyed this dual connection. It is said that he once invited Bukharin, then Soviet Minister for Education, whom he knew, to dinner in Trinity College, mainly in order to be able to make the introduction: "Comrade Bukharin—Lord Rutherford."

But in 1935, when he visited Moscow as usual, his passport was cancelled on the grounds that Moscow needed his services. When all appeals against that decision failed, the Royal Society agreed to sell Kapitza's special equipment to the Soviet Academy of Sciences so that he could continue his research. Replacements were ordered for the Mond Laboratory so that work in the same field could continue.

Personally, we were closest to the Blacketts. Patrick and Constance Blackett, both known to their friends and to each other as Pat, were a gregarious couple whose house was always full of friends and strangers. They took a warm interest in all of them. They had arranged for our accommodation in Waddington's house, but this was not an unqualified success. Patrick Blackett had spent some time in Germany and understood the political events taking place there. He was perhaps more concerned over the developments there than anyone else in Cambridge physics. In the autumn of 1933 the Blacketts moved to London, where Patrick had accepted a chair at Birkbeck College, the part of London University that taught mostly part-time students in night classes. He was the first of a series of Rutherford collaborators to leave and bring nuclear physics to the "underdeveloped" universities.

During the summer of 1933 many "non-Aryan" scientists from Germany appeared in England. Many more were anxious to come, once the aims and methods of the Hitler regime were becoming evident. It was also a time of economic depression and shortage of academic posts, and it would have been very understandable if the local scientists had resented the arrival of so many refugees who would compete with them for posts. But they received the newcomers with great kindness. British scientists, including physicists, took the initiative in setting up the Academic Assistance Council, which helped refugees, and, from funds raised by voluntary contributions, made grants to support them until they could find employment in Britain or elsewhere.

The "staff" of the Academic Assistance Council, later known as the Society for the Protection of Science and Learning, consisted of one

95

person, Miss Esther Simpson, who in 1933 started on a temporary appointment for three months. She retired a few years ago and today still follows the fate of the many people, her "children", to whom her care and advice have been a source of strength for over fifty years.

People seemed to feel particularly sorry for us. Genia's very obvious pregnancy and my lack of a job after the end of the summer sent ladies bursting into tears when looking at her. To us this worry seemed exaggerated. My fellowship still had several months to run, and we had saved a little money to last another two or three months, so we still had plenty of time to find a solution.

There were many advertisements offering university appointments, and at first I optimistically thought it should be easy to get one of them. But soon I discovered that there were many other applicants, and my chances did not look so bright. At one point a junior position in Cambridge was advertised, and this seemed promising. Hans Bethe was still in Germany, but of course wanted to leave, so I sent him a telegram suggesting he apply for this appointment, while also applying myself. But neither of us was successful.

Then an assistant lectureship in Manchester was advertised. I wrote to the professor, W. L. (later Sir Lawrence) Bragg, for information, and he replied very enthusiastically, making me feel that my chances would be very good, so I applied. In due course the official answer arrived by mail. It arrived at the Cavendish Laboratory before I got there one morning, and Nevill Mott, who knew my situation, got on his bicycle and in great excitement brought the letter to our house. However, it was a rejection. Bragg was apologetic: Manchester University had appointed Polanyi, another refugee but a very senior and distinguished person, to the chair of Physical Chemistry and had been violently attacked in the press for this. They could not continue making such appointments without making themselves unpopular. They did give Bethe a temporary post to replace someone on leave, but they could not do more. However, Bragg arranged for a two-year grant for me from a Manchester fund similar to the Academic Assistance Council. We felt a little embarrassed about accepting this grant, as we were not technically refugees, but finally persuaded ourselves that, as we evidently could not return to Germany, we were, in effect, refugees.

We had to find accommodation in Manchester, and went there for a few days to house-hunt. Upon our arrival, we looked near the railway station for some small hotel. Our experience on the Continent suggested that in a large city there should be plenty of hotels near the station. But we did not see any, except for the big Midland Hotel, which was beyond our means. Perhaps this was the wrong station?

But near the other station the situation was no better. By this time Genia was very tired, and I left her in the nearest place where one could sit down—the restaurant in Woolworth's. I then looked at the classified telephone directory, and was relieved to see several pages of hotels. I did not suspect that the word "hotel" in England usually means a pub, and I was surprised by some of the reactions to my phone enquiries. Eventually, I found that another category in the phone list, "boarding establishments & private hotels," was the correct source. It yielded a pleasant place, which also became our headquarters on later visits.

Wandering around, we saw some small but pleasant new houses. They were for sale, but the poster indicated one could buy them on instalments. We enquired at the office whether we could stay in such a house for two years or whatever time we were going to spend in Manchester, and then stop paying. We were assured this was possible, and the man promised to send us the papers. We went back to Cambridge pleased how nicely we had solved our problem.

When the papers came, we realised that we would have to buy the house with a mortgage from a building society. There was nothing to show that we could get out of the deal after two years, except by selling the house, which was fraught with uncertainty. Subsequent correspondence was not satisfactory, and in the end we gave up. It was a useful lesson that in real estate transactions one must read the small print and not go by what people say. By now Genia was in the maternity home, and I went back alone to Manchester and found a house to rent. It was what was known as a "modern semi-detached", cheaply and sloppily built, six miles from the university.

In August our daughter was born while we were still in Cambridge. We decided her name should be pronounceable in any language, since we did not know where we would end up living (and we had enough trouble with our surname!). As there was a French actress, Gaby Morlay, popular at the time, we settled on Gaby. The Rockefeller Foundation had a rule that its fellows must send them the results of their work, and I decided to send them a copy of the announcement of Gaby's birth. I heard later that they were not amused.

We decided to raise Gaby according to the instructions in the books of Truby King, then the fashionable texts on child rearing. But Gaby did not seem very happy, and it took Genia a little time to realise that the regime prescribed in these books did not provide enough food for the baby. She finally replaced the rules by common sense, and the child thrived.

As soon as we knew we would be going to Manchester we started

97

to acquire some furniture and other essentials. For this we went to the auction sales in the Corn Exchange in Cambridge, where, with a little study in the techniques of the auctions and a lot of patience, one could get nice objects very cheaply. We bought, for 15 shillings, a Victorian mahogany dining table with three extra leaves, which would eventually seat sixteen people, and, on a different occasion, we bought six chairs to match for 2/6d each.

Meanwhile, a constant stream of friends visited us that summer. Many of them had left Germany, or were planning to do so, and passed through Cambridge in their search of a future. We exchanged news and advice with all of them. Käte Sperling from Berlin also stayed with us for some time.

5

Growing Roots in England

Manchester. Working with Bethe

Eventually the time came to move. I went ahead to get the house ready and to find a charwoman. We had been given the address of a suitable help, and I went to call on her. I was surprised and charmed when she immediately asked me in and offered me a cup of tea, a gesture characteristic of the friendliness and informality of the Mancunians.

We had acquired the most essential furniture, including that for a spare room, in which Hans Bethe stayed for a year to share expenses. But there were new problems. We were not used to the methods then normal in England for heating, or rather not heating, the houses. We had some radiant gas fires, which heated the immediate area around the fireplace, and left the rest of the house damp and icy. There was no telephone, and of course we had no car. So life was not easy, particularly for Genia, who felt the absence of any close friends or relatives to consult about domestic problems.

In 1933 Machester was hardly an attractive city. The buildings had been erected mostly during the Victorian period and were in poor taste, and there were many slum areas. The new part, where we lived, consisted of cheap houses put up by speculative builders. Most of the older houses were black with soot, so that even the few attractive buildings in the centre were not easily distinguished. An unusual exception was the brand-new city library, which was white and circular, like a gigantic wedding cake.

All this was aggravated by fogs, of which we got a good supply that winter, sometimes for two or three days on end. They were so dense that on crossing a wide road you were never sure whether you had gone straight across, or had gone in a circle and were back on the side where you started. The fog (or its smoke content) even penetrated indoors, so that in the theatre it was hard to see the stage from the back of the auditorium.

But against all these drawbacks the warm and friendly nature of

99

the local population made the city a pleasant place in which to live. Manchester was famous for its liberal and free-trade tradition, for the *Manchester Guardian*, and for the Hallé orchestra; but during the economic depression of the thirties all these were in a bad way. There was not much free trade, the *Guardian* was generally late with the news because it could not afford enough correspondents, and the Hallé orchestra had lost its best players to the BBC.

Bethe and I acquired cheap second-hand bicycles for commuting the six miles to the university, a Victorian edifice in a rather seedy district not far from the city centre. I bought my cycle from a small shop near the university, and when I had paid the price, probably £1 or so, the shopkeeper offered me a receipt. I said this was not necessary, but he insisted: "When the police stop you and ask you where you got the bicycle, you need to show the receipt."

In October, when we had barely settled down in Manchester, I went to the Solvay Conference. These conferences, held every few years in Brussels, were very prestigious gatherings held to discuss the fundamental problems of physics. At the earlier conferences only the most distinguished and most senior physicists had been invited. This time it was decided to invite some younger people, as well—I suspect on the initiative of Paul Langevin, the great French physicist who became president of the conferences after the death of H. A. Lorentz of the Netherlands. I felt fortunate to be invited. Among those in my age group were also Nevill Mott, who had by this time moved to Bristol; Léon Rosenfeld, now back in Belgium; and George Gamow. Most of the great names in physics were there, too, and it was a privilege to listen to the debates.

The subject was the atomic nucleus, and since the preceding conference many things had happened: the discovery of the neutron and the positron, the use of artificially accelerated particles to disintegrate nuclei, and Pauli's hypothesis of the neutrino. It was an exciting conference. This was the only occasion on which I saw Marie Curie, who died the following year. I was very impressed with her poise and command of physics. She was then 66, which seemed to me very old, yet she was absolutely up to date on all technical details, and often corrected her daughter Irène and her son-in-law, Frédéric Joliot, on points of fact.

There was an amusing sequel to this. In 1977 a conference was held at the University of Minnesota on the history of nuclear physics. One woman student, who perhaps was writing a Ph.D. thesis on Marie Curie, asked a leading question: Was it not true that Madame Curie was a most unpleasant person, that by 1933 she was well past it and did not understand what was going on, and that she was invited to the Solvay Conference only because she would otherwise have made trouble? Hans Bethe, sitting next to me, asked if I was not going to reply. I said to him that I knew this was all nonsense, but I had no clear evidence to quote against it. Hans said, "Don't you remember how you returned from that conference full of admiration for Madame Curie and her command of up-to-date physics?" I got up and said I had forgotten, but Hans Bethe, whose memory I trusted, remembered my impressions of 1933, and I reported them. This was duly recorded in the conference proceedings.

The Solvay conferences were well endowed and provided the participants, and their wives, with travel expenses and accommodations in one of the best hotels in Brussels. This made the timing very painful for us: with a two-month-old baby, Genia obviously could not travel and had to miss the splendid occasion. Her position was even worse than that: almost as soon as I had left for Brussels, Bethe, who was staying in our house, fell ill with tonsilitis. She had to look after him as well as Gaby, and had to keep the two apart in case his illness proved infectious. While I was enjoying the intellectual atmosphere and social life of the conference, she was having a miserable time.

Even at other times, Genia had a hard life. She was getting very tired and really needed a restful holiday. That was just not possible, but we decided she should get away for two days at any rate—I could look after the baby that long. I presented her with a rail ticket to North Wales, and she went off with some misgivings. But when she returned she was refreshed and full of enthusiasm. She had walked a long way by the sea, and had stayed the night in the cottage of an unemployed miner, who was spending his time in the local library, and who knew more of Russian authors than many of our academic acquaintances. And the baby had survived.

In Manchester the Physics Department was on one side of the main university. It consisted of two buildings, of which the newer one had much of the inside covered with brown-glazed tiles, suggestive of a public lavatory. It was then normal to have only one professor in each subject in all but the largest universities. The physics professor in Manchester was W. L. Bragg. He was a handsome, well-dressed man, who might well be mistaken for a prosperous businessman. He was a brilliant lecturer and enjoyed lecturing, including giving popular lectures such as the evening discourses at the Royal Institution in London. He would take great trouble with his demonstrations for such lectures, and discuss the technicalities with his colleagues. He delighted in using an array of soap bubbles as the analogue of a crystal lattice.

I am not sure whether he invented the idea, but he certainly made good use of it. He was famous for having pioneered X-ray crystallography, initially together with his father. They shared the Nobel Prize for this work. Unlike some other father-and-son teams, it seems that here the son had a very major share of the ideas and the initiative.

By now the basic ideas of crystal structure analysis were settled, and Bragg was looking at techniques that would make the study of more complicated structures possible, and at the less obvious applications. The latter included the formation of superlattices in alloys, a subject of technological importance. He made a theoretical analysis of this with E. J. Williams. Williams was, next to Bragg, the best-known member of the Manchester staff, and was at home both with experimental and with theoretical work. He had worked on the passage of fast particles through matter, and had developed, with the German theoretician von Weizsäcker, a very simple and instructive method for calculating the radiation emitted when such particles pass through atoms. With Bragg he developed a theory of the superlattices. In an alloy of two elements, A and B, in equal amounts, the force between an A and a B atom is sometimes more attractive than between two like atoms. The atoms then tend to form a regular "chessboard" pattern in which the two kinds of atom alternate. If the temperature is raised, the thermal motion overcomes this tendency, so that above a certain temperature the atoms are distributed over the lattice sites at random.

The attractive force that tends to put an atom into a "right" as opposed to a "wrong" position depends on the arrangement of all other atoms in the neighbourhood, and an exact theory would therefore have to enumerate all possible arrangements of atoms, which is impossible. Bragg and Williams used what is now known as a "mean-field" theory, which makes the approximation that this force depends only on how many of the atoms in the piece of metal are in their "right" places.

Bethe and I found this problem challenging, and thought the mean-field approximation too crude. We found it difficult to do better, and made many unsuccessful attempts to find a method that was more accurate and yet manageable. But gradually the possibilities became clearer, and then Bethe saw the right trick to use in order to get a substantial improvement in accuracy with a reasonable amount of effort. He spent many late nights doing the calculations required by his scheme.

During that year in Manchester, Bethe and I also wrote some papers on nuclear physics, which for both of us were the beginning of work in that field. What got us started was a chance conversation with Chadwick, the Cambridge physicist who had recently discovered the neutron. He was then directing gamma rays at deuterium, i.e., heavy hydrogen, whose nucleus, the deuteron, consists of a neutron and a proton bound together, and expected that the nuclei would be broken up. This reaction of a system breaking up under the influence of radiation is called the photo-effect. When we met Chadwick, he had already obtained positive results in his experiment, but did not tell us. He simply said, "I bet you cannot make a theory of the deuteron photo-effect."

This was a challenge, and when we talked it over, we saw a simple way of looking at this problem. In order to describe the process one must know something about the force that holds neutron and proton together. There was good reason to believe that this force acts only over very short distances, short even compared to the mean diameter of the deuteron, and if that is true, one does not have to know much detail about it; it is characterised mainly by one number, which can be found from the known binding energy of the deuteron. Using the same idea, we could also describe the collision of a neutron with a proton and find how they deflect ("scatter") each other. We could also calculate the chance of the neutron being captured, to form a deuteron, emitting the excess energy as gamma radiation. This process is the inverse of the photo-effect. Some of our predictions agreed well with the experimental results, but the data for very low neutron energy did not fit the theory.

It was some time before it became clear what we had missed. The neutron and proton are spinning, and quantum theory says that their spins can either be parallel or opposite (i.e., they spin in the same or opposite senses). The force they exert on each other depends on their relative spin. When bound together in a deuteron, the spins are always parallel. But when a neutron beam meets hydrogen, the spins of the nuclei it meets will sometimes be parallel to that of the neutron, and sometimes opposite. The deuteron does not give us any information about the force in the latter case. This explanation was given some years later by Eugene Wigner, who never published it but mentioned it to Bethe during a ride on the New York subway. Bethe (with Wigner's permission) described it in a review article he was writing.

Bethe and I also enjoyed collaborating on some work on the neutrino, the hypothetical particle invented by Pauli to resolve the paradox of beta decay. Some radioactive nuclei decay by emitting electrons, and the observations appeared to show that this process violated the law of conservation of energy and other well-established principles of physics. All these difficulties would disappear if another particle besides the electron was produced in the process. It had to be a very elusive particle because it was not observed in any of the sensitive methods by which beta decay had been studied. At first the particle was called the neutron, but when Chadwick discovered the neutron, which is by no means elusive, Fermi christened Pauli's particle the "neutrino," using the Italian diminutive.

Fermi believed in Pauli's idea and formulated a quantitative way of describing it. He developed a theory to account both for the electron energies and for the mean lives of the beta-active nuclei in terms of the energy they lost in the process. As a result the idea had become much more tangible, and Bethe and I added some further points. By this time it was known that some nuclei emit positive rather than negative electrons, and we pointed out that instead of emitting a positive electron and a neutrino, the nucleus might catch one of the atomic electrons surrounding it and emit a neutrino. We also discussed the reverse process, in which a neutrino is absorbed by a nucleus and an electron is emitted. The chance of this could be predicted, and it turned out to be extremely small. A neutrino could, as we pointed out, pass through the whole of the Earth with only a negligible chance of being absorbed on the way. If this was the only way a neutrino could produce an observable effect, it was indeed elusive.

We thought neutrinos might never be observed, but we did not reckon with the advent of large atomic reactors, which produce enormous quantities of neutrinos, or with the ingenuity of experimental physicists. In the early 1950s Reines and Cowan set out to find reactions induced by neutrinos, and in 1956 they succeeded. As the neutrinos become faster they become less elusive, and with today's high-energy accelerators work with neutrinos has become routine. Bethe left Manchester after one year to go first to Bristol and later to Cornell University, where he is still active today.

Other People in Manchester

We remained in Manchester for a second year. One of the people whose company I enjoyed was Douglas Hartree, another theoretical physicist (in the ambiguous position of theoretical physics in English universities, he was actually counted as a mathematician). He held a chair of applied mathematics.

Hartree was a wizard with numerical calculations, long before the advent of the computer. The "Hartree approximation" and its refinements remain the most powerful method for determining the properties of atoms. He later became interested in machines that solve differential equations; today we would call them analogue computers. Such a machine, called the "differential analyser", had been invented by Vannevar Bush at M.I.T., and Hartree made a simple version for himself, built mostly from Meccano parts. He later replaced it by a more powerful version, which was properly engineered. I remember that on the day before the official opening ceremony, the technicians gave the machine a fresh coat of paint. Unfortunately they also painted the moving parts, so that the machine stopped functioning. Hartree and his students spent the night before the opening cleaning the paint from all the places where it was not wanted.

Hartree was a chubby man with the face of an overgrown schoolboy. He was rather shy, and in mixed company his red face would acquire a darker red hue before he managed an utterance. When, during a conversation on education, Mrs. Hartree praised the merits of coeducational institutions and commented that her husband had been educated at Bedales, a well-known coeducational school, and that this had greatly increased his self-confidence in social intercourse, we were amused by the thought of what he would have been like otherwise.

The Hartrees were kind to us and helped with advice and information where they could. On one occasion we attended a large reception at the university, and the Hartrees, who lived close to us, offered us a ride home. When we came out into the courtyard filled with a hundred or so cars, we asked which was their car, and Mrs. Hartree said airily, "The shabbiest and dirtiest car in the place." Genia, rather too promptly, asked, "Oh, is it that one?" It was.

We also saw a good deal of the Brentanos. He was an experimental physicist of great skill. He came from a distinguished Viennese family, but was somehow a Swiss citizen, raised in Italy. His wife was Dutch, and they usually talked French with each other. His advice to us was not to mix languages too indiscriminately in raising the children— "One has to have one language in which to dream." We had reached the same conclusion after noticing that Gaby was getting confused by the mix of languages. We tended to talk with Hans Bethe in German, to each other in Russian, and to visitors and the charwoman in English. We decided then to use only English with Gaby. Later we discovered that children can manage several languages easily, provided each person uses only one language with them. But this knowledge came rather too late, and our children missed the opportunity to acquire several languages without tears.

Brentano was a meticulously law-abiding person, but got into trouble with authority on every conceivable occasion. He never passed a customs check without the officers opening every piece of luggage and searching it from top to bottom. His wife came to going through the customs separately, not because she was smuggling anything, but because she was tired of the searches. We could never see the reason for this attention, unless it was that he was, and looked, so honest that officials did not believe this could be genuine.

There was Michael Polanyi, the physical chemist whose appointment had caused so much publicity. He was Hungarian but had been a professor in Berlin until 1933. He was always anxious to assimilate rapidly, and from the start avoided using any language other than English, at least in public. He wanted to change the name of his sons to Pollard, but the idea was abandoned. He had a deep understanding of the connections between physical chemistry and physics, and I found we had much common ground. He also had an interest in economics, and many years later transferred to a chair of economics. In 1933 he already had the hobby of studying the economic statistics of the USSR, and tried to read between the lines. He liked to talk with Genia, partly to check on his understanding of the Russian publications and partly because of her knowledge of the Russian way of life. On one occasion she could help without needing any special knowledge. He had found a discrepancy between the figures for the yield of grain and for grain consumed, and wondered whether there was some error or deliberate distortion of the statistics. Genia reminded him that he had forgotten to allow for the seed grain that had to be retained for next year's sowing.

We made friends with another chemist, though I cannot now recall his name. He was a man of rather Spartan habits, and I remember one particular incident. Once, when he was climbing the Matterhorn, he had an attack of appendicitis. He was able to descend, but, not knowing anything about Swiss medicine, travelled home by train and boat to have his appendix removed in Manchester. I do not know whether his scepticism about Swiss medicine was justified, but he certainly showed more confidence in his British doctor, though this did not necessarily reflect a uniformly high standard of medicine in England.

One evening we invited our chemist friend to dinner. We were puzzled when he stopped at the door and said, "My brother is not feeling well tonight." We expressed sympathy, but could not understand his hesitation. Then we realised that this was not our friend, but his identical twin brother, who (as we had no telephone) had come to bring his brother's apologies.

Professor (later Sir) Lewis Namier, the historian whom we met, was a great character. He was originally from Poland but had been in the British Foreign Office during the First World War. He was very fond of saying "we", and you had to be very alert in following the course of the conversation to know whether at the given point this meant the University of Manchester, All Souls College, Oxford, the Jews, the Foreign Office, or Poland. He was very active in helping Jewish refugees, and I believe he played an important part in setting up the Manchester fund that supported us. Immigrant visas could be obtained only for people with assured employment, or for whom some other means of support was guaranteed. The limited funds for support meant that only a limited number of people could be helped to leave Germany, and the immigrant committees had to make choices. This was a painful procedure. The times were getting worse for Jews in Germany, and stories were beginning to be heard about concentration camps where inmates were being forced to eat grass, or to sit in trees crying "cuckoo". (Information about extermination camps did not come until much later.) Namier was very scathing about Jews who had not yet grasped the situation, and who, in their applications for help, stressed what good Germans they had been. In one application a man tried to impress the committee with the fact that his father had given music lessons to the crown prince, to which Namier sadly commented, "He has not eaten enough grass yet."

When Namier came to dinner one evening we almost had a domestic calamity. Although Genia had never been taught to cook, she had become very good at it. Her mother was an outstanding cook, so Genia knew how good food ought to taste, and she soon discovered how to produce this effect, using Bethe and me as guinea pigs. She commented that, although both of us were ready to eat her less successful efforts without complaining, Bethe was of particular help by showing his enthusiasm very visibly when something was good. So, for Namier she had decided to roast a duck. But when she took the bird out of the oven, she realised that none of us knew how to carve it, and worse, we had no carving knife. She discreetly beckoned Hans Bethe to come into the kitchen, and while I entertained the guest, she and Hans each grabbed one leg of the duck and pulled. After being dismantled in this manner, the bird was artfully rearranged on a dish and served without mishap.

In the spring of 1934 I was invited to lecture at the Institut Henri Poincaré in Paris. This was an attractive prospect, and after Genia had missed the Solvay Conference, it seemed only fair that she should accompany me to Paris. We made arrangements for Gaby to stay in

107

a children's home for the period (which I think was for two weeks), and we enjoyed ourselves in Paris. One fly in the ointment was that the lectures had to be given in French, and my French was not really fluent. However, I managed somehow. I remember that at some point I was lacking a word and used the English term, prompting someone in the audience to supply the French equivalent. This was a word I was not familiar with, and I repeated it as best I could. From the faces in the audience, however, I gathered that my attempt had turned into a rather unprintable expression.

Still, I did better than R. H. Fowler. We were told that he had written out his lectures in what he believed to be good French, but when he read the first lecture nobody understood anything. So Langevin politely suggested that perhaps a little more idiom could be put into the text, and he sat down with some students to translate the remaining lectures into passable French. When Fowler read the next lecture, again nobody knew what he was talking about, this time including Fowler himself.

During this stay we were invited to dinner at Langevin's house. This was unusual, because it was then rare for guests to be invited into private homes, unless they were close personal friends. I suppose Langevin was unconventional in this, as in other matters (he was on the far left politically). We were anxious to behave correctly and asked our friends, the Solomons, whom we knew from Zurich, how long it was proper to stay. They said, "The rule is very simple. You wait until the cold drinks are served; then you have your drink and go." A very useful prescription, from which we profited on many occasions.

Of others in Paris I remember particularly Edmond Bauer, a theoretical physicist interested in solid-state problems, and a man of exceptional charm. He was Jewish and managed to get to Switzerland in time to escape the German occupation. We later became friends with his son, Etienne.

All this time we knew, of course, that our stay in Manchester was limited, and in any case we did not want to accept the grant for longer than necessary, so I made many attempts to find a position. At one stage a professorship was advertised in Raman's institute in Bangalore, India. Raman received a Nobel Prize for his discovery of the Raman effect, and he was a very strong personality. I decided to apply for this position, and, knowing that Sommerfeld was on friendly terms with Raman, I asked Sommerfeld for permission to give his name as a reference. Sommerfeld agreed and immediately wrote to Raman, sending me a copy of his letter. The letter said approximately: "Mr. Peierls has asked me to recommend him to you for the new professorship. He is a nice young man, who would have completed his Ph.D.

here if I had not gone off on sabbatical leave. While I am writing to you, I should also mention the case of Dr. X, another applicant. He is a man of great ability and has all the qualities you would want for this professorship. He is married and has two children, whereas Peierls is single" (which was not even true). I was not offended by this "recommendation", but thought it unusually honest of Sommerfield to send me a copy of the letter. In the end neither Dr. X nor I got the appointment, and from what I found out later about Raman's way of working, I think we were lucky.

My hopes were raised when I heard that Trinity College, Cambridge, had created a fellowship that was to be offered to a refugee and that I was under consideration. Then one day a young mathematician and his wife, who were also refugees, came to tea, and at one point they said, "Have you heard of Heilbronn's good fortune? He has got a fellowship at Trinity." Heilbronn was a mathematician. We knew that this meant the end of a dream. Genia and I looked at each other, and we were proud that we did not bat an eyelid.

A professorship was also advertised in Quito, Ecuador, and I considered applying, but the conditions of life and work there seemed very uncertain. I then wrote to Fowler, asking his advice about my prospects in England. I said I knew he could not promise me anything, but did he think I was foolish in hoping that sooner or later there might be a chance of a position? His reply was encouraging, and I did not try for Ecuador.

In the summer of 1934 we went to Leningrad to visit Genia's parents and to present the baby. While Genia stayed there, I went on a trip to the Caucasus with Landau (who by this time was back in Leningrad) and a friend of his. We walked through Svanetia, a strange country in the mountains, accessible from the north only by a bridle path over high mountains and from the south through a narrow gorge. Before the Revolution the government had not attempted to assert its authority over the Svanetians, who belong to an obscure Christian sect, which some believe goes back to the crusaders. European culture had hardly touched them. It took time even under the Soviet regime to bring these very individualistic people in line. Each house in the village has a high tower, and when the inhabitants were threatened by their neighbours, they would move to the top of their towers, pull up the ladders, and wait for the danger to pass. We made our visit during the second year that tourists were permitted, because now the country seemed safe for visitors. We travelled with a pack horse and a boy to look after it, and slept in schools or post offices, which were the most modern buildings, alien to the local tradition.

109

One night we were supposed to sleep in the post office, but the postmaster was out, and we had to wait for his return with the key. We decided to cook our meal in the meantime, and while the others were gathering wood and starting a fire, I went down to the river to get some water. As I scrambled up the river bank with my pail, I saw two men with a rifle at the top, who shouted at me in the local language and pointed the rifles at me. I tried to explain my presence, but they did not understand Russian, and I was rather uncomfortable until the word "tourist" met with comprehension. Next morning, I saw them again in the village square with their rifle. We asked the postmaster why the village needed armed guards. He explained that these men were not guards; they were from down the valley and were involved in a feud with another family. One of their members had killed someone in the other family, and now it was the duty of the victim's family to kill them. The fright I had the night before was probably nothing compared to the shock they must have had at seeing a stranger come up from the river!

A memorable conversation occurred on that trip. Landau's friend, an engineer, asked him, "What is this one hears about atomic energy? Is that just science fiction, or is there some real possibility?" Without hesitation, Landau replied, "It is a difficult problem. There are nuclear reactions that release more energy than they absorb; but if we try to bombard nuclei with charged particles, we cannot aim them, and they would have to travel a long way before encountering a nucleus. Long before that they are stopped by their electric interaction with the atomic electrons, which acts like friction. So only a small fraction ever hits a nucleus, and the energy released is extremely small compared to that needed to accelerate all those particles that miss. Neutrons are a different story, because they are not stopped by friction, and they go on until they find a nucleus. But so far the only way we know of producing neutron beams is by charged particles hitting nuclei, so we are back with the same problem. But if one day someone finds a reaction in which the impact of a neutron produces secondary neutrons, then we would be all set." Remarkably clear vision in 1934, just two years after the discovery of the neutron.

In 1934 I also attended a small conference in Geneva on the electron theory of metals. I presented two small papers, one of which concerned the question of melting. In a crystal the atoms keep their regular periodic arrangement over indefinitely large distances, a state of affairs we call "long-range order", whereas in the liquid there is no such long-range order. The existence of long-range order seems at first sight surprising, because even at low temperatures the motion of heat means that two neighbouring atoms will not be exactly in the right position relative to each other. The next atom will sense only the position of the previous one, with its small error, and will add its own error to that, so that the error will gradually increase and distant atoms get out of step. This is indeed what happens if we have only a linear chain of atoms, and such a one-dimensional system has no long-range order and no sharply defined melting point. But in three dimensions, there are many different ways of getting from one atom to another some distnce away, and not all the atoms along these different paths will be out of position by the same error. So we can understand why a real crystal in space has long-range order and a well-defined melting point. For the intermediate case of two dimensions, i.e., a plane array of atoms, which has acquired practical interest in recent years for surface layers of atoms, I predicted that there should also be no melting point. Many years later this answer was shown to be misleading, for reasons that would take too long to explain here.

My other comments arose because of a paper by a German physicist called Kretschmann, who was always finding fault with new ideas in physics. He had claimed that the current electron theory of metals was wrong for a number of reasons, one being that the approximation normally used in dealing with the collisions of electrons with impurities or with lattice waves was unjustified. I was irritated by this paper, and sat down to prove that the approximation was legitimate. To my surprise I discovered that in many cases it was not, if not exactly for the reasons claimed by Kretschmann. So it seemed that everybody's calculations on the electric conductivity of metals, and similar problems, were in doubt.

I mentioned this finding to Landau, who shared my concern. After some time he came up with the answer. Although the obvious derivation of the usual approximation was not valid, a more subtle argument could be used to show that, in most cases, the result was still right.

Old and New Friends

Among the people who joined the Physics Department in Manchester was a graduate student from Shanghai, Lu, who had a pretty young wife who was already a scholar in Chinese classics. She turned out to be a godsend for the City Library in Manchester. The library had a number of uncatalogued Chinese manuscripts, which were also hard to identify because many had missing title pages. Mrs. Lu set about labelling and cataloguing this collection, as one of her first acts on arriving; another was to buy herself a doll to play with. The Lus invited us to dinner and gave us our first taste of Chinese food, which we found delicious.

A more senior person who spent some time in Manchester was Eugene Wigner, who had come to visit Polanyi, his former teacher. A Hungarian by birth, he had worked in Berlin and Göttingen, and then moved on to Princeton University. He had already made outstanding contributions to quantum mechanics, particularly by showing the importance of symmetry for atomic physics, and by pioneering the use of group theory, the mathematical discipline for describing symmetries, for this purpose. However, his appointment at Princeton had come to an end; he told me at one point that this was because he was considered to be lacking in competence.

Wigner was already famous among physicists for his extreme politeness—politeness in form, at least, which was sometimes a rather transparent cover for very firm views. This combination is perhaps best illustrated by the story of an altercation he once had with a mechanic about his car, when he finally gave up with the words, "Oh, go to hell, please!" Another typical Wigner story is told by Sam Treiman of Princeton (where Wigner returned eventually). Treiman was beginning his appointment to a junior post in Princeton, and on his first day on the job he spotted Wigner in a corridor of the laboratory. He had met Wigner when he was being interviewed for the appointment, but he was not sure whether to presume on this slight acquaintance, which Wigner might not remember. He thus did not know if he should attempt a greeting. The problem was resolved for him when Wigner came up to him and said, "Good morning, Dr. Treiman, I am so glad to see you here. You may not remember me; we met at the interviewing board. I am Wigner." In Manchester we invited him to dinner one evening, and because of a misunderstanding, he came a day too early. It was impossible for us to pretend this was the right day, and we gave him a quickly improvised meal. His discomfiture at this serious breach of etiquette was striking.

During his Manchester visit we went to Cambridge for a day to hear about the latest developments in physics. We made our way around the laboratory separately, but we both visited Dirac, who was then doing an experiment. He had invented a method of isotope separation, and Kapitza had allowed him the use of a compressor. A hose from the compressor fed gas into a little brass "T" piece, and eventually lighter gas was to emerge from one of the arms of the T, and heavier gas from the other. This was not evident yet, but one could feel that the gas coming out on one side was hot, the other cold, so something nontrivial was going on.

Back in Manchester, Wigner complained that Dirac was so secretive; he would not explain the principle of his device. I was surprised because Dirac had been quite open with me. I had guessed what the principle might be, and Dirac had confirmed without hesitation that my guess was right. So I probed further and discovered that the following conversation had taken place: Wigner said, "It must have been very difficult to make that brass piece," and Dirac answered, "No, it was quite easy." That was all. Dirac had been asked a direct question and had answered it. Wigner, in his style, had requested information and had been refused. I bet Wigner that he would have been given the answer if he had asked explicitly. So, the next time I met Dirac, I asked him whether he would have explained the principle if Wigner had asked for it. He said, "I do not know." He did not like hypothetical questions. Our bet could never be settled.

Genia and I also made friends outside the world of physics. This included, in particular, the Shapiros. He (generally known as "Ship") was a young lecturer in English and had a fine appreciation of literature. He was (and still is) a perfectionist, never satisfied with his own work, and therefore never having anything major published. He and his wife, Pauline, a psychologist, became our friends for life. It was in their house that we awaited a telephone call from Leningrad that brought us some disturbing news. Genia's parents and her sister, Nina, had been exiled from the city to a small town some distance east of Moscow. One did not have to ask for a reason for this order; exile or arrest were then hazards that struck people at random, like lightning or disease. One tended to speculate about what factors might have contributed to this result, but this would never be known.

By this time Genia was expecting another child, and we decided to get some resident help. We engaged a girl who came from near Barnsley in Yorkshire, one of the mining areas that was suffering from severe depression. She was evidently undernourished, but it was difficult to get her to eat. Understandably she did not like the "foreign" foods we ate, and Genia tried to provide some acceptable alternatives. But habit was too strong, and all she would eat were potatoes with a gravy made from gravy salt. She was under strict instructions from her family to send home every penny she earned, and this was perhaps understandable in view of the needs of the family. But being permanently without money left her unhappy and grumpy, and eventually she left us.

Her successor, Olive, was an attractive, cheerful, and intelligent Irish girl who stayed with us for several years. She was given to occasional fits of moodiness and to occasional passionate love affairs, but these rare episodes always passed, and we became very fond of her.

While exploring Didsbury, the Manchester suburb in which we lived, we had noticed one street, Kingston Road, which seemed more attractive than the rest, consisting of a single row of houses with open spaces on both sides. In the spring of 1935 we discovered that a house was available on that street, and we found that the rent was no higher than for our "modern semidetached", so we decided to move. The house was old and badly in need of paint. At that time "do-it-yourself" was not yet common, but we took to doing the painting ourselves, with Genia doing most of it. The somewhat gloomy kitchen was brightened up with vivid orange paint.

The paint was barely dry when I was offered an appointment in Cambridge at the Mond Laboratory, the laboratory for magnetism and low temperatures built for Kapitza, who was unable to return from Moscow. The money earmarked for his salary was therefore unused, and Rutherford persuaded the Royal Society to establish two research fellowships, of which one was offered to me, the other to J. F. Allen, a Canadian experimentalist. This was great news. The fellowship was not a permanent appointment, but it was an appointment and not a gift from charity. Also, the salary was almost twice my Manchester grant, and Cambridge was still the centre of physics in England. So I accepted with enthusiasm.

By the time the appointment was confirmed, the birth of our second child was near, and once again I had to find a new family home by myself. This time the search was very successful. I spent a few days in Cambridge as a guest of Egon and Hanni Bretscher, our friends from Zurich who had meanwhile moved to Cambridge, where Egon had started work in the Cavendish Laboratory. Quite soon I saw a house for rent on the outskirts of Cambridge that was easily accessible. It was a single-story house (called a "bungalow"), well-built, and had a large garden. We spent two happy years there. It was later rented by David Shoenberg, a physicist at the Mond Laboratory, who eventually bought it and who still lives there, so we still visit the house occasionally.

Shortly before we moved to Cambridge, our son was born. This was the second of three occasions on which we had to move with a six-week-old baby. Our arrival at the maternity home had an element of drama. The taxi driver who took us there knew the object of the journey, both from the destination and from Genia's condition, and he anxiously drove the short distance as smoothly and as gently as he could. But this special effort had disturbed his routine. When he stopped in front of the maternity home, he forgot to put his gear lever into neutral, and the car gave a violent lurch forward as he took his foot off the clutch pedal. The poor man was conscience-stricken, as if he had committed a murder, and we had to assure him that no harm was done.

Cambridge. Mond Laboratory

In Cambridge, Rutherford had taken over the responsibility for the Mond Laboratory after Kapitza's departure, though much of the day-to-day administration was looked after by Cockcroft. There was much opportunity for getting to know Rutherford more closely and to appreciate his human qualities. A week or so after I had taken up my duties, I met him in the yard. He recognised me and asked how I was settling down. "Have they paid you anything yet?" I said I expected this would come at the end of the month. "Will you be able to last until then?" I felt the contrast with the situation in Manchester, where nobody had noticed that my grant was not being paid until finally, when money began to run short, I had to ask for it. Rutherford was a very busy man, and only marginally concerned with the Mond Laboratory, but he evidently remembered what it is like to be young and with limited means. I resolved never to forget his example, and I hope I have never done so.

Another side of Rutherford's personality was shown when he came to Manchester to address a colloquium. In introducing him, Bragg made some rather self-conscious remarks about the difficulty of being Rutherford's successor. At Senate meetings, he said, people were used to looking to the professor of physics for wise counsel, and then realised it was only he, and there was more in this spirit. The audience felt a little embarrassed by this. In his reply, Rutherford said, "Professor Bragg has expressed doubt about his ability to fill my chair. But," pointing to his own generous circumference and to Bragg's incipient middle-age spread, "I see he is well on the way to doing so." This brought the house down and relieved the atmosphere.

I continued working on order-disorder problems, which fitted in with the interests of the Mond Laboratory, and also with those of Fowler's group. In Manchester I had extended Bethe's method for treating superlattices to the case of alloys such as copper-gold, which forms a superlattice with the composition Cu_3Au, in which, in a face-centred cubic lattice, the gold atoms occupy the cube corners and the copper atoms the face centres. Fowler's group was interested in adsorbed layers, and I found that the same method could be used to handle the interaction between the adsorbed atoms. A number of related questions arose—for example, what would happen in an alloy in which the ratio of the constituents was not exactly the ideal one? One of Fowler's students, Colin Easthope, started working with me on these problems, and we got quite interesting results, which Easthope wrote up in his Ph.D. thesis. He was my first pupil, though I do not recall whether I was officially his supervisor.

I found that very fruitful inspiration often came from being irritated by someone else's work that seems wrong, unnecessarily complicated, or based on unreasonable assumptions. This was the case with a seminar talk I heard by a mathematician on the Ising model. This is a model of ferromagnetism, in which one has an array of magnets capable of two orientations and a force between adjacent magnets that tries to align them. This is mathematically equivalent to the superlattice problem that Bethe and I had discussed. Ising had solved this problem for a linear chain, and proved, correctly, that the model did not give ferromagnetism for this, because, while in the state of lowest energy, which must be reached at the absolute zero of temperature, all the magnets will be parallel; any temperature, however small, will spoil this alignment; and the system will then have equal numbers of magnets in both directions. The solution for the one-dimensional chain is very simple, and the speaker derived it in the course of his talk. But then he claimed that the same result applied in two or three dimensions and gave arguments which, he claimed, proved that this was so.

I felt sure he was wrong. However, rather than look for errors in his arguments, I decided to prove that, at a sufficiently low temperature, a two-dimensional Ising model will have a non-zero average magnetisation. This proof turned out to be reasonably simple. It taught me that if you feel really sure that something is true, you can ask yourself what makes you feel so confident, and then try to turn this reasoning into a formal proof. I was surprised to hear a few years ago from experts in statistical mechanics that the simple argument of my 1935 paper, with various generalisations, was still the only way to prove rigorously the existence of ordered states. But since then, more powerful methods have been found.

In the Mond Laboratory I saw much of David Shoenberg, who was then a graduate student. His father, who held a senior position in industry, was of Russian origin, and David was fluent in Russian. He worked on magnetic properties, and this led to work on the de Haas-van Alphen effect in bismuth, whose origin I had explained in Rome.

He found that many other metals showed the same kind of oscillations, but one had to work at lower temperatures and with stronger magnetic fields to see them. He eventually became the authority on this effect, which proved an important tool for studying the motion of electrons in metals. He was also working on the behaviour of superconductors in magnetic fields, and I was able to make a small step in the theoretical interpretation of the phenomena.

Jack Allen was working on liquid helium, which, below a temperature of about 4.2 degrees from absolute zero, shows a strange, and at the time very puzzling, behaviour. One aspect of this was that its heat conductivity was not only very large, but also seemed to depend on the magnitude of the temperature gradient. To study this further, I proposed an experiment that would allow measurements to be made with very small temperature differences. The idea was to use the helium liquid itself as a gas thermometer. A glass bulb immersed in a liquid helium bath and connected with it through a capillary tube would fill itself to a level coinciding with the liquid level in the bath. If the temperature of the helium in the bulb was raised a little, the gas pressure would increase a little, and this would push the level down. The very low density of liquid helium made this a very sensitive thermometer.

Allen and a student set up the experiment, and I joined them in taking readings. We had hoped that we would find clearer results than had been found by more conventional methods, but instead our results were more confusing and harder to understand than any others. At this point I left Cambridge, but Allen found the explanation soon afterwards. He decided to cut open the bulb, and found that, when heat was applied, the liquid would spurt out of the bulb like a small fountain. This phenomenon, which he called the "fountain effect", shows that in helium, unlike in other liquids, a temperature difference generates a difference in pressure. This discovery added one of the clues that eventually led to an understanding of the nature of "superfluid" helium. But it also meant that the beautiful experiment I had invented did not work, because the effect prevented the helium from functioning as a gas thermometer.

We were also friendly with S. Chandrasekhar, a very able young astrophysicist. He was then involved in a curious argument with Sir Arthur Eddington, one of the leaders in astrophysics. Eddington pioneered the study of the interior of stars by using the results of atomic physics, and thereby made astrophysics a serious quantitative subject. He also wrote a textbook on relativity, and organised the first expedition to check Einstein's general theory of relativity by verifying the predicted deflection of starlight passing close to the sun during a total eclipse.

Earlier, Fowler had pointed out that in certain stars, the so-called white dwarfs, the density of electrons was so high that the Pauli exclusion principle became important. In these stars, like in metals, the electrons would therefore obey a different equation than at lower densities. Eddington accepted this conclusion and used it in further work on the white dwarfs.

Then Chandrasekhar pointed out that, as a result of the electrons being spread out over different states because of the Pauli principle, most of them would, in fact, be moving with speeds comparable to that of light, and one had to use the relativistic laws of mechanics, which meant yet another change in the equation. To this Eddington objected strongly; it is difficult to see why. He attacked Chandrasekhar when he presented his results to a meeting of astronomers, as well as on other occasions. To all theoretical physicists it was obvious that Chandrasekhar was right. When they confronted Eddington with the usual proof of the relativistic equation of statistical mechanics, he took refuge in claiming that the enumeration of states in that argument was incorrect, because it used a simplified fictitious boundary condition. It therefore gave me pleasure to find a proof that the result was, to all intents and purposes, independent of the boundary condition. I published this in an astronomical journal. I don't believe it convinced Eddington.

A few years later Eddington, still in pursuit of the same argument, attacked Dirac's relativistic wave equation for the hydrogen atom, and Dirac, Maurice Pryce, and I wrote a joint paper to counter this. This was after I had left Cambridge, and I do not remember how this paper got written.

Contacts with the Cavendish

Although I was working in the Mond Laboratory, I had, of course, contacts with the nuclear physicists in the Cavendish Laboratory. Next to Rutherford, the senior person there was James Chadwick, Rutherford's collaborator for many years and discoverer of the neutron. On first acquaintance he appeared to be a man with a jaundiced view of life and of his fellow men; but when you got to know him, you found behind this facade great warmth and readiness to help. I remember one incident that occurred when I came to Cambridge for a day from Manchester, as I often did, to learn about current physics, and encountered Chadwick in the entrance of the laboratory, talking with some students. He greeted me and asked what I was doing there. I said I had come to look around, and if he could spare me a little time I would appreciate it. He looked at me over the top of his glasses and said, "Yes? What for?" I guessed this was not meant the way it sounded, and I was not put off. I explained my reasons, and we had a good talk.

He was a man of great energy, and not easily discouraged. In those days (and, for all I know, still today) the gates of the yard from which one entered the laboratories were locked at night. At one point Chadwick was engaged in an experiment in which readings had to be taken very late at night. It was unthinkable that the gates could be kept open for him, or that he might be given a key. So he brought a camp bed to the laboratory and spent the rest of the night there.

Charles Ellis was also a longstanding member of Rutherford's team. He gave the impression of a gentleman playing with research as a hobby, although his contributions to physics were solid enough. On one occasion he spent the best part of a year building a registering photometer with some students, used to measure the shape of spectral lines. Such an instrument could then already be bought ready-made; but this acquisition would have been a burden on the lab's budget, and, in any case, he could perhaps make a slightly better instrument than the commercial ones.

Mark Oliphant was a more recent arrival from Australia, and Rutherford had a particularly warm relationship with him. He had the same direct and outspoken manner as Rutherford. I did not really get to know him well until we both moved to Birmingham, and I shall say more about him later.

Among the refugees who had come to Cambridge was a graduate student, Maurice Goldhaber. He was exceptionally bright but a little naive, and had not yet acquired a very polished manner. He caused raised eyebrows by telling everybody, including Rutherford and Chadwick, what experiments they ought to be doing. It was particularly aggravating that he was usually right. He suggested the experiment of the photo-effect on the deuteron, and Chadwick invited him to take part in it.

John Cockcroft had been trained as an engineer, and, while he had an excellent command of physics, he was an engineer at heart. Thus he was in his element when he designed and built, together with Walton, the electrostatic particle accelerator. He also helped Kapitza in his problems with the big magnet. After Kapitza left, he practically ran the Mond Laboratory, while at the same time he supervised the building of a new high-voltage laboratory, which was to contain a commercially built Cockcroft-Walton set and a cyclotron. He was also bursar of St. John's College, and in that capacity looked after new college buildings and the restoration of old ones. Many of the old brick buildings in the college had been repaired with modern, factory-made bricks, which spoilt their appearance. When Cockcroft was driving in the country, he watched for dilapidated walls on farms that had been built with old bricks, and when he found any, he arranged to buy the old walls and have them taken to Cambridge.

I do not think I have ever met anyone else able to get as many different things done as Cockcroft. It helped that he was a man of few words, in speech and in writing. His letters were famous, often consisting of one brief sentence, in minuscule writing. He also could make up his mind quickly on small matters, as the following incident illustrates. The room I used in the Mond Laboratory had a drawing board, and on one occasion Cockcroft was working there on some drawing when the secretary came in, saying the architect was on the phone, wanting to know whether the light switches in the high-voltage laboratory were to be black or brown. (In those days switches were either black or brown.) Anybody else would have said, "Let me see, it does not really matter, but. . . ." Cockcroft did not lift his head from the drawing board. He said "brown" without any hesitation and went on with his work.

When I later was allowed to dine occasionally in St. John's College, I found that coffee in the "Combination Room" (as Cambridge senior common rooms are called) after dinner was the one occasion of the day when you could find him in a relaxed mood, and when he would chat in more than one sentence at a time.

My connection with the college followed after I became a member of the university. This was not an automatic consequence of doing research in the Mond Laboratory. It was felt that I should give some regular courses of lectures, and for this I had to have an M.A. degree. For Cambridge graduates this is a formality; they keep their names on a register for some time after graduation and then are automatically entitled to the degree. Members of the university academic staff have the degree conferred ex officio. But none of this applied to me, so how could I be allowed to lecture? As it turned out, academic bureaucracy is not only good in setting up these obstacles, but also in knowing how to get around them. The solution involved passing three resolutions, or "graces", as they are called, in the Regent House, the administrative body of the university. The first of these created a new unpaid university position, "Assistant-in-Research", at the Mond Laboratory; the second added this post to the list of appointments whose holders could be given an ex officio M.A.; and the third appointed me to the new post and ordered that I be given the M.A.

During my second year I was asked, probably at Cockcroft's suggestion, to take on the supervision of three physics undergraduates. In Cambridge the lectures and laboratories are university matters, while the colleges select the students, house and feed them, and look after discipline. They also provide tutorial teaching to back up the lectures. Each student has a supervisor who sees him, usually in a group of two or three, once a week in term time. When possible, the supervisors are fellows of the college (most colleges have fellows in most of the major subjects), but if there are more students than the fellows can handle, graduate students or research staff are brought in.

Nobody explained to me precisely what a supervisor was supposed to do—one just knew. However, not being Cambridge-educated, I did not know. So I did what I thought might be right, and I probably caused no irreparable harm to the pupils I had during their final year: one was Charles Kittel, now a leader in solid-state physics in Berkeley; the second was R. S. Rivlin, who achieved distinction in polymer research in industry; and the third, R. J. Huck, could not afford to become a graduate student at the time and became a schoolteacher, but he became a university lecturer later.

Dirac and Others

Paul Dirac did not count as a physicist. He was supposed to be an applied mathematician and belonged to the mathematics faculty. He always had the reputation of being very silent, but this is not an accurate description—he did talk, but only when he had something to say. What he did say was often striking, because his reactions were not like other people's, and they were never trivial. When you heard him speak you often realised that he followed the question in a straight line, while others, by habit, turned a corner. This description certainly applied to his physics, but it is also appropriate for his reactions to everyday matters.

There is a wealth of Dirac stories. I have already told the story of his conversation with Wigner about his experiment, which is as much a Dirac as a Wigner story. Incidentally, his method of isotope separation, which he did not pursue after Kapitza left, was remembered during the war, when isotope separation was a very real problem. A group of physicists in Oxford set up an apparatus based on his principle

121

and made it work. However, it turned out not to be competitive economically with other methods, and was therefore dropped.

One of my favourite Dirac stories was told by H. R. Hulme, who was doing theoretical research in Cambridge. He was walking with Dirac, when something rattled in his coat pocket. He apologised to Dirac for the noise, explaining that he had a bottle of pills and had taken some for his cold, so that the bottle was no longer full and rattled. After some reflection, Dirac said, "I suppose it makes the maximum noise when it is half full."

At a party in our house someone commented that all children born to physicists in Cambridge recently had been girls, more so than was statistically reasonable. Genia said, "It must be something in the air," to which Dirac added, after a pause, "or perhaps in the water."

Another story goes that a French physicist called on him, and struggled very hard to express himself in English. After this had gone on for some time, Dirac's sister came into the room and asked Dirac something in French, to which he also replied in perfect French. (Dirac's father came from Switzerland). The visitor was indignant. "Why did you not tell me that you could speak French?"—"You never asked me."

His lectures were as clear as his papers, but he did not have many research students. I suppose the reason was that he was not given to speculation. If a question in physics came up, he would say "yes" or "no" if he knew the answer, or "I don't know" if he did not. This is correct, but hardly conducive to an explorative discussion of an unsolved problem. This gives the background to a conversation reported by Gaby, our daughter, who in the 1950s moved to Cambridge. Mrs. Dirac said Gaby probably did not know many people there yet, so she might give a party and invite young people to meet her, perhaps some students. She turned to her husband: "Paul, do you have any students?"—"I had one, but he died."

But that was much later. In 1936 Dirac was still a bachelor, evidently a very eligible bachelor, to judge by the efforts of a number of physics wives who were trying to find him a match. Watching these efforts, Genia said, "If Dirac ever marries, it will be to an experienced woman, perhaps from the former Austro-Hungarian Empire." A few years later Dirac was married to a Hungarian divorcée, the sister of Eugene Wigner.

Among the bright young theoreticians in Cambridge was the Indian, Homi Bhabha. He came from one of the most highly educated and influential Parsee families and was related to the Tatas, who ran much of India's industry. He did important work on a number of subjects, including the theory of cosmic-ray showers and on wave equations for particles of higher spin. He was also a painter of considerable talent; his pictures have a shadowy, almost gloomy, quality. Bhabha returned to India to pursue academic research, and after the war created the Tata Institute of Fundamental Research in Bombay and remained its director until his death. In a country where many universities were still dominated by petty intrigues and personal ambitions, this was an institution in which academic standards prevailed, and it had an important influence on the training and attitudes of the young researchers. Later Bhabha took charge of atomic-energy research in India and started the development of nuclear power. He died in a plane crash in 1966.

Max Born also spent some years in Cambridge before being appointed to the professorship of applied mathematics in Edinburgh. For him, a mature man accustomed to directing a large department, it required some adjustment to settle down to a research grant in Cambridge, with an odd collaborator here and there. But he settled down very well, and felt, like many other refugees, that it was a rejuvenating process. He certainly showed the enthusiasm of a young man. He started a number of bold and speculative projects, such as nonlinear electrodynamics, which, it was hoped, would solve the problem of the infinite self-energy of the electron. In developing such projects, he usually saw the positive side and glossed over the obstacles. That is no doubt the right way to give a new idea a chance; if you worry too early over the difficulties you may get discouraged. On the other hand, ignoring difficulties may lead you to miss the point when it is clear the idea is unworkable, so that you continue with it long after it has ceased to be promising.

Born objected strongly to the name "applied mathematics" in place of "theoretical physics", and also to its inclusion as a branch of mathematics. He said, "It is certainly true that we use mathematics in our work, but physicists also use a lot of glass blowing. Would it be right to describe the Cavendish Laboratory as the Department of Applied Glass Blowing?" When he went to Edinburgh he succeeded in getting the title of the chair changed.

A frequent visitor to Cambridge was Leo Szilard. He was a physicist with a very original mind and a flair for invention. He held several patents, but I do not know whether any of them ever proved commercially viable. Almost as soon as the neutron was discovered, he thought of the possibility of a nuclear chain reaction and of its potential dangers. In 1934 he filed for a patent that described the laws governing such a reaction. For some reason, however, he also had the misguided idea that a chain reaction might be possible in lithium.

Szilard was given facilities in Oxford to carry on experiments with neutrons, and he made some important contributions to the rapidly growing subject of neutron physics. At the same time, he worked hard to assist refugees who had left Germany or were trying to do so. All this time he was staying in an hotel in London. As he kept complaining about being short of money, we suggested that he move into a bed-and-breakfast place. No, he said, that would not do, because one had to give a week's notice for such rooms, and he never knew when he might have to leave. So he stayed in his hotel for the best part of a year.

An important institution in the early thirties was the Physics Club. It was set up initially by the physicists from Cambridge who had left for other posts, mainly in London, and who wanted to keep in touch. It consisted of meetings at irregular intervals, perhaps once or twice a term, in Cambridge or London, to discuss some topical subject in current physics. Originally it was conceived as a private club with a limited membership; but the young people, including many of the refugees, could not understand why they were being kept out: there was plenty of room in the lecture theatre.

The pressure to keep the club closed came from an older generation, such as the theoretician Darwin and the experimentalist G. P. Thomson, who said that in the presence of strangers they would feel reluctant to ask stupid questions. The controversy lasted for a while, but as it was impracticable to have a doorman check the identity of members, more outsiders gradually appeared at the meetings. Eventually people got used to asking their "stupid questions" anyhow.

Our contacts with the mathematicians in Cambridge was more social than professional. We became friendly with Sydney and Rose Goldstein. He was an authority on fluid dynamics, and he had a strong sense of humour and liked to make points that at first seemed paradoxical. He would irritate his purist colleagues by asserting that the convergence of a series was neither a necessary nor a sufficient condition for it to be useful. He was right, of course. A series with a convergence factor of 0.999 is convergent but useless for calculation, and an asymptotic series, which does not converge, is well known to be frequently a powerful tool in numerical work.

A beautiful example of Sydney's quick humour came at a team party. His wife told a story about how she had called on Fanya Pascal (my friend Fanya Polyanowskaya from Berlin, who was also present) and found her in an argument with her landlady: Fanya was asserting that it was good for children to be "sick", the landlady was disagreeing violently. After a while Rose Goldstein realised that Fanya was saying "thick", which with her strong accent sounded like "sick", and she really meant "fat". Rose had some trouble reconstructing this story and had to be prompted a few times by her husband. When she finished she turned to him and said, "What would I do without you?" to which he replied, "I shall have to stick to you through sick and sin!"

During the Cambridge period Gaby reached the age of 4, and Ronnie that of 2. Both were happy and healthy children. Gaby started to look at things from other people's point of view at a very early age. Once she was playing in the garden in front of my open study window, and my replies to her questions must have been a little absent-minded, for suddenly she asked, "Would you like me to stop talking to you?" Her brother started talking rather early, and his first word was "daffodil". This was not an accident but the result of an intense effort on the part of Gaby, who spent long periods standing over his pram repeating "Ronnie, please say 'daffodil'," until he finally obliged.

We did have our worrying moments. Shortly after our arrival in Cambridge, when Ronnie was only a few weeks old, he was lying on a dresser, where Genia was about to change his nappies. He unexpectedly rolled over and off the dresser, and fell on the floor. This was quite against all rules: a child his age was not supposed to turn over yet! Fortunately, the fall does not seem to have done any harm. Another incident involving Ronnie occurred during an unguarded moment, when he grabbed a handful of soap powder and swallowed it. He frothed at the mouth and choked as his nose was blocked by the foam. I knew one should clear the nasal passages, but I also knew one could do damage if it was not done right. Our doctor was out of town, so I went to a doctor across the road, explained the situation, and asked whether he had some instrument to deal with this problem. He was not happy at my interrupting his dinner, but did insist on seeing the patient. By this time Ronnie was screaming blue murder and was red all over from the effort. The doctor took his pulse, which was a little elevated; took his temperature, ditto; patted him on the back, and said, "Never mind, old chap, I shall see you again in the morning." After making sure how to spell my name for the bill, he went back to his dinner. I saw that I would have to improve on the doctor's brilliant effort. I found some valve tubing for my bicycle, sterilised a piece, and pushed it up the baby's nose. This solved the problem.

Cambridge was a town for cycling. There were buses to get around, but they did not cover all parts of town and stopped running rather early at night. I used my bicycle a lot and thought it would also be

125

nice for Genia to learn to cycle. We had already tried this once in Manchester, where Bethe and I made an attempt to teach her, but the effort had failed. In Cambridge, Dirac took an interest in the problem, and declared that surely anybody could be taught cycling. So one Sunday we set out for the Gog Magog Hills, where we knew about a straight, level piece of road that had no traffic. Dirac and Genia went in his new car, and I rode my bicycle, pulling Genia's along. We managed to teach Genia to get on and stay on, but it seemed that any car within her field of vision had a fatal attraction for her. The bicycling lesson therefore ended when she approached Dirac's brand-new parked car, veered off the road, and headed directly for the vehicle. We held our breath as we anticipated a dreadful collision, but at the last second she managed to stop. This demonstration convinced Dirac, and he admitted defeat.

Another friend who took a great interest in the cycling problem was I. Fankuchen. He was an American X-ray crystallographer who had come to work with Bragg in Manchester. He and his wife Dinah moved to Cambridge about the time we did. They lived close to us, and we became good friends. He was very cheerful and uninhibited, and radiated great warmth. He had taught Dinah to ride a bicycle, and refused to believe that Genia could not be taught, as well. Dinah, however, took Genia aside and, lifting her clothes, showed all the bruises she had acquired in the process of learning, and that was enough to put Genia off, permanently.

6

A Provincial Chair

Move to Birmingham

In 1936 Oliphant was appointed to the chair of physics in Birmingham, but he delayed his move until October 1937. In the spring of 1937 he asked me whether I would be interested in a professorship at Birmingham. The answer was, of course, obvious. The chair did not exist yet; he was trying to persuade the university to establish one and wanted to show that indeed there were suitable candidates about. I went with him to visit Birmingham and to meet some of the science professors. As luck would have it, I came down with an attack of influenza before this trip, but recovered just in time to be able to go. Genia felt that I did not have a sufficiently respectable suit for this visit, so while I was still ailing she went out to buy one without me. It fitted, and served for the visit.

In due course the post was advertised, and I put in an application. Eventually I was invited for interview—a rather formidable affair. There were three candidates; besides me, there were Harrie (now Sir Harrie) Massey and Harry Jones, both outstanding theoreticians, so the outcome of this appointment was by no means certain. We all had lunch together with the Faculty Board, which was a large body consisting of all heads of the science and engineering departments. After lunch, the candidates were put in the common room, and were called in for interview (by the whole Board) one by one. My interview went off reasonably well, except for an answer that caused some difficulty. One person had asked me whether I was planning to acquire British nationality. It seemed obvious to me that someone in my position would wish to become British as soon as possible, and I replied that it took five years' residence in the country before one could apply. I learned later that this reply was regarded as evasive, as if I did not intend to become British, and by implication did not intend to settle in Britain. Fortunately, some members of the Board understood what I meant, and were able to convince the others.

I was informed immediately after the interview that I had the appointment. This was possible because in Birmingham the Faculty Boards made decisions on academic matters, while confirmation by the Senate (the body comprising all professors) was a formality, and the Council (the lay body constituting the legal authority) did not interfere in matters of appointments. All the civic or "red-brick" universities had similar constitutions, but in practice the power to decide academic matters rested with the Senate in some, and with the Council in others. I found the Birmingham system to be the most efficient.

Since the matter was decided on the spot, I could go home with the good news, which was a turning point in our fortunes. The professorship was a permanent appointment; it meant greater independence and the possibility of organising my subject in my own way. It also carried a salary 2.5 times that in Cambridge. I felt a little sorry for the competitors, but not too much, because they were sure to find good positions before long. Indeed, within a few years Massey had a chair at University College, London, and Jones had one at Imperial College.

One of the first things we did, in view of our impending affluence, was to buy an old car for £25 and to learn to drive. I essentially taught myself, practicing, as the law requires, when accompanied by someone holding a driver's licence. Most of the time I was, in fact, accompanied by a friend of Genia's who had obtained her licence in the days when no driving test was required, but who had never learned to drive! After I had passed my test I taught Genia. It is said that the most severe test of the stability of a marriage is whether it can survive the husband teaching the wife to drive (or vice versa). By this criterion our marriage seems to have come out with flying colours.

During the summer we made several visits to Birmingham to house-hunt, and to become acquainted with our new home town. We had much good advice from G. N. Watson, the mathematician, who was to be my closest colleague, and from the Shapiros, our friends from Manchester, who were now well established in Birmingham, where Ship was a lecturer in English.

It was immediately obvious that, if possible, one should live in Edgbaston. This is a part of town close to the centre, where most of the land is owned by the Calthorpe family, who leases it out for ninety-nine-year terms. This practice gives them some control over land use, and during the nineteenth century, when all adjacent areas of the city developed into miserable slums, the landowners allowed only attractive houses to be built, with wide spaces between them. We found such a house, built in the Georgian style, and rented it for the next five years.

We also felt that we could now afford a summer holiday and accepted the invitation of the Wooster family to join them in a holiday in South Cornwall. Peter Wooster was a crystallographer and had rather pronounced left-wing political views; we had many violent arguments. He and his wife Norah also believed in "progressive" education, which meant one's children must never be frustrated. This attitude did not become evident on our joint holiday, as their first child was still very small, but we witnessed many "progressive" episodes later. The boys had a wash basin in their room and a glass to clean their teeth. They frequently broke this glass and it was finally replaced by an "unbreakable" plastic beaker. It was not long before this unbreakable vessel was broken, too. The parents then replaced it with an enamelled iron mug, and this really resisted all attempts to break it. But in trying, the boys broke the wash basin instead. More trouble came during the war, when blackout regulations were enforced very strictly. At night the blackout curtains in the boys' room were left open to allow fresh air into the room, and the boys were under strict injunction not to turn on the light. But this was inconvenient, or they forgot. In any case, the light from the uncurtained window was visible for miles around, and attracted irate air-raid wardens.

South Cornwall is a very beautiful part of the country, with a mild climate and a surprising variety of subtropical plants. However, when we made some excursions to the wild and rugged north coast, we found this area even more attractive.

In the summer of 1937 I was invited to a nuclear physics conference in Moscow, and Genia planned to come with me. But we were warned that her presence might prove an embarrassment to her friends and relatives, so she did not go. I went by myself, stopping for a week or so in Copenhagen. I then went, via Stockholm and Helsinki, to Leningrad, where I met Genia's sister, Nina, who had by then been allowed to return to Leningrad. From there I went on to Moscow. The atmosphere in Moscow was very tense. People were arrested for no apparent reasons. It was even rumoured that the lists of people to be arrested were compiled from the phone directory, and some people unrealistically talked about getting their phones disconnected. Certainly disconnecting your phone would not do much to get your name out of the phone book! People were xenophobic, and all foreigners were suspected of being spies. The Russian translation of an English book whose author had been a secret agent in the First World War was being circulated everywhere. In his preface he wrote that the best time for spies to work is just before or during the outbreak of a war, when there is a general spy hysteria, and everybody suspects everybody else of being a spy; then it is virtually impossible to detect the real spies. Evidently the censor who had approved the publication of this translation had not read the preface. Landau was very worried by the state of affairs, a fact he mentioned only when we were walking in a park, and were secure from being overheard. Nevertheless, the scientific discussions at the conference itself were normal and fruitful.

After my return we prepared to move from Cambridge. On the appointed day, Genia and I set out in our car; the children and Olive were staying with friends. Fifteen miles out of town, the car broke down. We made arrangements to have the car towed back to Cambridge. We transferred all its contents to a rented car, in which we finally reached our destination—not a very triumphal entry!

Getting Down to Work

At the university I became joint head of the Mathematics Department with G. N. Watson; I represented applied mathematics. Watson had been the professor of pure mathematics and head of the department for many years, so sharing his authority suddenly with a young man cannot have been easy. I understood this, and did my best to be tactful. Watson went out of his way to make things easy for me. As a result the joint headship, which can always be a source of friction, functioned very smoothly.

Of course, I had to become accustomed to Watson's idiosyncrasies, which were numerous. He did not use a fountain pen, which, he claimed, would always leak in his pocket. Instead he used an old-fashioned inkwell and nib or a pencil for his correspondence; for longer letters he would use a typewriter. He did not drive a car because he did not like the fast speed limits; he used to drive in the days when speeds were about 20 m.p.h. He did not even like to be a passenger, and it was a sign of great confidence that he would occasionally accept a ride in my car. The family car was driven by his wife, and on holidays Mrs. Watson and their son would go by car, while he went by train. He liked trains, and the holidays were invariably spent in Teignmouth, where the railway line passed at the top of the beach. He would sit on the beach with his back toward the sea, so that he could watch the trains go by. He knew by heart practically all the timetables and routes, and the types of engines in use.

The Watsons lived in Leamington Spa, about 20 miles from Birmingham. The town was a stop for the fast trains between London and Birmingham, so he could get to the university more quickly than many residents of Birmingham. He would walk a few blocks from his train to the tram terminus, and then catch a tram to the university. He explained that for the walk to the tram he chose a way that avoided the bus routes: he disliked the big double-decker buses, which, he felt, were top-heavy and liable to fall on him.

Watson refused to use the telephone, claiming that he was slightly hard of hearing and that he could not understand people on the other end. However, he was generous enough to allow me to have a phone installed in the office we were sharing in the university, provided he was not expected to answer it when I was out.

Watson was a mathematician of distinction but a little old-fashioned even for the 1930s. He was known as the co-author, with Sir Edmund Whittaker, of *Modern Analysis*, a very widely used text of "classical" analysis. He had also written a book on Bessel functions, on which he was probably the world authority. He was always willing to help with difficult problems involving Bessel functions, but one had to promise not to tell him the application from which the problem arose—he did not want to know.

He used to work at home, coming to the university only for his lectures or for meetings. He had practically no research students other than a few former undergraduates who were working for an M.Sc. which Birmingham graduates could do by spare-time work. All the best candidates for Ph.D.'s in pure mathematics went to Cambridge, so that the Birmingham students were not of the highest caliber. There was one exception, a very bright student who for some reason could not get into Cambridge (I think he could not pass the Latin exam, which was then compulsory). Watson accepted him as a research student, and he wrote a good Ph.D. thesis.

Watson was very conscientious about his teaching duties, and he was the science faculty's expert on making up timetables. Each year he worked out the dates of term and vacation according to what had become known as the "Watsonian cycle". He also looked after another scheduling problem—the arrangement of practical physics laboratories. These were taken by many students, including engineers, chemists, and some mathematicians, and their practical work had to be spread over a number of days and could not clash with their lectures. The University Registry, which was supposed to make these arrangements, turned to Watson each year for a solution to the problem.

Compared to this complicated set-up, the timetable of lectures for mathematicians was simple. Each year Watson produced a notice, which was pinned on the board, giving the subjects, times, and rooms for the courses. He always signed this sheet personally, and after my arrival made me sign it as well. One year he had to leave before he could finish the sheet, and he asked me to complete it. I asked what I should do about signing it, and he said, "Forge my signature," meaning, of course, that I should sign his name, But I decided to take his instruction literally, and as I had plenty of specimens of his signature, it was not difficult to imitate it. Next day I drew his attention to the sheet, and he noticed nothing unusual. When I asked whether he had signed it, he recalled that he had not, and he was horrified.

The teaching duties of the department then consisted of teaching pure and applied mathematics to mathematics students and to students taking mathematics as a subsidiary subject. The latter, so-called "service teaching", applied to physicists, chemists, and several kinds of engineers. The "applied mathematics" was really elementary theoretical physics, comprising mainly statics and dynamics. For the mathematicians there were more advanced applied subjects, including electricity (mainly electrostatics) and hydrodynamics. All these were given by pure mathematicians, who naturally taught the subject from a rather mathematical point of view.

Watson suggested that for a start I should not take on a heavy teaching load, but get to know the teaching scheme, so that in due course I could recommend improvements. He suggested, however, that I take over the lectures on hydrodynamics, with which none of the others felt comfortable. I of course agreed to this small request and was not willing to admit that my knowledge of hydrodynamics was absolutely nil. I spent a good deal of time in the library cramming enough hydrodynamics to form the basis of a reasonable course of lectures. I came to like the subject, which seems to me very educational because it introduces the student to partial differential equations and to the field concept. It shares this with electromagnetism, but unlike the latter it does not bring in physical concepts that are unfamiliar to the student and sometimes difficult to visualise. I regret that hydrodynamics has by now almost disappeared from undergraduate syllabuses.

In addition to Watson and myself, the staff of the department included five lecturers. The oldest, Mr. Preece, had a great sense of humour and would even poke fun at Watson. He was a widower with a beautiful daughter. It was a terrible blow to him when she died of a thrombosis after a minor operation. Then there was Lumsden, a somewhat gloomy Scot but an excellent teacher. And there were two ladies, Norah Calderwood and Ruby Colomb. Miss Calderwood taught algebra at a rather elementary level. She was also an excellent pianist and a friend of Sibelius, whom she occasionally visited during vacations. She was Scottish, and there was an amusing incident when a visitor asked where she came from. "From Perthshire," she replied. This was followed by a number of strange questions from the visitor— did she not find the climate in Birmingham rather cold, etc.? It took some time to discover that he had understood she came from Persia! The youngest member of the staff was Bryan Kuttner, a Cambridge Ph.D. He was the only one of the lecturers who continued doing research, and quite respectable research, too. He was a little shy, and therefore not very sociable. Miss Calderwood attributed this to his being a relative newcomer to Birmingham: "He has been here only five years."

I was in close touch with the Physics Department, headed by Oliphant. He was a warm, informal, and direct person with a great zest for life, a loud voice, and a hearty laugh. He was happiest when he could roll up his sleeves and get to work on a piece of equipment. His instrumentation showed the influence of Rutherford's string-and-sealing-wax approach. Because of the developing needs of the experiments, Oliphant's projects were much more ambitious pieces of engineering than Rutherford would ever have contemplated. Even though they were sophisticated, he liked his machines homemade as far as possible, which made them more ingenious in design and cheaper than others; but they also took longer to build and had more teething troubles.

Of the other physicists, the first one we met was Martin Johnson, a lecturer of long standing. He had visited Cambridge before we moved, and had been at a party in our house. There he had said that our hospitality encouraged him to make a request: he knew it was not usual for a professor to visit the house of a lecturer, but would we pay him a visit when we were in Birmingham? This made us rather apprehensive of the Birmingham social atmosphere, but we soon found that his attitude was not shared by others. We did visit him, of course, and invited him and his wife to our house, as well. We discovered only later that the effect of Genia's forceful personality on the timid Mrs. Johnson was such that she had to retire to bed for a day after each visit.

In 1939 Philip Moon joined the Physics Department and our circle of friends. He is a very articulate man with a very broad knowledge of physics. As a nuclear physicist, he was concerned with the current problems and advances in his field, but he was also interested in "old-fashioned" subjects.

I was also asked to give lectures to physics students. The traditional applied mathematics they were taught in the Mathematics Department did not go beyond mechanics, and they were given a few brief courses on other theoretical subjects by physics lecturers, who had been trained as experimentalists, and were not at their best at presenting the theoretical topics clearly and intelligibly; but still, they were not too happy when an outsider came in to take over these courses. This resentment of lectures to physics students by theoreticians, who were not members of the department, never quite disappeared.

All these teaching duties were not heavy, however, and I had time for my own research. I had become very interested in the theory of nuclear reactions. In 1936 Niels Bohr had put forward his concept of the "compound nucleus", which had changed our picture of the structure of the nucleus. Until then, the neutrons and protons in the nucleus had been regarded as interacting weakly and moving fairly independently of each other. From this point of view, the experiments about collisions of neutrons with nuclei seemed completely unexpected. One would have predicted that most neutrons would be scattered by nuclei, and that capture with the emission of radiation should be a rare event. In fact, most slow neutrons get captured, and there is little scattering. Bohr explained this by assuming that the nucleons (the generic name for neutrons and protons) interact strongly, so that an incoming neutron will share its excess energy with many other nucleons, and none will have enough energy to escape. Re-escape of a neutron requires that all the available energy should by chance be concentrated on one particle. This takes a long time, during which it is likely that some energy will be emitted as radiation; after that escape becomes impossible, the neutron is truly captured.

Like most theoreticians, I immediately accepted Bohr's new point of view, and started to think about its consequences. I was joined in this by a student from India, P. L. Kapur, who had started to work with me in Cambridge and followed me to Birmingham. We worked out a general formula describing the results of a nuclear collision in terms of the resonances, i.e., the nearly stationary states of the compound system. I was worried that the result resembled an approach that Landau had described to me, and I thought perhaps I had just spelled out Landau's idea, which at the time I had not understood very clearly. I wrote to Landau, and he assured me that our method had no connection to his way of thinking about the problem. We now felt free to publish our results. Our "dispersion formula" became fairly well known, although a few years later Wigner and Eisenbud published an alternative method, which was used rather more widely. I still believe that our method has advantages. Kapur and I did some more work on other nuclear problems before he had to return to India. I lost touch with him, but I met him on a visit to India in 1950. It seems he landed in a job with such heavy teaching duties that he had no opportunity to do any research.

Another student who had started working with me was Fred Hoyle. He did not move to Birmingham, but came to visit me whenever there was something to discuss. He generally hitch-hiked between Cambridge and Birmingham, and he knew the roads and traffic conditions so well that he would announce his arrival for, say, 2:15 P.M., and promptly at 2:15 he would knock on my door. His Ph.D. subject was the theory of beta decay. Since Fermi's pioneering paper of 1934, in which he made a quantitative theory out of Pauli's idea of the neutrino, this theory had been the basis for the interpretation of the experiments. But there were several alternative forms for the Fermi interaction, and Hoyle sorted out what possible assumptions could be made, and what their consequences would be. One of his hobbies was climbing, and he did many of the difficult climbs on the Cambridge college buildings. This sport originated when students tried to get into or out of college after the gates were locked, but climbing over the walls became too tame, and the enthusiasts found more and more challenging tasks. Fred Hoyle kept in practice by going round his room without touching the floor, and his landlady had to get accustomed to the sight of a stockinged Fred Hoyle clinging to the picture rail or to similar precarious holds. He later turned to astrophysics and achieved popular fame through his BBC Reith Lectures, which presented the "continuous creation" theory then favoured by him and others.

For the first time since my student days, I found myself to be the only theoretician in my department, except for these few students, who did not stay very long. I had known what it would be like, and was not surprised. My intention was to select some of the brighter students, train them in theoretical physics, and eventually form a group. I knew this would take patience—it could not be done overnight. I realised later that this was not a good idea; it is too hard to educate a group in modern physics if there is only one teacher to learn from. In any case, within two years the situation was changed completely by the war, and later I had the chance to make a new start.

At age 30, I was fairly young to be a professor, and I probably looked even younger. This sometimes led to amusing confusion. When at the beginning of a term I came to the university carrying my M.A. gown (which one needed occasionally for formal meetings), I heard some worried undergraduates say, "Oh, do we need gowns?" And at a staff-student social, where one wore name labels, I danced with a girl student, who looked at my name and asked, "Are you a relation of the new professor?"

The administration of the university functioned rather smoothly, and the time spent on meetings and committee work was not substantial. I have already mentioned that the power to make decisions on academic matters rested with the Faculty Boards, and for a strong faculty that meant a welcome freedom to get on with their work. When the quality of a faculty had gone down, as was at times the case with the arts faculty in Birmingham, the system made it harder to remedy the situation. In Birmingham science (including engineering) was regarded as the senior faculty, which was unusual among English universities. This came about because the university had its origins in Mason's Science College, which was set up in the nineteenth century as a training college in science by Sir Josiah Mason, who had made his fortune in manufacturing pen nibs, presumably an early example of mass production. He was a freethinker, and caused a clause to be written into the statutes of the college that forbade any religious test being applied to students or members of the staff; the university later retained this clause. However, later, I believe it was during the war, the university received a donation to endow a chair of theology, and some questions had to be answered. Would the appointment of a professor of theology conflict with the founder's clause in the statutes? It was decided that it would not; a theologian would be selected only for the merit of his scholarship, not for his religious beliefs. If the most distinguished of the candidates was, say, a Buddhist, he would get the chair. By now the university has two chairs of theology. So far no Buddhist has been appointed.

The day-to-day business of the university was handled almost single-handed by the secretary, Mr. C. G. Burton. He was very experienced and knew the university inside out, but he tended to regard the university as a business, with the council being the equivalent of the board of directors, and the teaching staff being the employees. The story was told that he once came to the university late at night, and found Mr. Shakespeare, one of the lecturers in physics, busy with some experiment. He became very angry and admonished him for wasting the heat and light of the university with his "private" work.

Similar mistaken ideas about the nature of the university could be found among the members of the council. They were usually public-spirited businessmen, solicitors, and so on who were prepared to devote some time to university affairs, but they sometimes suffered from misconceptions about academic life. One member of council seriously proposed that they should investigate what proportion of his time each

professor spent on research, and then reduce his salary by that proportion. This man later became the treasurer of the university; he
evidently had learned a little, since no unreasonable actions resulted
from his term as treasurer.

The academic side of university operations also had a rather personal
touch. This was the result of the presence of Mrs. Brake, a very energetic and efficient lady, who was at first the registrar's secretary,
and later was promoted to assistant registrar and later deputy registrar.
She had the whole academic side of the university at her fingertips
and, except for the knotty scheduling problems on which she invited
Watson's advice, she took everything in her stride.

Oliphant had been busy getting support for equipping his nuclear
physics laboratory. The university had received a gift from Lord Nuffield, the motorcar magnate, to be used for a new building and the
construction of a cyclotron. The building was a small single-story
structure, except for a pit to house the cyclotron. Provision was made
for office space, which would include two offices for me and my
(future) collaborators; we would also get a machine room in which
to house our desk calculators.

I had, in fact, two research students in 1938-39. One was Hugh
McManus, who had graduated in physics but had theoretical interest
and ability. I suggested a problem to him in what would now be called
electro-migration, and he had made quite interesting progess when his
work was interrupted by service in the navy. He returned after the
war, but by this time there were no written records on his work, and
neither he nor I could reconstruct his results. So this work was lost
to posterity. The problem was not looked at again until about 1964.

The other student was Michael Wood, a mathematics graduate, who
intended to become a schoolteacher. His parents ran a private school
near Birmingham, and the idea of teaching came to him naturally. He
had been supported in his undergraduate studies by a so-called "education scholarship", which committed him to becoming a schoolteacher. I always regarded these grants as likely to damage the image
of school teaching. They gave the impression that if a student was
bright enough, he could get a state scholarship unconditionally; but
if he failed to qualify for one, he could still get a scholarship, provided
he promised to become a teacher. In any case, these promises were
usually unenforceable, since they were made before the student came
of age.

In Michael Wood's case, we felt he would benefit by spending a
year on an M.Sc. degree before starting on his teacher training. He
asked for the necessary permission, which was granted. My plan was

to work with him on building a differential analyser of the kind I had seen Hartree use in Manchester, and to make it largely from Meccano parts. With some advice and detailed drawings supplied by Hartree, we made good progress, but the work had to stop when Wood was also called up for service. Because of his interest in numerical problems, which had been stimulated by our work, he was assigned to Hartree's team, which was doing work of military importance. After the war he expected to return to teacher training, and enquired from the appropriate department when and where he would be able to resume this. To his surprise the answer was: "You no longer have to become a teacher; when we gave you permission to work under Professor Peierls for an M.Sc., we relieved you of your obligation." As a result he did not go into teaching and took a job in publishing instead. However, I believe that many years later he did become a teacher.

Life in Birmingham

We soon settled down to life in Birmingham. The city is much better than its reputation. For most people the name conjures up a grimy industrial city, and indeed there are parts for which this description is appropriate, but other areas are very different. Birmingham grew out of a conglomeration of small towns and villages. In fact, it developed because it was not a city. In the early days of the industrial revolution most of the Midlands were organised in cities with their guilds, whose restrictive rules made the development of industries difficult. The Birmingham area was free of these restrictions, so the new industries settled there. As a result it is still made up of different little centres today, with open spaces in between. Edgbaston is particularly rich in open spaces, and the university, built on land donated by the Calthrope family, is in a very attractive location. Birmingham prides itself on being an efficiently run city. Whereas in Manchester the local citizens would stress to newcomers the glories of free trade, the music, and the *Manchester Guardian*—all somewhat faded glories in the thirties—a Birmingham city councillor whom we met soon after our arrival said to Genia, "Lass, you've come to the city with the best sewers!"

We already had many friends there, among them the Shapiros. The Pascals came from Cambridge a year after us. I had known Fanya Pascal since our Berlin student days. Her husband, Roy, was now a professor of German, a distinguished scholar of German literature, and an exceptionally charming person, whose gentle manner won everybody's heart.

Among our new friends was S. Konovalov, a part-time professor of Russian in Birmingham who spent the rest of his time in Oxford. When it became difficult for him to retain part-time lodgings in Birmingham, he made our house his Birmingham base. He was interested in economics as well as in Russian language and literature, and edited a journal on Soviet economics. His group was joined by another Russian émigré, Alexander Baykov, who had come from Prague for what was intended to be a temporary stay, but the German occupation of Czechoslovakia left him stranded. He also stayed in our house.

The Hungarian physicist Egon Orowan, who had been working in Berlin, came to join the Physics Department for a few years, and we became good friends and often went on weekend excursions together. At his suggestion I studied an equation concerning dislocations, a fault in crystals which is of great practical importance in determining their strength. I wrote a short paper about it, which at the time seemed to have little importance, but I discovered years later that it had a considerable impact.

Soon it was time for Gaby to start school. Very conveniently, a private school was just across the road, and it was recommended to us. It was called the Edgbaston Church of England College for Girls, but in spite of the name there was not much religious pressure in the teaching.

With Gaby gone half the day, Ronnie was fretting. He not only missed his sister, but he envied her the learning. He spent much of his time at the window, hoping to get a glimpse of the exciting activities across the road. Eventually we persuaded the school to accept him in their kindergarten when he was only 3½ years old. On his first day, he was given some toys to keep him occupied, but he rejected them indignantly: "I have come here to work, not to play!"

During 1938 I made several trips to Copenhagen to discuss a problem of nuclear reactions with Niels Bohr and George Placzek. If a slow neutron collides with a nucleus, the resulting compound system has resonance levels, which are often much narrower than their spacing, so that they are well separated from each other. However, at higher neutron energies the width of the resonances increases and their spacing decreases, so that they eventually overlap. In this region of overlapping levels two different ways of expressing Bohr's idea of the compound nucleus formation gave conflicting answers. Which answer was right? In various conversations involving Bohr, Placzek, and myself, we gradually understood the solution to this puzzle, and it made an interesting point of principle. We now needed to write up our conclusions.

This proved a very difficult task. Bohr wanted to emphasise broad qualitative arguments, whereas Placzek and I felt that the point needed to be spelled out mathematically, which could be done using the method developed by Kapur and me. No doubt we were trying to make the paper too mathematical. I made several trips to Copenhagen to try and argue this out. Placzek visited Birmingham a few times. I remember one of these visits when, in his characteristic manner, Placzek was leaving for three days, always by the next available train, but never quite made it. The proposed paper was discussed when Bohr got an honorary degree at Birmingham and stayed with us overnight with his son, Aage. Finally it was agreed that we would send a short note to the journal *Nature* stating our results, but without detailed derivation, and we agreed on the text of this note without too much difficulty. The full paper was still not finished when the outbreak of war made further communication difficult.

During the war Bohr, Placzek, and I did eventually find ourselves in the same place, in Los Alamos, but we were preoccupied with other matters, so we did not return to the discussion of the paper until after the war. By this time various draft copies had circulated fairly widely, and the main results of the paper had been used in the literature, so it became the most frequently cited unpublished paper! We made another attempt to arrive at an agreed version, but we finally had to give up.

Refugees. War Threatens

In 1938 my father at last decided to leave Germany. As I mentioned earlier, he had been reluctant to make the move because of his age and financial worries. He now regretted that he did not leave earlier, at a point when he would at least have been able to take his savings with him. But now even that did not deter him.

We had hoped that he and his second wife, Else, would join us in Birmingham, and we started to look for a flat for them. But they decided to go to America to join his brother. While waiting for their American visa, they stayed in a boarding-house in Hampstead, London, where many refugees, including many of their friends, were temporarily residing. Father was not too well. His heart gave him trouble, but he recovered by the time the visa was ready. He and Else moved on to the New York area, where his brother, Siegfried, was happy to support them. He lived there until his death in 1945, and his prediction had been right: he was unhappy and never felt at home in his new environment.

It might here be appropriate to review the fate of my family. My brother Alfred had come to England in 1935. In Berlin he had become an expert on electric condensers, and he found a post near London in a firm that started to manufacture them. He took charge of that department, and in due course became the manager of the condenser factory. We were happy to have him, his wife Nina, and her daughter Vera within hailing distance. My sister Annie and her husband Herman Krebs emigrated to the United States at about the same time. Herman did not have any technical qualifications, but he was highly experienced in industrial administration. Our American uncle, Siegfried, helped him and Siegfried's son to start a factory making oil and petrol-resistant tubing for cars and airplanes, and the firm became very successful. They lived in Montclair, New Jersey, across the river from New York, and it was near them that Father and Else settled. Herman died a few years ago, but Annie still lives in the same house.

My mother's brother, Hermann Weigert, was a musician, and he was particularly gifted as an accompanist and repetitor. He had travelled much and settled in New York in the thirties, where he worked at the Metropolitan Opera. My mother's sister was married to a doctor in Breslau, where they remained; they perished during the war, probably in a concentration camp. Their two daughters did get away, one to England and the other to the United States. As to my father's side: his sister was married to my uncle Adolf, on whose sound business instincts I have already had occasion to comment. He had moved his capital from Germany in good time and was in New York by now. The writer Ludwig Fulda and his wife, Else's sister, could not face emigration and committed suicide when the Hitler regime became intolerable. Their son, my friend Carl, got to the United States in time and followed an academic career in law. On the whole, my family was fortunate in having most of its members escape Nazi persecution.

We encountered many refugees who had come to England and were trying to build a new life. Many of them had difficulty finding employment in the professions for which they were trained and had to earn their living by doing menial work. It was interesting to observe that the people with the highest professional qualifications, such as doctors, who were not able to practise before they had passed further tests and had to work as domestic servants in the meantime, did not complain much. The most bitter complaints about doing work that was "infra dig" and beneath their qualifications came from people such as small businessmen or lawyers whose qualifications had not been all that remarkable to begin with.

There were cases of people paying dearly for lack of imagination. We met a couple from Vienna, who somehow had managed to get a visa for Venezuela. They invested half their savings in the passage there, only to discover that Venezuela was very hot and humid, and that they could not stand it. So they spent the other half on getting back to England, and now had to be a "married couple" in domestic service.

Another interesting observation related to refugee children at school. At first they had a difficult time, finding themselves in schools with a different language, a different educational system, and different subject matter. But after struggling with these initial difficulties, almost all of them rose in a term or two to the top of their form. They cannot all have been exceptionally bright, and no doubt the explanation is that the process of encountering and mastering a new situation has a maturing effect.

In the summer of 1938 Olive decided to leave us, and we engaged a German refugee girl as *au pair*. Anneliese was an intelligent and energetic girl and got on well with the children. On leaving Germany she had instructed a shipping firm to send a big trunk containing her trousseau to England, but by mistake it was sent to Trieste. To recover it involved some paperwork, which included translating the contents list into English. I helped her with this but was stumped by the word *Zylindertücher*, which literally means "cylinder cloths". Anneliese had no idea what these might be. After doing some research, we discovered that these were cloths used to clean the cylinders of oil or gas lamps, and that they traditionally formed part of a trousseau.

Eventually the trunk arrived, and its contents were stored in a cupboard in Anneliese's attic room. The house had no central heating, and the attic was not wired for electric heat. We therefore provided an oil heater, but warned Anneliese to extinguish it before going to sleep, as the wick needed regular attention. But she did not like the idea of sleeping in a cold room and kept the burner going. One night she awoke in a fit of coughing. She switched on the light, and thought the bulb was dead, as the room was still dark. Finally she realized that the wick of the oil burner was too high, and the flame had filled the room with smoke and soot, so that the light was not visible. She quickly extinguished the burner and opened the window, but by now everything in the room was black with soot. Worried about her trousseau, she opened the cupboard door to look. The soot had not yet got

142

inside, but on opening the door it did. She spent a week cleaning the room and washing and ironing her linens and clothes.

In the spring of 1939 the situation in Europe looked depressing, but life continued as usual, in the hope that there would be some solution to the problems. For a period of a week or so there were no lectures in the university, to give students a break so they could rest a little before the start of examinations. On the contrary, however, the students used this period, which they called "Swot Week", for intense review. Genia and I decided we would use the free time to visit Scotland, although I had my doubts about taking this time off. There was going to be a British Association meeting in Dundee in the autumn and I was planning to attend it so we would have got to Scotland in any case. But Genia persuaded me to go: "Who knows what may happen between now and the autumn? Let's go while we can."

We had a glorious week driving around Scotland, sleeping in our car. This was not the unreliable car that had let us down on our move to Birmingham, but its successor, which served us until 1947. But the car actually did break down on this trip in a very desolate place in northern Scotland. We managed to contact a small garage, which sent out a car which towed us over hilly roads with gradients of 1:6. After he received the necessary part—which was sent by bus from a town 40 miles away—the mechanic completed the repair the same day, more efficiently and more cheaply than would have been possible in Birmingham.

Meanwhile, the country prepared itself for the impending war. The physicists organised themselves for work on radar, or radio-location as it was then called, though I did not know anything about that at the time—it was not a project for foreigners. I was aware only of the precautions taken by all residents. This included instruction in protection against gas warfare. We were all given copies of a handbook about gas, which started with the memorable statement, "Gases are of three kinds—solids, liquids, and vapours."

A young policeman came to lecture members of the university staff about air-raid precautions. Some rather worried old lecturers held up the proceedings with many questions: What could one do against a direct hit? Was there no way of protecting oneself? And so on. Everyone was getting impatient, and finally one of our staff, Mr. Preece, stopped the discussion by asking the lecturer, "I suppose you cannot promise these gentlemen absolute immortality?"

The threatening war did not come at once. Instead there was appeasement. It seemed that Hitler would have it all his way. I wrote to Hans Bethe in America that it looked as if Hitler would have to be stopped now, if at all. If it came to war, I would want to stay and take part in it as best I could. But if there was further appeasement, the future of Europe looked grim, and I would want to get out. I would be interested in any job in the United States no matter where and no matter what kind.

7

War

Birmingham in Wartime

Before my letter to Bethe had reached its destination, war had been declared. This made us "enemy aliens". However, there was no general xenophobia, and the restrictions that were immediately imposed on German residents were fairly mild, if sometimes a little illogical. The most inconvenient rule was that one was not allowed to own a car. I was reluctant to sell our car, because its market value was low, and we could never replace it without paying a lot more. The police were supervising these arrangements, and I offered to deposit the car or garage key with them, but they insisted that I must transfer the ownership of the car. We found a satisfactory solution. During the construction of the cyclotron, which was proceeding very much as a "do-it-yourself" job, there had been an accident. When the magnet was assembled from steel plates, a plate slipped and injured the legs of a physicist, Nimmo, and a technician. We offered Nimmo our car, which he was very pleased to have so that his wife could drive him around while he was disabled. It was understood he would return the car when we were again allowed to own it, but for the moment he was the owner. This arrangement satisfied the police. I then pointed out to them that we also had in our garage the car of our friend Roy Pascal, whose house did not have a garage. I expected they would require some arrangement by which I would not have access to the garage. "No," said the police inspector, "that is perfectly all right. You don't own that car." I found it a little difficult to visualise what actions by German agents these rules were trying to prevent. Other restrictions concerned the possession of maps, staying out late at night, and so on.

Quite soon, however, tribunals were set up to classify all enemy aliens into three categories: those in the first category were trusted, and freed from practically all restrictions; the second category were those about whom too little was known, and for whom the restrictions continued; and the third category were suspected of being enemy agents and were interned. We were placed in the first category, but my brother and his wife found themselves in the second category, which did not matter so much at the time but had unpleasant consequences later.

Our position improved further, quite unexpectedly, when in February 1940 my naturalisation papers came through. The machinery of naturalisation was practically stopped when the war started, but it seems my papers had been so near completion that they still went through. We were now British subjects, and freed from the restrictions.

Even this improvement in our status did not allow me to join Oliphant's radar team. He was anxious to have me work with them, but the authorities refused permission. In fact, in due course, when the new Nuffield building was devoted to secret work, I was no longer allowed access to it, and my new office, of which I had already taken possession, had to be vacated again.

The outbreak of war did not have any direct impact, but the country braced itself for the expected air raids. A blackout was in force, and one had to cover one's windows with dark curtains or shutters, if one wanted to have any light inside the house. Baykov seemed to be the expert on this, as he had already gone through blackout preparations in Prague. We followed his advice by improvising shutters out of black paper and strips of wood, but the system did not work well. He eventually admitted that his design had never actually been tried, since during his stay in Prague the blackout was never actually imposed. Official advice was also to paste strips of paper as a grid over large windows, to reduce the amount of flying glass in the event of an explosion. Further, we were urged to carry gas masks at all times, and for some people the mask seemed to become a talisman that would protect them from bombs. Others went to work with their lunch instead of their gas masks in the standard gas mask cases.

Petrol and food were rationed; clothes rationing came later. People were encouraged to move from the cities if their work did not require them to stay, and a scheme for the evacuation of children was started. The official scheme involved placing the children with families in the country, which often caused some friction, but was accepted good-naturedly for the most part.

Our children's school moved to a large country house near Shrewsbury, Attingham Park, and they boarded there. Our petrol ration sufficed to visit them every few weeks or so. An outbreak of whooping cough disrupted the school quite early after the move, and the children had to stay in bed under the supervision of a nurse. We visited one

Sunday, as did other parents, and when one little girl's parents turned to go, she broke into frantic tears. Not wishing to prolong the agony of departure, the parents left with a heavy heart. The nurse then asked the girl, "Why are you crying?"—"I did not want milk for my tea, I wanted cocoa!" ("Tea" was the nursery name for the evening meal.) We phoned the parents when we got home to give them the comforting message that it was not their departure that had upset the girl. By this time Ronnie was very articulate. For example, when the nurse took a group of children for a walk. Ronnie, then just four, said, "Nurse, I wish you would not walk so fast. You don't seem to realise that I have very short legs!"

The university lost many teachers who joined the armed forces or went into full-time war research. We also lost many students to military service; but the best students, at least in science, were allowed to postpone their military service and complete their courses. In general, the women students stayed, as did the foreign students, so the classes continued, though somewhat telescoped because of the shortage of staff.

Provision was made for air-raid shelters in the event of a raid during teaching hours. An underground corridor running through the university buildings was at first chosen as a refuge. The committee making such plans decided, by a majority, to keep men and women students separated during an air-raid alarm, because they had heard of cases of young men losing self-control in a crisis, and this could be embarrassing for any women present. Most of us considered this a ridiculous idea. The plan was never tested, however, because we never had any daytime raids. In any case, the university engineer pointed out that the corridor in question was full of pipes carrying high-pressure steam for the university heating system, and would not be a healthy shelter during a raid. I cannot recall what plans were finally adopted, but I believe the segregation was abandoned with the underground corridor.

When the war started, I wanted to do my part in the fight against Hitler. I found that as an "enemy alien" I would not be allowed to join the Civil Defence teams. Eventually I applied to the Auxiliary Fire Service and was accepted. The Service was started to help fight the many additional fires expected during air raids. A number of small stations were therefore set up to assist the regular fire brigade; they were manned during the day by a full-time staff and at night by part-time volunteers.

I acquired a uniform with helmet and axe, and started to spend nights at a station near our house. The duty shifts varied between every second night at critical periods and every fourth night during quieter times. Our station was equipped with a rather ancient car (the Service had gone around buying up cheap second-hand cars before the war) and a trailer with a pump. The car was not driven much but was started frequently, so its battery was permanently undercharged, and the engine had to be started by cranking. This required some know-how, but even our best efforts to get going during an alarm were not quite in line with one's image of firemen.

My colleagues were working class or upper middle class. The lower middle class were missing, probably because they were reluctant to be away from their families and property during a raid. We spent long hours at the station just sitting around, and a fair quantity of beer was consumed then. I was regarded as odd, less because I was German-born than because I did not drink beer. I have an aversion to beer— probably a reaction to my student days, when beer drinking was regarded as a sign of manliness, together with duelling and other habits of the student "Korps". I admitted to liking other drinks, including wine, and this prompted my station-house colleagues to play a practical joke on me. We were on duty on Christmas Eve, and everyone was merry and drank a good deal. One of the volunteers said he brought very special wine for me and hoped I would like it. He produced a glass full of a dark liquid, which, in fact, was a mixture of all strong drinks they could lay their hands on. I tasted the horrible stuff and, in answer to their questions, used noncomittal terms such as "interesting", "original", "not too mature". They watched me finish the glass, and expected me to end up under the table. They were impressed when I continued the conversation without any change in expression. I was never teased again about not drinking beer.

Later we did see duty in air raids. By this time the small stations with one crew had been combined into bigger ones with several cars. I remember one van whose choke was not working, so the engine was started by putting a rag into the air intake. But soon we received some real purpose-built fire engines. I reflected that most little boys dream of driving a fire engine with a loud bell (there were no sirens then), and I was one of the few to realise that ambition!

The work was undramatic. At big fires, we sometimes had to lay hoses from a canal or other water basin to get more water. This involved running back and forth, carrying hose reels—very hot and tiring work. On one occasion, when a paint factory was on fire, our job was to pour water on an adjacent building to prevent it bursting into flames from the radiant heat. Unpleasant, but not very dramatic. Another time, when the upper floor of a shed was on fire, I found an open ground-floor window through which we could spray water at the floor from below. After a while the floor and part of the wall collapsed, showering us with bricks. I had a dent in my steel helmet to show for the adventure, my companion was slightly injured on the arm, but he was only bruised.

On many occasions we were moved to other parts of town as reinforcements. When an air raid was concentrated in a certain area, perhaps the industrial north, the fire stations there were depleted, and engines and crews from other areas were moved in. Even when things in our area were quiet, one could look up into the sky and see the light of fires, the flash of bombs, and the bursting of anti-aircraft shells. From a distance all this looked terribly concentrated, and you would say to yourself, with a sinking heart, "That's where we are going." Once on the spot, we saw that there was much space between the bombs and the shell fragments.

I recall one scene in the north of Birmingham, in an area of intense activity. German bombers were dropping bombs, shrapnel burst from anti-aircraft shells, and fires blazed all over the area. Some firemen, who at the moment were not needed, were lying on the ground, sheltering under a solid shelf, when a van stopped. The chocolate firm, Cadbury, was sending their vans to offer refreshments to firemen and others working through the night. Two girls in steel helmets got out and bent down to proffer hot chocolate drinks to the sheltering men.

Driving through town during the night of a raid, one got the feeling that whole districts were destroyed. Some streets were closed because debris blocked them or because of the presence of unexploded bombs. By daylight one saw how many houses were still standing, but the effect was nevertheless eerie: the absence of wheeled traffic caused a depressing silence amid the debris, and one could hear only footsteps crunching on the ubiquitous glass.

Genia had become an auxiliary nurse. The hospitals were reinforced in anticipation of air-raid casualties. However, the number of casualities had been overestimated, and the number of homeless people was underestimated: in other words, human beings were tougher and brick and mortar weaker than expected. A typical example: A house in our neighbourhood belonging to a lady doctor was hit by a bomb. The doctor was found, still in her bed, on top of a heap of rubble. An ambulance appeared, but she insisted she did not need any medical assistance—but she could use a dressing gown!

Shelter for people whose homes had been destroyed often had to be improvised. One episode relating to this throws an interesting light on social habits. Our neighbour's wife was working for the Women's Voluntary Services, and at one point was assigned the task of recruiting householders for a scheme by which they would put a sign in their windows indicating that bombed-out people could come to the house and would be given temporary shelter, a cup of tea, etc. Her recruiting area was a slum district adjacent to our Georgian neighbourhood. She failed completely in her mission. The reason was that in that district, people in trouble could obviously go into any home and would find a welcome and whatever assistance was appropriate. What was the point of having a sign?

The summer of 1940 was unusually fine. The blue sky and bright sunshine contrasted sharply with the depressing news: the fall of France, the evacuation of the British Army from Dunkirk, and the prospect of a German invasion of Britain made this the blackest period of all. We heard about the Battle of Britain and dared not hope it would succeed.

The fear of a German invasion was justified, but not all the hasty measures taken to counter it were sensible. All road signs were removed so as not to assist German parachutists in finding their way. Around most towns and villages pillboxes were erected from which the roads could be covered with machine-gun fire, and preparations were made to fix tank traps at short notice.

One aspect of this general invasion hysteria was the internment of enemy aliens. Many of the Germans whom the tribunals had placed in the second category were now rounded up for internment. Certain areas, particularly port towns, were declared prohibited areas for enemy aliens. They had to move to other places, where, as strangers, they were regarded with suspicion, and were often interned. An old German-Jewish doctor we know was in a boarding-house in London when the police arrived to pick up all its residents for internment. The doctor interceded with the officer in charge, pointing out that one of the people they were taking was seriously ill and should not be moved. After some argument the officer agreed. Then the doctor said, "Now I must plead for myself. I have a weak heart." But the officer decided that enough was enough and the doctor had to go with the rest. Generally, the places of internment were improvised in a hurry, and there was often considerable hardship. It took some time before even the bare necessities were provided everywhere.

The army officers in charge of the internment were decent people, but they were the last to understand the problem of the refugees. We heard of one refugee camp in which considerable tension obtained because of a lack of tact on the part of the commanding officer. A new C.O. was appointed in his place with a reputation of being very diplomatic. On arrival he called a meeting of the internees and gave a talk, in the course of which he said, "I have my loyalty to my country, and you have your loyalty to your country. I have no respect for anyone who is not loyal to his country."

My brother Alfred and his wife Nina were interned and, after staying in some temporary camps, were sent to two different camps on the Isle of Man. Nina's daughter, Vera, stayed with friends. After a year or so, Nina was released and she and Vera came to stay with us. Alfred stayed in his camp until it was announced that interned men would be released if they volunteered for the army. They could serve in the Royal Pioneer Corps. Alfred volunteered and in due course became a soldier. He spent some time in army camps without doing anything very useful, but was allowed to take leaves so he could visit his family. Eventually he was released from the army, probably as a result of pressure from his firm, and he returned to his job.

In the summer of 1940 the University of Toronto invited the academic staff of the Universities of Birmingham and Oxford to send their children, and the mothers of young children, to Toronto. We accepted eagerly. We were not afraid of the raids, and in any case the children were reasonably safe with their school in the countryside, but we did fear a German invasion. If this happened, we, as former German and Russian, and both Jewish, would be in danger, and it would be good at least to have the children out of the way. Genia was also eligible to go, but she did not want to: "I could not bear reading in the papers about the fall of Europe; I want to be on the spot."

We explained to the children what was about to happen. They accepted the plan quite reasonably, and our assurance that the ice cream in Canada was excellent was hardly necessary. Ronnie, ever concerned about his food, had a question: "We are not going to stay in Canada forever?"—"We hope not, but why?"—"If the lady with whom we are staying should die, who will cook for us?" We explained that in that event someone else would be found, and he was satisfied. Gaby had no questions, but a comment: "You will be very sad if the radio reports that a ship evacuating little children to Canada has been torpedoed."

For the trip the children needed passports, and this required their signatures. So I set out to the school in Attingham Park with the necessary forms. Since our petrol allowance would not stand the extra journey by car, I took my bicycle with me on the train to Shrewsbury and cycled the five miles or so to the school. I felt slightly ridiculous going to this effort to secure the signatures of a six-year-old and a four-year-old.

Genia sent a letter with the children describing them and their background, and she also sent along some of their school books to indicate what they had been taught. Although we had no doubts about our decision to send the children away, parting was not easy when the day finally arrived. We left them on the boat in Liverpool and returned to Birmingham with heavy hearts. After a few days, when we thought they had already passed the most dangerous region of the Atlantic, we received a postcard from one of the mothers on board. The boat had spent several days in Liverpool Harbour and was only now passing through the critical zone. But all went well. On the boat the children became friendly with the large family of a Roman Catholic professor. On arrival the whole party was accommodated in a Catholic boarding school in Toronto, whose pupils were on vacation, while suitable homes were found for everybody. Our children were separated, but in related families of a brother and sister. They were charming people and have remained our friends.

In her first letter home, Gaby wrote, "Please, may we become a Catholic?" No doubt she had been impressed by her friends on the boat and the nuns in the boarding school. Religious tensions in Canada being rather strong, the hostess reassured us in a postscript that they were Church of England. We composed a diplomatic reply, but by the time it reached Gaby, she had forgotten the whole idea.

Is the Atom Bomb Possible?

In 1939 physicists were excited about the discovery of fission by Otto Hahn and Fritz Strassman in Berlin. Lise Meitner, a close collaborator of Hahn's until she had to leave Germany because of her Jewish origin, gave an explanation of Hahn's observations, together with her nephew, Robert Frisch. They estimated the energy liberated when the uranium nucleus is split. Frisch did the first experiment to show up the fragments into which the uranium nucleus had split, and, incidentally, proposed the name "fission" for the new phenomenon. It was suspected—and proved by several physicists, probably first by von Halban, Joliot, and Kowarski in Paris—that in this process further neutrons are produced, so that a chain reaction may be possible. Popular magazines at this time were full of stories and speculations about atomic bombs without paying attention to the technical details.

It was reassuring when Niels Bohr, together with John Wheeler at Princeton, worked out a theory of the fission process, and showed that fission by slow neutrons was entirely due to the rare uranium isotope of weight 235. This meant that the chain reaction in ordinary uranium would require a very large amount of material. In that case the neutrons would have to travel long distances in building up the chain reaction, and this would proceed rather slowly. As energy was released, the uranium would heat up and evaporate before the chain reaction had proceeded very far. Even if a chain reaction were possible, it would not lead to a bomb.

My own introduction to the technicalities of the chain reaction came by way of a misjudgment. I had not yet understood the basic feature of a chain reaction, which has a sharply defined critical size. The chain reaction proceeds when on the average more than one secondary neutron is produced by one initial neutron. If the size of the body is small, the chance of a neutron escaping without making a collision is high, and the average multiplication rate is therefore reduced. As soon as the piece of material exceeds the critical size, for which the escape fraction just equals the excess number produced, the chain grows indefinitely until circumstances change.

I had seen a paper by the French theoretician Francis Perrin in which he calculated the critical size in terms of the nuclear constants. He had assumed, as an approximation, that the size of the body is large compared to the mean free path, i.e., to the distance a neutron travels on the average before making a collision. I suspected that perhaps this approximation was responsible for the sharp distinction between sub-critical and supercritical conditions. This was a foolish thought, as I soon convinced myself, but it led me into trying to solve the problem more accurately. This was indeed possible, in a sufficiently simple case, in which the cross section, i.e., the chance of a neutron hitting a nucleus, did not depend on the neutron energy. This made my calculation seem rather academic, since fission had been observed only with slow neutrons, for which the cross section varies strongly with energy. But the calculation was very simple and could perhaps serve as a model for more realistic calculations.

I wrote a short paper about my results, but had some doubts about publishing it, as it could possibly have some bearing on the design of a weapon. I consulted Frisch, who had arrived in Birmingham in the summer of 1939. With war imminent and Denmark likely to be over-run by Nazi armies, Copenhagen did not seem a safe place for a Jewish refugee, so he had come to Birmingham to discuss a possible appointment. The outbreak of war prevented his return home, and he stayed on in a temporary teaching post. He saw no reason against having my paper published, since Bohr had shown that an atomic bomb was not a realistic proposition.

Then one day, in February or March 1940, Frisch said, "Suppose someone gave you a quantity of pure 235 isotope of uranium—what would happen?" We started working out the consequences. The work of Bohr and Wheeler seemed to suggest that every neutron that hits a 235 nucleus should produce fission. Since the number of secondary neutrons per fission had been measured approximately, we had all the data to insert in my formula for the critical size, and we were amazed how small this turned out to be. We estimated the critical size to be about a pound, whereas speculations concerned with natural uranium had tended to come out with tons. Our estimate turned out to be rather too low, because we did not know that some of the neutrons hitting 235 nuclei would be captured without causing fission, but the order of magnitude was right.

That still left the question how far the chain reaction would go before the developing pressure would disperse the uranium. A rough estimate—on the back of the proverbial envelope—showed that a substantial fraction of the uranium would be split, and that therefore the energy release would be the equivalent of thousands of tons of ordinary explosive. We were quite staggered by these results: an atomic bomb was possible, after all, at least in principle! As a weapon, it would be so devastating that, from a military point of view, it would be worth the effort of setting up a plant to separate the isotopes. In a classical understatement, we said to ourselves, "Even if this plant costs as much as a battleship, it would be worth having."

For all we knew, the Germans could already be working on such a weapon, and the idea of Hitler getting it first was most frightening. It was our duty to inform the British government of this possibility. At the same time our conclusion had to be kept secret; if the German physicists had not yet seen the point, we did not want to draw their attention to it.

Frisch and I sat down to write a memorandum stating our analysis and conclusions. It was written in two parts: one was technical and gave the arguments, and the other was nontechnical and summarised the conclusions. We discussed radioactivity and the spread of radio-active fallout. We pointed out that use of this weapon would probably kill large numbers of civilians "and this may make it unsuitable as a weapon for use by this country." But as there was no effective defence, other than the threat of retaliation with the same weapon, it would be worth developing as a deterrent, even if one did not intend to use it as a means of attack.

We did not entrust this document to a secretary. We typed it up ourselves, or rather, I did because I had a typewriter and was familiar with it. A funny episode occurred while we were working on the

154

memorandum in my office in the single-storey Nuffield building. It was a warm spring day, and the window was open. Suddenly, while we were discussing the wording of the document, a head appeared in the window, seemingly from nowhere. We had quite a shock. However, the "eavesdropper" was a lab technician who had planted some tomatoes along the south wall of the building, and was tending them in a spare moment. He had moved along bending over the plants and straightened up by our window. He had of course not paid any attention to what we were saying.

We made only one carbon copy of this memorandum. When these matters were no longer secret, the nontechnical part seemed to have got lost. Margaret Gowing reproduced the technical part in her book, *Britain and Atomic Energy 1939-1945* (Macmillan, 1964). Later, a copy of the second part turned up in Sir Henry Tizard's papers; it was reproduced in the biography, *Tizard*, by Ronald Clark (Methuen, 1965).

We did not know how to send a secret communication, or, for that matter, where to send it. We gave our memorandum to Oliphant, who promised to get it to the right person. The right person was Tizard, who passed the paper on to G. P. (later Sir George) Thomson, who was the chairman of a committee concerned with the possibility of a nuclear chain reaction. The committee was about to disband itself. They had studied mainly the effect of slow neutrons, for which the fast neutrons emitted in the fission process must be slowed down by means of a "moderator"—a light substance—whose atoms are set in motion by collisions with neutrons and thus take some of their kinetic energy. Many light substances are unsuitable because they capture too many neutrons, but carbon, in the form of graphite, seemed to be a candidate. The committee had overseen some experiments using uranium and graphite, and concluded that in graphite the capture was still too great. They saw no immediate prospect of success.

As a result of our memorandum the committee continued, and, in fact, it expanded its activity. At first we did not know anything about the committee, and all we heard was a message, via Oliphant, that the authorities were grateful for our memorandum, but that we would have to understand that henceforth the work would be continued by others; as actual or former "enemy aliens" we would not be told any more about it.

This ruling seemed ridiculous to us. I wrote a letter to the chairman of the committee, whose identity I did not know as yet, pointing out that Frisch and I had thought a great deal about the problems already and might well know the answers to important questions. Others, who had missed the point made in our memorandum, could perhaps miss other important points as well. The problem seemed urgent to us, at least until it had been shown that building a weapon was not possible. As a result of my letter, the ruling was changed, and it was decided to consult us fully. At first we were not put on the committee that discussed these matters; but later the committee structure was changed, with a small policy committee and under it a technical subcommittee, in which the technical questions were thrashed out. Frisch and I were made members of the subcommittee, and that seemed very satisfactory.

M.A.U.D. Committee

The name of the committee was the M.A.U.D. Committee, and that name has an amusing origin. At an early meeting the members tried to find a suitable code name that would not disclose the committee's purpose. At the same meeting, the committee was told about a message from Niels Bohr. When the Germans invaded Denmark, Lise Meitner happened to be visiting Copenhagen, but she was able to leave and return to Stockholm. As she left, Bohr asked her to send a telegram to a friend in England, saying that he and his family were all right and had come to no harm in the occupation. The telegram ended: "Tell Cockcroft and Maud Ray Kent." This seemed mysterious. If the recipient was supposed to know Maud Ray, why add "Kent"? If he did not, "Kent" was hardly a sufficient address. Someone on the committee therefore suggested that there was a hidden message here, perhaps an anagram. Someone actually "decoded" this anagram to contain a message about uranium. Frisch and I were sceptical. Knowing Niels Bohr, we felt he was quite unlikely to send a message in this way, and as for the "decoding" of the anagram, we wrote down half a dozen alternative "solutions" as plausible as the first. When we saw Bohr again during the war, we asked about the telegram but he had forgotten the whole matter. After the war we saw Lise Meitner, and she solved the mystery: the telegram had been truncated in transmission; the original form had had a complete address between "Ray" and "Kent", the address of a former governess of the Bohr family, whose address ended with "Kent". In any case, at the meeting this puzzle led to the suggestion of the name "Maud Committee", or M.A.U.D. to look more official. It was unfortunate that many people associated with it were convinced the letters stood for "Military Applications of the Uranium Disintegration"!

We became very friendly with Frisch, who came to stay in our house, where we had plenty of room after the children had left with their school. On weekends we would go for long walks in the country, often taking a train to some point in the hills around Birmingham and returning from some other station. On one such walk, Frisch, Genia, and I had counted on staying overnight in a small hotel in a village, reckoning that they would not be crowded at this time. But the hotel refused to take any guests. This was illegal, as hotels are obliged to accept travellers, unless all rooms are full, but there was no point in arguing. It was too late to get to any other village, so we had a problem. In a pub we talked to the local policeman and asked if we could sleep in one of the cells at the police station—a suggestion he refused to consider. But he introduced us to a local man who often rented a room to travellers. The man said he had a room, indeed, and it probably would be all right to put us up, though he had to consult his wife; we should come home with him when he left the pub. We stayed in the pub for a while, and heard Churchill's famous speech about "blood, toil, sweat, and tears" come over the radio. Nobody left until Churchill had finished. Afterwards, we walked with our prospective host to his house. The wife was quite happy to accommodate us, but explained that the bedclothes for the one spare bed were in her little girl's room and she was not willing to wake her up. We spent the night without sheets or blankets on a mattress covered with brown paper. Obviously I was in the middle of the bed, and therefore reasonably warm, and slept soundly, while Genia and Frisch carried on an intellectual conversation over my head.

Frisch and I spent much time considering various problems, such as the merits of different methods of isotope separation. The simplest method seemed to be that of thermal diffusion, developed in Germany by Clusius and Dickel. If a gas mixture is heated at one end and cooled at the other, one end will be slightly richer in the light component. This phenomenon, which had already been studied theoretically by Maxwell, is an interesting challenge to the theory, because for real gases it is practically impossible to predict how strong the effect is, or even at which end the lighter isotope will be enriched. As a coincidence, we found out much later that one of the few physicists who had made it his life's work to study this phenomenon was Dr. T. L. Ibbs, a senior member of the Birmingham Physics Department. The method is simple when it can be applied, but it is wasteful of energy and takes a long time to come into equilibrium. Eventually it was found that for the only gaseous compound of uranium, uranium hexafluoride, the effect happens to be practically zero.

After discussing a number of alternatives, we concluded that the

157

most promising method was to use gaseous diffusion through membranes with fine pores. This method had been used by the German physicist Gustav Hertz, but yielding only small amounts, even of gases for which the mass difference between the isotopes was much greater than the 1% difference between 235 and 238. The task is made more difficult because uranium hexafluoride is a very corrosive gas that breaks down into lower fluorides on contact with water vapour and therefore has to be protected carefully from contact with moist air.

Clearly it was most urgent to find someone to organise experimental work on isotope separation. Thomson vaguely mentioned a colleague of his who was available, but this frightened me as I knew the man, who was an exceedingly nice person but did not have the required energy or drive. I did know of one person who would be suitable: Franz (later Sir Francis) Simon at Oxford. He was a German refugee and an expert in thermodynamics and low-temperature work. I went to see Chadwick, one of the senior members of Thomson's committee, who had independently proposed that one should study the use of fast neutrons. He received me in his usual, somewhat distracted manner. When he wanted to consult some correspondence relating to our conversation, he would open a drawer in his desk containing a jumble of letters, each neatly in its envelope, and after a while he would find the right one. He agreed with me at once, and persuaded Thomson that Simon be brought in.

For a meeting of the Technical Sub-Committee in September 1940 I prepared a number of papers, giving details of the conclusions reached by Frisch and me to date, and of the reasons for them. Since the papers contained many mathematical formulae, and the committee staff had no facilities for dealing with them, I was asked to get copies made in Birmingham. It was agreed that the stencils for duplicating them would be typed by Oliphant's elderly secretary, Miss Hytch, and I would write in the equations. This presented some difficulties, because Miss Hytch worked in the Nuffield building, which by now I was not allowed to enter because I was not cleared for the radar work in it. The solution was for me to dictate the text into a dictaphone (the Edison-type dictating machine with wax cylinders) from which she typed.

The whole bundle of copies was then mailed to London—as secret documents, of course. However, this was a time of frequent air raids on London and the mail services were disorganised. Our papers were in a stack of mailbags at Euston Station, and there was no way of extracting them. Miss Hytch had kept the stencils, and was able to produce further copies, although handling used stencils, which are thickly covered with ink is a most unpleasant operation. By this method I was able to bring copies for everybody to the meeting.

Frisch moved to Liverpool to work with Chadwick on the nuclear data. Here the complications caused by his status of "enemy alien" became more aggravated. Liverpool was a prohibited area for enemy aliens, and he had to have a permit to live there. In addition, there was a curfew, and he needed permission to be out late at night, to possess a bicycle, and for doing various other things. All this while he was working on one of the most secret wartime projects! He describes these complications in his book *What Little I Remember* (Cambridge University Press, 1979) with amusement and without resentment.

I found that I needed more time to work on the many theoretical problems of urgency, and asked to be relieved of my teaching duties. This request was granted, and a young theoretical physicist from Imperial College, J. G. Kynch, was brought in to take over my teaching. He was a conscientious objector, and therefore neither in military service nor doing war work. His appointment was originally temporary, but he remained until 1952. A graduate student, W. Hepner, also came to help with problem classes. He was available because he was a foreigner. My preoccupation with atomic-energy work did not stop me from talking with him occasionally about nuclear physics, and we published one little paper with which I was quite pleased.

When France fell, Hans von Halban and Lev Kowarski, who had been working in Paris with Joliot, left in a cargo boat and came to England with the stock of heavy water that had been obtained from Norway from the only plant that produced heavy water in substantial quantities. Joliot decided to remain in France. The French group had concentrated on the project of producing a chain reaction with slow neutrons, using heavy water as a moderator. It is in some way the ideal moderator, since the deuterium is very light and therefore very efficient in slowing down the neutrons, and its rate of neutron capture is very small, as is that of oxygen. Its main disadvantage is that it occurs in nature only as a very small admixture to ordinary water, so that it has to be concentrated by a process of isotope separation.

Halban and Kowarski were given facilities in Cambridge to continue their work with heavy water. The team they recruited worked in conjunction with Cambridge physicists who were already doing experiments, supplementing the work of Chadwick. These included, in particular, N. Feather, Egon Bretscher, and the theoretician N. Kemmer.

Halban was a strong personality, single-minded in pursuing what he saw as the important objectives, impatient with obstacles and delays, and, some said, putting speed before accuracy. In the prewar days of rapid development of neutron physics, he wrote a number of papers with a Swiss collegue, Preiswerk. A disapproving worker in the same field jokingly talked about the papers by "Halbwerk und Preisan" (work half-done and advertise). Another lighthearted remark arose when the Cambridge group, during intervals of leisure, invented "famous last words" for all its members. For Halban it was "Make it priority". I do not remember any of the others except the one for Bretscher, who was inclined to complain about his health. Nobody could suggest the right phrase for him, but he supplied it himself when he came into the lab one morning with the words: "I don't know what's the matter with me today; I'm feeling so well!"

It was typical for the French group to have taken out patents on the production of power from fission at a very early stage of the development—no doubt on Halban's initiative—and further patents were applied for while Halban and Kowarski were working in England. Halban had great charm and was very good to the young people working with him. Of course it was always understood that he was the boss. He was of Austrian origin, had studied physics in Zurich, and later settled in Paris. He was married to a charming and vivacious Dutch woman, Els.

Kowarski was very different. A huge bear of a man, he never lost his Russian accent, although his command of English (and other languages) was remarkably sophisticated. He was slower in discussion than Halban, which caused Halban to conduct all negotiations with the authorities, who therefore tended to think of the group as "Halban et al." Kowarski resented this since his contribution to the joint work was substantial. Although he knew what was important, he could also devote a lot of energy and thought to trivia, and he was miserly in matters of small amounts of money.

When the government decided to support the work of the group, there was some doubt whether this was a proper use of resources during the war, since the slow-neutron chain reaction at which the research was aimed would not constitute a weapon, but only a source of power. It was decided that even a new source of power could have important military applications. Moreover, Feather and Bretscher showed theoretically that the new element, plutonium, which resulted from the capture of neutrons by uranium-238 in a slow-neutron chain reaction, might be as good a nuclear explosive as uranium-235, or even better.

There were a number of matters of common interest to be discussed with the Cambridge group, and I made several visits there. I was allowed a special petrol ration because in wartime conditions, cross-country journeys by train were exceedingly uncertain and time-consuming. However, I ran into trouble during one of these journeys, when I was accompanied by Genia. It was winter, and the roads were full of snow and ice. At first all went well, because the main roads had been gritted. But just after leaving the city of Coventry, the road, which went downhill, was not gritted, and the car, which was not going fast, slid out of control straight down the road and through a wooden barrier surrounding a new roundabout. There the car stopped, and we sat for a moment to recover our breath. We were not shocked, as one would expect to be, and we attributed this to having survived worse possibilities of danger during the war. Inspection showed that the only damage was a broken stub axle that held a front wheel. We thought it was lucky that the accident happened within hailing distance of the Rootes factory, where the car had been made. But when we phoned the factory, we were told that they would repair only government cars, and in any case their spare parts department had just been bombed and they had no supplies.

We found that no other garage in Coventry carried the right spare part, either, because, being so near the factory, they did not keep large supplies. We left our car and continued by train to Cambridge, where we arrived late at night, very hungry. We spent the night in the lodging house where our friend Egon Orowan was staying. He had moved from Birmingham to Cambridge where, in the Cavendish Laboratory headed by Bragg, he could pursue his interest in solid-state physics. It was much too late to find food in any restaurant, and Orowan's supplies consisted of a tin of sardines, which he offered us.

Next day I found a spare stub axle in a Cambridge garage. They had only one, for the left-hand side, which was just what we needed. We carried it back triumphantly by train, greatly impressing the garage in Coventry, whose mechanic wanted to know where we found it and whether we could get them any.

My closest contact, however, was with Simon and his collaborators in Oxford, because it was obvious that the isotope separation was the greatest problem that had to be solved. Simon grew up in Berlin, and had the typically pungent humour of the Berliner. He had served in the German army in the First World War. By the time I knew him he had a well-rounded body and very little hair, but a finely chiselled face. He was very perceptive in his dealings with people, and his students and collaborators adored him. In his work he combined a deep and detailed knowledge of physics and apparatus with strong common sense, which never allowed him to get lost in unnecessary

161

complications. I remember an occasion when we discussed a certain method, which I maintained would not work, while he felt sure it would. We got involved in a heated argument, when he stopped and said, "Now you argue for the method and I shall argue against it!"

He was rather sensitive to heat and cold, and we teased him that this was due to his preoccupation with thermodynamics. Like a thermodynamic state or phase, he had a temperature range limited by an "upper" and a "lower Simon point", but they were very close together. At meetings he would always have a cap and a scarf, and would put them on—with apologies—when it got too cold or too drafty for him.

Before 1933 physics in Oxford was not very strong, and the head of the Clarendon Laboratory, Professor Lindemann (later Lord Cherwell), knew this. When many first-class scientists in Germany lost their jobs, he saw the opportunity of helping them and at the same time strengthening his laboratory. There were no vacant posts, but he persuaded I.C.I., the big chemical firm, to donate money for a number of research fellowships, to which the refugees, selected by him, were appointed. In this way Simon was brought to Oxford, as were Nicholas Kurti, Simon's closest collaborator, and Heinrich Kuhn, a spectroscopist. Kurt Mendelssohn, another low-temperature expert who had previously worked with Simon, had arrived in Oxford earlier. In the course of time they were all given regular university appointments. Their arrival had transformed the laboratory into a world-class institution.

Kurti and Kuhn joined Simon in the work for the M.A.U.D. Committee, along with several graduate students. Prominent among these was H. S. Arms, a Rhodes scholar from America, who had come to Oxford for only two or three years. In fact, he continued to work in Simon's group throughout the war and stayed in England for the rest of his life, having married Simon's attractive secretary. There were plenty of problems to keep everyone busy—problems such as how to find or make membranes with sufficiently small pores; how to test the hole size of a given membrane; how to find the properties of the gas that had to be used, and how to handle the gas; and many others.

I also found many problems piling up on the theoretical side, and I could not deal with all of them fast enough. I got some help from unexpected quarters. Dirac, who had been interested in the problem of isotope separation since his earlier experiment, wrote a note that showed how to calculate the effort required to enrich a given amount of material to a given concentration of one isotope, and the contribution to this effort made by a given device. He introduced the concepts of "separation potential" and "separating power", which have become universally used to determine, without detailed design studies, how many units of a given type are needed to make up a plant to achieve a specified performance. Maurice Pryce, a very bright theoretician from Cambridge, who had worked under Max Born (and married his daughter) and who was now in Liverpool, obtained some useful results to estimate the efficiency of the explosive chain reaction.

But I needed some regular help—someone with whom I would be able to discuss the theoretical technicalities. I looked around for a suitable person, and thought of Klaus Fuchs. He was a German, who as a student had been politically active as a member of a socialist student group (which was essentially communist) and had to flee for his life from the Nazis. He came to England, where he worked with Nevill Mott in Bristol, completed his Ph.D., and did some excellent work in the electron theory of metals and other aspects of the theory of solids. I knew and liked his papers, and I had met him. He moved to Edinburgh, and when the war broke out he was interned and, with other internees, sent to Canada. The internees went in two boats, of which one, not the one carrying Fuchs, was torpedoed and sank. It had contained the records for both ships, so when the surviving ship arrived, there was no information about the internees. Because Fuchs was not Jewish, he was separated from the refugees and placed in a camp together with staunch Nazis, which he deeply resented.

After some time he was released, and he returned to Edinburgh. He had the kind of ability I was looking for, and I thought he might welcome an opportunity to participate in a project that was intended to forestall Hitler. I therefore asked whether he was willing to join us. I could not tell him what the project was until I had permission to do so, but I described the kind of theory needed in general terms, and he agreed to work with us.

When I asked for official clearance for Fuchs, I was at first instructed to tell him as little as possible—only what was absolutely necessary for his work. I replied that if I could not take him into my confidence, he would be of no use to me. In due course he got a full clearance, and he started work in May 1941. His appointment did indeed provide me with support in the research work that was as efficient as I had hoped, yet it turned out to have disastrous consequences, as is now common knowledge. I shall return to this story in chapter 9.

Fuchs became a lodger in our house, and he was a pleasant person to have around. He was courteous and even-tempered. He was rather silent, unless one asked him a question, when he would give a full and articulate answer; for this Genia called him "Penny-in-the-slot". There were a few brief periods when he felt unwell. He did not go to work, stayed in bed or on a deck chair in the garden, and showed no interest in food. But this passed in a day or so. We realised the significance of these attacks only much later.

With his help, my work was progressing faster. One problem that gave us difficulty was to estimate the equilibrium time of the isotope plant. This is the time it takes from starting up to producing output of the design concentration. This time is also characteristic for the time it takes the plant to respond to adjustments in operating conditions. If it is too long, perhaps of the order of weeks, the plant would be very awkward to operate. It was clear that the equilibrium time depended on the "hold-up", i.e., on the amount of material contained in the plant at any one time. An exact calculation was out of the question. Numerical calculation was too laborious. We knew the problem could be handled on Hartree's differential analyser, and we asked him to solve the equation for us. This could be done without explaining what the meaning of the equation was, thus avoiding the need for secret communications. Hartree agreed but warned us that it would take some time, as he was busy with other urgent problems, and some preparatory work was needed to put the equation in a form suitable for his machine.

Meanwhile we had to do some intelligent guessing. But I made what turned out to be a very unintelligent guess. The correct answer is that the equilibrium time is that time in which the accumulated output of the light isotope would equal the total content of the light isotope in the plant. I intuitively thought that, as the material moves up and down the stages of the plants, one had to multiply this time by a factor. As a result, I overestimated the equilibrium time, or, in other words, underestimated the hold-up that would be acceptable. As a result, Simon put great emphasis on compactness in the design of the units for the plant, avoiding unnecessary connections and wasted space, which would increase the hold-up. This was an unnecessary complication in the design, but at least some of the resulting features turned out to have advantages that were used in the postwar British plant.

A question that was discussed at this time was whether an efficient compressor could be made for the working gas. Since the gas was very heavy, the sound velocity in it was low, and the blades of the rotor (the "impeller") in the compressor could easily be made to move with supersonic speed in the gas. This, as well as the unusually large specific heat of the gas, constituted conditions not usually met in engineering practice. I tried to get some advice on this situation, and was told that one expert might be L. Rosenhead, a professor in Liverpool, who was now in a wartime research establishment in Cardigan. I arranged to consult him, and, since we were meeting during a weekend, Genia came along. We left in the afternoon, and by the time we passed Aberystwyth and started on the coast road to Cardigan, it was dark. Because we had only very little light from the almost completely masked headlights, the driving was not too easy. At one point we gave an army sergeant a ride. As he travelled with us, he warned me about the hazards of the road, narrow places, sharp turns, and so on. The crowning piece was: "Now we go steeply downhill; at the bottom is a sharp bend and a narrow bridge; I know this place well, because last week I drove a car over the parapet of the bridge." Shortly after this he got out, and from then on the road seemed quite normal. We said, "Lucky thing that we had him to guide us through that awful part of the road!" When we returned in daylight we discovered that the road was bad all the way, with bends and hills and narrow stretches; but driving in the dark "on the dotted line" (the practice of painting broken lines to mark the centre of the road was started then to help blackout driving), we had not noticed the bad road conditions until the sergeant pointed them out. Rosenhead was interested in the problem I had come to discuss, but he admitted that it went beyond his experience. He suggested various ways one might solve the problem, however, so the journey had still been worthwhile.

There is a sequel to this visit, which illustrates the vagaries of human memory. For part of the discussions, a colleague of Rosenhead's, a Dr. Slater, was present. In 1956, when I was visiting Cornell University, I called on Hilton, an English mathematician whom we knew well. He had another visitor from England, and introduced him: "Do you know Dr. Slater from Leeds?" I said, "I think we had tea together in Cardigan one weekend in 1941." I have a very poor memory for names, and can easily forget a person whom I met the week before, or even one with whom I have spent considerable time. What caused the exception in this case remains a mystery.

Tube Alloys

In the summer of 1941 the M.A.U.D. Committee wrote its final report. By now American physicists had used small samples of uranium-235 to measure its fission cross section, and they found it of the order of magnitude that Frisch and I had assumed, though it was a little smaller. There was now not much room left for doubt. The M.A.U.D. report concluded that an atomic bomb was feasible, and outlined the work that had to be done to produce it.

It was decided to increase the resources necessary for this work and to set up an organisation that could handle a larger project. The project received a new code name, "Tube Alloys". It meant nothing but sounded like a very dull but practical organisation. The chairman of the "Directorate of Tube Alloys" was W. A. (later Sir Wallace) Akers, research director of I.C.I., who was released by the firm for the duration of the war. He was a man of great energy and drive, very perceptive in his dealings with people, and an excellent chairman. His deputy was Michael Perrin, also from I.C.I., a chemist who had played a part in the development of polythene. He carried out the executive work with great efficiency and tact.

The minister responsible for Tube Alloys was Sir John Anderson, then "Lord President of the Council". He retained this responsibility when he later became Chancellor of the Exchequer. By a curious coincidence he was trained as a physical chemist and had done work on the chemistry of uranium, though this had no relevance to his connection with Tube Alloys.

There was a Technical Committee, but it was much smaller than the M.A.U.D. Technical Sub-Committee. Its members included Chadwick, Halban, Simon, and me, among others. It had taken some time to set up the new structure, which was understandable, since quite far-reaching decisions had to be made at a high level. Some people became rather impatient while waiting for a decision without being given any indication of what was going on. This slight irritation was aggravated when those members of the M.A.U.D. Committee who were not included in the new organisation heard nothing, while in effect their committee was dissolved and the new one set up. Oliphant, as usual very outspoken, made his irritation known. But the ruffled feelings were soon soothed.

At the first meeting of the new committee, two American visitors were present: Harold Urey, the discoverer of heavy hydrogen, in whose laboratory there were studies both about extracting heavy water and about the separation of uranium isotopes, and G. B. Pegram, a senior nuclear physicist. Both were from Columbia University. They were very impressed with how seriously the British government was taking the project. They sent a message back to the United States to this effect, and it is believed that this played a part in the decision to increase the pace of work in the States, which was taken about this time.

In Britain it was still too early for a decision about a full-scale isotope plant. It seemed doubtful that such a large project was feasible in Britain in wartime conditions. The alternative already in some people's minds was a joint project with the United States, involving a plant in the United States or Canada. In the meantime the research and development work went on at an accelerated pace. The number of theoretical problems also kept growing, and we gradually added a few computing assistants to the Birmingham team, usually mathematics graduates who did numerical work with desk calculators. Later we hired theoretical physics graduates or their equivalent.

We worked closely with the Oxford team, and I made frequent journeys there. I remember one occasion when there was a meeting at Oxford after a night of a heavy air raid on Birmingham, when I had been on duty with the Fire Service all night. I felt I had to go to the meeting, but was afraid of falling asleep at the wheel. I therefore went to the Students' Union, asking whether someone would like a ride to Oxford for the day, on condition that he talked to me to keep me awake. I ended up with three girl students, who took their obligation very seriously.

Among the minor improvements in the plant design was a method called the "rabbit". The use of eccentric names suited the sense of humour of Simon and others, and was encouraged by the necessity of using obscure code names. The rabbit principle consisted in dividing the output from each stage in the plant into three parts. The most enriched was the one that had diffused through the initial portion of the membrane, where the incoming gas was still fresh; the part diffusing through the end of the membrane, where the gas stream was already depleted, had about the same concentration as the input gas; and the one left without going through the membrane was the most depleted. The most enriched fraction was fed up to the next stage, the most depleted down to the previous stage, and the intermediate part was fed back into the same stage. The name was prompted by a paper published by zoologists, who had shown that much of the work on the metabolism of rabbits was invalidated by the discovery that rabbits eat at night the excrements produced during the day.

Another such name referred to the "roast pig treatment". This goes back to the legend that the delights of roast pork were discovered in China when fire destroyed a house with a pig inside. For some time, the story goes, the peasants burned down a hut with a pig inside whenever they wanted a sumptuous meal, and only later found simpler ways of getting the same result. The roast pig treatment at Oxford originated when some very delicate reaction did not function as intended. It involved uranium hexafluoride, or "hex" as we called it, which was always very carefully protected from any contact with air. Again and again the reaction was tried, without success. Then at a crucial stage in the experiment, someone dropped a tool on a part of the glass apparatus, breaking it and letting air in. Suddenly there was the desired result. The reason was never discovered, but the procedure was repeated whenever the reaction was needed. To be sure, instead of breaking the apparatus one opened a valve.

The meetings of the Technical Committee in London were convenient occasions for Halban, Simon, and me to exchange information and gossip, and we used to meet in a Danish restaurant called The Three Vikings for lunch before the meetings; soon we called ourselves "the three Vikings", making fun of our position as three very un-Vikinglike Jewish immigrants.

But throughout all of our lighthearted talk, we were perpetually conscious of the deadly serious business in which we were engaged. We were desperately afraid that the Germans would beat us in our objective. Of course everybody was anxious to know what progress, if any, the Germans were making with atomic energy. Early on I received a message from the intelligence people—indirectly, I believe through Perrin—asking if I had any suggestions on ways of finding out what the Germans were doing. I suggested keeping an eye on the movements of certain people who would probably be involved in any atomic-energy work, and checking whether they were away from their normal places of work, travelled to unlikely places, and so on. I appended a list of likely names, headed by Heisenberg.

The reply came back: "It is very interesting that you should mention this name, because he visited Cambridge shortly before the war, and we have no record that he ever left the country." I was shocked by this reaction and reflected that if this was a fair sample of British intelligence, the outlook seemed grim.

But then things changed, largely through the activities of Commander Welsh. I was told that, as a junior officer in Naval Intelligence, he once had to wait in an outer office while calling on his boss, and saw a secretary typing a list of names and addresses of scientists. He looked over her shoulder and said, "You have misspelled this name, and that man is not at X, but at Y . . . ." His boss appeared and asked why he knew so much about these strange people. Welsh replied, "It's my hobby; I have always been interested in scientists and their work." He was immediately picked to work on intelligence relating to atomic energy, and did so with great ability and understanding.

It was possible to gather some information from published sources, if one had some background knowledge. I spent a little time with the German journals, of which copies were obtained through neutral countries. I knew that each semester the *Physikalische Zeitschrift* published a list of the lecture courses in physics in all German universities. The lists showed that most physicists were in their normal places and teaching their normal subjects, which was completely different from the British or American situation. But there were a few exceptions. Heisenberg did not lecture, and a paper by a young man in Leipzig on a subject that would have interested Heisenberg acknowledged advice and help from others, but not from Heisenberg. This suggested that Heisenberg either was not there, or he was busy with something else. Another suggestive fact was that in the abstracting journal *Physikalische Berichte* certain people regularly abstracted papers on nuclear physics and on isotope separation. The picture emerged that Germany had no crash programme, no large-scale project that required a major participation by scientists. There did seem to be some atomic research going on, and Heisenberg and a few others were probably connected with it. On the whole, my findings were reassuring, but of course these deductions were no proof, and the matter was too serious to rely on speculation, however plausible. When the facts became known after the war, it turned out that my picture was reasonably accurate.

To America by Bomber. Tube Alloys Work Continues

By late 1941 we had a fairly free exchange of information with the Americans. We did not see all their reports, however, and we could therefore not get a clear picture of their ideas. It was decided that a delegation consisting of Akers, Halban, Simon, and me would visit the United States. The easiest way to travel was via Lisbon, with the flying-boat from there to America, and Akers and Simon went that way. Halban was not allowed to fly because of his heart condition, and he went by sea. It was decided that I should not travel via Lisbon because Lisbon was full of spies who watched the transients, and as my interest in nuclear physics was known, my travels might invite speculation. I was asked solemnly whether I would be willing to make the trip in one of the bombers that crossed the Atlantic to return air crews who had flown American planes to Britain. This apparently was not without danger; some people had lost limbs by frostbite because of a lack of heat on the planes. I thought that in wartime one should accept some risk and agreed to go.

The beginning of the journey was quite romantic. The planes would take off from Prestwick, near Glasgow, but this was a secret. The instructions therefore said: "A sleeper has been reserved for you on the night train to Glasgow. Get off at Kilmarnock and wait for further instructions." We were taken by car to the airport, where we were weighed, along with our luggage, and we were fitted with flying clothes to keep us warm on the plane. Then we were assigned rooms, since the plane was not going to leave that day. In fact, the weather en route was so bad that we could not leave for several days. It was strange suddenly to have time on your hands. In some ways we were already out of the country: we were not allowed to make phone calls and the meals did not show much of the wartime shortages—there were such unheard-of luxuries as bacon and eggs for breakfast. I decided to track down the origin of the story about loss of limbs through frostbite, and found that it was based on one case of a man whose flying boots were too tight and restricted his circulation; as a result he lost a couple of toes. This was sad, but I decided the trip was not as dangerous as I had been led to believe.

When the plane, a Liberator, finally took off, we were given oxygen masks, as the plane was not pressurised. The masks tended to freeze up and required some looking after; we were therefore not allowed to sleep. We were offered benzedrene tablets, in case we found it difficult to stay awake for the sixteen-hour flight.

After a stop in Newfoundland, we arrived in Dorval, the airport serving Montreal. I received a message that G. P. Thomson, who now headed a scientific liaison office in Ottawa, wanted to see me, so I arranged to fly on to Ottawa. It was evening by the time I got there, and it was very exciting to come down on the city, brightly lit in a clear winter air with the streets covered in snow. Even today I cannot get tired of the spectacle of coming down on a city at night, but this first experience was unforgettable, so great was the contrast with the blacked-out English towns and the rainy and damp English winter. That night I slept very little, after the excitement of my first flight and my first visit to North America, I flew on to New York the next afternoon.

In New York I phoned my sister, Annie, whom I had not been able to notify about my trip. When she answered the phone, I said, "This is Rudi."—"I don't know any Rudi."—"Don't you know your own brother?"—"Of course, but he is not here; he is in England." I eventually convinced her that it was me. I visited my father one evening; he was ill and very weak but pleased to see me, and at the same time I saw his wife Else and Annie and her husband.

Jointly or separately, our delegation visited many of the laboratories where atomic-energy studies were going on. I spent some time in meetings at Columbia University with Urey and with Karl Cohen, the theoretician who had been working on the isotope plant design. His results coincided with ours, with differences only in the details, except on the question of the equilibrium time, where his intelligent guess differed from mine. After a good deal of discussion I agreed that his guess was probably correct, and this was confirmed when a telegram from Fuchs reported that Hartree had now done the numerical calculation we had asked him to do, and the result showed clearly that Cohen was right, and I was wrong. Not much experimental work seemed to be going on with isotope separation, however. Only Dunning, a nuclear physicist in the Physics Department at Columbia, pursued such studies with energy and searched for possible membranes.

At Columbia we also met Fermi, who was doing experiments to find out whether a chain reaction in ordinary uranium, with a suitable moderator, was possible. Like Thomson's committee in London, he had found that commercial graphite had too high a neutron absorption to be used as a moderator. But he was convinced that the graphite was still impure. Certain impurities have such strong neutron absorption that they can spoil the chain reaction even when they are present in such minute quantities that no other physical or chemical method could detect them. He therefore hoped that further purification would produce usable graphite, and this hunch was later proved right. He was about to move to Chicago, where there would be better facilities for his work.

We then went to Chicago to meet Arthur H. Compton, whose discovery of the "Compton effect" had been of crucial importance in the development of the quantum theory. He was one of the senior people concerned with the planning of atomic-energy research. I told him that, as far as I could see, nobody in the American organisation was giving much thought to the actual weapon that would ultimately be produced.

The weapon depended on the physics of fast neutrons. Until then, Gregory Breit had been responsible for coordinating information about fission with fast neutrons. Because one could not talk about fast neutrons or fission for security reasons, he was described as "coordinator of rapid rupture". He was a great theoretical physicist who had done important and original work in nuclear physics, and would do more later. But he was also a very neurotic person and had an exaggerated concern about security. His way of coordinating the information was to lock all the important papers in a big safe, and let nobody get near them. Compton evidently was aware of the problem and knew that change was necessary.

I also went out to Berkeley to see Robert Oppenheimer. This journey was not without complications. I had decided to go out by train because I reckoned that long-distance planes were often delayed by weather, and by train one could count on arriving on time. The journey by fast train, or "streamliner", was to take one day and two nights from Chicago, and I looked forward to a peaceful day to collect my thoughts. On the day I was to leave, the streamliner did not go to San Francisco but to Los Angeles, so I arranged to fly north from Los Angeles. The journey by train was very comfortable indeed, but during the second night the engine of the famous train broke down, and we had to be hauled ignominiously by a steam engine for the last part of the way. We were hours late, my plane had gone, and the rest of the planes for the day were booked up. I had to go to San Francisco on the night train, and got to Oppenheimer a day late. So much for trying to play it safe!

I knew Oppenheimer from Zurich and had respected him, and now I was very impressed by his clear understanding of the problems of atomic energy. He had already considered most of the points Frisch and I had raised, and many that had developed subsequently. I stayed overnight with the Oppenheimers and was driven back to my train by Felix Bloch, who was living in nearby Stanford. He was then a somewhat erratic driver and I found the drive across the busy Bay Bridge more frightening than flying across the Atlantic.

Simon and I went to Charlottesville, Virginia, where Jesse Beams at the University of Virginia was the world's greatest authority on centrifuges. Centrifuging was one possible method of separating isotopes, and we discussed the state of the art and the prospects with Beams. We were not very optimistic, and indeed the method was not found practical during the war. Later, when stronger materials that could stand up to greater speeds were available, it became a competitor for the diffusion method. The buildings and the setting of the University of Virginia, which was founded and designed by Thomas Jefferson, are probably among the most charming anywhere.

Back in New York, I received a message from Compton, asking me to return for a brief visit to Chicago. It turned out he wanted to have a further talk about the plans for the fast-neutron work and the study of the weapon. In the end we agreed that it would be a good idea to put Oppenheimer in charge of this work. I do not recall whether he suggested Oppenheimer and asked for my opinion, or whether he asked me if I could suggest a name, but the conclusion was clear. Soon after, Oppenheimer was asked to form a committee to study the fast-neutron and weapons design problems.

While I was travelling around the United States, I managed to get

172

to Toronto for a weekend to visit Gaby and Ronnie. It was of course a pleasure to see them and to meet their foster parents. I was charmed by the Jephcotts, with whom Ronnie was staying. Dr. Jephcott worked in the city's public health service, but he was the academic type, a little absent-minded. His hobby was stamp collecting. His wife, Isobel, a warm and spontaneous person, is still now a great friend. Their two daughters were a little younger than Ronnie, which made him feel important.

Gaby's hostess was Dr. Jephcott's sister, Mrs. Sanderson, whose daughter, Nancy, was two years older than Gaby. They also had an older son. Gaby and Nancy were in the same class at school, as Gaby's English schooling had put her ahead. Arthur Sanderson, a cheerful, jovial man, was in the building materials business. He was the head of the firm started by the father of Dr. Jephcott and Mrs. Sanderson, who had emigrated from England as a young man. Gaby was happy and well cared for. If I felt a difference between the two households it was due to the exceptional warmth of Mrs. Jephcott. During my stay in Toronto I also visited some of the children of our friends, so I could report to their parents. I found that in most cases the families with whom they were staying were much like their families at home. The allocation of children to foster parents had been under the guidance of the psychology department of the University of Toronto, whose staff had of course never met the parents.

Back in England, we continued with our work under high pressure, but the situation was frustrating, since we did not know whether the British and American projects were going to be merged. We knew there were discussions about this possibility, but I did not know any of the details until I read Margaret Gowing's book long after the war. If no large-scale plant was going to be built in Britain, much of our work was academic; but it had to be pursued with urgency until a decision had been taken.

By the summer I was getting very tired and was in need of a brief rest, and so was Simon. He was on his own, since his wife had gone to Toronto with the children. Genia persuaded both of us to take a holiday together, and we agreed to go to Stroud, a place in the Cotswold Hills near Oxford. I went there by train, and Simon met me there by car. On the way to our hotel, as we rounded a bend, two young airmen on a motorcycle came in the opposite direction, took the bend too fast, and lost control. They collided with our car, and were thrown against a stone wall. They were fatally injured and died almost instantly. After this tragic adventure we did not get much pleasure out of our holiday, although Simon was in no way to blame for what had happened.

In October 1942 the lease of our house, which we had taken for five years, expired, and we decided to move. The house was too big for us, and as both Genia and I were out all day, it was troublesome to watch for leaking or frozen pipes and similar domestic problems. In one such incident we had been woken up by the noise of water running down the stairs. A pipe in a bathroom had been frozen and burst. Water covered the landing, and we had to get rid of it. Genia, our niece Vera, and I, still in our night clothes, swept the water out— one sweeping the water along the upper floor, one down the stairs, and one out of the front door.

By this time my brother Alfred was back home, and Nina, his wife, had joined him, but Vera stayed with us to continue her schooling. We rented a small flat and got rid of the extra furniture. All this was done in a hurry, as we were both working and could not take too much time off. Moving day ended with an amusing incident. We had gone to bed exhausted and had forgotten to lock the entrance door of the flat. The young policeman on the beat thought the flat was still empty, and while checking the stairs, found the door to the flat un-locked; he went in and entered the first room, which happened to be Vera's. When he turned on the light, she woke up and was terrified to see the policeman standing in front of her. She did not dare sit up, because, as it was a very warm night, she had nothing on. Both were surprised, and at last the policeman said, "Well, go ahead and scream!" But she did not.

Meanwhile the uncertainties about the future of the work continued. It was decided to transfer Halban's team, which was working with heavy water, to Montreal, where it was hoped they would be able to benefit from the proximity to the American laboratories. Halban thus started organising a laboratory in Montreal while Kowarski remained in charge at Cambridge. As the new laboratory became established, Halban invited Kowarski to come, too. But the status he would have in the new, large laboratory did not satisfy Kowarski, and he refused to go. His resentment, which had never been far from the surface, came out into the open, and there was a complete break between him and Halban.

At about this time difficulties in the relations with the American authorities were accumulating and eventually resulted in a complete breakdown of the exchange of information on atomic-energy matters. It therefore looked as if the British Tube Alloys project could get practical results only if Britain had its own plant. This was an unlikely prospect in wartime, but no decision was made.

We were still trying to add more strength to our theoretical group. We had a standing request with the Central Register, which was then allocating scientists to war-related jobs. They did send us some excellent young graduates, including Tony Skyrme, of whom I shall say more later. But the more senior people were either not good enough or did not have the right experience. We were therefore surprised one day to receive the particulars of a certain Boris Davison, who was a graduate of the University of Leningrad and seemed to know just the kind of mathematics we needed. He was born in the USSR but had British nationality. His grandfather, an English engineer, had emigrated with his family to Russia without giving up their British citizenship. Boris's father was therefore also a British citizen, and Boris had not left the Soviet Union until 1938, when he had to choose betweeen accepting Soviet citizenship and emigrating.

I immediately called him for interview. There appeared a small man in rather rumpled clothes, very polite and diffident, whose Russian was better than his English. He seemed to have the knowledge and ability that would be useful to us, and I invited him to join us, but suggested he should think it over. As I could not tell him the purpose of our work, I indicated its nature by showing him an integral equation that was giving us difficulty. He wrote a letter in the train returning from the interview, saying he did want to come, and enclosing the solution to my integral equation.

He indeed turned out to be a great asset. After a while I decided that his salary was inadequate for a man of his ability, and managed to get him a modest raise. When I told him, he was indignant; he had just meant to ask that his salary be reduced because he was not pulling his weight on the team. But he was eventually persuaded to accept the raise.

The reason for the state of his clothes was that he had spent a considerable time in a sanatorium, suffering from pulmonary tuberculosis. When he was discharged, his original clothes were no longer usable, and he was given what odd clothing could be found. Genia helped him buy new clothes within the limitations of wartime clothes rationing. The resulting wardrobe seemed acceptable in wartime England, but when he moved to Montreal it was rumoured that his ship had been torpedoed in the Atlantic, and he had swum the rest of the way in his clothes.

We had yet another adventure on a trip. I was returning late from a meeting in Cambridge with Genia and Fuchs in the car, and by the time we were half-way home, it was dark, it had started to snow, and we were very hungry and had little prospect of finding an open restaurant. In addition, the gearbox of the car was giving us trouble.

There was a small hotel along the way, and we stopped to ask if we could get a meal. The proprietor said he was sorry, there was nothing left of their dinner, but he could produce some bacon and eggs "if that was acceptable". (Bacon was then in short supply, and eggs were practically unknown.) In due course a waiter came in carrying an enormous dish piled high with rashers of bacon, and with more eggs than we had seen in months. Genia said she felt we were already dead, and this was some kind of Valhalla.

Thus reinforced, I decided to try to do something about the gearbox. I had never even looked inside a gearbox, and did not know its construction in detail. I took the lid off and looked inside—not an easy task, because the only light came from a torch held by Fuchs, which had a battery near the end of its life. I could not make out how the thing worked, but one link looked as if it was not in its right place. I pushed it a little, and the gearbox never gave trouble again. We made it home safely. The snow continued to fall, and by the next day the roads were impassable.

Some time earlier, George Kistiakowsky, a distinguished chemist who had also worked on explosives, wrote a report claiming that the explosion of an atomic bomb would do relatively little damage. He thought that the enormous energy it released would be used up in heating the air in a small volume to extremely high temperatures, and that the blast wave produced would be relatively weak. This was put to G. I. (later Sir Geoffrey) Taylor in Cambridge. Taylor was a remarkable man, whose research work covered many fields, experimental and theoretical. He had made important and fundamental contributions in each. Most of his work was in various aspects of fluid dynamics. In response to Kistiakowsky's challenge, he produced a very elegant theory which, with some simplification, gave an exact solution to the problem and showed that the blast wave would be as intense as one had expected it to be for the energy of such an explosion. In other words, Kistiakowsky was wrong.

In connection with this problem I had some correspondence with Taylor, and later met him in Cambridge. He was extremely charming and unpretentious. It was typical of him that, when his work on war committees in London meant frequent late-night returns by train to Cambridge, he would take his bicycle to the station and cycle to his home at the other end of town. When it was suggested that he apply for a petrol allowance for such journeys, he refused, saying it was not necessary.

Our correspondence referred to the theory of shock waves, of which I knew nothing, and I had to do some intense homework before I could understand his letters. This broadened my horizon in hydrodynamics. It would clearly be desirable to make his approximate calculation more accurate, but that was not an easy problem. First, one had to find the behaviour of air in conditions of extremely high temperatures and pressures, and then one would be left with an equation that could be solved only numerically. The first part was carried out in a study done jointly by Fuchs, Kynch, and myself. Kynch, who was teaching in my place, was not part of our team, but was interested in the problem.

This left the problem of the numerical solution of a partial differential equation, i.e., an equation with two or more independent variables—in our case, distance and time. No doubt mathematicians had already looked at such problems, but it would be difficult to search the literature. I decided to experiment with the simplest equation of this type, that of wave propagation with constant velocity, for which the exact solution is known. I tried a step-by-step method, in which you take the initial state as known at a chain of points a certain distance apart, and then determine approximately the state of affairs a certain time interval later. One can then repeat the process. I happened to choose the spacing of the points equal to the distance the wave would travel in the time interval I used. Doing a rough calculation, accurate to three decimal places, I reproduced the exact solution, as nearly as I could tell. So I repeated the calculation with five-figure accuracy, and my procedure again got the answer right to five figures. I then saw how to compare the result of my step-by-step process with the exact answer, and found that for the intervals I happened to have chosen and for the simple model I was dealing with, one gets the correct answer to any accuracy. If one makes the time interval smaller, one gets a solution of reasonable accuracy, but if one makes it larger, the procedure becomes unstable, and errors will grow with each step, and the ultimate answer will become nonsense. It was clear that these conclusions were not restricted to the simple equation I had taken as a model. I now felt I knew how to handle partial differential equations, but as the procedure was time-consuming, I put off trying the real problem. Nevertheless, the experience was to prove useful.

Contact with the United States Resumed

We suddenly got the news that many of the obstacles in the way of collaboration with the Americans had been cleared, largely by direct conversations between Churchill and Roosevelt, later embodied in the Quebec agreement. A limited amount of exchange of information was to be resumed. In August 1943 a group consisting of Chadwick, Oliphant, Simon, and me went to the United States again to resume the exchange of information. Oliphant had become interested in the possibility of isotope separation by an electromagnetic method, translating into an industrial scale the principle of the mass spectrograph, which had first led to the proof of the existence of isotopes. This method was being developed by E. O. Lawrence at Berkeley.

This time we travelled by the Pan American flying-boat service from Foynes in Ireland. This meant we had to be taken to Foynes by a British military flying-boat. On this short flight my place was under a pipe that leaked oil over my hat and raincoat, a painful experience in view of the fact that these garments had been specially cleaned to make me look respectable in America. Fortunately the weather was fine, and neither coat nor hat had to be used.

In Foynes we found that our flight to America would be late, and we went to the cinema in the nearby town of Limerick. I do not remember what film we saw, but one of the shorts preceding it was about the prospect of an atomic bomb, and mentioned a chain reaction in uranium, though this report was based only on speculation.

When Oliphant, Simon, and I were in Washington (Chadwick came a day later), we crossed a street while we were busy talking, without knowing that the police in Washington were now fining pedestrians crossing against the traffic lights. A policeman appeared, notebook in hand, and said in his most sarcastic manner "And where did you come from?"—"From England." He was taken aback a little. "When did you come from there?"—"Yesterday." We showed our passports to prove it. We were not fined. Later I asked a colleague from New York whether New Yorkers also fined people who crossed against the lights. He replied, "No, we run them down."

By this time the American atomic energy project had been put under the Army Corps of Engineers, the code name being "Manhattan District", with General Leslie Groves at its head. We met Groves at the beginning of our visit. He was a man of great energy, drive, and self-assurance, all of which he certainly needed in his job. He did not know much about modern science or about the nature of research, and he frequently expressed opinions or gave instructions that revealed this lack of understanding, and this was resented by the scientists. But one had great respect for his courage in taking on the responsibility for a project of an unprecedented nature, whose chances of success could be assessed only in terms of the scientific arguments.

He received us courteously and explained the arrangements, including the compartmentalisation, which now governed the American work. This meant that the work was divided into compartments: each

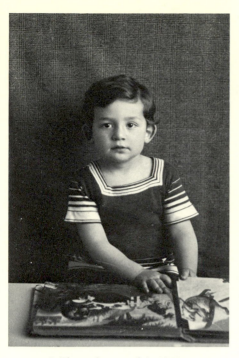

1. The author, aged 3, 1910.

2. The author with mother, sister Annie, and
brother Alfred, 1913.

3. Family home in Oberschöneweide, ca. 1914.

4. Arnold Sommerfeld on skis, 1927.   5. Lake Zurich, 1929. Ralph Kronig, Enrico Fermi.

6. Lake Zurich, 1929. Robert Oppenheimer, I. I. Rabi, L. M. Moitt-Smith,
Wolfgang Pauli.

7. Beach near Odessa, 1930. Pauli (centre) talking with Ya. I. Frenkel and I. E. Tamm.

9. Wedding day in Leningrad, 1931. Seated: Genia's stepfather and mother with the author. Standing: Nastya (household help), Nina (Genia's sister), and Genia.

8. Piz da Daint, Engadin, 1930. Gamow "working".

10. Leipzig, 1931. George Placzek and Werner Heisenberg playing table tennis.

11. Leipzig, 1931. Front: The author, Werner Heisenberg. Rear: G. Gentile, George Placzek, Giancarlo Wick, Felix Bloch, Victor Weisskopf, F. Sauter.

12. Skiing vacation, 1931. Ilse Thorner's brother, Genia, the author, Max Delbrück, Ilse Thorner.

13. S. Chandrasekhar with Gaby, 1934.

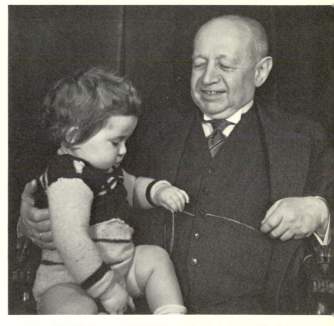

14. Christmas, 1934. The author's father with Gaby.

15. Family portrait in Berlin, Christmas, 1934. Standing: Nina (Alfred's wife), the author, Vera (Nina's daughter), Alfred. Seated: Hermann Krebs, Genia with Gaby, author's father, Else (his wife), Annie Krebs (author's sister). Sitting in front: Annie's children.

16. New York, 1943. Genia and the author.

17. Cambridge, 1947. James Chadwick (centre) in a cheerful mood, with G. I. Taylor on the right.

18. Tokyo, 1953. Dinner in Y. Fujioka's house.

19. Genia, ca. 1956. (Photograph by Lotte Meitner-Graf)

20. Moscow, 1956. Freeman Dyson (front, left), talking with I. Pomeranchuk and Lev Landau.

21. The author with Eugene Rabinowicz at a Pugwash Conference in Karlovy Vary, 1965.
(Courtesy Kurt Goldberger, Prague)

22. The author with C. N. Yang at a conference, 1969.

23. Retirement symposium, 1974. The author with Gerald Brown and Victor Weisskopf.
(Courtesy A. M. Kobos)

24. Retirement symposium, 1974. (Reprinted from *Rudolf Peierls and Theoretical Physics*, Pergamon, 1977)

25. Bonn, 1976. The author with Victor Weisskopf at a conference.

26. Golden Wedding, 1981.
(Courtesy A. Milhaupt)

27. Theoretical Physics Department in Parks Road
Oxford, ca. 1970.

member of the staff knew only what went on within his compartment; only very few people were allowed to look over the fence into the next compartment; and even fewer, more senior, people had knowledge about the more remote areas of the work. The object was, of course, to preserve secrecy.

We again visited laboratories, but were restricted to a certain number of them. The principle was that information would be exchanged only on those methods that were also being studied in Britain, so that use could be made of the information. In the places we did visit, the scientists freely answered all our questions. Their instructions from General Groves were, they told us, that we "could be told everything, but must not be shown anything". Nobody could quite make out what this meant, so it caused no problem.

At one of the meetings, Simon was being shown the arrangements for the isotope plant, and told the American engineers he thought they underestimated the problem of testing for leaks in a plant of such enormous size, in which any leak that could admit air had to be avoided. They told him, "You don't seem to appreciate American technology. Every American house contains a refrigerator. They are all filled with their working gas, freon, at the factory, and they never leak. We do know how to make things leakproof on a large scale." Simon was impressed, and after the meeting he returned to the apartment hotel where he was staying with his wife, who had come over from Toronto. She told him that the refrigerator was not working. He went to see the manager, who said, "I'm sorry, this can't be helped. You see, these refrigerators always leak and have to be topped with freon. But freon is in short supply because of the war, and we can't get the refrigerators serviced."

The one subject on which communication was more difficult was the progress of fast-neutron physics and the weapon design. This was Oppenheimer's field, and by now he was in Los Alamos, the laboratory in remote New Mexico that was devoted to these problems. I had a conversation with him in Washington, in which he explained that he was not allowed to tell me everything. He was accompanied by a senior colleague, evidently as a witness to what he was telling me.

I returned home again by bomber. Before leaving New York, I cabled home that I would be leaving soon. The cable arrived marked "sans origine" because it so happened that a troopship was leaving New York at the time, and the censor had deleted the words "New York". Genia assumed that it was sent from some air base, perhaps in Newfoundland, and that I was on the way. When I cabled again from Montreal that I would arrive soon (I could not, of course, give details), it looked as if I had gone back, and there was delay in my journey. In fact, this time we left at once and got to Prestwick in good time. One of my fellow passengers was a wing commander in the RAF, who was being taken by plane from Prestwick to Birmingham, and he offered me a ride. There was no time to phone Genia. The plane was a Wellington bomber, and I occupied the waist-gunner's seat. It was the roughest plane ride I have ever had, and I had difficulty keeping my seat. I found myself holding on to the machine gun and worried that I might fire it accidentally, but presumably it was not loaded. In Birmingham a car was waiting to take the wing commander to the railway station, and he again offered me a ride; again there was no time to phone home. At the station there was one taxi, which was a rarity, so I took it and arrived home unannounced. I was disappointed to find out from Vera that Genia had gone to the cinema, being sure I would not come back for a few days. Vera did not know to which cinema Genia had gone, but from the programmes in the local paper I could guess. Genia had a big surprise when she saw me walk down the aisle of the theatre.

The theoretical team was now more optimistic about a collaboration with the Americans. A new member had been added to our team. A. H. (now Sir Alan) Wilson was a very experienced theoretical physicist, with whom I had had an argument in 1933, and who had been the first to make a detailed theory of semiconductors. He had completed his work for another war research team, and joined the Birmingham group.

In October, Niels Bohr came to England. The story has been told many times how he escaped to Sweden, when the German occupying forces in Denmark had ordered the arrest of all Jews and other undesirables, and how he was brought to England in a Mosquito bomber, fainting from lack of oxygen when the pilot's instruction to put on his oxygen mask failed to reach him.

He spent a few days in London on his own before his son Aage was able to join him, and he was rather lost, being accustomed to having some member of the family look after him. Miss Vera Mayne, Akers's very efficient secretary, rose to the occasion. When Bohr had an important appointment with some minister, she typed the address and instructions how to get there on six pieces of paper and said, "Now, Professor Bohr, if you put one of these into each of your pockets, you are sure to find one when you need it."

The Bohrs also came to Birmingham, and were supposed to stay in our flat. We had dinner, when suddenly Genia had a massive haemorrhage, which turned out to be a miscarriage. She was taken to hospital, and the Bohrs went off to stay in an hotel.

After this Genia had repeated haemorrhages. One day I had a meeting in London, and when I came back I saw an ambulance standing in front of our block of flats. Fearing that they had come for Genia, I rushed to look, but saw another woman on the stretcher. Much relieved, I went upstairs, where Vera was waiting for me. "Where is Genia?"—"She was taken to hospital half an hour ago."

8

Manhattan District

Move to New York

Soon after this it was decided that we were to move to America. The British organisation was to cooperate with the American project, to discontinue work in England, except for items that could be of use to the Americans, and to send over a number of people who could assist the American project. From the theoretical group, Fuchs and I were to go to the United States, to work initially with the isotope-plant designers in New York; Skyrme followed a little later. As the stay was expected to be long, we were allowed to take our families. Alan Wilson stayed and took charge of the Birmingham theory group until it was finally disbanded.

We had rather short notice of the move and had to give up our flat, which was fortunately rented on monthly notice. We had to store or dispose of our furniture, and pack up what we were taking with us; our car was stored in an empty garage. Genia, who had been working in industry, had to resign from her job. She had left her work as a nurse when she was no longer needed, and trained as a fitter in one of the training centres set up for this purpose. She then entered a factory in Birmingham as a "marker-out and setter-off" and was soon promoted to forewoman in charge of an assembly shop, and then became a planning engineer. The managing director of the factory intended to make her his special assistant at about the time our departure ended her industrial career.

She was still too weak from her illness for any of the chores. I had to leave before the removers had collected our furniture, and my secretary kindly came to supervise this operation. Genia had gone ahead to London while I was doing the final packing. She was still so weak that she could hardly drag herself the short distance from the underground station to our hotel. I joined her there, and next morning we took the train to Liverpool and embarked on the *Andes*.

We were a large party, destined for a variety of American laboratories. Some were to stay only for a short period of discussions, the rest were going to join American research groups. The party included Frisch, who was to go to Los Alamos. His departure had been a tour de force. He was still a German subject since the Anschluss (the take-over of Austria), and he could not very well be sent as such to America by the British government. So his application for naturalisation was granted, and a certificate was issued; he took the Oath of Allegiance, which made him a British subject; he registered for military service and was granted deferment; he was issued a passport, on which he got an exit permit and a United States visa; he got a reservation on the boat; and he left—all within forty-eight hours. This would not have been possible without the efficient Miss Mayne, who had or-chestrated the operation, and had dispatched a breathless Frisch by taxi to the various offices.

The *Andes*, built as a luxury cruise liner, had been adapted as a troop transport. On the westbound crossing she was almost empty, so we all used what had been first-class cabins, which were now fitted with eight bunks for the officers. Genia and I had such a cabin, with some bunks facing at right angles to the others. Genia was very seasick, and as she found rocking head to foot less tolerable than rocking sideways, she changed bunks whenever the boat changed course, which was frequently, as we were following a zigzag course to evade German submarines. She was sure she would have to spend the rest of her life in America, because she would not be able to face such a crossing again.

We arrived in Newport News, Virginia, and went by train to Wash-ington. The first part of the journey was by a branch line in a ram-shackle train. Some of our party suspected that, to stop the train, someone put a rod through the spokes of the wheels—at least that was the way it felt. The train was also crowded, and Genia came back from an exploratory walk reporting happily that she had found an almost empty car, in which there were only two very nice Negroes. To her disappointment she was told that we were in the South of the United States, where transport was still segregated.

We arrived rather late in Washington, where hotel rooms had been reserved. Our room had a folding bed, which in the daytime disap-peared into a closet. It folded up when Genia tried to sit on it, but we were able to remedy the situation. She had more serious difficulty with the bathtub: when she turned on the tap, the handle came off. With great consternation, we watched the water level in the bath rise. Our appeal to the reception brought a handyman with tools to stop the water and replace the handle.

Next day we were received by Groves and went on to New York. Rooms had been reserved in the Hotel Taft in the Times Square area, and it was a depressing place: a noisy lobby full of milling crowds, narrow corridors in which one met rather unattractive characters. Friends remarked later that we were probably the first married couple to stay together in the Taft! Altogether, the neighbourhood of Times Square was unattractive. The stranger who has seen pictures of modern skyscrapers and elegant mansions and expects to find this style to be typical of the city soon discovers that only a small part corresponds to his image—in 1943 chiefly Fifth Avenue, including Washington Square, Central Park South, and Riverside Drive. We stayed at the Taft only one night, and then found ourselves a room in a very pleasant small hotel near Washington Square, where we stayed until we found an apartment.

My main contact was to be the Kellex Corporation, a subsidiary of a firm of plant designers, set up for the isotope plant. However, it would have been difficult for us, as foreigners, to be based in their offices, so we were given space in the British Supply Mission, a large organisation that dealt with British government orders for military supplies. Our offices were on the twenty-fifth floor of a building on Wall Street, and I felt like a real New York businessman, one of the crowd streaming into Wall Street every morning.

The Kellex offices were in the Woolworth Building, not far away. The building was famous because it had marked a new stage in the growth of skyscrapers. One problem it had faced was the design of lifts, since with increasing height the danger of a fall in the event of a mechanical failure or a broken cable became serious. The solution in the Woolworth Building was ingenious: the doors were so well fitted that they sealed the shaft pratically hermetically, and the lift fitted into the shaft fairly closely. A falling lift would therefore act like a piston, and compress the air in the shaft, and that would cushion its fall.

We spent much of our time discussing plant design and operation with the Kellex people. General Groves had given instructions that we were to be given all the information we needed. We had no problems except when dealing with new people. As soon as they realised we were from England, they became worried and felt obliged to ask their security officer for instructions. On some occasions the local security officer refused to give the required permission, and we had to appeal to Washington to have him overruled.

We soon discovered that it was too late for our elegant ideas for improving the efficiency of the plant to be considered. Orders had already been placed for parts, and these could not be changed. However, we could still make a contribution on the questions of the stability of the plant, which we had already studied in Birmingham.

Chemical engineers were accustomed to thinking about the stability of a plant, i.e., about the way it responds to small variations in the behaviour of its components; but they did not usually deal with a plant that, like the present one, has thousands of stages in series. Since conditions do not change much from one stage to the next, we treated the variations as continuous and thereby obtained differential equations, which were easy to solve. When we explained our method to the engineers in England who had been thinking about the plant, their reaction was that it was much too highbrow, and they would work out, on the drawing-board, what a small change in one stage of the plant would do to the others. After a day or two at the drawing-board they came back and said, "How was this about a differential equation?" Almost literally the same conversation took place with the Kellex designers, and again when we met the engineers from Carbon & Carbide, who were going to operate the plant.

Genia and I stayed in the hotel for about two weeks, during which Genia went to Toronto to bring back Gaby, leaving Ronnie until we had a flat. We celebrated Christmas in the hotel. Most of the hotel staff were black, and we learned much about their problems. While there was no official segregation or discrimination, it was in practice very hard for an educated black person to find a suitable job, and once we noticed a lift operator reading a mathematics book. In job applications, the employer was not allowed to ask about the applicant's race, and blacks with good qualifications would often get as far as an interview; but when they walked into the room they realised that they had no chance. Colleagues working in government laboratories told me that for civil service appointments no interviews were held, so as not to prejudice the chances of out-of-state candidates. As a result, nobody in these laboratories sacked his secretary since her successor might turn out to be black.

We ran into such a problem during our work. We had taken on a computing assistant and needed another. I phoned Hunter College, which had sent us the first girl, and asked if they could recommend another. The lady at the college said she had a very suitable girl, but she had to "warn" me that the girl was black. Did I still want her? Realising that I had never seen a black person in the building, I went to speak to the personnel officer in the Supply Mission. She told me that it would be impossible to employ black staff because the white employees, including those from Britain, would object. We could not in wartime afford rows or personnel disputes. "What is more," she said, "I must ask you to interview her and turn her down on merit; otherwise we risk being brought before a Senate Committee for practising discrimination."

But this game I would not play. I did not want to start any trouble, but I would not put the girl in the position of coming hopefully to an interview and being turned down for reasons that would be obvious to her. I told the personnel officer that if I interviewed the girl and she was suitable for the job, which was likely, I would recommend her appointment, and the personnel office could take it from there. She agreed, and I explained the situation to the college. I was wondering how Fuchs would react to this; I knew his feelings on these matters were if anything stronger than mine. But he took it very reasonably.

Genia found a flat on Riverside Drive, one of our favourite parts of New York, and collected Ronnie from Toronto. Next was the question of schools. We had come with the notion that in America every child goes to the neighbourhood school. This may be true in some towns, but it was certainly not so in Manhattan. The schools there were a "blackboard jungle", huge classes presided over by helpless old ladies; the papers often carried stories about knifings or even shootings. All our friends either sent their children to private schools, if they could afford them, or moved out to suburbs that had good schools. We did not seem to have the second option because there were no furnished flats to be found in the suburbs. We found a very good private school where the children were accepted. We thought that by living economically in other ways, we could manage.

The question of my income was complicated. When we left London, an official had explained to me what I would be paid, and asked if the salary was acceptable. I replied that I did not know about the cost of living in the United States, but we would try to live on the stated salary. When I received my first month's pay cheque it seemed reasonable, but for the second month the cheque was about $25. I was told that too little tax had been deducted the first time, and this was now corrected.

The rules were that people employed overseas by the British government were, in principle, liable to British income tax, but the rule was waived if the salary was less than £1,000 a year. If it was more, tax was due in full. My university salary, which was paid by Tube Alloys, was just above £1,000, which was therefore very unfavourable, taxwise. A cost-of-living allowance, based on one's salary, was added to the balance. I wrote to London, pointing out my difficulty and

186

asking that my salary be reduced below £1,000, which would make me considerably better off. But this somehow was against the rules.

So we decided we had to move into a suburb. We arranged to rent an unfurnished flat in New Rochelle in Westchester, and ordered the bare minimum of furniture. We had not yet moved to the new flat when it was decided I should move to Los Alamos. We were able to get the rental agreement cancelled and to stop delivery of the furniture. At the same time came a message from London that in view of the greater responsibility of my position in Los Alamos, my salary would be raised, and this would also get me into the next higher rate of allowances. So we were going to be well off, as life in Los Alamos was much cheaper than in New York.

I had already been at Los Alamos for a brief visit. At that time the laboratory was urgently required to obtain numerical solutions to the equations for the implosion, i.e., a shock wave travelling inward into the plutonium to make it supercritical. The equation for this was of the same form as that for the blast wave in air, for which I had done my numerical experiments. Computers did not yet exist, but Los Alamos had just received some punch-card machines, with which one could do simple calculations. It had not yet been settled how and on what problems these machines were going to be used. I therefore came just at the right time to explain the step-by-step method by which the equation could be solved and the limits on the size of the steps.

It was now summer, and New York was hot and humid. Commuting in a crowded subway train was not a pleasure in the hot weather, so the move to Los Alamos was very welcome. When the school term ended, Genia took the children for a brief stay at Cape Cod, in New England, to escape the heat. The prospectus of the hotel she had selected stated that it catered to a "restricted clientele". We were not yet aware that this phrase means "No Negroes, Jews, Italians, etc." Had we known, she would not have wished to stay there.

Life in Los Alamos

There were two reasons for the move to Los Alamos: we had finished what little we could contribute to the plant design and operation, and there was a request from Los Alamos to have me come there. All of us travelled by train. This applied to the top and bottom end of the scale. Groves would not allow the key people in the project, such as Oppenheimer, Lawrence, or Compton, to go by air because of the risk of accidents. On the other hand, the families were not important enough to rate the priority needed to get plane reservations.

Niels Bohr, who had left for Los Alamos earlier, had gone with enormous security precautions. He was instructed to get off the train before it reached Lamy, the station for Santa Fe, and was met there by a car. Then, on a lonely road, he transferred to another car, which took him to Los Alamos. Like other key people, he was not supposed to use his real name, and he became Mr. Nicholas Baker. This caused some complications. Before leaving New York, Bohr met George Placzek but said he had no time to talk now, as he was due for an appointment with the Danish consul. He said Placzek should phone him there, and they would meet later. Placzek thus phoned the consulate and asked to speak to Mr. Baker. He was told there was no Mr. Baker there. "But I understand he has an appointment with the consul?" No, he was told, the consul was talking to Professor Bohr. Placzek then realised that in the Danish consulate it would not make sense for Bohr to use his pseudonym, so he said, "In that case, may I please speak to Professor Bohr?"

Another story about Bohr/Baker is apocryphal. The Halbans were divorced and Els had married George Placzek. One day she met Bohr in an hotel lift. The story goes that she said, "Good morning, Professor Bohr. I do not know whether you remember me?" Bohr replied, "I am not Bohr, I am Nicholas Baker. But I do remember you; you are Mrs. Halban."—"No, I am Mrs. Placzek." It is true they did meet in an hotel lift, but Els was far too well trained to call Bohr by name in public, and Bohr surely knew about her new marriage. Still, it makes a nice story. On Bohr's subsequent visits to Los Alamos there was less concern; he went to the normal station, Lamy, and was taken to Los Alamos by the usual army car. There was even less concern on a later journey, when someone forgot to send a car for him at all.

We had to change trains in Chicago, arriving there in the morning and leaving at night. We spent the day with the Brentanos, our friends from Manchester, who now lived in Evanston, where he taught at Northwestern University. Our train west was the "California Limited", a train with the reputation of usually being late. It was said that when one day people in Lamy were pleased to see it arrive on time, they discovered it was the previous day's train. We had heard that the Bretschers' sleeping-car berths had, by mistake, been sold twice, and they had spent the first night sitting in the corridor on their suitcases. So we said, "Perhaps our accommodation will also have been sold twice, but if so, the other people can sit in the corridor!"

We got to the station early, and on to the platform as soon as it opened. The station concourse was packed with people and their belongings, reminiscent of a Russian railway station. The Brentanos helped us escort the children through the crowd. As soon as we got into our compartment, we put the children to bed. Sure enough, after a while some other passengers appeared and claimed the compartment. So they were indeed left in the corridor. When the conductor arrived, he told us that the ticket office had just made a mistake in writing out the tickets; in fact, our tickets were wrong, and we had a compartment reserved somewhere else. We were able to stay the first night, while the other people went to our reserved compartment. For the second night we had to switch.

The arrival at Los Alamos is always breathtaking. You come from the New Mexico desert, with its sparse vegetation of sagebrush and piñon, through jagged sandstone formations, to a border of wooded hills. The town is on a mesa—a plateau—surrounded by steep canyons. This situation, with the dry mountain air at the 7,500-foot altitude, and the view of distant mountains gave the town a beauty marred only somewhat by the army huts that made up most of the town. It had been a fashionable boys' school, and the log houses of the school were left, though they were dwarfed by the drab prefabs. The old log houses had the distinction of containing bathtubs, as opposed to mere showers, and the street on which they stood was known as "Bathtub Row". We were told, apologetically, that no room was left for us in Bathtub Row or in any of the houses nearby in the more desirable part of town. There was only a flat on the "other" side of town. We said, "Never mind; when we live there it will become respectable." Sure enough, when the Fermis arrived a little after us, they moved into the flat above us.

On our first evening there, the Oppenheimers asked Genia and me for dinner. This started with dry martinis, and we each had two. We did not then realise that the altitude substantially reduces one's tolerance for alcohol, until one gets acclimatised in a week or so. After dinner we found we had great trouble getting up from the table and walking home. This was only slightly aggravated by the fierceness of Robert's martinis.

He had strong views on questions of style in food and drink. Martinis had to be strong. Coffee had to be black. When coffee was served in their house, there was never any cream or sugar on the table. They would be provided on request, but the hosts started from the assumption that the guests would want to have their coffee the proper way.

Steak had to be rare (underdone), and this brings a story to mind.

Oppenheimer took the members of a committee to a steak house after a meeting. Everybody ordered steak, and the waiter took orders on how it should be cooked. Oppenheimer said "rare", and this was echoed by everybody in turn, until the waiter came to Robert's neighbour on the other side, who said "well done". Robert looked at him and said, "Why don't you have fish?"

Los Alamos had been set up to deal with the problems of weapons design and ultimately to make the weapon. It employed experimental physicists to determine the nuclear constants, theorists to calculate the behaviour of a chain reaction, chemists and metallurgists to work on the fabrication of the materials, explosives experts to design the fast compaction of the parts of the weapon, and many others. The place was so remote because of Groves's wish for isolation in order to preserve secrecy. His initial idea had been to lock the gates, so that nobody could go in or out until the work was completed. This proved impractical. He had expressed his idea by saying, "When the last construction worker has left, the gates will be locked." But the construction workers never left, so his statement did not become invalid.

Groves had chosen Oppenheimer as director of the laboratory. At first sight, this seemed a surprising appointment. Oppenheimer was a theoretician without experience of running an experimental team, or of any other major administrative responsibility. He was supposed to be a very academic type, more at home with poetry than with politics. But his appointment proved a great success. He had a very clear understanding of what were the important problems, and he was extremely good at summing up. His speed of understanding in a discussion was impressive; in talking with him you usually managed to complete only half your sentence, when he had already grasped your point and gave his reply. In dealing with people he was very perceptive and easily gained their confidence; this was one of the reasons why he had managed to attract such an impressive collection of people.

His wife, Kitty, evoked a rather more mixed response from the people, particularly the women, around her. As quick on the uptake as Robert, she had extremely strong opinions on many matters, and it was never hard to sense of whom she did or did not approve. She was a person of great courage, both in the saddle of a horse and when facing a hostile authority, as is clear from reading her testimony at the later "Oppenheimer hearings".

My recollection of Kitty bears little relation to the image conveyed in the recent BBC television dramatisation of Robert Oppenheimer's life. There she is shown attending a meeting of a Communist cell in California in the late thirties in a flowery hat. I have some doubt whether she would have attended that kind of meeting at that time, but I am sure she would never have worn that kind of hat, least of all on that kind of occasion. Most of the time she did not even own a hat. At a Solvay Conference in Brussels in 1953, when we were received by the King and Queen of the Belgians and the instructions were for ladies to wear hats, Genia and Kitty had a problem: they did not possess hats and had to improvise some suitable head covering.

The hat story illustrates Kitty's unconventional attitude and her indifference to the upper middle-class rules of behaviour; this, together with a degree of arrogance, may have caused resentment in some. But there were many who loved her personal charm and her frankness and admired her positive qualities.

It was a strange sensation to meet so many old friends from various phases of our lives in such an outlandish place as Los Alamos. Hans Bethe was the oldest friend there. He was now married to Rose Ewald, the daughter of Paul Ewald, a physicist famous for his work in crystallography. Bethe had worked in Ewald's department in Germany as a young assistant and had met his daughters, who were then children. Later the Ewalds left Germany and came to England, and Rose went to study in America. Hans met her again and married her. Their two children were born in Los Alamos. Rose is a very attractive woman of great energy, as well as a great organiser. Before her children were born she ran the housing office in Los Alamos.

Other old friends included Enrico and Laura Fermi and Emilio Segré, whom we knew from Rome. Fermi was now Mr. Henry Farmer when travelling. There was Victor Weisskopf, whom I had met in many places, and his charming Danish wife, Ellen. David Inglis, our skiing companion in Kitzbühel, was there also (now without the mark on his nose, where he had hit the snow). George Placzek was transferred from Montreal somewhat later, and brought Els, whom we had known as Mrs. Halban.

There were colleagues from England, besides Klaus Fuchs, who accompanied me: Egon and Hanni Bretscher from Cambridge; from Liverpool we had Chadwick, who was the head of the British group, Frisch, and Joseph Rotblat, a Pole who had been visiting Liverpool when war broke out and got trapped there; from Oxford was James Tuck, who had been Lord Cherwell's assistant for a time and had helped me explain to Cherwell what atomic energy was about; and from Birmingham there were Philip Moon and Ernest Titterton, one of Oliphant's pupils.

Some of our other friends came to Los Alamos from time to time. Niels and Aage Bohr came for prolonged visits. Oppenheimer, amused by the name Nicholas Baker, came to call him "Uncle Nick", and many of us adopted this term.

Another frequent visitor was John von Neumann, a brilliant mathematician, whom I knew from Germany. Although he was Hungarian, he did not have the extreme superficial politeness of many Hungarians. He liked good living and a good story. His mathematics was of the purest and most abstract kind, but he also understood physics and had written a book about quantum mechanics. He was extremely fast in solving practical problems, and contributed many useful ideas to the work of Los Alamos.

I. I. Rabi, whom I knew from Leipzig, came from time to time to keep a fatherly eye on the place. He is generally regarded as the wise old man of physics, and had already done the atomic-beam work for which he later received the Nobel Prize; he was now working on radar. He has the endearing trait of being very careful with small amounts of money, while being very generous in serious matters. During one morning's discussion he went with some of us to the snack bar for a cup of coffee and a doughnut. He rather liked the doughnuts, but before ordering a second one, he asked for the price. Since the answer was only five cents, he allowed himself the purchase. He had discussed the plans for Los Alamos with Groves at an early stage. When he saw what was being planned in the way of housing and other amenities, he said, "You are treating these scientists as if they were privates in the army. You should realise that there are fewer fellows of the American Physical Society than brigadiers in the U.S. Army." (This was correct, because not every member of the Physical Society is a fellow.)

The arrangements were probably improved somewhat as a result of this conversation, but they still left much to be desired. The houses were heated by hot air from a coal-burning furnace, and one thermostat served the upstairs and downstairs flats. Our living room contained the thermostat that controlled both our flat and that of the Fermis. We had to remember to set the thermostat to a higher temperature when we had a party, and perhaps a log fire, to prevent the Fermis from getting too cold; and to set it down when we opened our windows, or the Fermis would get roasted. Not all ground-floor tenants remembered these finer points, and there was a good deal of friction.

A more serious problem was that any excess heat from the furnace had to escape through the flats. If the janitors who stoked the furnace put in too much fuel, the rooms got unbearably hot, no matter what the thermostat setting. (Later the system was modified to remedy this trouble.) If there was any electrical or mechanical fault in the blower or in its control system, the furnace would get hotter and hotter, and if nothing was done, the house would catch fire. With wooden houses in a dry climate, this was no joke.

We were once close to this kind of disaster. We were awakened by a smell of scorching, and I went to the furnace room but was unable to read the thermometer. I ran back to get my glasses, and with their aid discovered that the mercury column extended to the very top, so the level was not visible. I ran to the nearest fire alarm—there were no private telephones—and some experts came to deal with the situation. In calling the fire brigade one faced an additional obstacle: the houses were numbered in the order in which they were built, so that house 145 might be next door to house 62, and the streets had no names. One could sometimes see firemen frantically asking, "Where is house no. X?"

Our house (and many others) had its front entrance facing the woods. This gave an attractive view from the main window, but it also meant a path through mud for most of the year. So everybody came through the kitchen door. As to the kitchen, the only cooking facility provided for those who had not brought a cooker with them was a wood-burning stove called the "black beauty", which was very difficult to operate. There was a shortage of housing so a rationing system was adopted by which people were assigned flats according to the size of their families. When Rose Bethe was running the housing office, she had a visit from a childless couple, asking to be put on the list for a two-bedroom flat. "You know the rules," she said. "Are you expecting a baby?" They blushed. "No, but we let nature take its course."

The housing office also allocated household help. These were mostly Indian women, imported by bus from the nearby Pueblo Indian villages. This, incidentally, often led to very friendly relations between the residents and the Indian villagers. The rules gave priority for domestic help to women working full-time in the laboratory. This was resented by women with small children, who claimed that their need was greater than that of childless women who spent eight hours a day in an office. Later, when some of the members of the committee that had made the rules had children themselves, they saw the point.

Security played a large role in the life of the place. The location of the laboratory was secret, and the address was a post office box in Sante Fe. The British were not allowed to use even that address; our mail was forwarded from Washington. Outgoing private letters were censored. The intention was not to catch spies, but to stop people inadvertently giving information away. Drivers' licences showed no name, but only a number. The school had a troop of Boy Scouts attached to it, and there was a problem in recording their achievements with the national headquarters, because a list of names might have disclosed a partial list of the staff of Los Alamos. So only numbers were sent. Perhaps: "No. 37 has passed the test in tying knots." Mysteriously, however, the Girl Scouts' names were not disguised.

The school was excellent. It had none of the troubles that had worried us about the schools in Manhattan, but the science teaching was weak. This paradox was explained by the fact that most of the teachers were wives of scientists and included some first-rate scholars. However, those with scientific qualifications preferred work in the laboratory, so teachers with poor science backgrounds had to teach science also.

The scope for leisure activities was limited. There was a cinema, but not much else. People with musical talents arranged music groups. Barn dancing was popular, and there was a "horsy set". There were also many parties, large and small. Being an army base, Los Alamos did not have a wine store, and drink had to be bought in Sante Fe. Whisky and gin were in short supply, but there was plenty of Mexican vodka. As most Americans like martinis, a mixture was made with vodka in place of gin, and nicknamed Martinovich. John von Neumann consumed fifteen of these one evening in our house. Next day he said, "I know my stomach has a cast-iron lining, but it must have developed a crack!"

On Sundays one could go for walks in the immediate neighbourhood or drive to one of the mountain areas for more strenuous walks. In the winter there was skiing, and in the summer one could swim in the Rio Grande, if the water level was high enough, or in some lakes. On our first Sunday, Genia and I went for a little walk near the town. On our way back we were stopped by a deep canyon—we seemed to have taken a wrong turn. We went back and tried another path, but again we could not get through. Yet we never lost sight of the town's water tower! It was hot and we were very thirsty, and finally Genia got tired and sat down on a log to wait for the sun to go down. I wandered around a little, and there, within fifty yards, was a road that led us home.

Tony Skyrme had remained in New York a little longer, but then joined us in Los Alamos. He had by now shown an unusual ability to see rapidly through complex mathematical problems. Before leaving New York, he had an adventure, which he reported on arrival. Walking through Central Park on a hot summer night without a jacket, he was stopped by a patrol searching for draft evaders. He could not show his draft exemption card, because the State Department had not yet issued it, and he had no other papers on him to prove his identity. He was taken into custody and handed over to the police. Here he was questioned, and they regarded him as suspicious because of his "guttural accent"—not a compliment for a young man educated at Eton and Cambridge! He was urged to confess that he was a German spy and spent the night sitting on a bench in the police station. In the morning (which was a Sunday) he was handed over to federal agents. He urged them to take him to his lodgings, where he could produce his passport, but this was refused, as was his request to notify the British consulate. Eventually he was taken to a federal prison, where he was fingerprinted, put into prison clothes, and told to wash floors. An Englishman serving a sentence in the prison expressed the wish to meet him, and they managed to get together. The man said, "Do you remember the Air Raid Shelter Murders in 1940? That was me!" On Monday morning he was taken to court, and the magistrate released him without calling for any evidence. Asked what had been the greatest hardship in this affair, he answered, "The way the meals in prison were eaten not from plates, but from metal trays with depressions for the different courses." He had not yet eaten his first meal in the Los Alamos cafeteria.

Besides meeting old friends, we made many new ones. We became very attached to Cyril and Alice Smith. He is a metallurgist, born near Birmingham but had settled in America long ago. He was now the head of the Metallurgy Division, concerned with all the problems of the properties and the fabrication of uranium and plutonium. Besides being an eminent metallurgist, he was also very interested and knowledgeable in the history of technology and materials, and he made this his specialty after he retired. His many books and articles on these subjects are of fascinating interest. Alice, an historian, taught in the school and later proved her ability as a writer.

We met Jane Wilson first through the school, where she taught English. She is a scholar with a passionate interest in literature and has strong opinions, which she states expressively and pungently in conversation and in writing. Her husband Robert, a very energetic and resourceful man, was the head of the nuclear physics division. He was involved in the task of dismantling a university cyclotron and re-erecting it again at Los Alamos, a very difficult operation that functioned without a hitch. He sometimes resorted to unusual measures. He found that members of his division wasted valuable time queueing in the barbershop, and his request to increase the number of barbers on the site was turned down. When he discovered that one of his technicians was a qualified barber, he ordered, through the laboratory

195

stores, a barber chair and other necessary equipment, including the *Police Gazette*, the customary reading material in barbershops. In due course everything arrived, even the *Police Gazette*, and nuclear physicists no longer had to queue for a haircut. Besides being an outstanding experimentalist and machine builder, he is a talented artist and has made sculptures in many materials. When in the 1970s he became the first director of the Fermi Laboratory near Chicago, his particular combination of talents created a highly efficient and successful accelerator laboratory that is also very pleasing to the eye.

Herbert Anderson was a longstanding collaborator of Fermi's, a very skilled experimentalist, and a very practical person. He was a bachelor, and often took us on excursions in his car. At first we had no car of our own, but we felt we should contribute petrol coupons when friends gave us rides, and we therefore bought a car, originally intended only to qualify us for a fuel ration. It was an ancient (1927), bright green Nash, which we bought from a horse dealer at the annual Santa Fe Fiesta. We therefore called it "Conquistador", and the children called it "Conkie" for short. It got us around, making the hilly journey from Santa Fe quite literally under its own steam, as it was inclined to boil. The army had a stable of horses that one could rent by the hour, and we occasionally went riding, remembering our experience in the Caucasus. But these horses, which were ridden by different riders in succession, were of an uneven temperament, and we decided to acquire our own horse. For this, we joined forces with Herbert Anderson, who also wanted a horse, and we jointly built a corral for two horses, to his design. We then went with him into the depths of New Mexico, to buy a cow pony. We got an extremely tough little horse, and also bought a saddle, which cost nearly as much as the horse. Herbert, who was a better rider, bought a half-thoroughbred. We took turns in feeding the horses and taking water out to them, and for this chore Conkie proved very useful.

One of the outstanding characters at the laboratory was Richard Feynman. He came to Los Alamos just after completing his Ph.D. work at Princeton, and was immediately recognised as a man of great ability. This applied not only to his theoretical physics, which certainly was impressive, but to many other things. He was very skilled in repairing typewriters and desk calculators, and the demand for his services became so extensive that Bethe finally issued an instruction that he was no longer allowed to do these repairs, as his theoretical work was more important. He also had the reputation of being a wizard in opening combination safes, but he confessed in his contribution to the *Reminiscences of Los Alamos* (edited by L. Badash,

J. O. Hirschfelder, and H. P. Broida; Reidel, 1980) that this was done by a trick. He had a unique ability to explain things using his face, his hands, and his arms in gestures that illustrated the mechanism of what he was talking about, always with a great sense of humour. He was equally good at getting across subtle points of physics as at telling anecdotes. On one social occasion on which he was functioning as entertainer, some women were overheard deploring the fact that he was wasting his time doing physics. By now his name is a household word in physics, because of his contributions to field theory, with their uniquely original approach, for which he received the Nobel Prize, and because of his talent as a great expositor.

Feynman was always chafing at the security rules, which seemed to him illogical, and he delighted in teasing the chief security officer. But one ingenious plan to make fun of him did not work. The weekly colloquium was always held in the cinema, which was outside the security area and therefore had to be specially guarded during such meetings. Feynman claimed that the precautions were not adequate and bet the security officer twenty dollars that he could drive a large truck close to the cinema without being stopped by the guards, and that if anyone did this with a truck full of explosives the whole scientific staff would be wiped out. His plan was actually to do nothing on the night in question, but he expected the security man to increase the guard on that night, which would allow Feynman to claim that twenty dollars was more important to him than the safety of the scientists. To his regret, the officer refused to take the bet.

At the time, Feynman's cheerfulness was hiding personal tragedy. His wife was dying of tuberculosis. Oppenheimer had arranged for her to be transferred to a hospital in Albuquerque, about 100 miles from Los Alamos, so that he could visit her from time to time. It seems they knew when they got married that she did not have long to live. Klaus Fuchs, who had bought a car, would often drive him to Albuquerque. The two men occupied adjacent rooms in the "big house", the residence for single people, and had become friendly.

The "big house" was one of the buildings of the old boarding school. In its school days, it had contained bathtubs, but these had been taken out in the adaptation. This was one of the many points of grievance contributing to the friction between the army and the civilians, and the situation figured in a joke. Groves had become concerned about the high birthrate at Los Alamos, which raised the cost of hospital services. No doubt this was due to the lab's unusually high childbearing age group, and perhaps to the fact that maternity services, as all medical care in an army camp, were free. Groves had requested Oppenheimer to see to it that his people did not produce too many children, but Oppenheimer did not regard this as one of his duties. Just then a paper appeared in a scientific journal, reporting statistical evidence that long immersion in hot water reduced male fertility. It was suggested that a copy be sent to Groves, pointing out that the absence of bathtubs was contributing to the trend he did not like. I do not know whether the article was actually sent.

In general, the civilians' grievances related to the security rules, which they felt were often arbitrary and illogical and to what they regarded as misplaced economies. I have already mentioned the weaknesses of the housing and shopping systems. By lack of foresight, there was also a shortage of electricity because of the constant increase in population, and by the increased demands of the laboratory itself. The output of the power station was raised by running the generators above their normal capacity, which resulted in boiling off the cooling water, thus straining the water supply. Later the power station had to resort to "load shedding", when different districts of the town had their electricity cut off for alternate periods.

From the point of view of the army, it was irritating to have to pander to the whims of these long-haired civilians who would not behave according to army traditions, and who were engaged in some mysterious activities not understood by most of the Army personnel. This applied particularly to the military police who had volunteered for special assignment, which many imagined would get them somewhere to the front line and near to real fighting. Instead they found themselves in the middle of the United States, guarding civilian installations.

Working in Los Alamos

In return for the isolation of the place, Oppenheimer had wrung from Groves the concession that there was to be no compartmentalisation within the laboratory. Every scientific member was allowed to know everything that went on in the laboratory, except for a few strictly military matters. This helped greatly to make the work efficient.

Oppenheimer arranged to hold weekly colloquia for all scientific members of the laboratory, at which one of the groups would present a report on its work. He would also announce any interesting news, such as the results of some crucial tests or the arrival of some samples of uranium-235 or plutonium. The meetings were held in the closely guarded cinema, which I already mentioned in connection with Feynman. Further details were discussed at meetings of the "coordinating council", which consisted of all group leaders plus a number of other senior people, including, for example, Klaus Fuchs.

Progress had been satisfactory in planning the use of separated uranium isotope for a weapon. When small quantities of plutonium became available, a major new problem arose. Plutonium has a very high rate of spontaneous fission, i.e., some of the plutonium nuclei will split up and emit neutrons even without any external stimulus. The obvious way to start off the explosion, which worked perfectly well for uranium-235, was to bring together two pieces of the material, each less than the critical size, so that together they are supercritical. This has to be done fast enough to keep the chain reaction from starting when the system was only just above critical, because then a very inefficient explosion would result. It was planned to shoot one of the pieces at the other in a gun barrel, and that was sufficient for uranium. But for plutonium it was not fast enough; the chance of one of the atoms undergoing spontaneous fission just after passing the critical stage was too great.

An answer had already been suggested as a possible refinement, which now became vitally important. It consisted in surrounding a shell of plutonium by high explosive and thus produce an inward detonation wave, which would collapse the shell into a compact shape. This "implosion" device, while simple in principle, posed great problems, because generating a converging spherical detonation wave is difficult, and it was not even clear whether such a wave would be stable or would get distorted into an irregular shape. The problem called for a great experimental effort, and it was carried out mainly by the division headed by George Kistiakowsky, the explosives expert. He has written an excellent account of this work in his contribution to *Reminiscences of Los Alamos*, already mentioned.

There was also a theoretical group, the "hydrodynamics group", to look into the problems of detonation waves and shock waves and their stability. This group was supposed to be guided by Edward Teller, but he insisted on devoting his time to a long-term project, the "Super", later known as the hydrogen bomb. After some arguments, he was allowed to carry on with a small group, although it was clear that this project could not contribute to the war. I was then asked to take charge of the hydrodynamics group.

This development was perhaps characteristic of Teller, whose thoughts are often leaps and bounds ahead of his plodding colleagues. While his ideas are always original and often brilliant, they are not always practical or timely. He pursues his ideas with great insistence,

199

and this makes him act at times like a prima donna. But, just as only an outstanding singer can afford to behave like a prima donna, he is an outstanding physicist. At home he is a fine and passionate pianist.

One could feel a certain tension between Teller and Oppenheimer. Perhaps the reason was that Teller was anxious to earn Oppenheimer's respect, not only as a physicist—which he undoubtedly had—but as a person. The complexity of this is well illustrated by the following episode. Lord Cherwell, who was a British cabinet minister, was making a rather official visit to the laboratory. In the evening Oppenheimer gave a party in his honour to which I should have been invited, since at the time I was in charge of the British group. But because of an omission by a secretary I did not get an invitation. Next day Oppenheimer discovered this, and came to me to apologise. "This is terrible," he said, "but there is an element of comfort in the situation: it might have happened with Edward Teller." I took this as a compliment, as it was obviously intended, but it was also an interesting token of the tension that surfaced many years later in the "Oppenheimer hearings".

I now found my knowledge of shock waves, which I had acquired in corresponding with G. I. Taylor, very useful. There was much more to learn, but I soon found my way, with help from Hans Bethe, who was heading the Theoretical Physics Division. Klaus Fuchs joined my group and we shared an office. One thing I had to get used to was the (then mainly American) practice of using only first names. At meetings of the theory group leaders, Hans Bethe might say, "This problem seems to be one for your group, Bob." As there were four or five Bobs sitting around the table, one had to watch carefully at whom he was looking.

Everyone was grimly determined to get on with their work. The date was approaching when enough fissile material for bombs would be available, and there was great pressure to be ready with all the necessary developments for making and detonating them.

Just at that time, Oppenheimer came down with chicken pox. He felt he could not afford to take time off at this moment, and he presided at meetings with a high temperature and an unshaven face, where the rash was visible under the stubble. He transmitted the disease to many of those present, and they carried it home to their families. For some time after this, he was not popular with the wives.

It was known that the required amounts of uranium-235 and of plutonium would arrive at about the same time. We were confident that the mechanism for assembling the supercritical amount of the former would give no problem, but there was much more room for doubt in the case of plutonium, which depended on the very complex implosion technique. When the first bomb of each kind had been produced it was therefore decided to test the plutonium bomb. This test would also confirm the general principle of the chain reaction and its effects.

A number of specialists with experience of the effects of blast waves were invited, including several people from England. Among these were G. I. Taylor, who immediately became very popular at the lab, and W. G. (now Lord) Penney. Penney's work had included studying the effect of German bombs on England, and he gave a talk about this to the colloquium. His presentation was in a scientific matter-of-fact style, with his usual brightly smiling face; many of the Americans had not been exposed to such a detailed and realistic discussion of casualties, and he was nicknamed "the smiling killer".

By this time Chadwick had moved to Washington, where he could be in direct touch with Groves and with other people concerned with the Anglo-American collaboration. He asked me to take charge of the British group at Los Alamos, which did not involve much responsibility. He also asked me to keep him informed of the progress of the work at Los Alamos. I therefore wrote letters at regular intervals in which I summarised, to the best of my knowledge, what was going on. I was a little doubtful about the appropriateness of this, because no secret information was supposed to be sent out from the laboratory without special permission. However, as Chadwick was in a sense a member of the laboratory, one could argue that he was entitled to the information. I decided to let sleeping dogs lie.

Then one day Richard Tolman, a distinguished elder statesman of physics who assisted Groves and occasionally visited Los Alamos on Groves's behalf, asked to see me, as he had a message from Groves. When he started, "I understand you have been writing letters to Chadwick about the work of the laboratory," I felt that here my chickens were coming home to roost. But he continued, "General Groves finds that Chadwick is often better informed than he is, and wondered if he could have copies of your letters." He added that, if these letters referred also to purely domestic problems of the British group I could of course omit the relevant passages from the copies for Groves. This made it clear that the intention was not to censor my letters. I was relieved, and highly amused. But, then, I have always prided myself on my facility for summarising.

Eventually all was ready for the test of the first plutonium bomb in the desert near Alamogordo. With other scientists not directly involved in the test, I was taken by bus to a hill about 20 miles from the point where the bomb rested on top of a steel tower. There was a long wait, as the weather conditions were unfavourable. Wind from the wrong direction could have blown the radioactive cloud toward inhabited places. If the wind did not change by dawn, the test would have to be called off, since much of the instrumentation to measure the effects depended on darkness. Finally, the news came through that the test would proceed. We had been given pieces of dark glass through which to look at the spectacle, and we were advised to lie on the ground to minimize any blast effect (somewhat exaggerated advice at our distance). The big moment came: a giant flash, and a fireball rising and turning into the by-now-familiar mushroom-shaped cloud. We were struck with awe. We had known what to expect, but no amount of imagination could have given us a taste of the real thing.

The sound took about two minutes to reach us. By this time some had thrown themselves to the ground. The sound, when it came, was not very impressive, perhaps like the sound of a rifle fired nearby. I overheard William Laurence, the science correspondent of the *New York Times* who was present to prepare an eventual press release, exclaim, "What was that?"

For all of us, the feeling of awe at the terrible power of this weapon was mixed with elation at the success of the work. Groves realised this, and he was afraid that any outsider who saw us would be aware that we had witnessed a very successful test. The plan had been to stop in Albuquerque for breakfast, but now Groves ordered our bus drivers to return to Los Alamos without stopping. He need not have been concerned, as by the time we passed Albuquerque the sleepless night and the long wait were showing their effects, and anybody not asleep on the bus looked worn out and depressed. An observer at this point would surely have decided that the test must have been an abject failure.

Everybody was anxious to know the energy yield of the weapon. It was evident that it was very large, but one could not get a quantitative answer by looking at the fireball. The first to come up with an approximate answer was Fermi. Watching the explosion from a distance of about 10 miles, he had prepared a few pieces of paper and let them go as the blast wave passed him. He watched the distance they were carried by the blast, and from this he could estimate the strength of the blast wave, and therefore the energy release. My respect for Fermi, always high, rose further as a result. But I am not sure what to admire more—his ingenuity in thinking of the method, or his control in letting the scraps of paper go at the right time. I think I would have been too excited and would have released them either too early or too late.

More accurate data were eventually obtained from the various instruments displayed around the test site, but the easiest method (and I believe the most reliable) was suggested by Penney, based no doubt on his experience in England. He had a number of wooden boxes prepared with circular holes of varying sizes, covered with paper. In a pressure wave of a certain strength, the paper over the larger holes is ruptured, while that over the smaller ones remain intact. The size of the largest holes still covered will therefore give a measure of the overpressure, and hence of the blast intensity.

Barely a month after this test came the news of Hiroshima. We knew this meant the war was over, and we knew that our work had contributed to this result. But with the feeling of elation there was horror at the death and suffering that must have resulted, though we had no details as yet. This reaction was intensified when we heard, only two days later, of the attack on Nagasaki.

Reflections about the Bomb

I am often asked, "Did you not know when you worked to help develop the atomic bomb what horrors it would lead to? You were motivated initially by the fear of Hitler getting there first. Why did you continue with the work after the defeat of Germany?"

These are not simple questions to answer. Nobody could look at the reports and the pictures about Hiroshima and Nagasaki with anything but horror, and nobody would feel any pride at having had a hand in bringing this about. But this was war, and in war death, suffering, and destruction are unavoidable. The number of casualties in the atomic-bomb raids were no greater than in a big fire raid on Tokyo. It is not the scale of destruction that gave war a new dimension with the introduction of the atom bomb; what was new was the ease with which the weapon can be used, with a single plane creating the kind of destruction that could previously have been accomplished only by a massive military operation. We knew the destructive powers of the bomb, and its radiation effects, and Frisch and I pointed this out in our first memorandum. We knew the ease with which it could be used, and therefore the terrible responsibility it would impose on the political and military leaders who would have to decide whether and when to use it.

We realised it was important to make certain that the decision makers understood the new situation, and all the consequences of the existence of the new weapon. We thought all this had been communicated. While I was in England the completion of the weapon was still too remote. In Los Alamos we had no immediate contact with the American authorities, but we knew that Oppenheimer was in contact with them, and we had confidence both in his understanding and his talent for clear exposition. We felt the leaders were reasonable and intelligent people, and would make responsible decisions.

In retrospect it is clear that these views were too optimistic. I do not wish to imply that the decision makers were lacking in good will, but we overestimated their vision and their ability to adjust to a drastically new situation. To me the obvious answer would have been to drop a bomb on a sparsely populated area to show its effects, coupled with an ultimatum to the Japanese government to negotiate for peace to avoid a large-scale nuclear attack. This would have involved killing some people and destroying some buildings, since otherwise the power of the bomb would not have been obvious; the effects visible after the Alamogordo test were frightening to the expert but not impressive to the layman. Of course such an ultimatum might have failed, but at least it would have been an attempt to avoid unnecessary casualties. It seems that this possibility had not occurred to anyone—at least it was never discussed in the high-level committees. What was discussed was a test to be announced in advance, with an invitation to observers (as was done later with a test at Bikini). This proposal was turned down because the reliability of the detonating mechanism was not assured, and if such a test failed, it would be counterproductive.

Given all the wisdom of hindsight, what should we have done? Should we have refrained from working on the atom bomb from the beginning, or stopped work after the defeat of Germany? The first would have meant an intolerable risk; at the later stage there was still a bloody and cruel war going on, which could have been (and was) shortened by the new weapon. Besides, once the phenomenon of nuclear fission was discovered and could not be undiscovered, and the possibility of an atom bomb was understood, it was inevitable that it would be developed sooner or later by someone. A general refusal of all scientists to work on nuclear weapons could not be achieved, unless there was a general failure to believe in the ability of their governments to handle the situation. I believe therefore that the idea of such a "strike" of scientists is unrealistic.

Or should we have insisted on keeping control over the way the results of our work were being used? This would have implied the arrogant assumption that we were better qualified than others to make the right political and military decisions, and in any case it could never have been achieved. My regrets are that we did not insist on more dialogue with the military and political leaders, based on full and clear scientific discussions of the consequences of possible courses of action. It is not clear, of course, that such discussions would have made any difference in the end.

This is the short answer to questions which would deserve a book by themselves.

Winding Up and Going Home

After the end of the war the pressure eased, and time was spent mainly on tidying up and winding up. We had plenty of holidays to our credit, and decided to take a brief vacation by driving to Mexico. We went in Fuchs's car, and also had Edward Teller's wife, Mici, with us. Later, when it turned out that Fuchs had been a Soviet agent (see chapter 9), while Teller was known to be an exponent of extreme anti-communism, this looked an odd combination indeed.

The journey started with complications. Fuchs had to go to a meeting in Montreal first, so we were to drive the car to Albuquerque, where he would meet us. Some of the tyres on the car were no good, and we had a permit to replace them with new ones, which were then rationed; but there was a strike of transport drivers, so tyres were practically unobtainable. We limped into Albuquerque, having acquired some suspect retreads from the horse dealer in Sante Fe who had sold us Conkie, and having had several blowouts along the way. A desperate search in the town eventually turned up new tyres at the last minute. We drove on, but the car broke down near the small Texas town of Marfa. Fortunately it had a very efficient General Motors garage, and after two days' enforced rest, we continued on our way. When we booked rooms in motels in Texas, and later in Mexico, we always got into arguments: the receptionists would offer us one room with two double beds and could never understand why we needed three rooms; but eventually they would give in to our insistence.

Crossing the Rio Grande into Mexico made an impressive contrast. On the Texas side the villages looked as if people were transients, growing some quick crops and dumping their rubbish until it was time to move on. Across the border the impression was of cared-for fields and gardens and settled inhabitants. Further south the new Pan-American Highway passed through country that until quite recently had been practically inaccessible. We encountered some people bringing their sick to the roadside for medical help, and we felt regret that we had to disappoint them.

We had only three days left for Mexico City, but that was enough to see some of the sights, including a bullfight, and to get an impression of the Mexicans' talent for shape and colour that is evident in the buildings, from the least important to the ceremonial, and in paintings and traditional dress. We knew that some of the very modern murals were in a baroque palace, now a college, and expected these different styles to clash, but we found that they made a perfect blend. Then we headed back to the north.

At Los Alamos the British group planned a party for their American hosts in return for all the hospitality they had received. The dinner, for which the whole British group pooled their ration points, was prepared by the wives and transported to Fuller Lodge, the log house dating back to the school days, which was the social centre. I nearly missed the party because I had gone back to England for a meeting of the Technical Committee to discuss the postwar plans for atomic energy. The bomber on which I returned to America was held up by weather and mechanical trouble for several days, and I finally got to Los Alamos on the day of the party, in time at least for a token contribution to the communal effort: I carved the meat for the party of over a hundred people.

Dinner was followed by an English-style pantomime, "Babes in the Wood", full of topical allusions. Frisch was a success as an Indian maid, and James Tuck was the evil witch Security. The colonel in charge of Los Alamos was overheard to remark that it appeared not to be true that the English had no sense of humour! After the pantomime there was dancing. One young English physicist who had arranged the lighting effects had drunk a little too much, and amused himself by throwing light bulbs from the balcony onto the floor; the first one narrowly missed hitting Kitty Oppenheimer. Here my position as head of the British group imposed some responsibility on me, and I had to persuade the young man to go home to bed.

The winter of 1945 brought severe frost without snow, and this caused the water pipes to freeze. The water was brought to Los Alamos by plastic pipes laid on the surface, as an economy. In the first two winters the snow had come before the sharp frost and had protected the pipes, but now the Army had to pay the price of its economy. It took a long time to deal with the problem, because the standard methods of thawing water mains, passing strong electric currents through them or building a fire under them, could not be used for plastic pipes. There were appeals to save water, which did reduce the consumption substantially. This success encouraged the authorities to continue appealing. They were disappointed to find there was no further reduction, but instead consumption rose again. They had not allowed for the fact that certain uses of water, such as washing your children, may be postponed but eventually become unavoidable.

The water pressure fell, and we were lucky to be living on a low part of the site so that there still was water in our toilet. Many of our friends honoured us with short visits. Eventually water was brought in by road tankers from the Rio Grande. Crawling up the steep and winding road, they tended to spill some of their cargo, and the road soon became like a skating rink. The water was put into the town's water system, after being heavily chlorinated. Occasionally we would get some long pink worms squiggling out of our water taps. They had lost their original red colour because of the chlorine, but they were still alive.

I had been asked by the editor of a new series, the *Penguin Science News*, to collect articles for an issue on atomic energy, in which there was then great interest. For convenience I chose authors in Los Alamos, and in due course got a number of excellent articles, with one exception: the article by Emilio Segré was not on the right level. It would have been a fine treatment for graduate students in physics, but not for the general intelligent reader, for whom the series was intended. I did not relish the prospect of going to Emilio and telling him his article was not acceptable, since he does not take criticism kindly; but I had no choice, as I had promised the editor I would find suitable articles. Emilio accepted the situation unhappily but with good grace. I invited Philip Morrison to write an article in place of Segré, and this worked out extremely well; I had chosen a man who later became a famous expositor of science.

Finally we were ready to leave. I handed over my duties as group leader to Fred Reines, who later became famous for the experiment in which he observed neutrinos. I had signed for a small amount of equipment in use by the group, mostly desk calculators and slide rules. Fred now had to sign for all of this, and we went through the list, making sure everything was still there. Everything was found to be in order except for one slide rule that was used by a young man who was on leave and whose desk was locked. When he returned he produced a slide rule, but the number on it did not agree with that on the list. Evidently there had been some clerical error. We reported this to the stores, expecting them to alter their records. Instead, a technician appeared with tools, scraped the number off the slide rule, and painted on the one on the list.

In our two years in America we had accumulated various items of household equipment, which, on going back to the postwar shortages in England, we did not want to leave behind. So we had some wooden boxes made (no shortage of wood in New Mexico) for these items and for four pairs of skiis. With all this and plenty of other luggage in tow, we set out for New York, where we expected to get on a boat home. We spent a few days in New York. My father had died early in 1945, but we saw our other relatives. There was also some shopping to be done, because the children did not have a single item of clothing that could be worn in England without attracting attention, and clothing was still rationed at home.

Then we were informed that the boat on which we expected to sail was cancelled, but we could get a cabin on a boat from Halifax, Nova Scotia. This meant a long train journey, changing trains in Boston. By now we had thirty-nine pieces of luggage, counting the boxes, and these were somehow ferried to the station and entrusted to the railway. Our train was due in Halifax in the evening, and we expected to spend the night on our boat; but at the last minute we were informed that there would be no embarkation until the following afternoon, and that all hotels in Halifax were full. We phoned ahead to an hotel in Truro, the last stop before Halifax, but they did not know if they would have a vacancy. When our train stopped in Truro, I ran across to the hotel. There was a room, so we tumbled out of the train with our hand luggage, before it left.

In the morning we went on to Halifax. There Gaby suddenly felt sick. We were rather lost in a strange town with a sick child. But I remembered that there was a university and that Henderson, the physics professor there, was a friend of Chadwick's. I phoned him for advice, and he invited us to spend the day at his house, where we were received in the most friendly manner. By the time we boarded the boat Gaby was much better. The crossing was rough again, but by this time dramamine, an anti-seasickness pill developed for soldiers on landing-craft, etc., had become available. With this, Genia survived the crossing but slept most of the time, since these pills make one sleepy.

We arrived in England with a problem. I had been offered a chair in Cambridge, but found it difficult to decide whether to accept the offer or stay in Birmingham. I did not know how the Cambridge system worked, having been rather on the fringes in my Cambridge time, and I did not know how Birmingham would develop in the postwar period. I felt I had to visit both places to make up my mind. But meanwhile we had no house and did not know where to look for one; we did not know where to look for schools; and we did not even know where to have our heavy luggage sent, so we had it stored in Liverpool. Genia and the children went to stay with my brother Alfred near London, and after accompanying them there I set out for Cambridge and Birmingham, having promised to take no more than seven days to make my decision.

In Cambridge I talked with Bragg, the head of the Cavendish Laboratory, who explained some of the administrative problems. One problem arose from the dual structure of the colleges and the university. Most of the academic staff held both college and university appointments, and there had to be some agreement about the level of pay from either source to ensure fair treatment and avoid inequities. Bragg was a member of the committee dealing with this and proudly explained that after (I think) twenty-four meetings they were near a solution. This vista of Cambridge committee work took me aback a little, but back in Birmingham on the evening of the sixth day I was still undecided. So I sat down with a large sheet of paper, drew a line down the middle, and wrote on the left all the reasons I could think of for staying in Birmingham, on the right all those for going to Cambridge. The list on the left became two or three times as long as that on the right. I knew, of course, that a different presentation could have altered the answer, because what is one reason or several reasons is quite arbitrary. But I had written the lists this way, and this showed me that I really wanted to stay, and so I did.

Now we could settle down again. It was impossible to rent a house, but we bought a house whose lease had only a few years to run. This served us for two years, until we found a better one. Genia arranged for schools for the children. Gaby went to King Edward's School, the most competitive girls' school in town. Ronnie probably could not have passed the entrance examination for the corresponding boys' school at that time because he would not have known the specifically English work expected, such as "money sums" in pounds, shillings, and pence. Instead he went to a small private school, West House, which turned out to be outstandingly good.

For me there was much to be done in organising my work, and my relations with the university. I knew from the past that the country had too few theoretical physicists, and that there were not enough centres to train more. It would make sense to build up a school in Birmingham. I had learned that this required a nucleus of staff of some experience, and since the undergraduate teaching of the subject did not require a large staff, I asked the university to create three research fellowships. The request was granted, since money was then reasonably easy to come by.

This meant that our activities would be rather different in character from those of the pure mathematicians, and it seemed inefficient to run both as a single department. A new department of mathematical physics was therefore set up, and the name of my chair was also changed to "mathematical physics", which got rid of the inappropriate "applied mathematics". But finding offices was much more difficult than finding money, and we had to exist in various makeshift quarters until in 1948 two ex-army huts were put up, which served us for a considerable time. By the beginning of the next academic year, October 1946, the three research fellows and an additional lecturer had been appointed, and the first seven research students had arrived. I started to make contact again with recent progress in physics.

I was now settling down to a steady way of life, no longer a bird of passage, though I still used every opportunity for travelling. In writing about the next seventeen years in Birmingham, I shall therefore abandon the mainly chronological presentation of the earlier chapters.

9

Settled in Birmingham

Domestic Life

I shall begin this chapter by writing briefly about our personal lives. We stayed in the short-leased house only until the spring of 1948, when we found a house we really liked. We were about to make a firm offer for it and pay the usual deposit when Genia got a phone message from the estate agent, saying that another prospective buyer was coming in the morning, ready to leave a deposit, but that we could have the house if we could bring our deposit before the end of the afternoon. There was not much time before the banks closed, and such deposits must be paid in cash. Genia tried to phone me at work, but I was not in my office, and nobody knew where I had gone. Several students got on their bicycles to try to find me. By a coincidence, my former secretary, who had left the job when she married Mel Preston, one of our research students, was having tea with Genia when she got the phone call, and from her experience could suggest places where it might be worth looking for me. I got the message just in time to cycle to the bank and carry an envelope full of banknotes to the agents. The house was ours.

Before we moved, our third child, Catherine, or Kitty, was born. For the third time we moved house with a six-week-old baby, though this time the move was only for a distance of two miles. Kitty arrived early, and Genia very dramatically went to the maternity hospital on the eve of a lunchtime meeting of the council of the Atomic Scientists' Association, of which I shall have more to say later, at our house. Genia had bought a goose for the occasion, and before departing for the hospital, she left instructions about cooking it. With these instructions, and with the assistance of Gaby and Ronnie, I produced quite a passable meal.

The new house was early Victorian in date but Georgian in style. It therefore had generous proportions, with the ground floor rooms having 12-foot-high ceilings. It was large enough to allow some sixty people to dance at our parties. It stood on an acre of grounds with many old trees and a large kitchen garden, surrounded by old brick walls. We had eight bedrooms and four rooms downstairs, counting a breakfast room, which became the children's playroom, but not counting the "butler's pantry". There was a cellar with a not very efficient central heating boiler, and a large garage with an old coachman's flat above it. The house, 18 Carpenter Road, was halfway between the city centre and the university, and about 1¼ miles from either. The district was typical of Edgbaston, with many similar houses in the neighbourhood. A golf course stood between us and the university. When I drove visitors home from the university, they felt sure we were leaving town and going into open country.

The house had plenty of room and plenty of storage space. From the start, some members of the department stayed with us; usually there were two, but sometimes more. This helped to spread the cost, and for them it was preferable to the usual lodgings. In addition, we could put up any members of the department or other friends who were in any kind of trouble. So there was always a large "family" at mealtimes. Washing dishes was a collective operation, usually with Genia washing and the rest of us walking in a large circle, picking up a utensil to dry when we passed her. When Gerry Brown stayed with us he introduced us to his favourite Norwegian song, which became the signature tune for washing dishes.

We frequently had parties. Early each term we had one for all the members of the department from research students up, and their wives, to help them become acquainted with the new arrivals. These were not dinner parties, but there were snacks, and word soon got around the department that it was advisable to have no dinner beforehand. The drink was usually cider, and we kept a six-gallon barrel in the house. This habit started during the war, when we discovered that with all the shortages, it was easy to get cider delivered in barrels. In fact, when we phoned to order a new barrel, the supplier, whose customers were mostly innkeepers, might say, "I can't get it to you today; will tomorrow morning do?" During the war, and in the difficult postwar period, this "delay" sounded quite incredible. In the more settled and more prosperous times that followed, the little place that so wonderfully kept us from running dry went out of business, like many good old things.

Christmas was of course a special time for parties. The family spent several days decorating the house, and we had a Christmas tree in the sitting room and a holly tree from the garden in the dining room. Our old dining table from the auction sale in Cambridge was put into full use. When extended it could seat about sixteen, and an additional trestle table increased the capacity to twenty-four. The table remained set over the holidays, and most days it was full. Christmas dinner would start at about 2 P.M., and the guests would leave in the late evening. One Christmas there was a blizzard in the afternoon, which we did not notice, sitting around a cosy fire with curtains drawn. For some of the guests, from Brazil and other warm places, this was their first snow, and they were very excited. But getting home was a problem; there was no public transport, and nobody had the right clothes or shoes for walking. A search of our closets produced an assortment of coats, scarves, galoshes, rubber and skiing boots, and everybody got home without too great hardship.

Other occasions for celebration included weddings. The wedding receptions for, I think, four members of the department were held in our house, although weddings in general were more frequent. We noticed that all our lodgers who occupied one particular room in the house were married either when they lived there, or shortly after they left. One of the last lodgers, Mel Leon, an American research fellow, seemed to be an exception from this tradition. When we went off for the summer, near the end of his time in Birmingham, he had no plans to be married. When we returned from our summer trip, however, we found that he had got married at very short notice just before returning to the United States to a Birmingham girl with whom he had been friendly. The wedding party was in our house, but without us. The reputation of our magic room was restored.

Large-scale entertainment was also called for during conferences. We had two large international conferences in Birmingham, in 1948 and 1953. The first of these was attended by some of our old friends, and the Oppenheimers and the Robert Wilsons stayed with us. At that time food rationing was still quite severe. The housekeeping therefore called for very careful management, and the fact that we had a child of six months added to Genia's problems. But all went well, and when the conference was over, and all the guests had left, Genia wearily sat down on our doorstep to rest in the nice summer weather. Alas, she sat on a wasp, and for a time after that sitting was impossible.

At the 1953 conference we were faced with the added problem that the university was short of money and could not help us with any entertainment expenses, so it all had to come from private enterprise. One evening we had a reception in our house for 160 people, and another evening a dinner for 36. For the dinner, we cleared the furniture from our dining room and borrowed folding chairs and trestle tables from the physics department. Gaby and Ronnie were very efficient waiters. The very successful evening was not even spoiled by the premature arrival of the Cockcrofts, who had mistaken the time of the invitation by an hour. Hearing that guests had come, Genia rushed down the stairs, forgetting that she had not yet put on her skirt; but she was caught and stopped on the stairs by Mary Flowers, who was helping with the preparations.

But more entertainment was needed, and we got the family and members of the department together to write a number of songs parodying Gilbert and Sullivan, which, with a choir collected from the department and friends, provided one evening's diversion. Lines from some of these songs became quite popular. One song, "Academic Career", ended with the lines ". . . and when you have ceased to contribute to knowledge, you may still be the Master of a Cambridge College". (This was at a time when a considerable number of physicists had become college heads.) Another song, lampooning the difficulties with American visas, referred to "fellow-nontravellers".

Running a big house brought some problems, of course. The central heating boiler used coke and had to be stoked several times a day. In cold winters we sometimes ran short of fuel, when the coal merchant could not supply us. In the postwar period you had to be registered with one particular coal merchant, and if he ran out no other would supply you. Small quantities of coke could be bought at the gas works, and a few times we drove there with boxes and sacks to bring back enough fuel to keep us going.

Then came the time to repaint the outside of the house. The Georgian front and side were plastered and the back was brick, but everything was painted and needed a fresh coat. We decided to do the job ourselves, and in the summer we rented some ladders; Ronnie did the top part, I did the middle, and Genia did the lowest. My part was the smallest, as I could not devote too much time to the enterprise. Genia had studied the types of paint available, and selected one that would be easy to apply and last long. The job took a big effort, but it was gratifying to see the house sparkling and clean; it was even more gratifying to see later that the paint lasted at least as long as that on the neighbouring houses that were painted professionally. On completion of the paint job, Genia rewarded Ronnie with a day of theatre in London, which included a matinee and an evening performance, and dinner at Simpsons in between. Compared to this outside work, painting inside was a routine job, at which Genia became an old hand. She did this work mostly at night, to reduce interruptions and to avoid encounters of people with wet paint.

Our last winter in Birmingham, 1962-63, was exceptionally severe.

214

In our street the six-inch water main froze; there had been a leaking gas main, and workmen digging for the gas leak exposed the water main. For some weeks we had to carry water in buckets from a hydrant around the corner. The water department had no way of thawing the pipe; it was too big to use the standard method of passing a current from a welding generator. They were so desperate that they even considered a suggestion I put to them, which was to attach a flexible hose to a steam generator, push the hose into one end of the frozen pipe, and, as the ice melts, push it further until it reaches the other end. They found a suitable steam generator, tried my method, and in a few hours we had our water supply again.

Family

From the house I turn to the family in it. Gaby became a pupil at King Edward's High School for Girls. At the beginning she had to work hard to catch up, even though in the Los Alamos school she had been two years ahead of her age and had taken a correspondence course in Latin. She was always ready to respond to a challenge. Once she had found her feet, she did not consider the school work exciting, and, in spite of her ability, was never higher than the middle of her form. This may have been in her nature, but it did not help that the teaching in an English girls' school was rather pedestrian; girls were not supposed to absorb as much, particularly in science, as boys. King Edward's was the most prestigious girls' school in the area, with entrance by a competitive examination; yet when we compared the material with that of the corresponding boys' school, the difference in level was obvious.

In her last year at school, Gaby decided to take the Oxford University entrance examination. Her teachers thought this was a waste of time, thinking she had no chance of getting in. But this was another challenge, and after a few weeks intense work, she not only gained a place at Oxford, but was the only one from her class to win an "exhibition" (a form of minor scholarship).

In the final examination she gained a second-class Honours degree. Her written work was on the borderline between second and third, and, as is usual, she was called in for a viva voce examination to settle the doubt. One of the board of examiners criticised one of her answers in a written paper. Being very observant, Gaby noticed a gleam in the eye of one of the other examiners, from which she deduced that he

215

agreed with her and not with his colleague. She decided to defend her position, and this no doubt determined the result.

After graduating, she took a job as a research assistant to a medical team, mainly doing statistics. But she was not satisfied with the work. Being very critical, and probably more intelligent than her bosses, she had no confidence in the soundness of their project. After a while she found a post with a firm of investment analysts with offices in Cambridge, where she expressed pleasure at working under a boss who seemed more intelligent than she. She did well in this work, and often found herself at meetings as the only woman in what was still a predominantly male profession. She met Charles Gross, an American graduate student in experimental psychology, and they were married in 1959 in Cambridge. At the Registry Office there was an amusing misunderstanding: while we were waiting in an anteroom, a secretary came to write down some particulars. After getting details from the bridegroom, she turned to Genia, asking her name, age, and so on. Genia was surprised that all this detail was required of a witness, when the secretary asked, "You are the lady who is getting married?" It was of course possible to rectify the mistake and prevent Genia from getting married to Charlie.

The wedding celebrations were held in Gaby's flat in Cambridge. All the food was brought from Birmingham, including the wedding cake, one of Genia's productions. It was decorated with the aid of George Bonnevay, a Frenchman in the department, who was not only a very able theoretical physicist, but a highly talented artist as well. He later died tragically in a mountain-climbing accident. His cake decorations included figures of monkeys, symbolising Charlie's experimental animals. At the party we had very efficient helpers, perhaps a little too efficient in pouring wine, because the wine ran out and more had to be procured in a hurry. It was a very successful party. Gaby and Charlie went to America, where Charlie had an appointment at M.I.T.

Ronnie profited greatly from the two years at West House. This was a small private school, mainly preparing boys for the entrance examination to the big public schools. Their system was to let boys work in mathematics and in classics at their own speed, using written material and consulting teachers when necessary. In other subjects they were taught all together, but each term the best in each form were promoted to the bottom of the next form, so they could never rest on their laurels. Yet the less bright ones were not made to feel inferior— the highest prize of the school was for improvement. In the two years Ronnie thus covered all basic mathematics up to simple calculus; he learned to read Latin poets, write English essays, swim, and, above all, he learned to work.

As a small boy, Ronnie was very absent-minded. This was evident in an episode that was long remembered in the family. The day before a wedding party, for which Genia was planning to do much cooking, our gas supply had been cut off for some emergency repairs, and now her cooker was out of action. Our domestic help offered to lend us an electric hotplate. She lived at the other end of town, and Ronnie was to go home with her and bring back the hotplate. The journey involved two buses. In due course Ronnie returned home without the hotplate—he had left it on the first bus. This tendency wore off gradually; today he is no more absent-minded than the average academic, or his father. He also was untidy, and, like most boys, did not take care of his clothes. One day he came home from school, where he had attended a chemistry class, and as he got off his bicycle, the seat of his trousers fell out. He must have sat in some acid. But all this changed suddenly when he joined the Army Training Corps at school, which involved keeping his uniform trousers well pressed. He studied the technique of ironing, and after he had mastered it, any delicate ironing job required in the family became his.

He had very broad interests but showed an early inclination toward mathematics and physics. This was coupled with an interest in making things, where, however, his dexterity did not always keep pace with his understanding. At one point he wanted to build a radio set and asked for money to buy the necessary parts. I agreed, but stipulated that he should design the set himself, rather than copy a design from the books. I suggested that, after he chose his valves, he should look up their characteristics and then decide on the specification of his other components from first principles. He did as suggested, and the set functioned nicely—for a time. Then a badly soldered connection shorted the high voltage through the valve filaments. He had to obtain replacement valves with his pocket money, and improved his soldering technique.

At age 13 he passed the "Ordinary Level" examination, normally taken at 16. Before he could take the next, or "Advanced Level", examination, new rules banned candidates from taking any examination before the age of 16. This was really intended for the O level, but since his birthday is in September the rule postponed his taking the A level. For the extra year at school his headmaster wanted him to take arts subjects, since he was good at these also. Ronnie did not want to drop the subjects of his main interest for a whole year, so the school arranged a special programme for him, which cut down the amount of time spent on mathematics and added some arts subjects. About this time he came to me and said that he had decided he liked physics more than mathematics, and within physics he liked the theoretical approach best, so, much as he hated the idea, it looked as if he would become a theoretical physicist, like his father.

He sat the Cambridge entrance examination and was awarded a scholarship at Gonville and Caius' College, but he was not allowed to come until he was 18. Since the applied mathematics course in Cambridge involved no physics lectures, he spent the extra year at Birmingham University, where he was given permission to take the first and second-year physics lectures. At Cambridge he found the college meals expensive and unattractive, so he and his friend, Graham McCauley, devised a way of cooking their own meals by fashioning an oven from an old biscuit tin attached to the gas fire. Their range of culinary experiments was limited only by the exclusion of onions and anything else with a strong smell, as cooking in the rooms was illegal. He took part in the activities of the Cambridge Union, the traditional debating society, and ended up being president of the Union, a very unusual distinction for a science student.

While Ronnie was at Cambridge, Hans Bethe came as a visiting professor, and invited him to come to Cornell as a graduate student. Ronnie was on the boat across the Atlantic at the time of his twenty-first birthday. The rest of the family sent him a message, combining a family tradition of cables in verse with the economy of words appropriate to a radiogram to a ship: "A comfortable majority! Your parents and your sorority."

At Cornell he was an active member of a Gilbert and Sullivan group and became friendly with another member, Penny Wilson. One Christmas he gave her a ride to her home in Maplewood, New Jersey, where he met her identical-twin sister, Julie, and they fell in love. He completed his Ph.D. in 1959, married Julie, and came to Birmingham. We did not go to the wedding, since they were coming over shortly afterwards, and we had met Julie earlier in New York. We again kept the family tradition with a rhyming cable:

> Old friend Cupid, never stupid, this time extra good,
> Tied up truly Ron and Julie in a shady Maplewood.
> We'd like to come across from Brum, alas we are not able—
> Too high the fare to get us there, so all our love by cable.

"Brum" was the colloquial name for Birmingham, where they stayed the next two years, while he held a postdoctoral fellowship awarded by NATO. They then returned to the United States. Their oldest child, our first grandson, was born soon after their arrival in Princeton, where Ronnie had a fellowship at the Institute for Advanced Study.

Sending Gaby and Ronnie to their universities had caused a financial crisis. As a short-term measure, Genia decided to take in a lodger on a commercial basis, in place of my collaborators, who were just contributing to the expenses. For a time we had a business woman, who owned clothes shops in a working-class area, for board and lodging. It was an interesting experience, meeting at close quarters someone from so different a walk of life.

As a longer-term contribution, I decided to write a popular book. I had started to write a book once before, in 1934 in Manchester, when a little extra income would have been welcome. It was to be a textbook on quantum mechanics, of which about one-third got written (and survives somewhere) before I was sidetracked. The new book was a nonmathematical, no-jargon account of physics, which I had thought about for some time, called *The Laws of Nature*. This time I did finish it, perhaps because there was a dictating machine available, on which I dictated the whole text right through; only a few odd pages had to be retyped. It was published by Allen & Unwin in 1955 and sold very well, including a number of translations. It did not earn me a fortune, but it did make a nice, if belated, contribution to the family financial crisis.

Perhaps the best part of the book is the dedication, which, following Genia's suggestion, reads: "To the Treasurer of Somerville College, Oxford, and the Bursar of Caius' College, Cambridge, but for whom this book would not have been written." (These are the officials who send out the bills for the students' fees.) I sent copies, of course, to the two college officers, and the Treasurer of Somerville was highly amused. The acknowledgment from the bursar of Caius' sounded as if he had not seen the point, and he had not when I met him months later: "I believe it has something to do with your son being a student here?" He was a bachelor living in college, and was unfamiliar with the ways, and the financial problems, of the rest of us.

Kitty, whose dramatic arrival has already been mentioned, grew up as a very pretty girl with a great practical sense. She had an amazing memory and great powers of observation. One summer, before we went on holiday, a newspaper had published a long list of holiday resorts and dates on which one of their reporters would visit each beach, giving a prize to children who recognised him. When we told Kitty the name of the resort we were selecting for our vacation (which had not previously been mentioned), she said, "Oh good, we shall be there when the reporter comes!" In another incident, a Swiss au pair had, on leaving, given a pair of shoes that no longer fitted her to our domestic help, Mrs. Jackson. Not until six months or so later, Mrs. Jackson came to our house wearing these shoes. Kitty was horrified: "But Mrs. Jackson, how *can* you wear Bertie's shoes!"

She was four when King George VI died. She had not heard of death before, and it worried her. When told that it was mostly old people who died, she insisted "But my Daddy is very new!" That night she could not get to sleep. "Mummy, you are teasing me. Only kings die!"

A typical episode took place when Kitty was nine. Genia had gone to Oxford for a day to visit Lady Simon, whose husband, Francis Simon, had just died. This was during school vacation, so Genia asked Anne, a research student staying in our house, to work at home and keep an eye on the children for the day. But almost as soon as she had left, Anne developed intense stomach cramps and became completely incapacitated. She asked Kitty to phone the doctor, but our doctor was not available. So Kitty decided to call the emergency services by dialling 999, and asked for a doctor. The answer was, "We don't send doctors, dear." Kitty said, "Then you better send an ambulance, because I have a very sick lady here." She then went to Anne: "The ambulance is coming; I shall pack a suitcase for you." She did, and it turned out that she had remembered everything Anne would need for a few days in hospital, except she forgot the slippers, and later was very embarrassed by this omission. When the ambulance men came they asked Kitty if there was a bedpan available. Kitty at first did not know what this was, but then she remembered—"a pot for grown-ups"—and found it. As the men departed with Anne, Kitty had the presence of mind to ask to what hospital they were taking her. Later a policeman called, as is usual with emergency calls, and asked for Anne's home address. Kitty did not know, but she went to Anne's desk and found some letters which had been addressed to her home, and gave the address to the policeman. After this episode we felt it was not important to provide babysitters for Kitty; she was more resourceful than most babysitters!

She went to several private schools in succession, but the standard of teaching was rather mixed. Particularly in arithmetic there was a tendency to learn mathematical operations as a ritual that had no explanation. After one change of school Kitty came home with the comment, "Miss Smith is wonderful! She explains things!"

But it soon became clear that Kitty had a peculiar phobia about examinations. The better she knew the subject, the worse her performance in the exam. As a result she did not get a place in the competitive King Edward's High School, and had to continue in private schools. This disability would cause her many problems later.

In 1949 we had another daughter, Joanna, or Jo, our only child who did not move house at the age of six weeks. Shortly before her birth, I was lecturing in Sweden and was naturally anxious to have news from home. Genia had no resident help, and if the new baby had arrived early, like Kitty, there would have been a problem. International phone calls were not as easy then as they are today, and the mail was faster than it is now. Yet I received no letter and was getting anxious. Finally a letter arrived. It was addressed to me c/o Professor Gustafson at the Physics Department of the University, Lund. But Genia's handwriting is not always legible, and the post office had read "Zurich" for "Lund". It reached the department in Zurich, where someone recognized the name Gustafson, and redirected it to Lund. The whole process took only four days—an impressive performance. And in fact, I returned home before Joanna was born.

As a small baby she gave a good deal of trouble, and our charming old Russian doctor suspected there was something odd about her, but he could not define it. He advised us to consult a famous paediatrician, Sir Leonard Parsons. When I returned from a brief meeting in America and phoned from London airport, Genia said she was about to go to Parsons. By the time I got home, I found her completely shattered. Parsons had told her that Joanna was a dwarf.

After recovering from the shock, Genia went to the libraries for all available information about dwarfs. "Achondroplasic dwarf" had been Parson's expression, which denotes the type with short arms and legs, frequently seen as clowns in the circus. She learned that, after overcoming various troubles with their health during their first year, dwarfs can look forward to a normal life and are usually of a cheerful disposition. Soon Genia had so good a command of the literature that Parsons, who was preparing a new edition of a book of his that contained a chapter on dwarfs, asked her to help him write it. It was clear that we should accept Jo's condition as a fact and not brood over it, and that we should try to get her to accept it, as well, and not to feel sorry for herself. The burden of putting these ideas into practice fell almost entirely on Genia, and the success is due in part to her, and in part to Jo's nature.

There were of course many problems. As a small child, Jo could not get up when she had fallen down, because the arms, with which a normal person pushes herself up, were too short. Genia tried various methods with her, and eventually worked out a technique for her to get up. But in many ways she was still awkward and clumsy. It was

221

important for her to learn to use her body to its best advantage, but nobody in the family had the skills to teach her. After searching everywhere, Genia found the solution in an article in a women's magazine. It described a Danish woman in London, a Mrs. Dane, who was a wizard in the physical education of handicapped children, and could often bring about great improvements even in the case of spastics. Genia went to see her and was greatly impressed. Jo was not yet three, but we arranged for her to stay in a home for children near London, from where she would be taken to Mrs. Dane for regular gymnastics lessons. Genia explained the plan to her, saying that just as Gaby was going to her "school" in Oxford to learn certain things, Jo would go to a school in London to learn to use stairs. A week later Kitty reported joyfully that Jo had learned to go up the stairs on her own, so she would not have to go to London! But we proceeded as planned, and Jo spent six months, with some interruptions, in London. When she came back, her movements were those of a dancer. She had also become very pugnacious, having learned from the other children in the home to assert herself.

Her outstanding characteristic was (and still is) her lively and cheerful personality. When Genia was out with the two small girls, passersby had eyes only for Jo, although Kitty was a very pretty and pleasant child. In fact, contrary to expectation, Genia had to build up Kitty to save her from being completely overshadowed by Jo. Jo learned to read and write early, and she always knew how to get around a difficulty. This was shown by an amusing episode. We were on holiday when Jo appeared and asked for the *Times*. When asked what she wanted it for, she said "I am writing to X, and I want to say I am having a good time; but I have forgotten how to spell 'time', so I want to copy 'Times' but leave the 's' off."

Kitty and Jo were always good friends. Kitty did not mind Jo being the centre of attention, and as a matter of course she gave assistance when necessary. The normal person does not realise the many occasions when being short can cause a problem, such as high door locks or handles, phone booths with high instruments, and so on. Gadgets can help; for example, we had a small folding ladder of aluminium made, which Jo could carry in her satchel and use to reach some of these things. She was very strong and absolutely fearless. At school she insisted on doing gymnastics with the others on full-size apparatus, which caused her many accidents. She was taken to hospital for an X-ray about once a term on the average, but never broke a bone. When her dancing class gave a public performance, she appeared in the costume of a poodle. Her stage presence was such that she got a round of applause just on her entrance. She also did not make it to King Edward's School, although she was bright enough. In her case the reason was that she was just not interested in academic subjects. So she, too, continued in private school.

Klaus Fuchs

Our most traumatic experience was the Fuchs case in early 1950. Out of the blue came a phone call from a journalist that Fuchs had been arrested and charged with giving secret information to the Soviet Union. Did I have any comments? I had no comments, but asked the man to get me more particulars. He rang back and reported that at the hearing Fuchs had been asked whether he had a lawyer to defend him, and he answered he did not know where to find one.

I decided that, whatever the merits of the situation, which still seemed quite unbelievable, he ought to have a lawyer to speak for him, and I took the next train to London. It was already evening, and the next morning I phoned the police, asking their permission to visit Fuchs. (Actually, no permission was needed, but I did not know that.) They were very helpful, but asked that I come to see them before going to the prison. I agreed and saw Commander Burt, the head of the "Special" (i.e., political) branch of Scotland Yard. The reason he wanted to talk with me was that, while Fuchs had admitted everything, he would not identify his contacts. If I saw him, could I try to persuade him to do so? This seemed to me reasonable, and I promised to do what I could. He also asked me whether Fuchs's pro-communist views had been evident. "No," I said, "he never talked much about his political views, but gave the impression that he shared our general views. I knew, of course, that he had been strongly left-wing as a student, but that is very common with young people." Burt laughed: "I know; my son is like that." He also expressed regret that a talented young man would have to be locked up for a considerable time, but that was the law, and nothing could be done about it.

I went on to Brixton Prison to see Fuchs. By this time he did have a lawyer, so my main errand had become unnecessary. We had a long talk. Yes, he had given secret information to Soviet contacts. He now regretted it, as he had since then learned to appreciate our way of life and our values. I expressed surprise that, as a sceptical scientist, he had been willing to accept the Marxist orthodoxy. He replied, "You must remember what I went through under the Nazis. Besides, it was always my intention, when I had helped the Russians to take over

223

everything, to get up and tell them what is wrong with their system."
Shaken by the arrogance and naiveté of this statement, I returned
home.

Genia decided to write him a letter pointing out the damage he had
done to people, particularly to his junior collaborators at Harwell, the
Atomic Energy Research Establishment, with whom he had built up
excellent relations, and who must now feel their confidence betrayed.
At the same time we were still wondering whether to believe the story.
We did not know exactly the nature of the charge, but we did know
that the only evidence to be presented in court was his own confession.
Could it be that he had a brainstorm and invented the whole thing,
or built up some minor indiscretion into a major crime?

Genia and I recollected many facts that seemed to be inconsistent
with Fuchs's involvement in spying. We remembered, for example,
that he had often drunk quite heavily in Los Alamos. He never got
drunk, but how could a spy take such a risk? Above all, he was about
to adopt a nephew of his, the son of his sister who had committed
suicide under the Nazis. The boy had been looked after by Fuchs's
father, who was getting old. With a dangerous secret hanging over
him, was it believable that he would tie a child so closely to him? We
decided to visit him again to ask about these contradictions. We saw
him on the day before his trial, though we did not know this at the
time. He could not really offer an explanation for his inconsistent
behaviour, but he convinced us that the charges were justified.

I formed the impression that his conversion from communism was
genuine. His communist friends in Germany must have instilled in
him a rather unfavourable picture of Britain, which life in Bristol and
Edinburgh, where he perhaps still associated with left-wing friends,
did not dispel. The internment, here and in Canada, must also have
caused resentment. It was only when he lived in a small and intimate
community that he saw the other side of life in our society.

Perhaps the process of understanding took so long because in our
intellectual circles we are curiously shy about saying what we believe.
Our style is not to use any words with capital letters. We don't mind
talking about what is wrong and what we want to fight, but we find
it much harder to talk about moral principles and about what is right.
Our behaviour follows quite firm rules, but somehow we feel it is bad
taste to spell them out, and they have to be discovered by observing
how we act.

During the trial the dates of Fuchs's various contacts were mentioned, starting with his visit to the Soviet Embassy almost as soon as
he started work in Birmingham. All these coincided with the myste-

rious periods when he was feeling unwell, as Genia remembered. He was sentenced to fourteen years in prison, of which he served the usual two-thirds, after earning maximum remission as a model prisoner. On release he went to East Germany, joining the atomic-energy research laboratory in Rossendorf. He evidently reverted to his belief in communism, which was perhaps prompted by the British government's decision to revoke his British nationality. He became deputy director of the laboratory, and by an almost unbelievable quirk of fate found himself acting as director when his boss, Dr. Barwich, defected to the West.

I learned later that, in the course of tracing the source of leaks from Los Alamos, the evidence indicated at one stage that a theoretician in the British group was responsible, which pointed to Fuchs and me. I must therefore have been under great suspicion for a time, but at no stage was I made to feel it. Public opinion in Britain, while shocked by the affair, showed no hysteria. This cannot be said of the press. One of the Sunday papers ran a front-page headline reading "Perturbed Men", with photographs of a number of refugee scientists, including mine, over a story claiming that we were all afraid of antirefugee prejudice triggered by the Fuchs affair. I wrote a firm reply headed "I Am Not Perturbed", which they were decent enough to publish.

Naturally the affair brought us much attention from the press, and many requests for comments. I always refused to comment, saying I would make any public comment in my own time and in my own way, but I was willing to help them get the facts straight, if they would not quote me. After agreeing to this, several papers printed long statements attributed to me that had no similarity to anything I said. Genia chided me for talking to them at all, and when the *News of the World* phoned to speak to her, she firmly refused to say anything. Next Sunday the *News of the World* ran a column in quotes under her name. You cannot win.

Research

Most of my time in Birmingham, as well as during the later years in Oxford, was spent on research, and on looking after research students. In this respect I kept my interests very broad, though the general tendency for physicists, even theoreticians, was now to specialise and to regard themselves as solid-state, or nuclear, or high-energy physicists, and so on, if not even narrower—as specialists in magnetism, or in the optical properties or ionic crystals, say. I never followed this fashion. Perhaps this was because I did not like to choose, or because I followed, conservatively, the practice that had been common in the early days of quantum mechanics.

There is an old definition of the specialist as a man who learns more and more about less and less, until he knows everything about nothing, whereas the generalist learns less and less about more and more until he knows nothing about everything. This description of the generalist is only a slight exaggeration of my approach. So instead of moving, like a bird of passage, from one place to another, I was now moving from one subject to another in the same place. I believe there are advantages in having some generalists: science would lose if all scientists were narrow specialists; it might be even worse if all were generalists.

Research in theoretical physics serves, in principle, two distinct purposes. One is to consolidate and extend our knowledge of the basic laws of nature, mainly by analysing and interpreting experimental results and suggesting further kinds of experimental tests. The other is to apply these laws to practical situations, and to devise ways of exploiting them for useful purposes.

In the actual day-to-day work of the theoretical physicist these two aspects become closely intermingled. We do not convince ourselves that the laws we have formulated are correct, or rather that they are a good approximation to the truth, by the single "crucial" experiment, though this can certainly strengthen our belief in a particular interpretation. Firm confidence arises from the command over practical situations that the application of these laws gives us.

The engineer's facility for designing electric machinery, the physicist's success in building accelerators for particles moving with speeds near that of light, and the functioning of nuclear power stations leave no doubt that our knowledge of the laws of electromagnetism, of relativistic mechanics, or of nuclear physics is adequate. A deeper study of the underlying causes can, of course, bring further refinements.

Studying applications is usually not just a matter of formal problem solving. In any real situation in the laboratory or in industry there are many more factors than even the most powerful computer can take account of. The theoretician has to decide which of these are essential for the purpose in hand. He has to find the right question to ask of the laws of physics, and that is often more difficult than finding the answer.

One of the subjects in which I retained an interest was quantum electrodynamics, and more generally quantum field theory. I still pursued the idea of changing the theory so as to get rid of the infinities.

The infinite self-energy is due to the fact that the electron is a point charge, and if, as Lorentz had in mind, one could assume it to have a finite size, the self-energy would be finite. But a rigid body is not compatible with relativity, basically because it is spread out in space but not in time, whereas relativity insists on treating space and time in the same way.

Our idea, which was pursued in collaboration with Hugh McManus, who had returned to Birmingham, and John Irving, the new lecturer, was to set up a theory in which the equations were spread out in time as well as in space. In a classical framework this is easily done, and the resulting equations seem quite satisfactory, but we saw no way of translating them into quantum theory. I kept worrying about this problem, and in 1952 found a new way of introducing the quantum rules, which did not obviously exclude the "non-local" theories; but I was unable to prove that this would work for the McManus type of equations. I came back to the problem in 1954, with Max Chrétien, a postdoctoral visitor from Switzerland, and we found a new form of the theory, more adapted to treating the electrons as waves. We still could not carry out the complete programme of introducing quantum rules, but a guess at the nature of the quantum equations suggested that the infinities were getting worse than in the local theory. In the latter there are two infinitely large terms that cancel each other approximately; in our equations one of these was made finite, so that a larger difference remained. Of course, if a quantity becomes infinitely large, it does not matter how quickly it grows; but what we had achieved was evidently no improvement.

Meanwhile it had been discovered that the infinities were no obstacle to progress. If the mass of an electron is made up of its intrinsic, or mechanical, mass and its self-energy, which by Einstein's relation $E = mc^2$ also contributes to the mass, only their sum, the total mass, is observable. If one of these contributions is infinite, there is nothing to stop us assuming the other also to be infinite with the opposite sign, so that the total can be finite. Subtracting infinities is not a very clean operation, but the essential step was to see that in any practical situation involving electromagnetic effects the answer could be unambiguously expressed in terms of the total mass of a free electron, without worrying about the mechanical mass and the self-mass separately.

This conclusion was stimulated by experiments (Lamb and Retherford) showing a small displacement of one of the spectral lines of the hydrogen atom, which called for an explanation. Several people tried to calculate this displacement from the existing theory. It turned out that the displacement, expressed in terms of the real electron mass, agreed well with the experiment. This procedure was put on a systematic basis by Julian Schwinger and Richard Feynman. Some of the basic ideas had been put forward independently by S. Tomonaga in Japan, who had to work often in shelters during air raids. Since then calculations using this new quantum electrodynamics have been carried out with increasing accuracy, and they agree with experiments whose accuracy even exceeds that of the theory. This impressive success is achieved in spite of the infinities, but I would still feel happier if there were a theory in which the infinities did not appear at all.

Of course we learned the new methods, and several of the members of the department made contributions to their applications. I discussed their work with them, but I did not work in this field myself. Much of the work was inspired by G. E. ("Gerry") Brown, who arrived in 1949 and of whom I shall say more later, and then by Paul Matthews, lecturer from 1952-57. Interest gradually shifted to the application of similar methods to the new fields representing the new particles that were being discovered, and this was reflected in a number of studies in the department. Here, too, Matthews and others took the lead.

Nuclear physics had been one of my interests before the war. Now better experiments at higher energies were providing information about the forces that hold the nucleus together, and techniques for analysing these experiments were required; I made a modest contribution to these. The question came up whether nuclei were capable of rotating, and some learned papers gave proofs that this was not possible, just as an atom does not rotate as a whole. But the experiment showed that some nuclei do rotate, and the problem was now how to describe this rotation and to estimate the moment of inertia, which determines the rotational energy. One way of tackling this problem was proposed in a paper I wrote with Jean Yoccoz, a young Frenchman. The method of this paper was improved much later by David Thouless and me.

The success of the concept of the compound nucleus, consisting of strongly interacting nucleons, which Niels Bohr introduced in 1936, had mesmerised everybody into believing that there was no chance of describing nuclei in terms of the more or less independent motion of individual nucleons, the so-called shell model. Therefore the success of this model in 1959 came as a great surprise. Some of us, notably Brian Flowers and later Gerry Brown, studied various applications of the model. Some of these techniques had been developed earlier by Herman Jahn, the most senior of my first batch of research fellows. There was also the problem of understanding why the shell model worked and how it could be reconciled with Bohr's compound-nucleus model. I devoted much time and thought to this problem, but was never satisfied with the results. I had students working on other problems in nuclear physics.

Before the war much of my work had been in solid-state physics, but there had been a great expansion of work in that area, so that I felt out of date, though there were a few problems I could suggest to students. I recovered my connection with solid-state physics in an unusual way. In 1953 I gave a course of lectures on solid-state physics at the summer school at Les Houches, which I will describe later. This required, for once, written lecture notes, which I decided to turn into a book. In writing the notes, and in later revising them for the book, I realised that many of the problems I had regarded as open questions fifteen years earlier were still unsolved. This related in particular to problems in the theory of conductivity. I therefore decided to return to these problems, and started discussions with colleagues in the department. Geoffrey Chester, who on arriving in 1956 had worked on liquid helium (which is traditionally treated together with solid-state problems, though it is not very solid!), became interested, and so did Armin Thellung, a visitor from Switzerland, and Sam Edwards, who had come in 1953 with experience in field theory and nuclear physics. From their work and that of several students resulted important clarifications.

In the course of tidying up the material for my book, I looked carefully at the way the atoms in a metal crystal hang together, partly as a result of the almost free electrons moving between them. I noticed that in one dimension, i.e., in a linear chain, the periodic structure, with all distances between adjacent atoms equal, is not stable and will always suffer some distortion. This seemed at first a very bizarre result, and I wondered whether there was a flaw in my reasoning. I put my argument to Maurice Pryce, then in Oxford and one of the most critical theoreticians I know, but he could not see anything wrong. So I put the argument in my book. It seemed an academic point, as there are no one-dimensional metals in nature. Some twenty years later, when experiments on nearly one-dimensional organic crystals, in which molecules are arranged in long chains, showed a novel type of transition, my old result was remembered. The "Peierls transition" or "Peierls instability" has now become a standard term. I prefer the first version, which does not appear to suggest that I am unstable.

In this summary of the main topics of concern to the department I have omitted some items that are hard to categorise, and a few that are too complicated to explain in a few words.

229

Members of the Department and Their Problems

These activities were carried out by a large number of people spending various periods of time in the department. Some 180 members passed through the department while I was there. Many of them were research students, of whom the British ones were usually supported by research studentships on government funds. We were unable to give any financial support to foreign students, with very rare exceptions. They depended on support from their home countries, except for a few grants from the British Council, for which they had to compete with candidates in all subjects and destined for all universities. We had a few lectureships, whose numbers rose slightly during the period, and research fellowships, which decreased in number, plus occasional special grants. Many of the foreign postdoctoral visitors brought their own grants.

Considering the reputation of Birmingham as an ugly industrial city, one could feel sure that those who chose to come did so for the physics, not to have a good time. This is true in spite of a conversation we had with Jean Yoccoz, after he had returned to Paris, and with his wife, who had been in Birmingham with him for part of the time. We asked how they were, and were told, "Oh, it is so hard to settle down in Paris after you have been in Birmingham!" No doubt they were referring to the atmosphere among physicists, and not to the beauty or attractiveness of the city.

Although, as I have said, Birmingham was much better than its reputation, conditions for visiting scholars were difficult. Accommodation was very hard to find, particularly for people with families. For those from overseas, we usually had to try to find accommodation before their arrival, and sometimes we had to ask them to give us carte blanche to act for them, since available places tended to be snatched up very quickly. We sometimes had to act even on behalf of people moving from elsewhere in England. Before Paul Matthews moved from Cambridge, Genia had shown him a variety of houses to find out what he liked. When a suitable house came on the market, he could not come to inspect it, as his wife was in the maternity hospital; Genia therefore had to phone him for authority to buy the house on his behalf. However, Matthews had no telephone in Cambridge, so we had to phone a colleague of his. He in turn cycled to Matthews' house to get him to phone us before the deadline set by the house agent.

We could usually get some help from the university's lodgings warden with these housing problems. Her main duty was to find lodgings for undergraduates, but she did what she could for more senior people.

230

The available accommodation always had some drawbacks, mostly relating to inadequate heating. In the forties and fifties central heating was still the exception in England, and one could not find it in furnished houses or flats at a modest rent. For visitors from warmer climates, or from well-heated America, this was specially painful.

During a particularly cold winter, Baqi Bég, a very bright postdoctoral Pakistani, and his American wife Nancy were living in a flat across the road from us, and were miserably cold. We always had some people staying in our big house, but usually only single people. As we had some room to spare and felt sorry for the Bégs, we asked them to stay with us. As they moved, I noticed Mrs. Bég carrying a heavy suitcase across the road. Her husband had evidently not yet lost the Eastern prejudice that it is infra dig for a scientist to carry baggage. So I said, "This is too heavy for you, Nancy; let me take it." After that he carried the rest.

The visitors had many other problems. They often had to adjust to a new language, and to a different way of life; they were not familiar with the system of medical care, of shopping, of schools. Sometimes the baggage they had brought on the boat took a week or two to arrive from the port, and they were short of essentials. Some had their first children in Birmingham and were badly in need of advice. All these problems tended to land on Genia's shoulders, and she was quite busy as a general counsellor to newcomers. She had not forgotten her own problems in Manchester and the value of every little piece of advice and help she received, so she was in a good position to know what was needed. She referred to these Birmingham-born children as her "grandchildren by proxy". She keeps a warm interest in their careers, and sees them with pleasure when we meet them on our travels.

If I now try to look back at the multitude of names and faces, I remember most of them very clearly, though I would be rather hazy about dates if I did not have some records to help. But some individuals single themselves out in my memory, for various reasons; some because we formed particularly close friendships with them; some because of the special nature of their work; and some because of especially amusing episodes involving them.

Senior Collaborators

Gerry Brown arrived late in 1949 after completing his Ph.D. under Gregory Breit at Yale, which apparently had been a rather gruelling experience. Breit was a theoretician of great merit, but he ran his

231

group and his students in a very dictatorial manner and in accordance with his many prejudices. Gerry blossomed in the very different atmosphere of our department. He became one of our lodgers, and in domestic matters he displayed the same enthusiasm and determination as in physics or teaching. He was a keen gardener and reproached us for the wasteful practice of burning weeds. One should leave them on top of the soil, where they would dry up and decay. He tried this on some vegetable beds he tended, and was surprised that the weeds refused to dry up but took root again, the English climate being rather different from that of his home in South Dakota. At parties he proved himself an excellent dancer, often unconventional and wild: he could do a passable imitation of a Cossack dance, and another dance involved skipping over a handkerchief held in both hands, a feat our children and the au pair girl struggled for days to imitate.

In research he was equally passionate. Early in his Birmingham period he started to work with students, whom he infected with his enthusiasm and perseverance. He also found time to learn languages, including Russian, German, and later Danish. He stayed in our house until his marriage in 1952 to Traudl, a very attractive and strong-willed German girl. Their wedding reception was one of several held in our house. By the time he left in 1960 to go to Copenhagen, he had been a research fellow, then a lecturer, and finally a second professor.

Max Krook was one of our original research fellows. He is a South African who did astrophysics in Cambridge and then returned to Capetown. He now wanted to extend his knowledge of modern theoretical physics. He also stayed in our house for two periods, but at one time he stayed with Kynch and his wife in a flat. He then went away for a time and returned to Birmingham while the Kynches were away. He needed a suitcase he had left in their flat, and went to fetch it. The lady on the floor below was surprised to hear steps, as she knew the Kynches were not there. When she looked out there was a big man coming down the stairs with a suitcase, who smiled at her apologetically and said, "I am Krook." For some time after this experience she refused to stay alone in her flat.

Krook was a great Bohemian; he was also rather absent-minded. When he volunteered to paint the floor of his room in our house, together with Ronnie, they ended up painting themselves into a corner. In the course of time he became more practical, and more "bourgeois". He is now a professor of astrophysics at Harvard, and during a visit there we found him very concerned about his property, and about little boys who were damaging his garden.

He became very friendly with Bruno Ferretti, who came from Rome for a year. Ferretti was the only senior theoretician left in Rome when Wick emigrated to America, and he took his responsibility very seriously. He followed all developments in fundamental physics in detail and worked out many of the answers for himself.

He and Krook made a curious pair, Krook being tall and solid, Ferretti short and slight. They did some good work together, including a new method of solving the Schrödinger equation. At one point they resolved to take a short vacation together, and agreed to meet at a certain time on Sunday morning to discuss the details. Each of them thought they were meeting at the place of the other. So Ferretti went punctually to our house, where Krook was then staying, found nobody at home and sat patiently on the doorstep to wait for Krook, who had at the same time, but by a different route, gone to Ferretti's lodgings, and was sitting on that doorstep. After waiting half an hour, both decided to give up, and returned home, again by different routes.

Ferretti gave a course of lectures to our graduate students, which were excellent but hard to understand because he used the Italian names for the letters, and when, in discussing an equation, he referred to "acca vu" the students had trouble recognising this as $h\nu$. His first lecture was inaudible: the wooden dais was very resonant, and while he lectured he would march up and down in his heavy boots so that the sound of his steps drowned out his voice, except for one word at the end of each traverse, when he turned. I drew his attention to the difficulty, and he promised to remedy it. I expected he would try to keep still, but he knew that ingrained habits are not so easily abandoned. For the next lecture he turned up in galoshes.

The youngest of our initial research fellows was Tony Skyrme. He married Dorothy, a lecturer in the Physics Department. They chose to have a proper wedding, with grey top hats and all. Max Krook was to be best man, and this raised a question: how could one make sure that the absent-minded best man would not lose the ring before the ceremony? Genia had the solution: put the ring on the side of his glasses. When the minister called for the ring, he was slightly startled to see the best man take off his glasses, but the ring appeared and all was well. The wedding reception was in our house, of course.

In 1948 Skyrme moved to Harwell and worked on many topics. Perhaps his best-known work is the invention of the "Skyrme force", a simplified version of the nuclear force, with which one can do simple calculations to explain many properties of nuclei. Recently another very abstract concept he invented has become famous under the name "Skyrmions". After a visit to Australia, the Skyrmes stopped in Malaysia on the way back; they found it attractive, and Tony accepted a three-year appointment at the University of Malaysia. From there he returned in 1964 to become my successor in Birmingham.

Dick Dalitz joined us in 1949. He was then still working on his Cambridge Ph.D. thesis, but he was so mature that he was immediately given a research fellowship. He was already then of impressive ability, and tackled every problem with a thoroughness that let him find the points that others had overlooked. He is by now a well-known authority in particle physics, and is much in demand for review articles or lectures. He always insists on making these completely comprehensive—perhaps sometimes more than the occasion demands. Each of the reviews therefore requires a considerable effort, and since he finds it difficult to refuse an invitation, he often finds himself hard-pressed for time. One of his most important pieces of work was the proof that one particle, the K-meson, had different decay modes, which, if the law of parity conservation held good, could not belong to the same particle; this was an important step in the discovery of parity nonconservation. After a stay in the United States and a brief further period in Birmingham, he held a professorship in Chicago; but in 1963 he returned to a Royal Society research professorship in Oxford.

In Birmingham he was involved in the famous episode of Walter Kohn's briefcase. Walter Kohn, then a young but distinguished Canadian theorist, was in Birmingham for a brief visit. Dalitz looked after him, and brought him to our house for dinner in his ancient, almost vintage, Austin 7. All of Kohn's luggage was left in the open car while it was parked in the drive of our house during dinner. When they left, there was no briefcase. This was a serious problem, because the briefcase contained Kohn's passport, tickets, and a year's work. Nobody knew for sure whether it had been in the car or left somewhere else. They drove around, retracing all their steps, and, finding no briefcase, finally decided it was stolen and went to the police, who were not very hopeful. By this time the Austin 7 had broken down, so they took a taxi to explore the neighbourhood of our house: perhaps the thief had discarded the briefcase after taking any valuables. The taxi shone its headlights into every drive, and this attracted the attention of the local policeman on the beat. It turned out he had arrested the thief just outside our drive—a shabbily dressed man, just released from jail—and the shiny American briefcase had looked incongruous.

A very unique and imaginative member of the department was Freeman Dyson. Much detail of parts of his life can be found in his excellent book, *Disturbing the Universe* (Harper and Row, 1979). After the

234

war he was a pure mathematician of distinction in Cambridge. There is a story, perhaps apocryphal, of a conversation he had with Harish-Chandra, then working in theoretical physics. According to this story, Harish-Chandra said, "Theoretical physics is getting very complicated. I have decided to change to pure mathematics," with Dyson replying, "I agree that theoretical physics is becoming very complicated. I have therefore decided to become a theoretical physicist."

He came to ask my advice, and among several good ways of getting into the subject I suggested he go to Cornell to work under Hans Bethe. He did move to Cornell. There he made an important contribution to the new quantum electrodynamics, by proving the equivalence of the procedures of Schwinger and Feynman, and proving that all the terms in the infinite series introduced by them were satisfactory. He came back to England for two years, which he spent as a Royal Society Research Fellow in Birmingham. Incidentally, it was no accident that so many British physicists returned to England for two years after a stay in America, because those who had entered the United States on an exchange visitors' visa were not eligible for an immigration visa before they had spent two years elsewhere.

For the first year Dyson stayed with us. The children made fun of his slow and meticulous way of eating, which they claimed included carefully peeling each pea. He had periods when he felt that he had run out of imagination, and that he would never again have an original idea in physics. At such times he would seriously talk about changing his profession, perhaps to study medicine. But each time, the next challenging idea appeared before long, and all such doubts were forgotten.

He had never taken the trouble to get a Ph.D., and it seemed to us an attractive idea that he might get a doctor's degree from Birmingham. He was by now too distinguished for a mere Ph.D; and the right level was clearly the D.Sc. In many universities this can be given only to their own graduates, but for some technical reason Dyson was not eligible for a Cambridge D.Sc. In Birmingham this degree was also restricted to Birmingham graduates, but I had qualified in Manchester for a D.Sc. and did not see why Birmingham should be less generous. I persuaded the university to abolish the restriction, but in the end Dyson did not stay the full two years. He had taken one term off, and to ask for yet another concession would have been too much. So he never got a regular doctorate; by now he has no doubt honorary doctorates instead.

Another lasting friendship developed with Brian and Mary Flowers. I first became aware of him as a promising and lively experimentalist at Harwell. After a wartime undergraduate course at Cambridge he had been directed into experimental nuclear physics, but his heart was in theoretical research. Eventually he was seconded for two years to Birmingham for theoretical research training. So, in 1950, a dashing young man with a sporty red M.G. appeared in Birmingham.

This was at the time when the nuclear shell model had become a promising tool, and Flowers made this his field. Several students followed his lead, and many contributions to the subject resulted. At the time the shell model and the "liquid drop" model pursued particularly by Aage Bohr in Copenhagen seemed mutually exclusive alternatives, and this caused a mock rivalry between Aage and Brian. Each teased the other about the weaknesses of his model, but they were the best of friends. We could exploit the new liberalised rules resulting from the abortive attempt to get a Birmingham D.Sc. for Dyson to get one for Flowers.

He and Mary married while he was in Birmingham. Mary had been the wife of Oskar Bünemann at Harwell, but was divorced. Before the wedding she stayed with us while the divorce was becoming final, and wedding arrangements were made. Mary has unlimited energy and is always perfectly organised. Perhaps these qualities came out most obviously many years later, when at a large party in their house one of her sons ran into a glass door: he was given first aid and taken to hospital, the blood was wiped up, and the party continued.

Brian makes decisions easily. He knows that nothing in life is perfect, that you can never find the ideal solution, but have to accept a good approximation and stick to it. He is good with people and is always aware of their problems. If they need help or just warm interest, he and Mary will take great trouble. With these qualities he rose rapidly in status and responsibility. On returning to Harwell, he was put in charge of the Theoretical Physics Division. Cockcroft, the director of Harwell, felt he was taking a chance in this promotion because of Brian's lack of experience, but I encouraged him to go ahead.

After Harwell, Flowers moved to Manchester as professor of theoretical physics and soon found himself head of the Physics Department. From there he went on to become chairman of the Science Research Council, a high-level administrative position with great responsibility for the government support of scientific research. While in this hot seat, he received a knighthood. Our message on that occasion read:

Endowed by the British Lion
With (official) birthday powers,

Her Majesty made you Sir Brian,
So Mary becomes Lady Flowers.
The aim of our message, quite terse,
To express our greatest delight
From Lady to Lady, in verse,
And, ditto, from knight to knight.

(I had received a knighthood a few years earlier.)

After serving his term at the S.R.C., where he was succeeded by another former member of the Birmingham department, S. F. (now Sir Sam) Edwards, Flowers became rector of Imperial College, and later a life peer. Now Lord Flowers is active on innumerable committees and commissions. In their position, he and Mary have to do a great deal of entertaining, and they do so with the same warmth and consideration, whether the guests are royalty or undergraduates.

In 1951 there appeared Luigi Radicati with an Italian postdoctoral research award. He had somehow arranged his own accommodation in a guest house for missionaries, and therefore we had not enquired about his family; since he did not mention a wife in his correspondence, we assumed he had come alone. At a dinner party in our house, it suddenly came out in conversation that his wife was in Birmingham, sitting alone in the guest house! Genia rushed there the next day and found Gianna Radicati, who could do with some help, as her English was not yet very good. The oldest of their many sons, Luca, was born in Birmingham, and he is another of Genia's "grandsons by proxy", whose wedding we attended a few years ago. Luigi's tastes are unusual for an Italian: he dislikes pasta and adores plum pudding, perhaps because he has an American grandmother. He stayed for more than two years, and during that time tackled some basic problems in nuclear theory. I like discussing physics with him, because our intuitive reactions to unsolved problems seem to be almost identical.

Boris Davison returned to the department for a year in 1953 for complicated and not altogether pleasant reasons. When he left Birmingham in 1943 he went to Montreal and developed a very productive collaboration with George Placzek. Placzek wanted Boris to accompany him to Los Alamos, but the doctors doubted whether Boris's health would stand the altitude. He went there on a trial basis, but after a few weeks had to return to Montreal. After the war he went to Harwell and became a very useful member of the theory division. But in 1953 the authorities became worried about having a Russian-born man in the highly secret Harwell laboratory—a man whose parents were still in the Soviet Union. Perhaps the worry was

237

that he might be blackmailed into disclosing secrets by threats to his parents, but more realistically it was fear of adverse publicity if his position became known. It was decided that he had to leave Harwell, though he was not told the reason. He was seconded to our department, where he took a very helpful interest in many of our problems; we were happy to have him, though we deplored the reason. Then he was offered an appointment at the University of Toronto, where he had been anxious to go. He died there in 1961.

When in 1957 Paul Matthews left Birmingham to join his friend Abdus Salam at Imperial College, I persuaded Leonardo Castillejo, at short notice, to move from University College, London. The son of a Spanish father and an English mother, he is completely bilingual. I had refused to accept him as a student because we had too many students at that time, and I regretted it later. He has a great knowledge of field theory and particle and nuclear physics, but he has not published many papers because he finds it difficult to write. This probably reflects a very critical attitude toward his work, with which he is never satisfied. He never wrote a Ph.D. thesis, and his best-known work is a joint paper with two co-authors, who no doubt did the writing. But he is always willing to help with other people's problems, and many of his thoughts appear in the papers of others.

David Thouless had done his undergraduate work at Cambridge, his Ph.D. at Cornell, and he stayed on in America for some years, until he came to Birmingham in 1959. He had done important work in nuclear physics, particularly in getting general exact results for problems involving many interacting particles, an area in which many competent theoreticians have come to grief by not thinking deeply enough. He later applied his command of many-body problems to the theory of solids. I came to respect his judgment; when we disagreed over a problem, I knew from experience that he would probably turn out to be right.

At first he was rather shy and awkward, and also not very practical. His arrival in Birmingham was typical. He and his wife were to bring some old furniture, borrowed from his parents-in-law. They transported it in an old trailer towed by their car. On the way the trailer collapsed, and it took him some time to make emergency arrangements to collect the furniture. When his wife was expecting a child he had his car parked in front of the house, ready to drive her to hospital. When the moment came, the car refused to start, and he had to wake up a neighbour to do the driving.

His subsequent movements are an odyssey worthy of a "bird of passage": he went from Birmingham to Cambridge, returned to Birmingham as second professor, and after that held positions at Kingston, Ontario, Yale, and Seattle. He is now back in Cambridge as a Royal Society research professor.

In the fifties academic visitors from the Soviet Union rarely stayed for more than a week or two, and it was a pleasure when two Soviet scientists came to stay for six months each. A. M. Baldin was the first, in 1958, and V. M. Galitsky came a year or two later. Baldin was a very sociable person, with an excellent command of English, but even so there are always pitfalls in the usage of the language. Leaving the department one day, some of the young people invited him to join them for a drink, and he accepted. On the way someone mentioned they were going to a pub, and he asked what this term meant. It was explained that it was short for "public house". He became indignant and said he was not going to any such place! (In most European languages "public house" is a term for a house of ill-repute.)

He stayed in a small boarding-house used mainly by transient businessmen. He delighted in a conversation that regularly took place at breakfast, with minor variations, typically as follows: His neighbour would notice his accent and ask where he was from. "From Russia."—"When did you leave there?"—"Two months ago."—"What are you doing here?"—"Research in nuclear physics at the university." "Who brought you here?"—"The Soviet government." The visitor would depart, shaking his head in bewilderment.

Interchange with Poland was easier, and we did have Polish visitors in the late forties. Of these, Marian Günther was a great character. He always had problems with landladies, not for lack of good intentions, but because he often did not appreciate their position. His first landlady had told him in good time that she was going away for Christmas. When, shortly before leaving, she asked him what arrangements he had made, it emerged he had not understood that he could not stay in the house on his own. In other places he was thrown out because he came home very late without a key and had to awaken the landlady. When the situation was explained to him he would say, "I am so shameless" (meaning he was ashamed), a phrase that became part of our family jargon.

About this time the University of Birmingham was violently attacked in a speech in the House of Lords by Lord Vansittart, who claimed the university was full of communists. He singled out for special mention a certain Canon Cope who was on the university staff, and who, he said, had written a leaflet advocating that all opponents of communism should be liquidated. He called him the "murderous Canon".

I did not see the leaflet in question, but I am sure that this was not a fair summary.

As luck would have it, Günther was just then a lodger in the "murderous" Canon's house. The Copes were worried about further publicity in case the media discovered the presence of a man from Poland who, in his black leather jacket, fitted the image of a communist spy. They were too kind to ask him to move, but made him promise that, when alone in the house, he would not answer the phone or open the door to anyone. Then one day Mrs. Cope returned home to find a commotion outside the house. There was a man with a van to deliver a large parcel. Günther was talking to him through the window, but refused to open the door, true to his promise. The caller was really a delivery man, not a disguised reporter, so there were no ill-effects.

But now Günther really had to move. At a party in our house he realised that he had again forgotten his house key, and by now he had learned that it was not a good idea to ring the bell in the middle of the night. So he accompanied some of the other guests home, then took a circular bus route a few times around town, and finally sat on the doorstep until a reasonable hour in the morning. When he finally rang the bell, the very puritanic landlady threw him out because he had been out all night.

Nina Byers is a Californian who came to Birmingham in 1956 as a research fellow with a Chicago Ph.D. She received quite an accolade: while Pauli was visiting Birmingham, he spent an hour or so talking with her, and said afterwards, "That is a *very* clever girl." With Pauli's known attitude toward women theoreticians, this was praise indeed. She also stayed in our house, and we became, and remained, very fond of her. Her problem has always been her sense of time. She finds it hard to allow enough time to get from one activity to the next. This usually makes her late for appointments, and the number of planes she missed must be legion. If on her travels she arrives anywhere on the day she is expected, it is regarded as a miracle. She is now a professor in Los Angeles and continues, with her students, to contribute to the new particle theories, about which she is as enthusiastic as the youngest researcher.

Erich Vogt arrived from Canada with his wife and two children and another on the way. They coped with all the assorted domestic problems; Genia lent them a very large and very old pram, in which Erich propelled first two and then three children. He has tremendous energy, great even in proportion to his huge size. So the effort spent on domestic problems did not detract from his concentration on the theory of the nucleus. Many years later he came from the University of British

240

Columbia in Vancouver, where he is now a professor and directs the "Triumf" accelerator, to spend a year in Oxford. By this time there were five children, of whom four came to Oxford with the parents. Genia was proud to have found four different schools to suit each of the four children. We happened to visit Vancouver at a time when Erich was host to a small conference. He arranged an excursion for some eighteen people to Mount Garibaldi nearby. Typically he not only produced the food for the party's picnic lunch, but carried it up the mountain on his back; he graciously allowed his younger collaborators to carry the water supply.

P. K. ("Pasha") Kabir came from Cornell as a research fellow. He is an Indian, the son of a Hindu mother and a very distinguished Muslim father who was a minister in the Indian government. This background gave him familiarity with Hindu and Muslim, as well as Western, culture, and it makes conversation with him very interesting. It is also interesting to talk with him about physics. One of his favourite occupations is to think deeply about the basic laws of physics, their consequences, and ways of testing them. Each time we meet I know he will bring up questions which I can answer only sometimes, but which are always instructive to think about.

In Birmingham he bought a huge ancient Jaguar, in an elegant white colour, and optimistically talked about driving it to India. When the car failed to go the $1\frac{1}{4}$ miles from our house to the university, having to be pushed half the way, the ambitious project was dropped. He returned to India for a time, but found the ways of the universities too uncongenial. He had realised the lower salaries and difficulties in everyday life, and was prepared to accept them, but he found he could not work there, and returned to the West. He married an American artist, and is now a professor in Virginia.

Graduate Students and Others

I have already mentioned Hugh McManus as a prewar and postwar research student. He stayed on as a research fellow, and as lecturer, until 1951. He was a good lecturer, but he had some trouble getting started in the morning. Some claim that he was seen running up the drive to the university at 9:05 A.M. for a 9 o'clock lecture, with his pyjama trousers showing beneath his flannels. On another day he rushed breathlessly into the lecture room and hurriedly started writing on the board, before an amused roar from the students made him aware that a lady mathematics lecturer was already writing at the other end of the board. He had forgotten that they had arranged to swap lecture times.

He went from Birmingham to Chalk River, the Canadian atomic energy laboratory, where work started even earlier in the morning. He was never able to catch the official bus to work. This led to a memorable conversation with the director, W. B. Lewis, who called him in to request better timekeeping. McManus pointed out that he worked longer hours than most people; he did arrive late, but stayed much later than everybody else in the evening. "I know you do," said Lewis, "but unless you keep the same hours as other people you cannot interact with them. And we get paid according to the amount of interaction. For example, among the best-paid are television person- alities, who interact with millions; and hermits, who interact with nobody, do not get paid at all." I do not know Hugh's reaction to this argument. He is now a university professor, where presumably he can make his own schedule. He is also married and has a family, which usually keeps one to more normal hours.

Stuart Butler came from Australia as a research student in 1949. He made his mark by developing the theory of deuteron stripping. This is a collision of a deuteron with a nucleus, in which the neutron is captured and the proton goes on. The observed patterns are a tool for obtaining information about the state of the nucleus. He came to Birmingham with his wife, Miriam, and their first son, John, was born there. Later John developed a brain tumour, and though the parents consulted the best medical authorities, they received very pessimistic prognoses. We very much admired Miriam and Stuart for the way in which they coped with this appalling situation. But the disease did not progress as drastically as had been feared, and eventually a surgeon in Sydney was able to operate successfully. It was a great pleasure for us, on a visit to Sydney, to attend John's wedding, where another guest was the surgeon who had saved him.

Walter Marshall started as an undergraduate in Birmingham. His Welsh school had not given him the best preparation, and we initially had some doubt whether he would manage the difficult undergraduate course in mathematical physics. He soon proved that he was up to it and obtained an excellent degree. As a graduate student, he came to me and said he had not realised how much more material there was beyond what had come up in the undergraduate course; he would never be able to get on top of it. I assured him that this reaction was not unusual, and that he would be learning things faster than he realised. Not many months later he was so well informed that I got used to consulting him when I wanted to know whether a problem in his area had been treated before. He would consult his notes and usually produce a reference to a relevant paper.

He had a good Ph.D. thesis ready after two years and was offered a job at Harwell. I was usually sceptical about students leaving after two years' research training, but I did not oppose it in his case because I knew that the theory division at Harwell under Flowers would have a congenial atmosphere in which he could mature further. He became a very productive solid-state expert, and succeeded Flowers as division head. He went on to become director of Harwell. Even in that position he still kept some research going. He found time for this, although he insisted on making himself familiar with all the facts underlying any decisions that were being discussed. But he had to give up research when he became the chairman of the Atomic Energy Authority. Today he is Sir Walter Marshall and the chairman of the Central Electricity Generating Board, whose duties are rather far removed from what he learned at Birmingham.

In 1954 Stanley Mandelstam applied for a place as research student. His application was late, and we already had our full complement, so it seemed that we would have to turn him down; but he looked so good that we decided to make an exception. He was a South African who had studied at home but came to Cambridge for a further degree. Our first impression of his ability was soon borne out, and in one year he completed a paper that was of the standard of a Ph.D. thesis. But even the rather flexible regulations of Birmingham University did not allow anyone to get a Ph.D. in one year, so the thesis had to remain in cold storage for another year. In fact he stayed until 1957, and worked with Dick Dalitz and others on particle physics. Because Genia had many relatives called Mandelstam, she decided there must be some family relationship. But as he was so young, the only suitable relationship that came to her mind was that of a grandson, and she always refers to him as her grandson.

Stanley went from Birmingham to Columbia University, and later to Berkeley. He made a name for himself in the study of the mathematical nature of the quantities appearing in field theory. The terminology he introduced became standard usage. In 1960 we persuaded him to come back to Birmingham as a second professor, and he provided valuable inspiration to many students. He returned to Berkeley in 1963, attracted by an environment with many more experienced people of similar interests.

Elliott Lieb was an American graduate student, sent to us by Viki Weisskopf, who knew him as an undergraduate at M.I.T. Weisskopf felt that, as the young man was very bright but very highly strung, the Birmingham department would provide the right education for him. At the time we had a Japanese research fellow, S. Yoshida, who would hardly open his mouth in English. Lieb was very interested in Japan and the Japanese language, and I arranged for him to share an office with Yoshida. At the end of the year Lieb spoke very good Japanese, but Yoshida still would hardly say a word in English. I later discovered from Japanese colleagues that he was equally taciturn in Japanese. Lieb spent a year in Japan, where he tried to follow the local customs, which is not always easy. I heard of one party in the department in which he was working at which everybody was in Western dress, except Lieb, who was in Japanese garb. He became a respected authority on statistical mechanics.

A very charming, newly married couple from Portugal, João and Costanza da Providencia, had some landlady problems. They cooked highly spiced foods, and the smell was always too much for landladies. Because of one such instance, a new place was found for them by the university's lodgings warden. They were to move in the evening, and when the time arrived, João realised he had lost the piece of paper with the address on it. Luckily, I was able to contact the lodgings warden, who was at a party, for help.

This seems to have been the general pattern with the Providencias—crises were always resolved at the last minute. We were almost certain that they had a special guardian angel. One typical situation when the guardian angel was on the job was during a journey in Europe. The Providencia family got on the wrong train because of a confusion between Genova (the Italian for Genoa) and Geneva. A conversation with other passengers revealed this just in time to get the luggage and the family out of one train and into the other. He returned to Coimbra, Portugal, and built a small but lively group.

Themistoklis Kannellopoulos came from Greece as a research student. He was rather older than the usual student. He had been in the Greek army during the war and fought against the Italians. For a time we also had an Italian, Villi, who had been an officer on the other side. The two former war enemies exchanged stories about the front, but without any animosity. When Kanellopoulos arrived in Birmingham he found lodgings, and then wrote letters to his family and friends announcing his safe arrival, and giving his new address. He had already obtained stamps, and set out to look for a mailbox. He looked for one on the walls of houses, as was normal on the Continent, and missed the typically English pillar boxes. Finally on one wall he saw a receptacle labelled "Litter", evidently an unfamiliar grammatical form of the word "letter", and he deposited his letters there. They all

244

arrived in Greece. He continued to mail letters in this fashion until he discovered the right way. He was, for some years, the head of a new research institute in Athens, but upon a change in the political situation in Greece he left, and he now lives in Germany.

Jean Lascoux, a very bright Frenchman who is well-read in literature as well as in physics and mathematics, was a research student from 1955 to 1958, and stayed with us most of that time. He was inclined to make impulsive decisions, and when they resulted in trouble, he would sadly comment to himself, "Pas réfléchi!" This phrase, too, has remained in our family's vocabulary.

But impulsive decisions did not always give him trouble. He had a very old motorcycle, and one day decided to ride it to France. At that time one still needed special papers (*carnet*) to take a motorcar or cycle abroad, and also, since it was the busy season, one needed a reservation on the ferry. He had neither and just rode down to the ferry in Southampton, but, as fortune would have it, there was room for just one motorcycle. When he went through customs in France, he was told he would have to pay duty on the motorcycle, since he had no *carnet*. "How much is the duty?" The customs man looked at the cycle, consulted some colleagues, and decided the cycle had no commercial value, so the duty was nil.

When Lascoux had enough material for a thesis, he found it difficult to set pen to paper, and it looked as if there would be no end to the process of writing. Here Genia intervened, and announced that he would get no food until after he showed her ten pages of writing each day. "I don't care what you write, and you can tear it all up afterwards, but you have to write." The method worked, and a good thesis was completed within a reasonable time. Some of his results are still not in the literature, since when he left Birmingham on completing the thesis, no one pressured him to produce a paper for publication.

The same method had to be employed again for the thesis of Alfonso Mondragón from Mexico, who was a student from 1957 to 1960. He had done an excellent piece of work, but he also had difficulty in getting down to writing. At the time when his stay in Birmingham was nearing its end, and my family and I were about to depart for the summer to Chalk River in Canada, he had produced, under pressure, only a draft thesis, which needed substantial rewriting. There was now a problem: if he departed for Mexico, with nobody around to bully him, the thesis might never get finished. Then we had a bright idea. Air France was operating a service to Mexico via Montreal, so it would be possible for him to stop in Canada without additional expense. We had a large house at our disposal in Chalk River, so he came to stay with us for a few weeks, and, with Genia's "encouragement" the thesis was rewritten.

His stay in Birmingham was marred by medical problems. He had a mild form of epilepsy, but this was kept under control with medication. Even though he had very good medical advice in Birmingham, he still suffered a very bad attack one day and fainted in the street; he was rushed to hospital. The incident suggested that his condition was getting worse, and made us all unhappy. But then the real explanation was found: the pharmacist had made an error, and instead of tablets that suppressed his disease, he had been given some that aggravated it. When this was corrected, his improvement continued, and by now he is free of any trouble.

Delawar Husain, from East Pakistan (now Bangladesh), applied first for admission as a student from a mental hospital in London, where he had gone with a nervous breakdown after starting research in one of the London colleges. The cause seemed to be homesickness and loneliness in the impersonal atmosphere. After some hesitation, we decided we had probably a better chance of helping him than other places, and we accepted him. He soon settled down happily, and became very popular in the department, especially in his telling of Scottish jokes. Within a year he was completely at home and took care of new arrivals, showing them around and helping them buy clothes appropriate for the local climate, as he had been helped before. We discovered that he was very musical, but had never heard any classical Western music. We played him some Bach records, which left him quite shattered. He soon became an enthusiastic supporter of the chamber concerts in the university. He wrote a good thesis, working with David Thouless, before returning to Dacca.

James Stuttard posed an interesting problem. He had taken an undergraduate course in mathematics and had qualified for a Pass (i.e., not Honours) degree, but was still short of a subsidiary subject. He was an epileptic and lacked self-confidence, probably because of an overprotective family, who, for instance, would not let him lift a teapot in case he had a seizure while holding it and might scald himself. I heard that after the end of his studies he could find a job only as porter in a grocery warehouse. We then needed someone to do numerical calculations on a desk calculator (the university did not yet own a computer), and I called him in to offer him the job. He was hesitant, so I told him to think it over, but to let me know soon: "I would rather have you, but if you don't want the job I shall have to take someone else, and the others won't wait indefinitely." He was surprised: "Why would you rather have me?" I explained that I thought he would do the job well, but if I was wrong and he could not do it, he would have to go. "Don't think we are offering you the job because we are sorry for you!" He took the job and proved to be excellent at it, careful and patient, and with some sense for the numbers he was handling. Before he started, I had a problem with the secretary. At the time we had a very young secretary, who objected to his coming because she was afraid of his seizures. I explained to her that he was a good man for the job, and it was a uniquely good job for him, but if she did not like it she could resign. She saw the point and apologised for her reaction. When the university computer made his job redundant, the computing department took him on to do numerical work for them.

Other students from far-away places included Young-Nok Kim from Korea and Maurice Wong, S.J., a Chinese Jesuit from Manila. And there were many others. I fear I have already strained the patience of the reader by fondly recalling people and events, and I must apologise to the many colleagues and students whose names do not appear here. Any memorable episodes in which they were involved must have faded from my memory.

Outside physics, a very interesting person in the university was Lancelot Hogben, famous as the author of the best-sellers *Mathematics for the Million* and *Science for the Citizen* (George Allen & Unwin, 1936 and 1938). He came to Birmingham as Professor of Zoology, but later changed to Medical Statistics. This change reflected the breadth of his interests. Apart from biological subjects and basic mathematics, he was also interested in languages and experimented with a new international language, "Interglossa". He was also quite a craftsman and had made some very attractive furniture in his spare time. After his marriage to the statistician Enid Charles was dissolved, he fell in love with a Welsh schoolteacher. He learned Welsh and started writing in that language. He was very articulate in private discussion, and I found it surprising that at meetings of the University Senate he spoke rarely, and when he did his remarks seemed to have little connection with what previous speakers had said. This disparity was explained when he told me that at gatherings of more than a few people he was unable to speak unless he had written out his remarks in advance.

We also acquired many friends outside the university, including Lovis and Penelope Barman. Lovis was an important person in industry, and later left Birmingham to join the board of Rolls-Royce. His wife, who is a former ballet dancer and taught ballet in Birmingham, became a very close friend of Genia's. They have many interests in common, including the ballet, as Genia has been a balletomane since her youth in Leningrad. Their eldest son married a girl from one of the Quaker families who are part of the establishment in Birmingham. We were surprised to find wine served at the wedding reception, since Quakers are usually opposed to drink. It was explained to us that they make exceptions, but they do draw the line at champagne.

10

Teaching

Graduate Students

During all these years, I regarded teaching as my main responsibility. It seemed to me that teaching was the primary duty of a university professor. Of course it was also important (and enjoyable) to do one's own research and to contribute to the progress of one's subject, but most of this was done in collaboration with research students, and therefore it became indistinguishable from teaching.

In graduate teaching, the first consideration is, of course, the selection of students. Decisions about candidates from our own or other British universities were easier, because there was ample evidence and they could be called for interview, though even with the best information the selection process was not infallible. It was harder to select prospective students from overseas. We could not call them for interview, and the recommendations of their teachers were hard to evaluate if we didn't know much about the teachers' background and style. On the whole, we were fortunate in the choice of foreign students. Many of them came with graduate scholarships from international bodies or from organisations in their homelands that often were highly competitive, so the students had passed some quite severe selection processes already.

We had a useful procedure in Birmingham for dealing with students whom we had accepted for a Ph.D. course, but who were not able to produce work of the necessary standard. After about one year the students were required to write a small dissertation on the level of an M.Sc. thesis. The work was evaluated as if it were an M.Sc. thesis; but as long as the student continued with research training, the degree was not awarded, and the work could therefore be used as part of the Ph.D. thesis. But if the student wanted to leave, either because he had reached his ceiling, or for any other reason, he was entitled to the Master's degree. Because the degree was awarded strictly on the basis of a thesis written and approved for the purpose, the prestige of the

249

degree was upheld and it did not look like a consolation prize for a failed Ph.D.

Choosing a field, and a specific problem, for a student was another important task. We usually waited until the student had spent a little time in the department, and perhaps worked on some minor problem, so that we could judge his way of thinking and his specific abilities. There was usually no shortage of research problems once a student had demonstrated his specific talents and interests, though we sometimes recalled the famous remark by Max Planck, when a student asked him to suggest a problem: "My dear man, if I knew of a problem, I would solve it myself!" Some students had firm ideas about what they wanted to do, and if they seemed sensible and feasible, we encouraged them in their choice. Not surprisingly, this was rare, since it takes some experience and knowledge of the literature to find a question that has not yet been answered and looks interesting and not impossibly difficult. There were always some cases where the project given to a student proved unprofitable, but usually it was discovered in time to change the problem; and even so, the student had not completely wasted his time, because even the unsuccessful attempt was a valuable experience.

In choosing a field for a student, I did not think that I was settling the student's line of work for the rest of his career, nor even that he would remain in academic research. A good research training in any live field provides a good start for research of any kind (and even for many other kinds of work). The experience of finding out what a problem is about, reducing it to basic questions that can be tackled, collecting the available information, and trying to formulate clearly what it is that one has not understood are activities common to all forms of research. If we knew what the student's career interests were, we usually tried to choose a research field close to his prospective future concerns.

In the case of foreign students, particularly from developing countries, it was often not easy to predict their futures. Sometimes we worried whether it was right to encourage them in research on subjects very far from anything likely to be of interest in their home countries. Usually we felt that their research experience would be generally useful, but we would still have preferred to make the choice with more information. I remember the case of one student who raised this problem himself. He was a student from the West Indies and was finishing a thesis on particle physics. He expected to obtain a teaching post in the University of the West Indies, and he did not expect to continue in the same field, as he would not have anyone with whom to discuss his work. He came to me for advice. I asked him what was going on in his university in experimental physics. It turned out they had a strong group that worked on the physics of the upper atmosphere— an appropriate topic in view of their location at a lower latitude than most research stations. I suggested the student might like to get some experience in the theory of this work before going home, and this suggestion was welcomed by the physics professor in the West Indies, whom we consulted. We arranged for an extension of the student's grant so he could spend a year in the Radio Research Laboratory. I have not heard of his further progress, but my guess is that he did well.

We did not assign an official supervisor to each student, since a change might be necessary if the student's subject changed, or if another senior member of the department became interested in working with the student. In the official university records my name went in as supervisor for every student, which simply meant that I was willing to answer questions about him. This very informal way of working was possible because no fee was paid to the supervisor for each student, as is the case in some other universities.

I felt it was important to encourage students to rely on their own judgment about what were correct arguments, and not to accept the opinions of their seniors, though in most cases the senior person turns out to be right. One such situation developed when W. J. Swiatecki, a bright student who came in 1946, expressed the wish to work on Milne's then new "kinematic relativity". I told him that I regarded this theory as completely wrong, but that he need not accept my opinion. We agreed that he would continue reading Milne's book, and when he had understood enough of it he would give a seminar talk to explain it to the others; however, he would use only part of his time for this study, and during the rest of the time he would look at another problem I had suggested. As I expected, he never gave the seminar talk; in studying the book carefully, he discovered for himself the serious flaws in the theory.

The amount of time I spent with each student would vary with the student and the state of the work. Sometimes there were periods of weeks when the student would be reading or doing calculations, and then there might be times when we would meet daily, arguing about the next step or how to get over a difficulty. Sometimes the student would come proudly to present a solution to a problem, which I intuitively knew could not be right. Then we had to look at each step in his argument, until we could locate the error (or until he could convince me that my intuition was wrong). I seem to have a knack for putting my finger on the place in a long calculation where something has gone wrong. H. S. Arms claimed that I could see a mistake through a three-foot brick wall.

Most students learned much from talking with each other. This applied to conversations with those working in the same field, who could tell each other about facts or methods they had found in the literature, or about tricks they had invented themselves. But it also applied to discussions with students in different fields. Learning about what goes on in other fields can often be helpful in suggesting different points of view for your own work, and in any case it counters the tendency to excessive specialisation. In assigning desks in the department, I would usually try to mix students from different fields. They would get to know those working in their own field soon enough, and in this way they would also meet others. Of course, other factors had to be considered in assigning rooms: inveterate pipe smokers should not share rooms with those irritated by smoke; and those who, like some Americans, liked their rooms heated to 80 degrees, should not have to share with fresh-air fiends.

Besides personal discussions, we had of course lectures and seminar meetings to help in the education of graduate students. The lecture courses served two purposes: to give each student the background in the particular field in which he was to work, and to provide the minimum necessary information about other fields. The first was needed almost as soon as a student started, but there were not always enough students in the same field to make a lecture course for this purpose worthwhile, and they often had to learn these techniques by word of mouth from their supervisor, and by reading. For the other purpose, lectures were essential, but they did not necessarily all have to come in the student's first year. We tried to vary the subjects from year to year, so that over three years—the normal time a student spent in the department—they covered a reasonably wide range. This differed from the practice of many other universities of concentrating the lecture work in the student's first year. This means that he does not make a real start in research during that year, and the final decision on whether he should be encouraged to complete the training for the Ph.D. may have to be made without seeing him do research, or may have to be postponed.

Seminar meetings similarly served two purposes. The general seminar of the department covered all aspects of theoretical physics, and we tried to get the speakers to present their material in a way that would be understandable to all. The group meetings, on the other hand, were intended for highy technical discussions of the specialists in each field. The practice of having these specialised meetings developed gradually as the size of the department and the number of people in each field grew. Not all seminar talks were of the same standard. Some of the talks were given by graduate students as an essential part of their training, and they could not yet be expected to be accomplished speakers. Sometimes their talks concerned questions to which the answers were not yet available or not clearly understood. It was then the job of the senior people to help clarify the issues by asking questions or making comments. This process was well described by Oppenheimer in an interview with *Time* magazine: "What we don't understand, we try to explain to each other."

Over the years, as the amount of material to be digested and the number of papers to be read in each field kept growing, students became reluctant to attend lectures or seminar meetings on subjects not immediately related to their research. This is a phenomenon observed in all research schools. I remember a student arguing, "There is a shortage of research jobs, and my chance of getting one depends on my writing a first-rate thesis. Any time spent on other subjects only distracts from that purpose." My answer was: "Research jobs are short, and you cannot be sure of getting one to continue work in the narrow field of your thesis. A general knowledge of theoretical physics will widen the range of jobs open to you, as well as enable you to do your job better."

A colleague in another university tried to apply pressure by making it known that in the oral examination for the Ph.D. he would feel free to ask questions on any subject recently discussed at his departmental seminar. This did not have any effect; it probably lacked credibility, because the students did not believe that they could be failed in the exam for not answering such questions. I used a different device: I reminded students that most of them would eventually want letters of recommendation from me. The usefulness of such letters was much increased if I could say that the candidate had wide interests, but I could not say this unless I had evidence, such as their participation in general seminars. This did have some effect.

When a student working under my supervision had finished his work, it was essential that he write his thesis himself, though I would give advice on the presentation; foreign students sometimes needed help with the English. But when it came to writing a paper for publication, I insisted on vetting the text fully myself, since I remembered how badly my own early papers were written when I had no help from professors. This meant that the writing was best done before the student had left Birmingham. But the funds supporting the students were often barely sufficient to keep them in residence long enough to complete their research and write a thesis—usually three years—so the text of the publication often had to be settled by correspondence. In some cases the student failed to write the paper, and good work remained unpublished; in a few cases I finally wrote it up myself as a joint paper with the student.

The question of joint publication always involves a difficult judgment. Almost any thesis contains some ideas and suggestions by the supervisor. When are these substantial enough to make the supervisor a co-author? I always remember the story (perhaps apocryphal) of the German professor who said, "I never published my work under my own name. When I was a student, my professor published my work under his name, and now I am putting my name on the work of my students." I regarded this as a cautionary tale, and if I erred it was generally in the sense of not including my name as author when it would have been justified. I discovered that this is not necessarily to the student's benefit. If he is credited with more originality than he deserves, he may later find that too much is expected of him. In addition, my habit of withholding my name from a paper became known, and people suspected that all papers by my pupils were perhaps in part my work, and that all students with whom I did publish joint papers had contributed very little. Good intentions do not always produce good results.

When the student finally was ready to leave, he would often need advice about applying for positions, and usually one would have to write letters of recommendation. I felt that it paid in the long run to be honest in such recommendations; praising a candidate more highly than was justified would not only bring my recommendations for other people into question (they would be "renormalised", the physicist would say), but the candidate would also suffer, as he might find himself in a job to which he could not do justice. I learned, in fact, that no harm was done in mentioning some adverse factors, provided they were not major disqualifications for the job in question, because they showed that one was writing about a real person, and writing with some realism.

The problem of finding positions for departing students underwent a serious change during my Birmingham years. In the beginning there was a strong demand for trained scientists, including theoretical physicists, because the universities were expanding, and new universities were being started. Few people had been trained during the war, though some of those who had worked in war research could adapt their experience to academic research. There was also a great demand from industry and from government research laboratories such as Harwell, but most of the able students went into university posts. It became the accepted norm to such an extent that people got used to the idea that a Ph.D. from a good university entitled the holder to an academic career. I always knew that this could not last, because if each university teacher produced even one good Ph.D. candidate per year who would himself go into university teaching, there would be a fantastic growth rate, which no educational system could absorb. In the end the number of people being trained would have to be reduced, or a greater fraction would have to go into other types of work, such as work in industry or administration. This was another reason that I insisted that students get a broad coverage of the subject.

In the end, the change came about much more suddenly than I had expected, because a number of factors happened to change at the same time: the expansion of the universities stopped; the job market in industry was curtailed by the growing economic crisis; and the number of trained people had grown to a level that approached saturation. This made the problem much harder for our departing students, and I had to write many more letters. I do not know of any former students who actually failed to find a position, but many had to accept rather different work from what they would have chosen.

Undergraduate Teaching

Lectures to undergraduates and the organisation of their studies were other important functions of the department. Under the Birmingham system we had to look after a range of different courses—from theoretical physics courses for mathematics and physics students to pure and applied mathematics for engineers, chemists, and others requiring mathematics as a subsidiary subject. The latter, the so-called "service teaching", made great demands on the ability of the lecturer, because he had to make the subject attractive to students who were often not interested in it, and who were not necessarily chosen for their ability to absorb mathematical arguments. These courses were usually taught by the most experienced lecturers. New and inexperienced lecturers would start with specialised postgraduate courses for our own students, which made the least demand on teaching ability. They might then graduate to final-year undergraduate courses, and so on, until, having proved their teaching ability, they would be allowed to teach service courses.

The service courses were shared with the mathematicians, as each course would contain a mixture of pure and applied mathematics. I remember my first experience with such a course, in 1946, just after returning to Birmingham. A lecturer in pure mathematics had left at short notice—I believe after a disagreement with Professor Watson. There was nobody else who could conveniently take over his lecture course, and I therefore felt obliged to take it on. I had never given that particular course before, and with my other courses it added up to thirteen lectures a week for that term.

In my normal lectures I usually surprised people by lecturing without writing out the text beforehand. It is perhaps a weakness that I find it very difficult to lecture from a written text. I cannot just read the text, because reading and sounding as if one knew what one was talking about is a difficult art, which I never mastered. Writing out the text and memorising it is equally difficult. I tried on some occasions to write out a draft, and then to follow the general trend of it, without trying to reproduce the text verbatim. With this, too, I ran into trouble, because in writing the draft I had used some turns of phrase to lead from one thought to another, and I clearly would have liked to repeat these, but as I had varied the wording in talking they would not fit in.

Because of this disability I learned to speak freely, using perhaps a sheet of notes listing the order in which I wanted to present the points, and of course with notes of any numbers or formulae I wanted to quote without deriving them. This makes it possible to adjust the presentation to the reaction of the audience. In general, one gets a feeling from the listeners whether an explanation or an argument has got across, and if necessary one can try a different explanation. Sometimes this impression of the audience reaction can be deceptive. I remember particularly a course to mathematicians and physicists, in which a certain student always sat in the front row. It seemed evident that she followed the lecture especially well. When I reached a difficult point she looked worried and thoughtful, and when I produced the solution her face lit up with understanding and pleasure. Alas, the examination at the end of term demonstrated that she had not understood a word—the expressions on her face had just been instinctive responses to my mood.

My way of lecturing could occasionally give trouble when I thought there was an obvious argument to obtain a required result, and then found the argument was not valid, or I could not reconstruct it. I do not believe such occasional lapses do any harm; in fact, they show the audience something of the mental processes of the lecturer, more so than a very polished presentation, which makes every step look obvious and easy. Of course, if this type of trouble occurs too often it will confuse the audience. Roger Blin-Stoyle, who attended some of my graduate lectures, reminded me recently of an occasion when I could not reconstruct an argument in a lecture, postponed it until the next time, and at the next lecture still did not get it right!

In working out a derivation or in solving a problem on the blackboard without notes, one can make algebraic errors. A small amount of this is also useful because it encourages the audience not to accept the speaker's statements unless they are seen to be correct. It can also help to keep an audience alert. Once, when a class of students seemed particularly lethargic, I told them that I would make a deliberate error in the next piece of work I would be presenting, and that this would lead to a manifestly wrong answer: they should catch me out if they could. Of course the error was subtle and they did not spot it. But when the wrong answer appeared, they started speculating where I might have gone wrong, and they got near the right answer. In any case, they were paying attention.

Attendance at lectures was compulsory, a rule I did not like. However, I could understand why: most of our students were supported by maintenance grants from public funds, and no one would know if they were truant unless their presence at the university was checked. This could no doubt be determined by the examination results at the end of the academic year, but by then they might have had a year's free ride. But it was clear that some students could learn their material more easily from books than from lectures. I therefore made it known that I would be willing to excuse attendance provided students told me what books they were using to learn the material, and provided they attempted to solve the problems set by the lecturer. It seemed to me essential to give them this option; however, it was an academic point, because in all those years there was only one student who asked to be excused from lectures, and because of his poor performance I advised him against dropping the courses.

It had been clear to me from the start that Birmingham offered no suitable course for future theoretical physicists. The courses for physicists did not contain enough mathematical techniques and theoretical material, and the Mathematics School did not contain enough physics. No one offered a course on quantum mechanics. In the late 1930s this was generally the case in British universities, except in Cambridge, where a lecture course on quantum mechanics was in Part III of the Mathematics Tripos. I therefore decided to start a new school of mathematical physics, and obtained approval for it. Since we could not obtain additional teaching staff, we formed the new programme mainly by a selection from existing courses. This proved quite convenient, and the only additional course required for mathematical physicists was a final-year course on quantum mechanics, which I would teach myself.

The first year of the new option was practically identical with the first year of both the mathematics and physics schools. This was a great convenience, because it allowed us to postpone the decision on admission to the new school until after the first year. The plan was that each student would have to be accepted either by physics or by mathematics, and he would continue in that school unless he was accepted for mathematical physics. While the school was new we wanted only very good students, because we could not be sure what the demand for its graduates would be. Also, the students would have to carry a very heavy load of lectures. For the bright students the work of one of these courses would help them understand others, and therefore the load was bearable. But a student with a more pedestrian attitude might get into difficulties.

From the start the new school went well; we had a small number of bright students. The course could not, however, develop fully because the requirements of military service allowed most students only two years at the university. The final-year course did not come into existence until after the war. The school never became very large, but its students were always of high quality, and many of them became graduate students in my department or elsewhere.

In teaching undergraduates who were not aiming at an academic career—and they were the majority of our students—I felt that the most important requirement was not only to make them understand the language of mathematics, but to teach them to translate physical or other problems into that language, and to translate the solution back into practical terms. This is a situation with which pure mathematicians are not always familiar, and it was therefore the aspect of the teaching in which we, as theoretical physicists, could be particularly useful.

Later I decided to start a one-year diploma course for mathematics graduates who wanted to learn these particular techniques of applied mathematics. The response to this course was disappointing in numbers, because we could have handled more than the three to five students who came each year. They did, however, include some who made us feel that the effort had been worthwhile.

One of them was Hong-Mo Chan, a Chinese who had graduated in pure mathematics in Hong Kong, and who came to us for the diploma course. He turned out to be very bright, and during the year acquired a good understanding of theoretical physics. He stayed as a graduate student and obtained a very good Ph.D. degree. The terms of the scholarship that had brought him to Birmingham—and his conscience—demanded that he return to Hong Kong, and he was appointed to a junior teaching position at the University of Hong Kong. He decided to institute a course in theoretical physics there. His enthusiasm infected some of his senior colleagues, and before long they were turning out graduates in the new subject. At that time the "Commonwealth Scholarships", grants that brought graduate students from the British Commonwealth to British universities, were fairly new; they were for all Commonwealth countries and for all subjects. There were usually four or five such grants from Hong Kong, and in some years a substantial fraction of those went to theoretical physicists trained by Chan and his colleagues. All this, of course, took a lot of hard work in addition to Chan's enthusiasm. It seems the University of Hong Kong authorities did not support him to the extent his success deserved, and after some years he returned to the West. He is now doing elementary-particle research at the Rutherford Laboratory in England.

Another interesting case was Daniel Jonah, who came from Sierra Leone, where the opportunities for an advanced education were very limited. He went to a school for Seventh-Day Adventists, and fortunately one of his teachers was an able mathematician. He recognized Jonah's ability and took him under his wing. Jonah won a scholarship to Britain and obtained a mathematics degree from a Welsh university; he then came to us to take the diploma course. He seemed to have research potential, and was anxious to get research training. The subjects studied in my department did not seem right for him, but we recommended him to the Chemical Engineering Department, where a team was doing theoretical work on the structure of liquids. He obtained the Ph.D. and returned to Sierra Leone, where he is now a lecturer at the university in Freetown. There he carries a heavy teaching load and has no opportunity to discuss his research interests with anyone else. But in spite of these handicaps he has managed to continue his research and has published a number of papers in reputable journals.

The part of the teaching duties that I liked less than the rest was examining. I did not object to marking papers, which is a routine job, but the setting of papers requires thought and imagination. It is not always easy to judge how difficult a problem may be for a student who misunderstands its point, or how a small error in solving an equation may get the candidate into deep waters. Sometimes one thinks of a really nice and amusing problem, but by the time one has read fifty mostly poor attempts at answering it, its attraction seems to have disappeared.

Most of the usual examinations in mathematical subjects suffer from two faults: they put too great a premium on speed, and they contain too much "bookwork", i.e., they put a premium on memory. Speed is much less important at the university level than is depth of understanding. In fact, the student with a deep knowledge of the subject will often see possible complications and lose time. I therefore always pressed for a reduction in the number of questions to be answered, so that a bright student would be able to complete the paper in less than the allowed period. Bookwork, the repetition of arguments given in the lectures and textbooks, allows more sophisticated material to appear in the papers, but it does not really test the candidate's understanding. I usually tried to allow only questions that could not be completely answered by citing passages from books or lectures, but there always had to be some new point, however slight, to test the students' capacity for new thought. Of course one had to allow some credit for just reciting the bookwork; otherwise the results for weaker students would be too devastating.

We often debated other methods of testing students. One attractive idea was to let students write the examination papers in their own time, making use of any books. With this method it is hard to ensure that the student has answered the questions himself and has not been told by other students or more senior friends what to write. In addition, this method, which was used in some summer schools in which I taught, often makes a fair assessment difficult unless the examiner is familiar with all of the literature in the library. Otherwise it is impossible to judge whether a passage written by the student represents his own thought or is copied from a book. This makes a difference if the passage is a brilliant insight, and even more if it is a foolish confusion. At an advanced level the best method is, of course, to set each student a little research problem, which he can do with perhaps some advice. But for the large classes of beginners this is not practicable.

11

Travelling and Other Sidelines

Conferences

Although I had settled in Birmingham during the postwar period, I still had many opportunities to travel. Apart from family holidays, the occasions for these trips were usually conferences, summer schools, and other scientific visits. The number of journeys was so large that I could not possibly list them all, but I shall give some examples.

We had two international conferences in Birmingham, one in 1948 and the other in 1953. It is a sign of the rate of expansion of physics that even in 1953 it was possible to have a conference on both nuclear and high-energy physics, and still have time for leisurely discussions about the most interesting topics. We chose to run these conferences in an unconventional way: there were to be no set programmes and no contributed papers. For each half-day session there would be a topic, an introductory speaker who was to present his views on the topic in as provocative a way as possible, and a chairman. After the introductory talk there would be a free discussion. Colleagues to whom we mentioned the idea thought that the meetings would run out of steam; few people would be ready to get up and comment freely in front of an audience of three hundred or so. This fear proved groundless; we never ran out of discussions, and the chairmen had to be firm to keep the meetings under control, and stop people talking at too great length, or to come up with lectures which they had prepared, and which had little connection with the topic under discussion.

Another objection we encountered was that people would not get their travel expenses paid (we had no funds to pay the fares for participants) unless they were presenting a paper. We dealt with that by informing people who wished to present a paper that we had no scheduled papers, but that we would be pleased to have them take part in the discussion and express their opinions. This proved quite adequate to get their expenses paid.

We also had more applicants than we could accommodate, so we had to ration places. This was difficult; in fairness to the people turned down, we had to be firm with gate-crashers. It was usually my job to deal with such cases, and fortunately there were few. The only time we had a problem was when some Italian graduate students had been told by their professor just to come, and we could not very well send them back to Italy. I compromised by barring them from the opening session, where indeed every seat was taken, but allowing them to stay for the rest of the conference. When at the beginning of the Kyoto conference in 1953 the organisers asked about my experience in running a conference, I told them, "There are only two difficult things: one is to stop people coming to your conference, and the other is to stop them giving papers."

An important series of conferences were the "Rochester Conferences" on high-energy physics. They started in about 1950, when the rapid developments in quantum electrodynamics and the experimental results with the new accelerators led to very intense activity by theoreticians and experimentalists. Robert Marshak, the chairman of the Physics Department in Rochester and a very energetic person, whom we had known in Los Alamos, decided to invite the experts in the subject for a conference lasting a few days. On this first occasion there were, I believe, some thirty participants. The meeting proved popular and was repeated annually for a number of years. Soon the conferences lasted for a week, and the number of participants grew until a rigid selection had to be made. Each country or region thus organised a committee that decided how many places could be allocated to each department, and on a few occasions I served on the committee allocating places for Europe. Soon the job of organising these big conferences every year became too onerous for the hosts at Rochester, and the "Rochester Conference" was held in different centres on each occasion. It is now held only every other year. On one occasion, when the meeting was in Vienna, it was decided, as an experiment, to allow anyone who wanted to participate to attend. About one thousand people came.

In 1950 a theoretical physics conference was held in Bombay, where the Tata Institute for Fundamental Research had recently been founded. Afterwards we were the guests of the Indian authorities on a tour of some of the famous sights of India, ending at Bangalore, where the annual meeting of the Indian Association for the Advancement of Science was held. Raman, the discoverer of the Raman effect, for which he obtained the Nobel Prize, was there, as his laboratory was in Bangalore. He was indeed a very capable experimentalist, but did not like the accepted theories; in particular, he claimed that Max Born's fundamental work on crystals was all wrong. At this meeting he was going to present a new theory that explained the scattering of X-rays by crystals and would replace Born's. He asked that Rosenfeld (who was also present) and I should come to hear this talk: "I would like you to be my guinea pigs." I said, "We don't mind being guinea pigs, but will we be allowed to squeak?" It turned out that this was a justified worry, because Raman's talk lasted an hour and fifty minutes, and the room was available for only two hours. Raman had criticized Born's work in particular for using the so-called cyclic boundary condition, which is not realistic, but makes calculations easier. I had time only to state that this condition gives correct answers and that I could prove it. I offered to write out a proof if he would publish it in his journal. He agreed, but when I sent him the paper, he first argued that it was incorrect, and later that the question was not important, anyway. But I got the paper published in another Indian journal, since it seemed important to counter Raman's influence on the young students in India.

Another important and unusual conference was held in Kyoto, Japan, in 1953. It was a general theoretical physics conference, held in two sections, nuclear physics and solid-state physics. It was my first opportunity to see Japan. I went there by the Comet I plane, the first jetliner in commercial service, which later turned out to have a risk of crashes due to metal fatigue. At the time I travelled there had already been two accidents, but the cause was unknown. One theory had been that excessive air turbulence had caused one accident near Calcutta, therefore when our plane ran into heavy turbulence near Calcutta, I worried a little, but nothing happened.

A small number of the participants had been invited to speak at two public meetings sponsored by one of the daily newspapers, the *Asahi Shimbun*, and the conference organisers had asked us to accept because the newspaper had given generous support to the conference. We expected the audience to consist mainly of university students, but when we got to the hall there were about five thousand school children. The level of the talks we had prepared was quite unsuitable, but we could not change them, because the talks were to be translated sentence by sentence, and the interpreters worked from a previously prepared typescript. So we had to go through with it. The meeting was long, with about five half-hour talks (with the same amount of time for the translation), but the audience, who could not have understood much, sat patiently through it all. The last speaker was Tomonaga. His first sentence brought the house down. One of our Japanese colleagues told us what he had said: "I am going to speak Japanese!"

I had met Tomonaga previously in the West, but got to know him well at the conference. He was a great physicist and a person of enormous charm, very quiet and polite, but possessing a very subtle sense of humour. At the banquet at the end of the conference, the chairman suggested that a person from each of the nationalities represented say a few words in his language. This seemed a nice idea, but in practice it became rather wearing to hear the same rather obvious sentiments in twenty or so languages. When it was Tomonaga's turn he said a few words in Japanese; but he changed to English for the benefit of the foreign guests and said, approximately, "We are very pleased to have our colleagues from the West with us, because we have learned so much from them, including modern physics. But with the good things they have brought us also some bad ones, and one of the worst is the after-dinner speech!" And he sat down.

I shall always remember another remark of his made many years later, when he was visiting England. The conversation was about Japanese cities, and Genia asked him, "How can you explain that the Japanese, who are so sensitive to beauty, have allowed Tokyo to become such a mess?" He replied, "You must remember that, while we are, as you say, very sensitive to beauty, we are insensitive to ugliness, whereas you Westerners are less sensitive to beauty, but very sensitive to ugliness."

It was a pleasure to meet some of the young Japanese research workers and students who attended the conference in vast numbers. At the same time there were practically no scholarships to support students, and very few positions for mature researchers. They all had to earn their living somehow and think about physics in their spare time. The numbers were particularly impressive in theoretical work, probably in part because it is hard to do experimental work on a spare-time basis, and perhaps also because the fame of the Nobel laureates Yukawa and Tomonaga had created an attractive image for the subject.

I spent most of my time in the nuclear physics section but gave a paper to the solid-state section. I arrived early in the solid-state lecture hall, and heard most of the talk given by the preceding speaker, Lars Onsager. He had an extremely original mind and well deserved the Nobel Prize he was awarded later. But his mind worked so fast and was able to deal with such subtle arguments that he had difficulty explaining his ideas even to normally competent theoretical physicists.

He was talking about the anomalous diamagnetism of metals, the so-called de Haas-van Alphen effect, on which I had done some basic work in 1933, and on which some of my students were still working. Onsager put forward an ingenious method for interpreting the experimental data on this effect and for directly deriving results about the motion of the electrons in each metal. As I listened to his talk I understood his trick immediately, because I was very familiar with the background, but I also realised that most of the audience had understood nothing. So I abandoned the talk I was going to give, and instead gave an explanation of what it was that Onsager had done.

After the conference we were takan to Osaka, where the second of the public meetings sponsored by the *Asahi Shimbun* was to take place. The meeting happened to come at the height of a typhoon, so many people were unable to get there, leaving an audience of "only" about three thousand. After the meeting we were entertained by the staff of the newspaper in an elegant restaurant. The typhoon had caused a power failure, so the dinner was served by candlelight, and the food was prepared by somewhat improvised techniques. Traffic was disorganized by the storm, and the geishas arrived late and had to serve in their street clothes instead of the traditional costume. All this made for a more intimate glimpse of Japanese life than a visit under more normal circumstances would have given us.

News of the typhoon reached England, and Genia was worried whether this would delay my return. She therefore asked the Birmingham newspaper if they had information about traffic conditions. The journalists tried to find out, but reported that no information was available, except that there were no reports of British casualties. When the evening paper appeared it had my portrait on the front page under the headline, "Birmingham professor missing in typhoon." When Genia saw this, she knew at once that it was a result of her phone call, but such is the power of the press that even so she felt very depressed!

There was indeed some difficulty with the flights from Osaka to Tokyo, but the *Asahi Shimbun*, who regarded the speakers at their meetings as their special guests, helped me get a plane reservation to Tokyo, and they looked after me there. My plane to London was delayed, and I had a free evening, so Y. Fujioka invited me to dinner in his house. He was an old friend, as we had been together in Leipzig in 1928-29, and he was now the secretary of the international conference. The dinner consisted of sukiyaki, the meat-and-vegetable dish cooked at the table. He explained that his was not a traditional Japanese house, because otherwise we would not be sitting on chairs, "and my wife would not be eating with us." He did not notice that she actually was not eating; she was present to replenish the sukiyaki pot, but there was no place laid for her, and she did not sit down!

In 1955 I attended the conference on "Atoms for Peace" in Geneva. It was exciting for me not so much for its scientific content, but because it was the first occasion after the war at which we could speak at length with scientists from the Soviet Union. We had had a few contacts earlier, particularly the year before, when the thaw initiated by Khrushchev had allowed a number of Russians to come to London for a meeting of an organisation called Parliamentarians for World Peace. Among them was M. A. Markov, a theoretical physicist who knew all our friends among the Russian physicists and brought us news of them; he also knew Genia's sister, Nina, and promised to send her a message. But the Geneva meeting was an occasion at which nuclear and high-energy physicists from East and West could actually exchange ideas and results; for example, it was the first time that we heard about Soviet accelerators. The main subject of the conference was, of course, nuclear power and the use of reactors for research, which was not really my field. In some sense the conference was like a huge trade fair. Some of the smaller countries did not want to be left out and had hurriedly set up atomic energy commissions consisting mostly of their military men, since they were the only ones who knew anything about atomic energy. I heard that one of these gentlemen had submitted a paper entitled "Military Aspects of the Peaceful Uses of Atomic Energy". It was not accepted.

In the evenings there were discourses on general topics by distinguished speakers. One of these was Niels Bohr, who, as always, was listened to with great attention, particularly as he had thought more deeply than most people about the future and about the dangers of nuclear weapons to the whole world. The conference had an elaborate system of simultaneous translation. In general, when the address was in English, the English channel was connected to the speaker's microphone. But during Bohr's talk the earphones for the English channel carried the voice of an interpreter reading Bohr's text. I never discovered whether the interpreter did not realise Bohr was speaking English, or whether he decided his reading would be more intelligible than Bohr's.

The East-West thaw in scientific relations continued, and in 1956 there was a conference in Moscow to which a considerable number of scientists from the West were invited. For me this was an especially welcome occasion, because Genia's sister, Nina, came to Moscow, and I was able to hear all about the fate of Genia's family. We had had no contact with them for eight years, and no detailed communication for much longer. I heard that neither parent was still alive, and that both had gone through very hard times. Genia's stepfather had spent some time in prison in conditions of great hardship, and on release had been exiled to a small town in Kazakhstan. Nina had, after the war, worked as a biologist in Moscow and, when the parents moved to Kazakhstan, she joined them and looked after them. She also took up an appointment in the local public health service, which involved introducing hygienic measures to primitive people. She liked this work, which involved travelling to remote areas by horse, camel, or truck, and continued in Alma Ata after her parents died.

It was also a great pleasure to meet my old friend Landau again and to hear of his ideas. He was then involved in discussing the basis of quantum field theory, and he maintained that he could disprove the theory, in spite of its great successes in accounting for all observed electromagnetic phenomena. He had by now become a very successful and popular teacher, and he was surrounded by a crowd of his students and collaborators. Since too many people wanted to become his pupils, he selected them by giving each candidate a problem and telling them, "When you have solved this problem, you can come and work with me." Some knew how to tackle the problem and brought back the answer in a week or so; some realised they had to study some more, and took a year or longer to solve the assigned problem. Many never came back.

In discussions with his pupils he was very severe and could wield devastating criticism. Nevertheless, the members of his group adored him and felt, rightly, that they derived enormous profit from working with him. This was demonstrated years later when he was seriously injured in a car accident. His friends and pupils worked in relays to obtain any available medicine, food, or other comforts for him, and they ran errands for the doctors in their frantic efforts to save his life. His life was indeed saved, but he never recovered to a point where he could enjoy life, let alone continue his contributions to physics.

During the conference I had an amusing conversation with Freeman Dyson, whose many accomplishments include a fair knowledge of Russian. He expressed surprise that Bogolyubov, another distinguished theoretician, had much closer personal relations with his students than Landau. This observation seemed incredible to me, as my impression was the very opposite, and I asked Dyson for his reason. He said that he had noticed that Landau's students called him by his surname, whereas Bogolyubov's students would use his first names, Nikolai Nikolaevich. What Dyson did not know was that the rather formal and respectful address in Russian is to use the Christian name and patronymic, and that the use of the surname without title is much more familiar. Besides, the students had surely not said "Landau", but "Dau", his nickname! Such are the pitfalls in knowing a language without knowing the customs.

The conference provided a simultaneous translation service for the foreign visitors, since their number was small. When the visitors talked, a Russian colleague would translate sentence by sentence. One such talk was by Keith Brueckner, an American theoretician who had initiated an ingenious but rather complicated theory, but his presentation was not always easy to follow. After a sentence or two, the translator gave up and said this talk should be translated by a theoretician. A theoretician took his place, but gave up, too. Finally, I was asked if I would be willing to do the job, and as I was familiar with Brueckner's work, I was able to do it.

Being in Moscow in 1956 was an exhilarating experience. There was a feeling of liberation from the oppressive Stalin regime, and every day people felt free to do things they would have been afraid to do the day before. But things often became a little chaotic, because the people had no experience with voluntary discipline. It was noticeable that even the scientists in meetings tended to disregard the instructions of their chairman, and pedestrians in the street would ignore the signals of policemen. I feared that, if this went on, the authorities would eventually have to return to a sterner regime. Indeed, this happened very soon in Hungary.

Summer Schools

Summer schools are meetings that last anywhere from a week to two months, and a number of lecturers give lecture courses to introduce the audience to some topics, usually chosen from a special field that has developed rapidly in recent years, and in which many students want to be brought up to date. The audience usually consists of research students but also includes some more senior people who want to broaden their experience to cover a new field.

One of the first series of summer schools of this type, and the first one in which I participated, was the French summer school at Les Houches, near Chamonix in the French Alps; its purpose was to introduce French students to quantum mechanics. At that time quantum mechanics was still not taught in French universities, and with the centralised education system, by which the syllabus of all university courses is under the control of the French Ministry of Education, it was difficult to introduce reforms. The idea and the initiative for the school came from Cecile Morette de Witt, an original and energetic French theoretician, married to an American.

I was invited to lecture at this school for a month in 1953 on the quantum theory of solids. I had not really been active in this field since the 1930s, and found this a good occasion to review my ideas on the subject. The lecturers were required to produce lecture notes, which would be reproduced and distributed to the students. I usually do not like writing out my lectures in advance, but agreed this time, on the understanding that I could take the notes as read and use the lectures to comment on them. I enjoyed the course and, as I mentioned earlier, I used the lecture notes as a basis for a book.

The school consisted of a barn that is converted into a lecture room, near to an hotel, where most of the students stayed and had their meals. We did our own housekeeping. I had most of the family with me, and we were given a small house a little way above the school. Our house had more space than we needed, and two students stayed on the top floor. They were nice young men, and one played the guitar very well. Their names were Philippe Nozières and Pierre-Giles De Gennes. In time both became famous theoretical physicists. Generally, students at Les Houches tended to work very hard, because for many of them the two months in the summer were a unique opportunity to build up their knowledge. Even the Saturday morning lecture had a full complement. But weekends were spent on strenuous walks or climbs in the mountains.

That summer the school faced practical difficulties. There was a very general strike in France, which affected the railways, the mail, the banks, and so on. The lecturers were to be paid by the school, but there was not enough cash for everybody. The hotel was taking in cash from tourists and helped the school pay at least those lecturers who were leaving, so that they could get home. By good fortune we had established credit with the local cooperative shop and could buy our food there. Some mail was sent to a post office across the border in Switzerland, and people took turns to collect it. But letters that were already on the way when the strike started took a long time to arrive. One of the first to get the delayed mail was Cecile de Witt, the director of the school, who had a lot of mail waiting for her in Paris. Her husband left the school early, stopped in Paris on his way to America, picked up the mail, and posted it back from New York to the Swiss accommodation address!

One of the letters that reached us rather late contained the information that my plane to the Japanese conference would leave a day earlier than planned. Fortunately, I still had enough time to get back to England for it, so we set out with Kitty and Jo in the car; there was no room for Ronnie, and he was going by train with some of the luggage. As we passed Vevey, on Lake Geneva, the car had a serious mechanical breakdown, and Genia had to stay to drive it back, while I took the children home by train; a message caught up with Ronnie just in time to get him to join us on the same train. The girls were then aged 4 and 5, but the journey caused no problem. Ronnie had to look after the girls at home until Genia returned.

In 1956 Genia and I went to a summer school in Mexico City, the first of a series of Latin-American summer schools. It was organised by Marcos Moshinsky, a Mexican theoretician of Russian origin. He is a great authority on the theory of nuclear spectra. His very charming wife unfortunately died a few years later. Other lecturers included Joe Levinger, an American theoretician who later spent a year in Birmingham. The mathematician Atiyah was in town for another meeting but stayed in our hotel, where we started an acquaintance that continued many years later when we were both in Oxford. Students in the school included Shelley Glashow, now a Nobel laureate for his work in particle physics; Martin Blume, who later became a solid-state expert at Brookhaven and a friend of Ronnie's; and André Martin, a cheerful young Frenchman who is by now well known for his many contributions to field theory.

R. G. Thomas from Los Alamos was another lecturer, who had come with a motorcycle that was specially low-geared for use in mountains. He had hopes of riding up Popocatepetl, but this proved too difficult. One day he was riding around in Mexico City, when a little boy ran out in front of him and was knocked over. The boy got up and shook himself; that would have been the end of the affair, if it had not happened just outside a police station. The police immediately took Thomas, the boy, and the bike into custody, following a practice that is normal in most Spanish-speaking countries. The boy was taken to hospital to determine whether or not his injuries would last longer than a specified time, because in law this determines the gravity of the offence. The hospital's X-ray tube had broken down, and instead of sending him to another hospital, they kept him under observation, which took the whole day. In the evening Thomas phoned to ask us for the papers for the bike, which were in his hotel room. He also had not had any food all day, so we took him some. A Cuban professor knew a Mexican senator, and they both came with us. At the police station the boy looked very glum, giving one the impression that he really had been hurt. Genia asked him whether he had had anything to eat, which he had not, so we gave him a good helping. He cheered up at once; there was nothing wrong with him except for the hunger. The senator pointed out to the police inspector that Thomas was a very distinguished scientist, sent by the U.S. government to lecture, and got the answer, "Yes, I know. We are very honoured to have him with us." But it took a few days and the intervention of several influential people to get him released on a few dollars' bail. When the case came to court, it collapsed because the essential witness, the little boy, could not be found. Not wanting to be involved with the police, he had given a wrong name and address.

We met the rector of the University of Mexico, Professor Carillo, a great character. He was by profession a civil engineer and also a member of the Mexican Atomic Energy Commission. In that capacity he attended the American atomic-bomb test in the Pacific, to which a number of foreign personalities had been invited to watch. He told us that when his boat returned to Oakland Naval Base, he saw his wife on the pier and told her, "I am glad to see you, but you need not have troubled to meet me here; I would have taken a plane home tomorrow," to which she replied, "No, you have been at sea for a month with only men, and were exposed to all this radioactivity—I would not let you spend a night in San Francisco without me!" He added that he told this story as light relief in some lecture about atomic energy, at which his wife was in the audience. She told her neighbor, "But you know, this radioactivity is very much overrated."

At the time of the Mexican summer school there were still restrictions on the amount of money we could take abroad, and there was some misunderstanding about the amount I would be paid for the lectures. It looked as if we might run short. I remembered that there was always a demand for translators by the American Physical Society, which publishes translations of the Russian physics journals. This work was quite well paid; I did not usually do it, because it would take too much time, but in Mexico I was not too busy, and the editor was willing to let me do just enough work that summer to fill the gap.

In 1958 I was invited to a summer school in Banff, in the Canadian Rockies. The programme sounded attractive, and it seemed an ideal spot for a family holiday. But the plan had to be cancelled because too few of the invited lecturers had accepted. (A few years later it did work out, and we spent a summer in Banff.) But by a strange coincidence I had no sooner learned about the cancellation than an invitation arrived for a summer school at the University of Colorado, in the American Rockies, which did, after all, provide us with the hoped-

271

for holiday. This was the first in a successful series of Colorado summer schools. The first one was not trouble-free because of delays in confirming funds and in making arrangements with the lecturers. As a result the public announcement was late, and there were practically no students. The audience at the lectures consisted of some local students and faculty who happened to be around for the summer, a few special students who were paid for taking lecture notes, and the other lecturers. The lack of students was of course disappointing, but for the school it was a kind of dress rehearsal; and the audience, while small, was intelligent and appreciative.

Besides exploring the surrounding mountains, we went swimming in a little reservoir in the neighbourhood. A group with a motorboat gave lessons in water skiing, so I decided to give it a try and in due course mastered the art. I was very pleased when, back in England, I saw the profile of an industrialist in the paper, which singled out for special mention that he had learned to water ski at the age of 50. I had just learned it at 51!

Among many other summer schools, there was the one at Ravello in 1963. It was actually a spring school, being held during Easter vacation. The host was Caianiello, the theoretical-physics professor in Naples. Ravello is a beautiful spot on a high escarpment by the sea, and our meetings were held in a palace. At the time of our meetings a film crew was shooting a film in the grounds of the palace. The action in the film was supposed to be taking place in spring, but that year spring was late. They could not put off the schedule of filming, so artificial flowers were planted all over the grounds. The film crew and the actors, who included Rossano Brazzi and George Sanders, stayed in our hotel, and at mealtime there was one long table for the physicists and one for the film people. After a while George Sanders came to sit with us. Physicists, he said, were much more amusing than film people. I suppose it was just the change of company that attracted him.

Other Visits

I did not often go away on longer visits, although university regulations made provision for such "sabbatical" absences. My reluctance was due mainly to the problem of research students. One could not just abandon them for long periods, and to arrange for someone else to supervise them was not always easy. (It was no longer possible to dispatch all one's students to another university, as Sommerfeld and

Heisenberg had done when I was their student.) I did, however, make a few such visits. The first was to the Institute for Advanced Study in Princeton in 1952. I stayed there for a semester, which in their schedule meant just over three months.

The Institute had become a very important centre for theoretical physics (as well as pure mathematics and many subjects in the humanities). Its director was Robert Oppenheimer, and under his guidance the place flourished. It had rather few permanent members, and, at least in physics, a large number of short-term visitors, who spent there anything from a semester to perhaps two years. Among the permanent physics members was C. N. Yang, who was then working closely with his friend, T. D. Lee. They later won the Nobel Prize for their prediction that the law of conservation of parity might be violated. Shortly after this they fell out, and nobody else understood the reason. All that the people at the Institute noticed were the loud and angry voices in Chinese emerging from the room used by the two, followed by Lee's departure for Columbia University. Yang remained at the Institute but later moved to the State University of New York at Stony Brook.

The other permanent members were Abraham Pais and my old friend George Placzek. Pais is a Dutchman who got his training during the war under the German occupation—a difficult achievement. He has an original mind and made a number of important suggestions in physics. His taste in physics problems is very personal, and one can never be sure that he will be interested in a problem that seems to one topical and exciting. George Placzek did not have a very satisfactory position after the war, until Oppenheimer, who appreciated both his understanding of physics and his human qualities, invited him to the Institute. At the time he was doing pioneer work on the use of neutron scattering for studying the structure of crystals and other substances. This method has since become a very important research tool. He had a very able young Belgian, Léon van Hove, working with him in this field. Van Hove continued for a time in this line, becoming an authority on neutron diffraction, before turning to other subjects. Of course Oppenheimer, besides being the Institute's director, was also a permanent member of the physics group. He was very much in demand as an adviser to various government bodies, and this left him too little time for research. But he followed the current fundamental work and presided at most of the seminars, where his gift for clarification allowed him to sort out many difficulties and made the discussions very fruitful. His great gift for criticism also showed up on these occasions. When a speaker came up with a wrong argument he was likely to be stopped by Oppenheimer, and often this would get the discussion back on the rails. But he was by no means always right, and there were occasions when a perfectly sensible speaker found himself contradicted at every step. One needed great confidence in one's own reasoning (or great stubbornness) to persist.

I enjoyed my colleagues at the Institute and learned much from both the permanent members and the transients. I had brought projects with me for which I just needed time to think and calculate. One of these was a way of expressing the basic rules of quantum mechanics in a new form, which was applicable to situations to which the conventional rules could not be applied. I was specially pleased about this because Freeman Dyson, whose judgment in such matters I respected, had assured me that such a thing was impossible. I also used the opportunity to work on my scheme for introducing a finite size for the electron, and thus avoiding the infinite self-energy. This was the scheme that later proved unworkable, but one could not tell until it had been studied in detail. The Institute's setup, however, was not congenial for all the visitors. If they were looking for collaboration and advice, they were unlikely to get it from the permanent members, and it was a matter of luck whether they could find the right kind of help from other transients.

During my stay in Princeton I attended the New York meeting of the American Physical Society, which was then an annual event at about the end of January. These are huge meetings (and have become bigger since then) at which every member of the society has the right to present a paper. These papers are usually limited to ten minutes, but even then there is not enough time without having a large number of sessions run in parallel. The talks one is interested in seem to take place simultaneously in different sections, or at nearly the same time in rather distant locations. I also found that the amount of information that can be conveyed in ten minutes, or the enlightenment from the ensuing discussion, is not really useful. Some speakers, particularly young and inexperienced ones, try to condense much information into their talk by writing out the text and reading it at top speed, and by using slides containing many graphs or equations. The result is of course that the talk conveys no information whatever to the audience.

Nevertheless, these big meetings serve some useful purposes; one used to be the job market: chairmen of physics departments would use the meetings to watch for young people looking for posts. I believe the conferences no longer serve that function, since there is now such heavy competition for appointments that the selection tends to be made earlier in the year. I found it useful to go to the talks of people whose names I knew from their papers, and so to discover what they looked like. I could then look for them in the lobbies and discuss common problems with them. In recent years even this approach has become difficult. The meetings have become so large that it is almost hopeless to try to find a particular person among the crowd. I remember one occasion when I saw a colleague to whom I wanted to talk as he was going down on an escalator while I was going up. I never passed him again. At the later conferences the best plan was to make the most of accidental encounters with acquaintances.

The next time I took sabbatical leave was in early 1959, and I spent a semester at Columbia University in New York. This again was an opportunity to get on with research work that had been vaguely in my mind, but had been put aside under the pressure of routine work. It was also an opportunity for new contacts and new ideas. There were many interesting people in the department, including T. D. Lee, whom I already knew from Princeton; Giancarlo Wick, an old friend from Rome; I. I. Rabi, the wise old man of physics; and many bright young people. Hugh Burkhardt, who had just done a Ph.D. in Birmingham (and would return later as a lecturer) was there. So was Steven Weinberg, who later became famous and earned a Nobel Prize through his work on the foundations of the modern synthesis of electromagnetic and weak interactions. He was a pleasant young man, with quick reactions and a somewhat bitter sense of humour. I must confess that I did not spot the great ability that became evident later.

I gave a course of lectures for graduate students. It was interesting to learn how the American teaching system works. One very obvious difference is that students tend to be more argumentative, asking questions and disputing the lecturer's statements. They show much less of the British students' respect for the lecturer, something one must make a great effort to combat in England. My lectures were the second part of a course on nuclear physics; the first semester's lectures had been given by Rainwater, a well-known physicist who had played an important part in the development of the ideas about rotational states of nuclei. I had his lecture notes; they were very concentrated and seemed to contain a very large amount of detail for one semester's course. I struggled to understand them so I could build on them. But I soon discovered that the students had not understood much, though I did not decide whether the lectures were too hard or the students too slow. So I returned to my more modest ideas about the material to be covered, and it seems the lectures went down well.

I did not find the Pupin Laboratory, the Physics Department of Columbia, a very easy place for social intercourse. It was a tall building, with the offices spread over several floors, so that one did not often run across people. I believe in all my time there it happened only once that on going out to lunch I encountered a colleague with the same intention, so that we had lunch together. Of course it was always possible to make an appointment to join someone for lunch, and I certainly did that if I had a definite topic to discuss. But this does not replace the casual encounters common in other places.

Once a week we took part in a ritual to have lunch at a Chinese restaurant. Besides Madame Wu, the great nuclear experimentalist, and T. D. Lee, the department had many other connoisseurs of Chinese food, and ordering was always a matter of serious and prolonged discussion.

Life in uptown New York was in many ways like life in a small town. I stayed within walking distance of the university, and often did not use any public transport for weeks on end. In the local shops everybody knew everybody else, and at the small post office the line was slow because everybody had to exchange the local news with the woman behind the counter. Once, as I was waiting my turn in a long queue, a girl who was a few places ahead of me finished her purchases, and after she left the queue she remembered that she had forgotten to ask for ten 2-cent stamps. She stood there wondering whether she would have to go back to the end of the queue. By this time my turn had come; I made my purchase and also asked for ten 2-cent stamps, which I passed to the girl. She looked up in surprise and said, "Spring must be in the air!"

One of the speakers in the departmental colloquium was V. A. Fock, an eminent Russian theoretician. He had shown great energy and courage in defending the theory of relativity in the Soviet Union when it was attacked as being contrary to dialectic materialism. In doing so he had studied the basic principles of relativity, in order to understand them quite clearly, and he thought that he had understood some points that had been missed by everyone else and thus gave a new presentation of the theory. After his talk we took him to dinner in the Faculty Club. By this time Fock was very deaf, and he carried with him an old-fashioned black-box hearing aid, whose batteries were perpetually failing. This made dinner conversation difficult. One of the party was L. H. Thomas, a very able and original theoretician who was perhaps a little professorial in manner. He had just been elected president of the Lions Club in his suburb, and was being congratulated all around. Somebody suggested he explain to Fock about the Lions, and he launched into a long description. Fock did not realise he was being addressed, and he had switched off his hearing-aid to save the batteries.

I could have remedied that, but I did not think the story of the Lions would have got across. So I did nothing, and the speech by Thomas, in which he explained that the Lions had made it their purpose to do everything possible for blind people, fell rather flat. There was a silence, which I broke by saying, "How interesting that they use Lions for this now; they used to use dogs." I do not think Thomas liked the remark.

Genia had not come with me to New York. She did not want to leave the small children for four months, and she knew it did not make sense to bring them. Going on a sabbatical visit with small children creates many problems; housing is more difficult, and the children catch all the local infections to which they are not immune. The mother is busy looking after them and does not see much of the place. The father is preoccupied with all the little domestic disasters, and gets distracted from his work. Instead, Genia came half-way through the period for a few weeks' visit without the children. For such a short time it was easy to make satisfactory arrangements for them. By this time I had worked hard, and felt able to take some time off; I had also saved up my visits to other universities, so that we could travel together. This worked out very well. An extra bonus was that she could meet our prospective daughter-in-law, whom Ronnie had met in the Gilbert-and-Sullivan-like encounter reported earlier. Genia always advised younger wives to follow her example in dealing with sabbaticals, but they did not often heed her. However, when they returned from their family sabbaticals, they often said, "Now we know what you meant!"

During my previous stay in Princeton, Genia had not come for such a visit, partly because of domestic problems—this was the time when Jo had gone to London for her physical training—but largely for lack of money. My third sabbatical leave was from Oxford in 1967; I shall come to this later.

Other Contacts. Harwell

In 1945 the Atomic Energy Research Establishment was set up at Harwell to carry out basic research aimed at the development of nuclear power and at the possibility of developing nuclear weapons. The actual industrial aspects of nuclear power were the responsibility of another establishment at Risly in Lancashire, and the design of nuclear weapons, when it was decided that this should proceed, became the task of the weapons laboratory at Aldermaston.

I became a consultant to Harwell, and served on some of its committees, including the one charged with the design of the isotope separation plant, for which I used my experience of work on the design of such a plant during the war. I therefore paid frequent visits to Harwell, including many social visits to our friends there. The first director of Harwell was Cockcroft, on whose efficiency I have commented earlier. Although he was universally respected, he would occasionally create a little friction because of his failure to communicate. He tended to be extremely brief in speech and writing, and while this allowed him to get through an incredible amount of work, his staff often complained that they did not know what was on his mind.

His second-in-command was Herbert Skinner, a well-known experimental physicist, whom we had known since the thirties. He was more forceful in conversation than Cockcroft; he tended to hold strong opinions, often more conservative than those of most physicists, and was never reluctant to make them known. His lively personal contacts with the staff of Harwell made up for Cockcroft's detachment. In 1949, after Chadwick had resigned from the physics chair at Liverpool, Skinner succeeded him. J. M. Cassels, a very bright young experimentalist, joined him and became a second professor in Liverpool. The personalities of the two men were not very compatible, and there was a good deal of friction. Blackett commented "What can you expect when an angry young man is supposed to work under an angry old man?"

Erna Skinner, Herbert's wife, came from a central European background. She was a brilliant conversationalist with a wide knowledge and appreciation of literature, and became particularly friendly with Genia. The Skinners were very sociable, and we often visited them, with or without our children. For many years we spent Christmas together either in their house or in ours.

Other friends at Harwell included Klaus Fuchs, who had become the head of the theoretical physics division, until the shattering blow of his arrest in 1950 (see chapter 9). He was not replaced as division head for some time, and for a while Maurice Pryce, then the professor in Oxford, acted as part-time head. He was well qualified for this because of the breadth of his knowledge and interests. He could be a devastating critic, and it is said that after each of his visits to Harwell someone had to go round to comfort the young people he had seen and assure them there was still a chance they might turn out to be competent theoreticians.

When Pryce went to America for a year's sabbatical leave, I looked after the division on a part-time basis, though this was not as easy from Birmingham as it was for Pryce from Oxford. Eventually Brian

Flowers took over the division, as I have already mentioned. I continued as occasional consultant to Harwell, but the problems with which I am concerned became more specialised and more marginal.

For a number of years I was a consultant to the Nuclear Power division of the English Electric Company. I went there a few times a year, and found their problems very varied and interesting. It so happened that several members of their theoretical physics group were former Birmingham students, and we found it easy to speak a common language. They usually brought up their queries in a form I could understand and followed up my suggestions.

The best man in the group was Glen Schaefer, a Canadian who had been a student in Birmingham. He had worked with Gerry Brown on a difficult problem in the then new quantum electrodynamics. His Ph.D. thesis on that subject was ready when Hans Bethe was in Cambridge, and we chose him as "external examiner" for Schaefer. He liked the thesis, but was a little doubtful about the candidate's general knowledge; in the oral examination, he had given satisfactory answers to questions relating to the thesis, but he had not responded as well on other matters. In the end it was decided to pass him, and it was therefore very rewarding to see him doing first-rate work in a field completely different from that of his thesis.

Schaefer actually changed his field again. He was a keen bird watcher, and on vacation trips he liked to go on bird-watching expeditions. In order to extend his observations to nighttime, he built himself a radar set, which could spot birds in the dark. The pictures he got were not sharp enough to identify the species of birds from their shape, but they showed the rhythm of their wing movements, and that was usually enough for identification. This project became known, and soon the University of Loughborough offered him an appointment to do work on this borderline field between electronics and zoology. I found this a gratifying confirmation of my view that good research training in one field can be good preparation for research in anything else.

In the 1960s the nuclear power research of the English Electric was reorganized. The theoretical group was split up, and its members assigned to various engineering groups that needed theoretical help. As a result my role as consultant became less useful and my connection with the firm came to an end.

I tried to make other similar contacts with industry. I was always convinced that the experience and way of thinking of theoretical physicists could be useful in more practical fields, and my experience during the war, in the contacts with English Electric, and in other casual encounters tended to confirm this. I enjoyed these problems, and such contacts were also useful in demonstrating to my students that their talents could be put to good use outside the narrow academic field. I regretted, therefore, that I was not more successful in my search for other such arrangements.

Various activities outside the university kept me busy as well. I served on different committees, including the council of the Royal Society. This is an unusual body, in that its forms are very democratic, but in fact the power to make decisions rests very largely in the hands of the officers. Council members normally serve for two years, whereas the officers' term is much longer. In any organisation it takes some time before a new member becomes familiar with the procedures and can exert his influence, and this is not a negligible fraction of a two-year term. I actually served for only one year, because during the following year I was going on one of my sabbatical leaves, and therefore would not have been able to attend the meetings regularly. My contribution to the work of the council was therefore not great, but I did what I could.

Another body on which I served for a time was the board of NIRNS, the National Institute for Research in Nuclear Science. This was a government-funded but independent body that operated the Ruther-ford Laboratory, which was to provide a high-energy accelerator and other facilities for use mainly by the universities who could not afford to build such equipment. I enjoyed the meetings under Lord Bridges, a very experienced and skillful chairman. He knew exactly at what point to deflect a discussion that was getting confused and would invite one or more of the members to look into the question and give a report.

The work of the board was on the whole very easy, as Gerry Pick-avance, the director of the laboratory, knew his job, and his proposals were always sensible. Under his direction the main accelerator func-tioned well, and many useful experiments were done with it, though these included no great discoveries. The machine was closed down when the experimental programme demanded more modern acceler-ators, and the work of the British teams is now carried out in foreign laboratories, mostly at CERN, the European laboratory in Geneva, and in America. The laboratory continues with other duties.

Other committees I served on were concerned with publications. For some years I sat on the Papers Committee of the Physical Society, including a period as its chairman. This was at a time when, in postwar conditions, paper and printing facilities were short, and the size of the journals was limited. This meant that we had to be very selective in accepting papers, and to ensure that they were as brief as was consistent with clarity, and as clear as possible within a reasonable length. We therefore had all papers refereed strictly and insisted that authors complied with the changes requested by the referees. Although the paper shortages have eased, these established traditions have continued, and I believe that the papers in English journals compare favourably in brevity and clarity with those, for example, in American journals.

Immediately after the war there was great public interest in atomic energy, and I lectured and broadcast on such subjects on many occasions. I then noticed that many of the questions from the audiences did not relate to the danger of nuclear weapons, or the blessings of nuclear power, but to the underlying physical laws. How was it possible for nuclei to be held together by pi-mesons, when no such mesons existed in a normal nucleus? I liked to answer such questions, but to answer them in depth was impossible during a short question period, because they are part of a long story. One has to go through a chain of successive steps of reasoning to make the explanations intelligible. This was my motivation for writing my book *The Laws of Nature*, which tried to tell the story without mathematics and without jargon. I enjoyed writing it, and it was reasonably successful.

12

Problems of
Nuclear Weapons

My work on nuclear weapons had ceased in 1945, but not my concern with the problems they created. Like most of the people who had worked on this project, I was aware of the possibilities for the future. It was clear to us that nuclear war would be an unthinkable disaster, and we hoped that recognition of this danger might open up a way to eliminate war. At first the United States had a monopoly of these weapons. Perhaps they would make wise use of it in the interests of international order. This was the time when an American committee under Lilienthal wrote, largely on the initiative of Oppenheimer, a proposal for the international control of atomic energy. In England the scientists who had worked on atomic energy, and many others, formed the Atomic Scientists' Association, with the aims of educating the public on problems concerning atomic energy and to work for an acceptable form of control. We were enthusiastic about the Lilienthal proposals, though there were details that needed elaborating.

The Lilienthal report eventually led to the "Baruch Plan" proposed by Bernard Baruch to the United Nations. It was essentially the same plan, but the presentation had lost some of the elegance of the original proposal, and some of its generosity. Doubtless Baruch was aware of the difficulty of getting the United States Congress to accept the plan, and he therefore stressed the features that made it look favourable to American interests, and these naturally made it look less attractive in Soviet eyes. Looking back, I now believe it made no difference. There never was a chance of getting such a plan accepted by the Soviet Union. Any such plan necessarily implied a surrender of some part of national sovereignty, and in face of the temporary U.S. monopoly of nuclear weapons this would appear too humiliating in Soviet eyes. When we began to understand this, I said that perhaps when the Russians had their own nuclear weapon they would be easier to talk with. Some of my friends, particularly Americans, were horrified by this thought; to them a Russian nuclear weapon would be utter disaster.

The Atomic Scientists' Association, or A.S.A., spent much time discussing forms of international control that would be acceptable to all sides, and some of our proposals attracted favourable comment from all sides of the political spectrum. The association was run by a council, and its officers, besides the president and the secretary, included a number of vice presidents. These were distinguished scientists; among them were some known for their left-wing views, while others were solid citizens such as Sir George Thomson, and Conservatives like Lord Cherwell. Cherwell supported the A.S.A. for a time, though he disagreed with some of its views, and eventually this led to difficulties.

Cherwell used to say that scientists should not meddle in politics, and it apparently never struck him that such a statement by a professor of physics who had long been an adviser to Churchill, and for a time a cabinet minister, sounded odd. I had a disagreement with him at an international conference on nuclear physics in Chicago in 1951, during a discussion of the problems of nuclear weapons. In the course of the discussion the French physicist Pierre Auger expressed the idea that it might be good for stability if there were a third power besides the United States and the Soviet Union, and that perhaps India could play this part. Cherwell regarded this idea as complete nonsense: India may be a large country with many people, but that was not the point. What counted was only economic strength and military potential, and in these respects India was nowhere. When my turn came, I could not resist saying, "I cannot follow Lord Cherwell in his Marxist interpretation of history." He never forgave me.

Besides being concerned with international problems, the A.S.A. tried to contribute to public education on atomic energy matters. There was much demand for such information, and many of us gave talks to many diverse groups. The association also organised an "atomic train", an exhibition mounted in railway carriages, which travelled around the country, stopping in many towns. In each place some members of the A.S.A. or other volunteers would act as guides. One of the first exhibits was a model of a helium atom, showing a light symbolising the nucleus, with two smaller lights revolving around it, representing the two electrons of helium. Brian Flowers was the guide, when an old lady asked him, "Do these electrons always keep going around in the same direction?" Brian said they did. "Then how do you reverse the train?" But in general, the exhibition met with a favourable and intelligent response.

The officers and council members of the A.S.A. were largely people

283

who had been involved in the atomic weapons project during the war, but others also gave valuable service. Nevill Mott was president for a period, and Frank Nabarro, a theoretician in the Metallurgy Department at Birmingham until he moved to Johannesburg, was editor of the *Atomic Scientists' News*, the journal of the association.

But in the 1950s the association ran out of steam. The trouble was that too much of the burden of running the organisation was carried by the older people, who had been directly involved in atomic-energy work. We did not attract enough young people. This was perhaps because the younger people did not feel that they had any particular expertise in the subject. More important was the feeling that, however important the international problems, there was little that a British organisation could do. The future depended essentially on what the United States and the Soviet Union were doing. We might try to persuade our government to use its influence with the "superpowers" in the right direction, but this prospect was too remote to attract enthusiastic support. There was also friction because some of the vice-presidents objected to statements being made without their approval. Finally the association was wound up.

By this time a new, international activity was taking place in the form of the Pugwash conferences. These originated in a manifesto written by Bertrand Russell and signed by Einstein just before his death. It called on scientists of all countries to save the world from nuclear war. This resulted in a series of conferences on "science and world affairs". The first of these was financed by the Canadian industrialist Cyrus Eaton, and was held, at his request, in his birthplace, Pugwash, Nova Scotia, from which the conferences take their name.

Cecil Powell, the Nobel laureate physicist, was the first chairman, and Joseph Rotblat became secretary-general. Rotblat had shown great concern about nuclear weapons ever since he had left Los Alamos in 1945. He had been active in the A.S.A. while the organisation seemed to have some hope of acquiring influence, and he now made the Pugwash conferences his main concern. He was secretary-general until he retired from this office in 1973, and even afterwards he continued to devote much of his time and energy to Pugwash.

The conferences consist of scientists from many nations, including the USSR and other communist republics, as well as the United States, Britain, and other Western countries. They also include scientists from Japan, India, and many of the developing nations, and at first there were also some Chinese. The term "scientist" is here used in the European sense of including scholars who are not natural scientists, though the majority of the participants are, with physicists particularly prominent.

The conferences do not vote to pass resolutions, but all their statements are by consent of all, or nearly all, those present. One might think that with such rules, and such a mixed composition, the conferences would never be able to express anything but trivial sentiments. When I attended my first Pugwash conference in 1960 in Moscow, I did not expect much. I was surprised and gratified to see how much good sense could come out of such meetings in spite of their limitations.

In the discussions the dominant theme is disarmament, but other related sujects, such as measures to reduce international tension, means to reduce the risk of accidental nuclear war, and international scientific cooperation, are included. The conferences do not aim at publicity, but try, in the first place, to reach an understanding of the issues, and to determine the factors impeding agreement in the views of the nations involved. Any insight gained in this way is transmitted by the participants to their governments as far as possible, and there have been instances in which this information has been of help to the official negotiators.

For example, at a conference in India in 1964 we discussed anti-ballistic missiles, and the scientists from the West tried to convince the Russians that such a missile defence would have a destabilising effect and would lead to an escalation of the arms race. It seemed at the time that we failed to get the idea across. But years later, at a press conference, Millionshchikov, the senior Russian member, recalled this discussion and commented that we learned much from each other, and that he passed the lesson on to his government. Although he could not say what effect his communication had, these were the ideas that are now incorporated into the SALT I agreement.

One should not, of course, overrate the effect such conferences can have. The arms race is still with us, and at this time is proceeding at an accelerated pace. But the issues are so vital that even a small chance of exerting an influence in the right direction is worth much effort.

Perhaps Pugwash was of particular importance in its early days, when there were very few informal meetings across the ideological divisions, and some people argued that later, when the cold-war atmosphere eased, and many different groups conducted such discussions, Pugwash had lost its raison d'être. But the international climate changes, and today, after the events in Afghanistan and Poland, contacts are more difficult than before, and it is again important to maintain a proved channel. It is also a fact that in such discussions scientists seem to understand each other more quickly and more completely than others. This does not imply that they are less prejudiced than other people, but their profession trains them to listen carefully to views opposed to their own. If a physicist makes a statement about a theoretical problem or about experimental data, and this is contradicted by a colleague, he will be anxious to debate this in detail because he knows that, if he is right, this will become clear in the discussion, and if he should be wrong, the sooner he finds out the better.

It also helps that many of the scientists from different countries know each other personally, or through their work, and have confidence in each other's integrity. Of course our discussions take place in a real world, and one could not expect that a Soviet scientist would at the meetings express views contrary to his country's official line. But if he holds unpopular views he may remain silent. Particularly in the case of familiar figures such as the late I. E. Tamm, or the late L. A. Artsimovich, I could feel absolutely sure that they would never express views in which they did not believe.

The conferences were run by a "continuing committee" of which Cecil Powell was chairman. He was not only a great physicist, but a person of great charm, warmth, and sense of proportion, and his efforts did much to create what we call the "Pugwash spirit". After his death I chaired the committee meetings for some years, and I deputised for him earlier when he was unable to attend. I was in the chair at a number of meetings at times of great tension, as at the height of the Vietnam War and after the invasion of Czechoslovakia, and these occasions were a valuable lesson in patience.

The conferences work in groups. Each group is assigned a specific topic and produces a report on its discussions and on any conclusions reached. In the end the whole is summarised in a statement from the conference. At first this statement was approved by a plenary session of the whole conference, but it proved too troublesome to discuss wording in a large meeting, and the drafting was then delegated to the committee. Even this was hard enough, particularly since the statement was required for a press conference that usually had to be held the day after the end of the meetings. Many times the committee sat through the night settling the text of the statement.

Another topic that was debated at the conferences was the "North-South" problem, i.e., the needs of the developing countries. To ensure an informed discussion this made it necessary to have the developing countries well represented. Since travel funds are not easily available in these countries, this caused financial problems. Fairness also made it necessary to add members from the developing countries to the committee (now renamed Council), which has become almost as large as the early conferences.

To me, and to many others, this was not a desirable change. There is no doubt that the problems of development are of great importance, but it is not clear that the Pugwash conferences are the right forum for discussing them. Many of us feel that the emphasis on these problems may detract from the primary object of Pugwash, which is the avoidance of nuclear war. Of late the tendency has been to restrict the work on development problems to issues concerning the security of developing countries, and that seems a good move.

The selection of participants from each country is usually in the hands of a national Pugwash group, which is also responsible for paying the travelling expenses of its members, and for organising and hosting conferences and symposia in their countries. These groups do not get any official support and their members' subscriptions are nominal. They therefore have severe problems in raising the necessary voluntary support. In the case of the British group, we find in addition the same difficulty we experienced in the A.S.A.—the advancing age of the active members and the failure to recruit a sufficient number of young people. The group is now busy trying to remedy both these difficulties.

My own conclusion from the experience of these conferences, and from watching the international negotiations about arms control, is that the problem is made difficult by the insistence on balance and on verification. On the face of it the idea that any arms control agreement should leave the two sides in approximate balance seems very reasonable, but in reality it creates prohibitive difficulties. In the negotiations between the United States and the Soviet Union, and their allies, it is evident that the geographical and strategic situations of the two sides are different; that their nuclear weapons, the means of delivering them, and their intelligence organisations are completely different; and that therefore any evaluation of the relative strength becomes highly speculative. Recently there has even been a tendency to subdivide the problem by trying to balance strategic weapons by themselves, and by treating intermediate-range missiles in Europe separately, and this division makes the problem even harder.

In fact, everyone now knows that nuclear weapons are not suitable for fighting wars, since a large-scale nuclear war would be suicidal for both sides, and that the only purpose they serve is as a deterrent against nuclear attack by others. For this purpose the stockpiles of weapons held by both the "superpowers" are grossly excessive, and their relative size is of no consequence. If one side has enough weapons to wipe

287

out the cities of the other ten times over, their security does not suffer if the other side can do so twenty times. Each side could therefore safely reduce their armour substantially without regard to what the others do. Only if this process were to reach a point where it is doubtful whether the remaining strength is an adequate deterrent would one have to look at the number and power of the weapons. It is hard to understand why this simple truth is not evident to the leaders on either side. Perhaps they are still thinking about military strength in traditional ways, appropriate for tank forces or battle fleets, and have not yet understood that *nuclear weapons are not battleships?*

Verification would be desirable, as it would reduce mutual suspicion, but to be complete it would require a very pervasive inspection of each country, which the Soviet Union, with their traditional suspicion of foreign intervention and of spies, would never accept. The development of reconnaissance satellites, and the recognition of their role in the SALT I treaty is a welcome development.

Another very worrying factor is the presence in Europe of so-called tactical nuclear weapons, and the doctrine of NATO that these be used in response to a non-nuclear attack that cannot be stopped by conventional weapons. There is no clearly definable distinction between tactical and strategic weapons, and there would be an intolerable risk of escalation to a full nuclear war.

13

Oxford

Departure from Birmingham

In 1961 I was offered the Wykeham Chair of Physics in Oxford, which since the war had in effect become a chair of theoretical physics. This was a tempting offer because of the quality of the intellectual life in Oxford, and because after over twenty-four years in Birmingham (though with interruptions) it seemed time for a change. Yet I was apprehensive of the more complicated structure of the university, and the somewhat ill-defined status of theoretical physics. I knew that Oxford, with its great history, was more influenced by tradition, and I expected that it would be much harder to make innovations. In a sense I was spoilt by Birmingham, where, in academic matters, departments were free to do as they liked, within reason.

After the usual agonising period, I decided to take the plunge. When I was asked for my reason, I would quote the need for a change and add that if I had been in Oxford for so many years I would probably have liked to move to Birmingham. But I also added that, in the prospect of running a department in Oxford, there was a challenge like that of a mountain climber who might say, "I have done this mountain, now let's see if I can do the north side in winter." I now feel that this comment was not fair to Oxford.

I needed some assurances, however, that I would get the necessary support. It was essential to get such assurances before I accepted the chair, because once I had accepted, I would have lost my bargaining power and would have had to rely on persuasion. The promises I wanted included a new readership and some space for theoretical physics, which was scattered over odd rooms in the Clarendon Laboratory and in some other university buildings. These negotiations took some time because they were outside the jurisdiction of the Electoral Board, which was to make the appointment. Eventually it was all settled, and I accepted early in 1962. But I felt I needed some time

289

to sever my ties with Birmingham and postponed taking up the Oxford appointment until the autumn of 1963.

The Birmingham department gave me a very warm send-off. They had a big party with various humourous sketches and presented a film that parodied my Birmingham career. Some shots had been taken of me walking to and from the department; others showed me cycling between home and university, but my part was played by someone else wearing my hat and coat, which he had "borrowed" for awhile.

I had hoped that my postponement of the move would allow the university to appoint my successor in time. However, the negotiations took longer than expected. When I left, Geoffrey Chester agreed to act as head of the department for a year before moving to a post at Cornell University, and Tony Skyrme, who had accepted the chair, did not return from Malaysia until after that.

In Oxford, theoretical physics had traditionally been part of the Clarendon Laboratory, but recently it had become a separate department; this made sense because experimental physics had become divided, with nuclear physics becoming a department of its own, and the Clarendon retaining all other physics, particularly low-temperature and condensed-matter work, as well as microwave, electronics, and spectroscopy. Theoretical physics was concerned with all these topics, and it would not have been right for it to "belong" to either of the other branches.

Arriving in Oxford was very different from my beginnings at Birmingham, because in Oxford theoretical physics was a going concern. My first obligation was evidently to avoid interfering with the good work going on there and to encourage it, before starting any new developments.

The senior people in the department included D. ter Haar, who had been in charge during the year when there was no professor. He is a Dutchman with experience in many fields, particularly in statistical mechanics, and had trained many research students. He is a good linguist, and besides his research and teaching he did a good deal of translating and editing. With all these activities his time had to be well organised, and he often retired to his college room where, at that time, he had no telephone and was saved interruptions. After my arrival, we often had practical matters to discuss because he had been the acting head of the department, and it turned out that the best time for this was about 8:30 A.M., after we had both taken our children to school. The phenomenon of two theoreticians finding this a congenial time must be somewhat rare. Ter Haar is a lively debater; at meetings he had a tendency to ask very aggressive questions of the speaker, which did not always make him popular. In recent years his interests have moved to plasma physics and astrophysics.

Roger Elliott was the leader on the theory of solids, in which he had made a name for himself, and he was working with many students and more senior visitors. He, too, has the ability to get through large amounts of assorted work without appearing to be rushed. This facility came to serve him well when he later became very active in university administration. He became my successor in 1974.

David Brink was the leading expert on nuclear theory. He is an Australian, with a Swiss wife, and in 1963 he already had a reputation for originality and a very flexible approach to problems. He also was a prolific source of inspiration for graduate students.

The strength of the department was further enhanced by the arrival of Dick Dalitz as a Royal Society Professor. He had been at the University of Chicago; but he was persuaded to accept the Royal Society Research Professorship and to choose Oxford as the place in which to hold it. He came at first only for a trial period, keeping open the option to return to Chicago, but in the end he settled down in Oxford and had many excellent pupils.

John C. Taylor was appointed as the new reader, and he, too, worked in particle physics and field theory. He is a rather quiet person whose depth is not immediately apparent; but he has excellent judgment, which he manages to impart to his students, and he has contributed many original ideas to his subject. He returned to Cambridge in 1980 as a professor.

Besides Dalitz there were other friends from the Birmingham days. Robin Stinchcombe was in a temporary post when I arrived, and later became a regular lecturer and fellow of New College. He was a Birmingham product; his main interest is in solid-state theory. He has a very modest and self-effacing manner, which hides a good deal of confidence in his indeed very considerable ability. For a time he had very heavy teaching duties, conducting some thirteen hours of college tutorials a week besides giving lectures for the department and keeping up his research and looking after that of his students.

Leonardo Castillejo came to Oxford when I did, and stayed as a lecturer for a number of years. He eventually returned to University College, London, as a professor, almost as soon as his new house near Oxford was completed. Two other friends from Birmingham, Ian Aitchison and Jack Paton, came later. Both added to the strength of the elementary-particle side of the department and have become very popular members of their colleges.

291

University and Colleges

The structure of the University of Oxford is very different from that of Birmingham, and in a way it is completely unique, differing in important respects even from Cambridge. In both universities the colleges play an essential part. They are responsible for the selection of undergraduates, for housing them and looking after them, and for tutorial teaching. Lectures, laboratories, and examinations are the responsibility of the university (in science subjects carried out largely through the departments). The tutorial teaching carries great weight, even more in Oxford than in Cambridge. In the humanities, lectures are hardly of any importance, and there is no general syllabus that ensures that all aspects of the subject are covered. In science there does exist a scheme of lectures. The terms of appointment of the teachers contain an obligation to give a specified number of lectures, but nobody has the authority to tell them on what subject to lecture; the person responsible for the lecture list usually has to use a lot of persuasion to get the right coverage.

Each college has a complement of fellows covering the main subjects, and they teach their students singly or in pairs. This involves only an hour or two a week, but the students are made to read and to write essays or work problems for their tutors. I have known physics tutors who would never send a student to a lecture course unless they have previously gone over the subject with him in tutorials. When the college has no fellow with the right expertise, or there are more students than the relevant fellows can handle, some additional people who are not regular fellows are appointed college "lecturers" to do the additional teaching, or graduate students are used for the purpose; but in general a fellow keeps an eye on the arrangements.

Most college fellows also hold university appointments, and vice versa. A college fellowship without a university post represents a heavy financial burden for the college, if the fellow is to receive an adequate salary. A university appointment without a college fellowship is usually unattractive, both because the fellowship involves an additional income (but also additional teaching duties, which can be heavy) and because of the feeling that you are an outsider if you do not take part in college life. Therefore, wherever possible, new appointments are made jointly to a college and to a university post, and there is an elaborate system for deciding which college is to be associated with a vacant university appointment. This often makes the selection process very involved, because the college and the university department or committee may have different preferences among the applicants. The head of a department has to learn the art of negotiating with a college in a way that makes the college arrive at the right choice without feeling it is being pushed.

Professors are in a somewhat different position. They are not allowed to do any college teaching. From the point of view of the college, they are therefore parasites. They do not receive a salary from the college but share all amenities, including free meals. They sit on the governing body, and while they perhaps contribute wisdom and experience to its deliberations, the tutorial fellows often fear that the professors might exert undue influence in it.

Each professorship is by statute assigned to a definite college. There were complications when men's and women's colleges could not appoint fellows of the opposite sex, and in each case the statutes had to make the provision that if a woman was appointed to the chair she would become a fellow of a certain women's college. Now, with the restrictions gone in most colleges, such clauses are no longer necessary, and the statutes are being changed gradually to reflect the times.

My chair, the Wykeham Chair of Physics, is attached to New College, as its name indicates; Bishop Wykeham was the founder of the college. However, while the name gives the impression of an old tradition, the chair is a recent foundation; I was only its fourth holder. In spite of my occasional feeling of being a parasite in the college, I enjoyed (and still enjoy) my association with it. Apart from the beautiful setting and the amenities, fellowship of a college gives one the opportunity of close contact with leading scholars in different fields; New College has certainly had a good supply of these.

When I joined the college I was aware of the peculiar status of a professorial fellow, and in replying to a welcoming speech at my first formal college dinner, I used the analogy with the position of a son-in-law in a family: each arrives by a selection process not under one's control, except for a veto right that is seldom used, each is received with goodwill and the hope that he will prove to be an acceptable member of the family.

The college is particularly strong on the side of the humanities, but it contains also many excellent scientists. Each college has a spirit of its own, which is not always easy to describe. New College has a liberal attitude toward all problems, and, in a lighthearted style, does not appear to take itself too seriously. The warden, or head of the college, Sir William Hayter, a former diplomat and one-time ambassador to Moscow, was an embodiment of this style. His lodgings in the college were furnished in exquisite taste. He and Lady Hayter had for most of their lives stayed in embassies or diplomatic quarters not entirely under their control, and enjoyed the opportunity of creating an environment to their own taste.

While the warden is elected to serve until his retirement, a "sub-warden" serves for one year, in strict rotation according to seniority. His duties are not onerous, except when the warden is unavailable or when a new warden is to be elected. However, by curious college tradition, the sub-warden (and in his absence, the most senior fellow present), not the warden, presides at the formal dinner table and in the common room for the traditional port-and-dessert session. In fact, the warden is a member of the senior common room only by invitation, and he symbolically keeps his gown when moving to the common room after dinner, whereas all others discard it. This is evidently a residue from the times when there was tension between warden and fellows, now forgotten. But the ritual, like many old traditions at Oxford, is strictly observed.

There is another ritual at the post-prandial sessions, where port is served in the common room. The fellow (or if the attendance is large, the fellows) of lowest seniority in the college has to serve the dessert. For a year or two after joining the college, a fellow is likely to be doing this chore every time he is present on these occasions. I found this amusing, but there were actually fellows who, on joining the college at a mature age, resented having to do such a menial task.

On the basis of seniority, my turn as sub-warden would not have come until after my retirement, but, through a rearrangement of the sequence, I was given the opportunity to serve. The duties were indeed not heavy, the most difficult of them being the after-dinner speeches to welcome new fellows or new honorary fellows, and on other occasions. I discovered that, rather typically for Oxford, there was no record of the sub-warden's duties, except that each received from his predecessor a usually rather vague letter on the subject. Here perhaps my German education asserted itself, and I made an effort to compile a list of the various things a sub-warden was supposed to do and when and how to do them. I was sure the list was not complete and could be improved. I understand that today, after ten years, my list is still in existence and, with a few amendments, still in use.

College meetings usually proceeded in a businesslike manner, but one could never tell what items would involve a lengthy debate. Important matters of policy were often settled rapidly, and quite trivial items could lead to a prolonged and heated debate, as on the occasion when the question whether the window boxes around one quad should or should not contain geraniums took an hour's discussion.

Shortly after I joined, New College became divided on the issue of a proposal by the late Harry Bell to admit women students. As far as I know this was the first such proposal in any of the Oxford colleges. It involved a change in the college statutes, and therefore required a two-thirds majority of the fellows. We agreed to study this proposal further and to get the reaction of the University Council and of the women's colleges; at the end of the academic year the matter was to be decided by a vote. It so happened that on the day of that college meeting, I was in Washington, taking part in a small Anglo-American meeting to discuss some questions of nuclear disarmament policies and related issues. This was a two-day meeting, but at the end of the first day I found that all the questions of concern to me had been disposed of, and I was not needed on the second day, which was the day of the crucial college meeting. So, *if* I could get on a plane to London that evening, *if* the plane was on time and the traffic to Oxford not too bad, *if* the discussion preceding the vote was prolonged, and *if* the support of the motion was short of one vote, it would be worth the effort. I decided there were too many ifs, and indeed it turned out that the motion missed the required two-thirds by more than the number of absent fellows.

The matter was raised again some years later, when five other colleges decided to admit women. In New College we again failed to gain a two-thirds majority, but we agreed to amend the statutes to allow women members in principle, and as a result the first woman fellow was elected, a decision greeted with much bitterness by some. By now New College, like nearly all other colleges, has accepted women students.

One of the most charming personalities in college was Sir Christopher Cox. He was, until his retirement, a senior civil servant concerned with education in the British Commonwealth. In his frequent travels to the former colonies he was received as a friend everywhere. When he ceased to work full-time, he came to live in College, while still pursuing his travels. He did not teach, but took a close and very warm interest in the students. His extensive correspondence contained many letters to and from men who had been students over the years. He remembered them all and spoke of them with his characteristic enthusiasm. Whenever possible he spent some weeks in the summer in the "chalet", a rather primitive place in the Alps, where parties of students and fellows go for vacation trips, mixing fresh air and mountain walks with reading parties. He did not dress elegantly but treasured an extensive collection of ties, and at official dinners he and I often compared our more outrageous specimens.

In college the conversations at the High Table are not too lively, since its width makes cross-table conversation difficult, so one is restricted more or less to one's two neighbours. The best place for inspired talk is over coffee in the common room. These conversations have a style of their own, usually erudite, always provocative, and often teasing. The undoubted master conversationalist was Anthony Quinton, a philosophy tutor. Guests invited to dinner were in for a treat if he was present and at his entertaining best. Not surprisingly, he is much sought after for television quiz programmes and the like. He has now moved to Trinity College as its president, and has been awarded a life peerage.

Herbert Nicholas, a reader in political science and later professor of American history, is very knowledgeable on international affairs, and I enjoy talking with him. One sentence, characteristic of his wit, has remained in my memory. In an article about the situation in Vietnam at the time of the war, he said, "The United States government would be well advised to pay attention to the traffic sign outside its embassy in Grosvenor Square: 'Do not enter box unless your exit is clear.' " He is a bachelor and lived in college until he took up residence with his two sisters.

John Bayley taught English in New College until he was appointed to a chair that made him a fellow of another college. He has an encyclopaedic knowledge of literature in many languages and a great love for poetry, including Russian poetry, which he used to discuss with Genia. With a slight stammer, he is the image of the absent-minded professor, and he is indeed absent-minded, but he is all there on things that matter. In 1973 he visited Egypt with his wife, the novelist Iris Murdoch. After she had given some invited lectures in Cairo, they intended to see the pyramids and other sights. But when they were driven to a meeting with a lady guide, he jumped out from the front seat of the car to open the door politely for the ladies, tripped over a seat belt, and broke his leg. This disposed of the sightseeing plans. When he returned to Oxford, I had just come back from Seattle with a foot injury, and we compared notes about the finer points of negotiating the steep and polished stairs in the college on crutches.

Another interesting figure around the college is Dr. B. Juel-Jensen, a medical man of Danish origin. Though he is not a fellow, he has certain dining rights and can often be seen at the High Table or in the common room on Sunday nights. Besides being involved in various kinds of medical research, he is the university medical officer, and among his duties is inoculating members of the university who are about to travel to tropical countries. For this he is well suited not only because of his medical expertise, but because he is an inveterate traveller himself. His many journeys have included a number of expeditions to Ethiopia. He also has an impressive knowledge of English literature, particularly of a certain period, whose dates I do not recall. One evening there was a visitor in College who seemed to be an expert in that particular period and held forth about it with great authority and aplomb. It was a pleasure to watch "J.-J." (as he is generally known) quietly correct the visitor on most of his facts and, very politely, show up his ignorance.

The present warden of the college, Arthur Cooke, is a physicist of considerable achievement. Even before he was chosen as warden, he had become involved in university administration, where he was much in demand because of his efficiency, even temper, and tolerance. These qualities served him equally well in College, to such an extent that he was asked to serve for some years beyond the normal retiring age, although this meant changing the statutes. His wife was German and happened to be a school friend of Hans Bethe's. She died before he became warden, so he had to bear the considerable weight of a warden's social obligations on his own.

Running a Department

The relations of the university and its faculty boards and departments to the colleges are of course more complicated than my brief summary shows, and on arrival in Oxford I had to learn all the relevant procedures. This did not prove too difficult, as long as I kept my eyes open and asked the advice of the right people. I was particularly proud of one achievement. Graduate students from outside had to go through a ceremony of "matriculation" before they were recognized as members of the university. This could be done only after their admission had been approved by the proper Faculty Board, for which the paperwork was not always available in time, particularly for students from abroad. If a student missed the date for the matriculation ceremony, he would not count as resident for that term, which could prolong the minimum time for completing his course. There was a remedy: one could appeal to the vice-chancellor to use his discretionary power to admit a student for a limited period, and this would give the board enough time to complete the regular procedures. I had found this out very early, and a few months after my arrival, I could explain the solution to the senior tutor of a college, who had accepted one of our graduate students and did not know what to do about the matriculation requirement. This solution was typical of Oxford procedures, which turned out to be not nearly as inflexible as I had imagined. Within wide limits many unusual things are possible, as long as one knows how to go about them.

I had a more serious worry at the beginning. The accounts for the Theoretical Physics Department had been handled by the accountant of the Clarendon Laboratory and his staff. Just before I arrived, there had been some personal grievances in that accounting department, and by way of protest the assistants decided to stop working on the theoretical-physics accounts, which were beyond their normal duties. So, even before the beginning of my official appointment, I was, at no notice, faced with the problem of paying our bills, and particularly the wages of the cleaners, which involved complicated procedures about tax and insurance deductions. The accounting staff were not even prepared to explain to me what had to be done. I was lucky in finding someone who gave the right advice. The University Chest (this is the quaint Oxford name for the university treasurer's department) were willing, and indeed anxious, to conduct the accounts of departments. I was at first concerned whether this would mean some loss of independence, but I found the Chest ready to run things entirely according to our wishes. This was a happy solution to an embarrassing problem. I later found the arrangement much more convenient than it would have been under the old system, since the ways of the Clarendon Laboratory—a large experimental department—were not really suitable to our needs.

The department moved into a pair of old houses in Parks Road, appropriately between the Clarendon and the Nuclear Physics Laboratory. We were worried that the physical separation from the experimentalists might reduce our contact with them, and to counter this possibility we agreed that there would be no afternoon tea in theoretical physics: those who wanted a cup of tea in the afternoon (and that was practically everybody) would have to join one or the other of the experimental departments. At first it was thought that this should also apply to morning coffee, another obligatory custom in British research; however, we felt there was a need for the theoreticians to get together by themselves, too, so we did arrange for coffee in our own building.

After a while I noticed that the senior members of the department and the postdoctoral visitors did not get to know each other as well as they had done in Birmingham. Thinking about this phenomenon, I came to the conclusion that in Birmingham people had lunch together more. In Oxford all the permanent staff belonged to colleges, where they got an attractive (and usually free) meal, and where they could meet colleagues from other disciplines. They could not be expected to forgo this privilege frequently. Visitors, on the other hand, usually did not get college attachments, and they ate lunch in a number of widely scattered places. I decided that the remedy was to have an informal luncheon for all postdoctoral members once a week. We thought of having this in a college, but found that it would have been complicated and expensive. Instead, we arranged for some bread, meat, salads, cheese, and fruit to be sent in from a local delicatessen, and we bought some wine to accompany it. There was no need for waiters; the members would lay the table and set out the food. Ordering was not difficult because this happened only once a week, and there was no great need to vary the menu. People signed on the day before, and a secretary passed the order to the shop according to the numbers, by a set formula. At first we even washed up after lunch, but later someone was persuaded to come in to do the dishes. These lunches proved popular, and the cooperative nature of the enterprise added to the attraction. The custom is still in practice after more than twenty years.

The department grew as several posts were added in one way or other, and we had an increasing supply of good graduate students and visitors. Eventually there were too many for the Parks Road houses, and we acquired a floor in a house around the corner, which went against my original insistence on having the whole department under one roof. However, by this time the department was well integrated, so the slight division was tolerable.

Naturally we—meaning mainly Genia—wanted to look after the social contacts, mainly for the new arrivals. This problem was eased in Oxford by the existence of the "Newcomer's Club", an organisation built up by Lady Wheare, the wife of the head of Exeter College. It would get from departments and colleges the names of new arrivals with families and arranged to associate each with some established neighbours, who would keep in touch with them and give help and advice where necessary. This care was available to all, from senior visiting professors to students.

But we still felt a need for getting the new people in the department acquainted with each other and with the old hands. We could not continue the kind of parties we had in Birmingham, because our Oxford house was much smaller and the department was larger. So instead, we had an annual party in the department, usually early in the academic year, when the need to meet people was greatest. It was held on a Saturday evening, and the whole of that Saturday was spent in a communal effort to decorate the rather unattractive premises appropriately. The walls were covered with paper (the tail ends of rolls of newsprint discarded by the local newspaper were very handy for this) and covered with "murals" by any talented artists in the department. The furniture was rearranged to make room for circulating and passing food and drink. Lighting effects were arranged and flowers were displayed. For those who took part in these preparations, the day was almost more fun than the party in the evening. The food was prepared by Genia, and assembled on the Saturday by her and some helpers. Everything was in bite size to obviate any need for plates or cutlery.

We remained in close touch with the two other physics departments. Undergraduate courses and examinations were common; prospective theoreticians took a special option in the final examination, which was based mainly on final-year courses. These were in addition to all the other work done by physicists, except for part of the laboratory work. We also took part in the lecture scheme for graduate students in nuclear physics and in the Clarendon, and we had our own set of lectures for theoretical graduate students.

The head of the Clarendon was Brebis Bleaney, an expert in microwave work, who had also applied microwave techniques to resonance processes in magnetic salts and similar systems. He is a quiet, soft-spoken man, with surprising glimpses of a biting sense of humour showing through a gentle exterior. He did not take administrative responsibilities lightly and often seemed unhappy. A few years ago he retired from his professorship and from the directorship of the laboratory, continuing his research as a Senior Research Fellow of the Royal Society. He visibly blossomed after shedding the duty of running a large laboratory.

Other contacts in the Clarendon Laboratory included Nicholas Kurti, a friend from the wartime days of atomic energy work. He was originally from Hungary, but does not have the extreme and often superficial politeness in manner of many Hungarians. He is distinguished in low-temperature physics and magnetism, but in his spare time he is also an outstanding cook, an activity to which he applies his knowledge of thermodynamics and other relevant parts of physics. He has given many lectures on subjects such as "Physics in the Kitchen", with demonstrations, and has appeared on television. He has had many letters published in the *Times*, and when he thinks that something needs doing, he often goes and does it. For example, one evening the automatic barrier at the station car park did not function, and the button to call assistance could not be found in the dark. Many people with cars were trapped, so Nicholas broke the wooden barrier, leaving a note with an explanation and his name. The railway had him taken to court and fined. He had many letters expressing admiration for his action and indignation at the railway, though no one offered to share his fine. Another member of the Clarendon was R. Berman, also a former member of the Tube Alloys team, who made careful measurements of heat conduction in nonmetallic substances and verified the prediction in my Ph.D. thesis.

Denys (now Sir Denys) Wilkinson was the founder of the Nuclear Physics Laboratory. He is a very gifted experimenter with a fertile imagination and also a very witty speaker. He had to choose between Cambridge, where he had been a student, and Oxford, where the proximity of the Rutherford Laboratory and other institutions with modern accelerators provided better opportunities for research in nuclear and particle physics. A new accelerator in Cambridge would have made it possible for him to work there and to revive the Cambridge tradition in nuclear research. An attempt was made to obtain a government grant for such a project, but no confirmation could be obtained by the time he had to make his decision, and he settled on Oxford. Eventually the grant was approved, and he was able to build the planned machine in Oxford. The result was a large department with people working both in nuclear physics using the new accelerator and in particle physics using the Rutherford Laboratory and facilities elsewhere. Two new professors were added to help run this large department: Donald Perkins, an expert on neutrino experiments, who led the high-energy group; and Ken Allen, who became responsible for the nuclear-structure group.

The Nuclear Physics Laboratory, while mainly an experimental department, contains a theoretical group under Peter Hodgson, with whom I had contact earlier through the A.S.A., in which he was very active, and later through the Pugwash conferences. He came to the nuclear physics lab originally to carry out numerical calculations to assist the experimenters, and his group was then known as the Nuclear Computing Group. But inevitably the group's interests widened, and it became a nuclear-theory group, thus in principle overlapping with some of the activities of my department. But in fact there is no conflict of interests, and both groups are happy to exchange ideas. In academic life one finds many illogical arrangements working well, and it would be a mistake to take such demarkations seriously.

Secretaries

The functioning of a department depends much on the efficiency and personality of the secretary. I remember more secretaries than I could possibly write about. My first secretary was Mrs. Roberts, who worked for me part time during the war when I started on atomic-energy work. She was a very sweet matron and commuted from the businessmen's suburb of Barnt Green. However, I soon needed a full-time secretary, and Margaret Leighton arrived, a tiny person who looked so frail that one feared she might collapse any moment. In fact, she was very tough and coped quietly and efficiently with the rapidly growing paperwork of the group.

After the war the office was started by Mary Whittaker, who had served in the Women's Air Force and brought to us the crisp efficiency of the Service. She left after less than two years, when she married Mel Preston, one of our Canadian research students. Her successor was Sheila Vann, a very intelligent, cheerful, and outgoing lady who rapidly made friends with all members of the department. We lost her also through marriage, but to an "outsider". Eventually she and her husband separated and he died, leaving her responsible for his debts. We encountered her in Sydney, where her two daughters live, and where she had started in a new job and a new life.

A few years later I appointed a well-educated and rather glamorous young lady secretary. Before she could start on the job she had a serious car accident and spent a few months in hospital. We kept the job for her, managing with temporary help while a gallant junior secretary, Gillian Rose, took on more than her share of the work. But by the time the patient was discharged she became engaged and never took up the job.

When I arrived in Oxford, the senior secretary was Miss Sybil Owen, Irish and a great character. She was a tower of strength in the difficult business of finding accommodation for our visitors and their families. She found a house containing three flats and arranged with the owner to let us choose tenants for him, provided we kept the flats occupied. They were simple and reasonably cheap, so they were within the means of even the less well-off visitors, and a great boon to the department. She also had a very shrewd knowledge of the many students in the department, and had very definite preferences. Those she did not approve of were dealt with in rather draconian ways: there was, for example, a notice on her door saying she was available for issuing stationery, etc., only from 10:45 to 11:00 A.M. She also had a habit of bursting into my office, while I was talking with people to bring up a minor question of no real urgency with the preamble, "Before I forget it. . . ." She was convinced that other people in the university did not know their jobs, and she made them feel it. I learned soon enough to conduct business with the administration and other departments myself, thus avoiding the need to soothe ruffled feelings.

302

Miss Owen was succeeded by Miss Margaret Bradfield, who was of Anglo-German extraction and was educated in Germany. She was in many ways the perfect secretary—an excellent typist, an infallible proofreader, bilingual in English and German, and had an old-fashioned German attitude about her work and her duties. She was also a near-professional pianist. Her perfectionist attitude toward work meant that she could never trust any junior secretary, and insisted on doing everything herself. As a result she was overworked and became depressed and moody and eventually decided to return to Germany. She had always deplored the work habits of young English people compared to what she had known in Germany. Alas, she now found that young people in Germany had changed, too, and were often careless and disorganised. To make matters worse, she was the victim of a misunderstanding and did not get the post she thought had been promised to her; so she returned to England. Her post in my department had been filled, and she found great difficulty in getting another one in spite of her excellent qualifications, as she was by then over fifty years old.

Research

My position in research underwent a gradual change, which had started in Birmingham and accelerated after my move to Oxford. Because of my reluctance to choose a narrow field in which to specialise, I found it increasingly hard to keep up with the current developments in all areas. This was in part because of the rapid rate at which new concepts were generated in some areas, particularly in particle physics. Even though many of the new ideas were transient and did not find a permanent place in the accepted scheme, one had to understand them to take part in the topical discussions. Another cause was that, with my advancing age, it became harder to follow, understand, and remember other people's ideas. I felt that I could no longer contribute actively to particle theory; but I kept myself informed in a general way about what was going on, and occasionally was even able to help people with advice or criticism.

Sometimes I envy the specialists, particularly in recent years, when spectacular advances in particle theory have been made. The ideas of Steve Weinberg, Abdus Salam, and others have made possible a satisfactory description of the so-called weak interactions, which are responsible, for example, for the phenomenon of beta decay. According to this theory, the weak interactions and the well-known electromagnetic field are different aspects of one underlying set of physical laws, and many applications of these laws have been well confirmed by experiments. The most spectacular confirmation came when two new particles, the "intermediate vector particles" which, according to the theory mediate the beta decay, were found at the European laboratory, CERN, with masses and with a behaviour very close to the forecasts.

There has also been much progress with the problems of the "strong" interactions, which are basically responsible for holding nuclei together. Novel ideas have brought much order into the wealth of experimental data on particle physics, though the theory is not as yet in as tidy and exact a state as that of the electro-weak interactions, largely because of mathematical difficulties. In Birmingham I had already left the direction of particle research in the hands of experts such as Stanley Mandelstam. In Oxford, with people such as Dick Dalitz, J. C. Taylor, and many younger colleagues, there would have been even less sense in my interfering.

To a lesser extent my situation was similar in solid-state physics or, to use the modern name, condensed-matter physics. Here the growth of new fundamental concepts was less spectacular than in particle physics. One of the major revolutions here resulted from the explanation by Bardeen, Cooper, and Schrieffer, in Illinois, of superconductivity, the last fundamental phenomenon to resist previous attempts at explanation. In condensed-matter problems the growing complexity was due largely to a wealth of sophisticated mathematical techniques for solving problems involving many particles.

In Oxford, Roger Elliott and others were the obvious leaders in this field. However, I felt I was still able to contribute to parts of this subject, and to guide research students. One of the areas was transport theory, the description of such processes as electrical or heat conduction. Here there was also a tendency to apply elegant modern techniques, but I found that these were often too ambitious and could not be carried through without assumptions of questionable validity. Sometimes young and enthusiastic investigators would apply such techniques to problems that had been solved long ago by old-fashioned and somewhat pedestrian but valid methods. When they obtained different answers by use of "modern" methods they accepted them, without reflecting that there were good reasons for believing the "old-fashioned" answers.

I felt less out of date concerning nuclear theory, though here, too, many new concepts and new techniques were developing. I had a number of students working on problems in that area, and the department had experts in this field, in particular David Brink and later also Brian Buck; in our sister department, we had Peter Hodgson and others.

Another general line of research in the department is plasma physics, the physics of gases in which many or all atoms have lost their electrons and therefore have become electrically charged. Plasmas are particularly important in fusion research, i.e., in the project to generate energy by a controlled version of the reaction that fueled the hydrogen bomb. Plasma physics is also very important in astrophysics. The first kind of plasma physics was done in the department by W. B. Thompson, who held a chair of theoretical plasma physics for some years. The astrophysical applications were studied by ter Haar.

While the Oxford department became more clearly divided into distinct groups with different research interests, no categorization in academic matters is ever complete or logical. I became interested in some older problems that do not belong in any of the areas I have mentioned. One of these was the question of the momentum of light in a refractive medium, about which there had been a controversy since 1909, and was revived more recently by some very clever experiments. I did some work on this problem with a student, Michael Burt, and we published a paper in 1973. This turned out to be wrong, which put us in the company of some very eminent authorities who had also erred on this subject. My next paper in 1976 was nearly right, more progress was made in 1977, and I have recently given what I hope is the last word on the subject.

In line with my change of attitude about my work, my research publications since the move to Oxford have been outnumbered by review articles, book reviews, and historical notes.

Colleagues and Students

I shall mention some more of the people in the Theoretical Physics Department, though here again they were so numerous that I can choose only a few, selected quite arbitrarily.

W. B. Thompson was a somewhat exceptional member of the department. He worked on plasma physics, and had been a member of the Culham Laboratory, the place set up by the Atomic Energy Authority to develop fusion power. In 1963 he was appointed to a new chair of theoretical plasma physics at Oxford, and joined the department. So, in a sense, he was with us, but not of us. In 1965 he left Oxford for the University of California. He is a Canadian and very lively, with a booming voice that made him specially popular at all social occasions where the entertainment included singing. When he left, and no successor could be found, the chair was transferred to applied mathematics, and its connection with our department ceased.

We had many senior visitors. Some of them were old friends who had spent some time in Birmingham, but there were also many new ones. Micky Engel was an Israeli who did research in nuclear theory. He was completely deaf, but could do some lip-reading in Hebrew, though not in English. He therefore had difficulty following seminar talks, but he managed to get the gist of the talks from the equations and diagrams on the board or on the screen, and when he missed something important he was never shy to pass a piece of paper to a neighbour and ask, "What did he say?" Even though many deaf people are bitter and suspicious, Engel was cheerful and had very warm relations with everybody.

Bulent Atalay, a nuclear theorist of Turkish origin, came for a year from Virginia. He is also a talented artist and published a book of drawings of old houses in Virginia. Since he happened to be in England during Jubilee Year, he was encouraged to present a copy to the Queen, and it was very well received. He used the visit to Oxford to produce a similar set of drawings of Oxford, and they capture the spirit of the place very well.

Rainer Beck came from Germany. He, too, worked on the nucleus. He was taken ill; the doctors at first suspected meningitis and put him into the isolation hospital. His trouble was then diagnosed as a brain aneurism and he was told that it would be necessary to operate, as the condition was dangerous; however, a later examination showed that it was not safe to operate. He coped well with these traumatic developments. When he was discharged from hospital he was very weak, and Genia took him to our house to convalesce. She advised him on a regime of exercises, starting very gently and increasing them gradually. She was delighted that he did exactly as he was told and recovered quickly. His health has been all right so far, with only occasional brief relapses.

Jeremy Bernstein is a well-known American theoretician who works on particle physics, but he is even better known as a contributor to *The New Yorker* magazine, for which he has written many "profiles" and other stories about science and scientists. E. L. Tomusiak came twice from Canada. The first time he came, we, together with R. K. Bhaduri, a very charming Indian, developed a possible approach to nuclear binding energies. Some part of this work was unfinished when he returned to Canada, and he completed the calculations together with a student, B. G. Nickel. This resulted in a joint paper by Tomusiak, Nickel, and myself. When Nickel later came to Oxford I was able to welcome a co-author whom I had never met! He had meanwhile changed his field to the topical subject of phase transitions, and had made a name for himself in that area.

Of our students I must certainly mention Christopher Llewellyn Smith. He was an undergraduate in New College, where he was regarded with a kind of proprietary interest, because he was the seventh member of the Llewellyn Smith family to study in the college, though he was, I believe, the first scientist among them. He did his research training under Dalitz and rapidly rose to become one of the leaders in particle theory. He has more breadth than some particle theorists, who tend to feel that nothing outside their own subject can possibly be of interest, and his talks are a model of clarity. As a student of Dalitz, who in turn was, in a sense, my student, I regard him as my spiritual grandson, and so I was doubly pleased when he was elected a fellow of the Royal Society. He is now a reader in the department.

Another brilliant student was Anthony Leggett, who started as a student of classics, where he did well, but turned to theoretical physics. He did excellent research in condensed-matter physics and served for many years in the University of Sussex, where he was promoted to a professorship. He has now moved to a prestigious professorship in America. Other students who have done well in academic life include Christopher Michael, also in particle physics, who is now a professor in Liverpool, and Michael Moore, in condensed-matter physics, who is a professor in Manchester. Christopher Pethick divides his interests between condensed matter and astrophysics, and his time between Copenhagen and Illinois. Frank Close, who contributed many drawings and paintings to the decorations for the departmental parties, is now doing research at the Rutherford Laboratory, and has been successful in writing popular, or nonspecialist, expositions of particle physics.

My own last student was George ("Yura") Kirczenow. He came from Australia, but his parents were Russians who had met in a displaced-persons camp in Germany at the end of the war. He is bilingual and combines the very informal manners of Australia with some very Russian habits; for example, Russians worry about food contamination and Yura still washes oranges before peeling them, a habit picked up from his Russian grandmother. His work on condensed-matter theory has gone well, and he has held university posts in the United States and Canada.

A. K. Das came from East Pakistan (now Bangladesh). In his first

307

year he had worked under another member of the department, but somehow this did not go well and I took him on. I suggested to him the problem that McManus had tackled in Birmingham in 1939, but of which no record remained. This went well, and he produced an excellent thesis. It would have been good for him to spend another year or two in the West to acquire more experience before returning home, and we had already made arrangements for that when the Pakistan Atomic Energy Commission, who had provided the grant that had brought him to Oxford, asked him to return. He did go back, but after a few years he lost his job, probably because he was a Hindu in a Muslim country. Since then he has moved around Europe and North America, holding fellowships and temporary positions.

Often the problems raised by research students are far removed from scientific ones. Keith Ellis, for example, had made a good start working with Jack Paton on a problem in particle physics, and then decided to leave after the end of his first year. He explained he had spent a vacation in Italy, and had become so fascinated with Italian life and language that he had the urge to spend time there. It turned out there was no girl friend behind this, as we at first suspected. Perhaps, we thought, this had been his first time abroad, and therefore the experience had made such a deep impression, but we heard that he had already spent a year abroad in voluntary service. So it must have been a case of genuine affection for the country. There was no reason why he should not satisfy his urge without losing his contact with physics. I got in touch with Italian friends who arranged for him to join a research group in Rome. His research scholarship was transferred and his father agreed to help him with the higher cost of living. He did complete a good thesis there, and when I ran into him afterwards in an American university, I was told by his professor that he was doing well.

One day I was surprised to receive an application from Moscow. It was from L. J. Sibanda, a black Rhodesian who had studied at Moscow State University. Africans in Moscow are usually sent to the Lumumba University, and the fact that he was at the more select university suggested that he was well thought of. He also had gained an M.Sc. there—I had not known until then that there was such a thing in Moscow. He sent a very favourable letter of recommendation from his supervisor, so we accepted him. But when he arrived his expected scholarship had not materialized, and we had great difficulty finding him some other means of support. As a Rhodesian citizen, he should theoretically have sought support from the Rhodesian government, but clearly as an African who had spent years in Moscow he had no chance of getting anything there during the Smith regime.

Before I started him on research, I ought to have tested his knowledge; but I was sufficiently impressed by his qualifications and recommendations to put him at once on a problem in nuclear physics, as his master's thesis had been on the nucleus. But he did not make much progress, and I gradually realised that he had not grasped some of the fundamentals. So we went back to more and more basic matters, and it turned out that he was very ill-prepared. I never discovered the reason for the enthusiastic recommendation from Moscow; perhaps it was a case of misguided kindness. We lowered our target for his work, but even on this reduced level he had not made much progress when his grant ran out. He evidently could not get a doctor's degree, but he submitted a thesis of sorts. The examiners had the power to grant him a master's degree if the thesis did not merit a D.Phil. and they were prepared to do so once he had corrected a few errors in the thesis. I discussed the revisions with him, but he abruptly disappeared from Oxford and went abroad. When I finally made contact with him, he explained that his thesis was in a waste basket somewhere in Oxford. His case was my worst failure.

Conferences and Summer Schools

Journeys to conferences, summer schools, and other physics-related visits continued from Oxford at the same rate as from Birmingham. Among many conferences I might mention the first conference of the European Physical Society in Florence in 1969. Florence had been chosen because there was to be a new conference centre, which was to be specially equipped for our purposes. Alas, the centre was not ready in time, and the meetings had to be held in the beautiful old palace of the Signoria. For the participants this setting was far more attractive than a modern centre, but it must have caused headaches to the organisers, who had to improvise projection and amplification facilities. One of the opening speeches was given by Blackett. He told us that he had been married many years before in the same hall; his wife was in the audience, as was a lady who had been a witness at the wedding.

The conference consisted of plenary sessions as well as many parallel sessions. There were only invited speakers, and no contributed papers. I enjoyed the plenary sessions, but regretted the parallel meetings. Most of the speakers at the latter had made an effort to make their talks intelligible and interesting to all, not only to the specialists in the field. But with many lectures to choose from, and not being able to attend them all, most people drifted to the meetings about their own fields. I had a peculiar difficulty at that meeting: the organisers had considerately sent out an excellent plan of Florence, but it did not carry any indication that it was not in the conventional orientation—that is, it had its north at bottom left. We had come by car, which happened to have a compass on the windscreen. Trying to follow the plan, I became hopelessly confused. Even after I had found the source of the trouble I could never get the picture of the city straight in my mind, and I lost my way each time we were trying to return to our hotel in Fiesole.

Another memorable occasion was a conference in Göttingen in 1966 to celebrate Hund's seventieth birthday. He had been one of my teachers, and was held in great affection by all physicists. The celebrations included many speeches and lectures (including one by me), the award of a medal by a government representative, and the conferment of an honorary degree by someone from another university. In his reply he said approximately, "You are making such a fuss of my reaching the age of seventy. But there is no great merit in getting old. In fact, in our time there have been so many occasions to lose one's life with decency that a person who lives to an old age may have looked after himself a little too well." I missed Hund's eightieth birthday, but met him shortly afterwards at a conference in Bonn, at which both of us were members of a panel to discuss the future of physics. After a lunch party, taxis were called to take the panel to the meeting, but Hund declared that he preferred to walk. He got to the meeting in good time.

In 1972 there was a conference in the International Centre for Theoretical Physics in Trieste to discuss the history and the basic concepts of quantum mechanics. Most of the founders of quantum mechanics who were still alive were present, including Heisenberg, Dirac, Jordan, Wigner, and many others. This made for very interesting lectures and discussions. The conference banquet was in honour of Dirac's seventieth birthday. The principal speaker was Lord (C. P.) Snow, who did not strike quite the right note for the occasion. Even after further speeches the atmosphere remained cool. Genia was getting impatient and said to Casimir, the chairman, that she wanted to speak, too. He replied that he could not permit that. But she grabbed the microphone and said "I am speaking against the wishes of the chairman, but nobody has mentioned the names of all colleagues from the same generation who are no longer with us. Let us drink to the memory of Pauli, Schrödinger, Fermi, Oppenheimer . . ."—a long list of distinguished names and good friends. Her speech was well received, also by Casimir, and the spirit of the gathering changed, with many more impromptu remarks. The published conference proceedings report Genia's speech, starting with "I speak with the permission of the chairman . . . ."

There were also many more Pugwash conferences, and I attended most of them. The one in 1972 was held in Oxford, and I was the chairman of the local organising committee, while Genia planned the ladies' programme and the social events. Pugwash had developed the tradition of having, every five years, a large conference to which all past participants are invited, and at which future policy is decided. The Oxford conference was one of these, and there were about three hundred participants, so that the total numbers, including wives, guests, staff, and so on came to near four hundred. There were many problems both with the preparations and during the conference. Three groups of student helpers were at the three terminals of London Airport to meet the visitors and guide them to special buses; but one of the contact points with the parked buses closed down earlier than expected, so contact was lost, and only the efforts of the bus company in sending a car out to meet the "lost" bus and turn it round saved the situation. We found that the college where visitors were staying had no way of helping them with their luggage, and all student helpers were at the airport. So some of us had to step in and carry the luggage of the less able-bodied visitors, to their surprise. Added to this were the usual misunderstandings, cancellations, breaking down of office equipment, and so on. When asked how the conference was going, my reply was, "We stagger happily from crisis to crisis." We were fortunate in having found an outstanding conference administrator, Mr. Miller, who had just retired as clerk of the Examination Schools, where our meetings were held. He had extensive local knowledge, and put in long hours of efficient work.

In 1974 we celebrated the centenary of the British Physical Society (now absorbed by the Institute of Physics) and the French Physical Society. The two organisations had the happy thought of celebrating the occasion by a joint conference in the Channel Islands. The scientific programme of the conference was excellent and enjoyable, but had its share of small things going wrong. One of these occurred when Sir Nevill Mott gave a talk. The slide projector was one of the kind that is controlled by the speaker, and Mott, who does not like gadgets, eyed the control that was handed to him with suspicion. He said, "Well, I suppose I shall have to use this," and pressed the button, whereupon the slide carriage jumped out of the projector with a loud clatter.

The conference banquet presented the organisers with an unforeseen snag. Their intention was to follow the British tradition of toasting the Queen preceding the formal speeches. Because of the binational nature of the occasion, it seemed proper to include also a toast to the French president. But the French physicists, who regarded their president primarily as a political figure to whom most of them were opposed, objected to this plan. Could one therefore do without any toasts to heads of state? The lieutenant-general of Jersey, who was to be a guest at the dinner, objected; if there was no "loyal toast", he could not attend. I do not know how the problem would have been resolved; but as it turned out, shortly before the conference began, President Pompidou died. There was now no French head of state to be toasted, and some words of regret at his passing, inserted in the right place, did not offend anyone.

Of many summer and spring schools of my Oxford years I might mention the one in Sitges, a seaside resort near Barcelona, in the spring of 1974. This was organised by L. M. Garrido, the professor of theoretical physics in Barcelona. He had come to Oxford to ask my advice on how to improve the contacts between Spanish and other theoreticians, and I suggested the idea of running summer schools. Before Sitges, one had been held in Mallorca, which had been successful from a scientific point of view but was hampered by the effects of the tourist season. In Sitges the season had not yet started, and things worked well. The theme of the conference was the statistical mechanics of nonequilibrium phenomena, and my last student, George Kirczenow, whose research was in that area, was appointed one of the editors of the published record of the meeting.

In 1974 Antonino Zichichi, the originator of the very successful summer schools on particle physics in Erice, Sicily, invited me to that year's school. I was no expert on particle physics, but I was to give an historical talk on "The Glorious Days of Physics". I liked the idea and collected a series of snapshots of physicists from the late twenties and thirties, which the Clarendon photographer, Cyril Band, turned into attractive slides. Although I was to give only a single lecture, Genia and I were able to stay in Erice for the two weeks of the school. The charming and unspoiled town, situated on top of a mountain and therefore surprisingly cool, had fallen on lean times, until the summer schools, which brought many visitors, started a revival. Besides the particle-physics school there are now many other courses on many subjects, and they run practically all year. My lecture went well, and since then there has been a continuing demand for it. I have lost count of the number of occasions on which I have given similar lectures, usually called "Reminiscences of the Early Days of Quantum Mechanics", and the audience reaction to them led to the idea of writing my memoirs.

Other Visits. Seattle

In the spring of 1966 Genia and I spent a month or so visiting Brookhaven, the inter-university laboratory containing a particle accelerator that is too big for any one university. The availability of other kinds of equipment there makes the physics research very varied and interesting. The laboratory is on Long Island, about 50 miles from New York City, and close to the sea. One of the special attractions for us was, of course, to have Ronnie and his family close by; he is on the staff of Brookhaven, and lives a few miles away. His sons were then aged 5 and 3: Tim, thin, thoughtful, and musical; Ben, cheerful, round, and cuddly.

Genia went home a week before I did. When I awoke on my last morning there, I found that half my face was paralysed. I saw a doctor who conducted some tests and indicated that it was probably only a local infection. But by the afternoon my eye was getting irritated, because it could not blink, so I went back to the doctors to see if they could suggest a remedy. There was a different doctor this time; she conducted further tests and thought it might be a brain spasm. She prescribed an anti-coagulant and advised me to fly home as planned. She did not tell me how to treat the irritated eye, but I put a patch over it, and that solved the problem. I sat up all night in the plane, worrying a little about the possibilities. Genia met me at the airport and was horrified that I had been travelling with a possible brain spasm. I went to a good doctor in Oxford, and he established at once that the diagnosis was nonsense; I had a case of "Bell's palsy", an infection of the facial motor nerve. This turned out to be due to shingles, which normally attacks the sensory nerves and causes severe pain; but in my case there was no pain, just the disability. The nerve, it turned out, was completely destroyed, but in a year or so it regenerated itself very largely.

That was not the end of my medical troubles. I also developed at the same time sudden and severe bouts of fever, without any other symptoms. The doctor at first suspected Hodgkin's disease and then an auto-immune condition, but later that was ruled out by specialists in Seattle. Now it is believed that I have Mediterranean fever, a rare inherited condition found among people in the Mediterranean area and among Sephardic Jews. I had not known that I was of Sephardic origin, but Ronnie reported that he had heard from the aunt in New York that we came from a Sephardic family. He had not mentioned it before because he assumed that I knew. In any case, I have by now learned to control the condition, and it is only a minor nuisance.

Of other visits the most significant was a six-month sabbatical in Seattle in 1967. I had already been there for a month in 1962 to attend a summer "workshop", and had come back enchanted with the situation of Seattle, surrounded by water and by mountains, and I was most enthusiastic about the people in the physics department of the University of Washington. Their senior theoretician, Boris Jacobsohn, had directed the workshop, and I enjoyed my contacts with him. He had a deep knowledge of many branches of physics, on which he tended to comment with a very dry sense of humour. He was also a very keen mountaineer and skier. On an excursion into the neighbourhood of Mount Rainier, the beautiful extinct volcano whose white cone rises to 14,000 feet from sea level, some of my photographs were spoiled by a too-bright reflection of sunlight from Boris's bald head.

When I received the invitation to be a visiting professor in Seattle in 1967, I accepted with delight. The Battelle Distinguished Professorship was supported by the Battelle Memorial Institute, an industrial research organisation that was setting up a new research and conference centre in Seattle and was kindly disposed toward the university. I was the first holder of this chair. I had looked forward to meeting Boris Jacobsohn again, but just before we left Oxford we heard that he had died of a heart attack on a ski slope. He had known about his heart trouble, but had wanted to continue an active life, whatever the cost.

Kitty and I went to Seattle first, because Genia's sister was visiting and wanted to stay on a little longer. We were met at the airport by members of the Geballe family. Ron Geballe had been chairman of the Physics Department for many years and was largely responsible for creating the active and friendly atmosphere in the department. In American departments the chairman is usually appointed from among the professors, and his functions vary widely. In some departments the term of office is very short, and the holder is then usually a rather junior person who looks mainly after the paperwork; the real influence then generally rests in a rather undefined way with some senior members of the department. In other departments the chairman serves for a long time, and although decisions are taken by the whole staff, the chairman acts as a leader, and this was the case in Washington. In any case, a selection of the eight Geballe children, who then ranged in ages from about 6 to about 24, accompanied Ron and Marj, his wife, a very warm person of tremendous energy. They told us that Ruth Jacobsohn, Boris's wife, was at their house and anxious to see us. By the time we got there, in time for dinner, it was 6:30 P.M., which meant 2:30 A.M. London time. But the good company made up for the jet lag, and we stayed awake. I was asked to take over the lecture course Boris would have given, which dealt with symmetries in physics. This was a new subject for me, but I managed the course passably.

At the end of January I attended the New York meeting of the American Physical Society, and Genia met me there. We took the occasion to visit Princeton and call on Robert Oppenheimer. This was two weeks before his death, and he evidently knew he was dying, but he was very calm. We talked about the old days, and we agreed that he could have saved himself much trouble if he had resigned from the Advisory Committee of the Atomic Energy Commission when the commission refused to act on the committee's advice about the hydrogen bomb. As the chairman of the committee he was specially blamed for opposing the hydrogen bomb, and as a result his position became untenable. He said, "You know, there is the attitude that says 'As long as I keep riding on this train, it won't go to the wrong destination'!" He was always able to find the right phrase for a situation, even about himself.

We made many friends in Seattle, and I found the activities in the department very stimulating. From there we made a number of visits to other universities and to Los Alamos. It was interesting to see Los Alamos again after twenty-two years, and to meet many old friends. But we were disappointed by the appearance of the place. When we first arrived in 1944, we felt that the army huts were an eyesore in the uniquely beautiful landscape. Now we almost wished the army huts were back. When the war ended, the land was owned by the government, and it would have been possible to plan a unique town of architectural distinction, fitted to the beautiful environment. Instead, people built their houses in a hodgepodge of styles, and usually too close together, to save on pipes and services.

During our stay in Seattle, the Battelle Institute had a symposium on dislocations. These are faults in crystals, which are very important for the mechanism of plastic flow. In 1939 I had written a paper on the suggestion of Orowan on the force resisting the movement of such a dislocation in a perfect crystal. It had really been his idea—all I did was formulate and solve the equations representing his model. I had wanted this to be a joint paper with Orowan, but he refused. The matter did not seem important at the time, and I did not take much more interest in the problem of dislocations. At the Battelle symposium I discovered that this paper had become one of the classics in the field, and that many papers at the symposium referred to the "Peierls-Nabarro force". Nabarro had extended my argument, and had also corrected a major algebraic error in my paper. He continued to work on dislocations. I was invited to speak at the conference dinner, and took the occasion to tell the history of that force.

Seattle became a kind of second home, and we returned for a month or two in most of the following years. I became particularly interested in the work of Greg Dash and his group on monatomic layers (i.e., layers at most one atom thick) of gases such as helium on solid surfaces. These experiments lead to very interesting results about two-dimensional physics, and I took part in the discussion of the theoretical implications.

In the summer of 1973, while visiting Seattle again, I had an accident. Genia and I were walking in the neighbourhood of Mount Rainier during our last weekend there. Descending by a steep path covered with loose sand I slipped, and in falling, I twisted my ankle, resulting in a torn ligament. After the initial shock had passed, I found I could still walk by putting as little weight as possible on the damaged foot. Supported by Genia, who was also carrying my pack and cameras, we made it slowly down the 2,500 feet to the parking lot. Our rented car was an enormous convertible, which Genia had never driven, and she did not relish the prospect of having to drive down the hairpin bends of the mountain. So I managed to drive. As my right foot was the injured one, I had to go easy on the accelerator, so the trip back to Seattle was slow. There were hospitals closer to Rainier, but we did not trust them. An excellent Seattle surgeon repaired the torn ligament, and we eventually returned home with my whole leg in plaster. In due course my foot was as good as new.

Other journeys during the Oxford period included many visits to the Institut des Hautes Etudes Scientifiques in Bures-sur-Yvette near Paris. The institute was founded by the mathematician Léon Motchane, and was inspired by the Institute for Advanced Study in Princeton, if somewhat smaller. Motchane, whom I had first met in Paris in 1932, had consulted me—as well as many others—about his project, and in 1963 I was invited to join the scientific advisory committee, which met about twice a year. The institute contains pure mathematicians and theoretical physicists, and I was naturally more concerned with the problems of the physicists. The permanent physicists were then Louis Michel and David Ruelle.

Michel is well known for his work in many fields, including the weak interactions. He and his large family are perhaps greater globe-trotters than we are, and they are masters at the peculiarly French art of packing a large family and their belongings into a minute car. Ruelle is an authority on statistical mechanics. The institute also has a stream of visitors and is well set up to provide for them, because it rents two blocks of flats and a group of small houses. The furnishings and general administration of the housing were looked after by Mlle. Roland, the charming and highly efficient secretary of the director. She is now Mme. Motchane. When Motchane retired he was succeeded by Nicholas Kuiper, a Dutch mathematician. After many visits—including to neighbouring institutions, when we were also allowed to use the institute's accommodations—we now feel completely at home in Bures, and the morning walk to the baker to get fresh French bread for breakfast has become automatic.

Domestic and Family

We needed a place to live in Oxford. In the summer of 1962, a year before we moved, I was going to the summer meeting in Seattle; Genia drove me to London airport and stopped in Oxford on the way back. There she saw a house that would suit us, and as Oxford houses do not remain on the market for long, she bought it, informing me by a telegram: "Don't get kittens, bought a house." The injunction was hardly needed; I would not have worried unduly, as I have great confidence in her judgment in matters of real estate. The house was on Boar's Hill, some 5 miles from town, and had beautiful views over the Berkshire Downs. We did not need it for another year, but we knew it would be easy to find tenants. Indeed, a Canadian physicist who came to the Clarendon Laboratory found the house suitable. He and his family moved in one week after we obtained possession. During that week the house was furnished, curtains were put up, and the main room was given a coat of paint.

The actual move, a year later, was a major operation, because the Birmingham house had practically unlimited storage space, and therefore we had hardly discarded anything during the fifteen years in the house—"this might come in handy some time." Also, much of the old furniture, including some of the items acquired in 1933 in the Cambridge auction sales, would not fit in the Oxford house. We let all our

317

young friends pick out what they liked among the discarded items, gave to charity what seemed to be usable among the rest, and finally got a contractor to dispose of the remainder. He carted away seven big truckloads of rubbish.

When we moved to Oxford in 1963, Kitty was fifteen. Because of her exam phobia, we had a problem finding a school, and we decided instead to enrol her at the Oxford Polytechnic. She took their courses for two years, but did no better at exams than before. She would have liked to become a doctor, but this was ruled out because of the many exams. Instead, she was taken on by the university Physiology Department as a temporary technician, hardly more than a bottle washer. She did extremely well in this work and was gradually given more responsibility. When she came with me to Seattle in 1967, her recommendations were such that she was accepted at once in a medical department. She remained in Seattle for another year after we returned, and at the end was setting up a laboratory course for graduate students; her activities also included doing open-heart surgery on baboons.

After her return to England she continued in her career as technician, even after she married Chris Coppin, then a graduate student in physiology. He decided to get a medical qualification, initially with the intention of extending his research to clinical work. But he succumbed to the attraction of the medical profession and of the care of patients. He and Kitty visited us in Seattle in 1975 and he was so attracted by the Pacific northwest that he applied for a post in Vancouver. After some initial hurdles with Canadian regulations and examinations, he established himself there as an oncologist, specialising in chemotherapy. Kitty is continuing her career as a high-level medical technician, after an interruption while her two children were small. Pippa and Andrew are our sixth and seventh grandchildren, whom we enjoy visiting whenever we are in the neighbourhood.

Jo at first continued her schooling in Oxford, but we felt that in adolescence, with the problems caused by her disability, a girls' school was not the right place to develop her personality. We sent her to Millfield, probably the most expensive boarding school in the country, but one that was geared to cater to the unusual. She was one of eighty girls among eight hundred boys. In her two years there, she matured and gained confidence in dealing with people. But she failed her exams, basically because she was more interested in people and in theatre than in academic subjects. There seemed little sense in her cramming to gain university entrance, since she would still not have been interested; instead she took a secretarial course. In this she did exceptionally well and at once gained a job of personal secretary to the head of a university department in Oxford. She was a very efficient and popular secretary, and in her spare time had an intense social life. Although not a student, she worked for the student newspaper, *Cherwell*, and was an invited member of the OUDS (Oxford University Dramatic Society). At the age of twenty-one she married a student, Chris Hookway, whom she had met while they were playing the accompaniment to a college theatre production—she playing the drums, and he the guitar.

Chris became a graduate student in philosophy, first at the University of East Anglia in Norwich, where he had no scholarship, so that Jo supported him. She worked as a secretary in the diocesan office of the cathedral. When she talked about her work it sounded like pure Trollope. They later moved to Cambridge, where Chris was awarded a research fellowship after obtaining his Ph.D. He is now a lecturer in philosophy in Birmingham.

Jo decided, after several secretarial jobs (one happened to be in the Department of Applied Mathematics and Theoretical Physics at Cambridge) and after taking courses in the Open University, that she wanted to take a full-time university course, after all. She was accepted by a Cambridge college as a "mature student" and gained a maintenance grant. Three years later she graduated in anthropology. Meanwhile Chris had moved to Birmingham, so for two years they had a "commuting marriage". Anthropology did not, in present circumstances, seem a bread-and-butter profession, so she took a course in computing, and is now doing very well as a senior programmer.

Our first five grandchildren also live in North America. Ronnie has been on the staff of the Brookhaven National Laboratory for many years. Of his two sons, Tim remained a thinker and a musician. He graduated from Yale summa cum laude in computer science. He also studied music but decided to make computers his profession and leave the music for enjoyment. We were amused, during a visit to New York in 1983, to watch him perform with a small group in a night club. He and a friend had written the text and the music of a number of songs, which had had great success at Yale, hence the New York engagement. He is now a graduate student at Cornell, where his brother, Ben, is an undergraduate majoring in biology.

Gaby and Charlie lived for many years in Cambridge, Massachusetts, where Charlie first taught at M.I.T. and then at Harvard. He was later appointed to a professorship in Princeton. They had two little girls, Melanie and Monica, but Monica died in an accident at the age of two. The family had gone for a holiday to New Hampshire, and took the cog railway to the top of Mount Washington as a treat for the children. On the downward journey, some points were wrongly set, probably by an inexperienced young summer employee; as a result the train left the rails and ran out of control downhill. The little girl was killed, and Charlie had an arm badly broken; the rest of the family were shaken but unhurt. They had two more children, a boy, Derek, and a girl, Rowena. Melanie graduated from Barnard College in Urban Studies; Derek has recently entered college, and Rowena is still in high school. When the younger children were 3 and 5, Gaby decided to study law, which in America means graduate study. After completing her three-year, full-time law course, she is now working for the State of New Jersey. She and Charlie have separated but remain on friendly terms.

I was awarded a knighthood in the 1968 New Year's Honours List. One might argue that these old-fashioned honours and titles are bad because they create barriers between people. However, in my case it brought at least the advantage that the official form of address, "Sir Rudolf", is easier on people who cannot spell or pronounce my surname. When Genia relayed the news by telephone to her sister in Leningrad, most of the time of the phone call was taken up with peals of laughter at the idea that Genia would now be "Lady Peierls".

The award was the occasion for a cheerful celebration in the department, at which I was presented with a decorative sword, with an inscription that ended ". . . from the Officers and Men at 12 Parks Road" (the address of the department).

Among the many letters I received I treasure one from the Department of Education and Science, the government department responsible for the universities. After congratulating me, it pointed out that on the occasion of the investiture at Buckingham Palace, I was entitled to claim second-class rail fare to London and back for myself and any members of my family attending the ceremony, and for myself also a day's subsistence.

14

"Security" Troubles

On a number of occasions I experienced difficulties with the problem of security clearance. Basically, the need for clearance comes from the desire of the government to keep communist sympathisers and other potentially disloyal people out of sensitive jobs. In occupations concerned with military secrets one appreciates the need for such measures and sympathises with the people charged with the "vetting". If we could fail to recognise the views and activities of Klaus Fuchs, a close personal friend, the task of the outside investigator must be hard indeed. But the problem of ensuring the loyalty of people entrusted with sensitive, confidential information is sometimes confused with a desire to keep "undesirables" from entering the country or any particular profession. This shows a failure to appreciate that the strength of a stable democracy rests on its citizens' understanding of the basic issues and their ability to reject simplistic extreme ideologies. Marxist or fascist ideas are not like an infectious disease that can be contracted by exposure to it. On the contrary, familiarity with them helps to give a firmer basis to one's own convictions, and makes one's arguments against such ideas stronger.

My first encounter with such problems was in 1951, when I applied for a U.S. visa to attend the Nuclear Physics Conference in Chicago. My application met with a long delay, and I heard informally that it was going to be refused. This was of course during the McCarthy era, when such refusals were very common. Chadwick, who had official contacts, told me that the reason for the delay was probably due to some statement in the files that I had been seen at a certain date in a place where I was not supposed to be (and where I certainly was not). The problem was solved by a coincidence: at approximately the same time, there was to be a meeting in Washington on the declassification of papers about atomic energy, to which I was to go as one of the British representatives. I thus had the status of "government official" and was entitled to a visa. Once in the United States, I was able to go to the Chicago conference.

Early in the following year I was to go to the Institute for Advanced Study in Princeton, and I thought naively that after having been granted a visa once, it would be easy to get another. However, there again was an inordinate delay, and I was getting ready to cancel my visit to Princeton when the visa came through at the last possible moment. I do not know what went on behind the scenes to get the visa for me.

Another disturbing episode occurred about 1953, when Oliphant had resigned from his chair in Birmingham to go to the new Australian National University in Canberra. A suggestion was made that the faculty board should invite Cecil Powell, the discoverer of the pi-meson and one of the outstanding physicists of the country, to succeed Oliphant. The dean of the faculty and I were encouraged to call on Powell and sound him out about the prospect. He was quite interested, and made only one major condition—that he should be able to bring his research group with him, which was exploiting the photographic emulsion technique he had developed. Their rather modest equipment was provided for by a government grant, and their need for space could be met, so it looked as if the proposal would be accepted. But then someone pointed out that Powell had rather left-wing views and was, possibly, a member of the Communist Party. This turned many of my colleagues against him, some on general principle, others because they feared that his presence as head of the department would result in the loss of government research contracts. I was shocked, because the work of the department had nothing to do with military secrets or with politically sensitive problems. I came close to resigning from the university, and I would have done so if I thought that political prejudice was mainly responsible for blocking the appointment. However, some members of the Faculty Board were opposed because they feared he would concentrate on the work of his own research group and not take the responsibility for the big machines in the department seriously enough. I disagreed (and indeed, when some years later Powell was one of the U.K. representatives on various committees at CERN, the European accelerator laboratory, he pulled his weight very well), but this was a substantive argument, on which reasonable people could hold different views. Powell did not get the appointment, and Philip Moon was appointed to the chair; he proved to be an excellent head of the department, but this did not diminish my concern with the behaviour of some of my colleagues.

The Oppenheimer case of 1954 was by far the most serious of these security troubles. I was only a distant spectator without direct involvement, but the affair was a great shock to me, as it was to many other scientists. Briefly, Oppenheimer had made many enemies, in-

322

cluding some in the Strategic Air Command, when he argued for more effort on defensive measures and for tactical nuclear weapons. He had upset Lewis Strauss, who was now the chairman of the Atomic Energy Commission, by making him look foolish in hearings before a congressional committee investigating the possibility of exporting radioactive substances. The General Advisory Committee of the AEC, of which Oppenheimer was chairman, had opposed a crash programme to build a hydrogen bomb. He was accused of disloyalty and his security clearance was withdrawn. When he appealed, a quasi-judicial board was set up to examine him. In three weeks of gruelling hearings, every facet of his activities was discussed, including some early indiscretions, which had long been known to the authorities.

One of many witnesses was Edward Teller, who was asked whether he thought Oppenheimer was a security risk. The question clearly meant whether he might be disloyal to the country, or might sympathise with a foreign government. Teller evidently could not assert anything of the kind, and said so in his testimony. However, he added, "In a great number of cases I have seen Dr. Oppenheimer act . . . in a way which for me was exceedingly hard to understand. I thoroughly disagreed with him in numerous issues, and his actions frankly appeared to me confused and complicated. To this extent I feel that I would like to see the vital interests of this country in hands which I understand better, and therefore trust more. In this very limited sense I would like to express a feeling that I would feel personally more secure if public matters would rest in other hands." (From *In the Matter of J. Robert Oppenheimer*, M.I.T. Press, 1971.)

The three-man board resolved by two votes to one to condemn Oppenheimer for lack of enthusiasm for the hydrogen bomb programme, but found no evidence of disloyalty. The AEC knew that any ruling against a scientist for his views on technical questions would cause concern among scientists. They therefore did not accept the findings of the board, but decided to bar Oppenheimer from access to classified information because of "grave defects of character". One member of the commission, the physicist Henry de Wolf Smyth, disagreed and wrote a minority report. In 1963, when the McCarthy era was an embarrassing memory, Oppenheimer was awarded, as a gesture of reconciliation, the Enrico Fermi Prize, a high-level award then conferred by the president of the United States on the advice of the AEC.

As a footnote to this story I might recall the remark of George Placzek, then a member of the Institute for Advanced Study. At the height of the crisis, a representative of the AEC came to offer Placzek a research contract on some problem within his field of interest. Placzek terminated the conversation by asking, "Who do you think I am?"

Then, in 1957, another irritating episode occurred. I was still a consultant to Harwell. I was not concerned with very weighty or very secret problems, but I still had clearance. Then, when my appointment as consultant came up for renewal, I received a letter saying that for reasons of administrative convenience I would no longer be able to see classified documents. There was something odd about the letter, and I enquired whether this was really a routine measure, or whether there was more behind it. In reply I was told that the same action was taken in all cases of senior consultants whose contracts were coming up for renewal. This was technically correct, because mine was the only contract due for renewal at the time. In fact, there had been a message from American security asking that I be given no more access to American secret documents. Eventually I was told about this, because there was to be a conference at Harwell with American scientists, and if I had turned up to attend, I would have been refused admission. Actually, I had no intention of going there.

I was not upset by the American ruling. One knew they were inclined to act on unsubstantiated reports, and after the Oppenheimer affair I felt I was in good company. I also had no regrets about seeing no more secret documents. But I did resent that the Harwell authorities had tried to deceive me on this matter. Presumably the message from America specified that I should not be told, but they could have insisted that they must tell me, as in the end they did. The incident showed that I did not have the full confidence of Harwell, and I resigned my consultancy. After my move to Oxford, when the proximity to Harwell led to frequent contacts, I reconsidered my position. By now all the people involved in the offending episode had left, and there seemed no point in keeping up resentment against an abstract body. So I became a consultant again, but no important secrets have come my way.

The inclination to see Reds under the bed can reach grotesque proportions, as I discovered in 1979, when a book, *The British Connection*, written by the journalist Richard Deacon, was about to be published by Hamish Hamilton, a very reputable publisher. The book dealt with the alleged activities of Russian revolutionary agents in Britain since 1889. It contained many unsubstantiated allegations against well-known people, including, for example, a completely unfounded slur on Lise Meitner, the well-known nuclear physicist. But nearly all the individuals mentioned were no longer alive, so it was safe to make careless remarks about them, since in English law there is no libel against dead people. But for some reason the author thought I was dead, too, and made some extremely damning and quite unjustified statements about me. These statements were mentioned in a prepublication review in a student magazine, and some of my shocked colleagues brought them to my notice. The review had been published before the book, because the book had been delayed. Another person about whom unpleasant things were said in the book complained to the publisher and the pages concerning him were replaced. Because of this I was able to take legal action very early, and a writ was served on the publishers and the author a few days after publication. The matter was settled out of court very promptly; the distribution of the book was stopped at once, so that the few copies that were sold are now collector's items. I received a "substantial sum" by way of damages. The speed of action was impressive: the settlement was announced in the High Court just thirteen days after I first consulted my solicitors. The publishers could have reissued the book in amended form, but they decided to abandon it.

News of my legal action leaked out, and I was approached by many reporters. Usually one does not comment in public when legal action is pending, but when a journalist asked for my reaction to the statement that I was dead, I could not resist the temptation to say, "It is about as accurate as the rest of the book." My favourite comment on the episode was made by Paul Foot in the *New Statesman* (vol. 98 [1979], p. 129): "Something really must be done to protect ordinary working journalists who want to write books about espionage, but who can't possibly have access to obscure reference works such as *Who's Who*, *Burke's Knightage*, or the telephone directory."

15

Retirement

Reaching the Limit

In 1974 I reached the age of 67, which in Oxford (as in many other universities) is the age of compulsory retirement. When I was younger I was sceptical about a rigid retiring age. There are wide variations in the effect of age on people, and logically each person ought to retire at the time when he is becoming less efficient than his likely successor. But I began to realise that the individual judgments necessary to make such decisions would be very hard to arrive at in the academic world. Some institutions have provision for continuing an appointment for a few years beyond normal retiring age, but usually this has to be done at rather short notice and therefore makes it impossible for the individual to plan his life. By the time my own retirement approached I regarded the fixed age as sensible.

My departure was marked by a symposium organised by Ian Aitchison and Jack Paton on behalf of the department, and attended by some two hundred present and former members of the Oxford and Birmingham departments, as well as old friends like Hans Bethe and Viki Weisskopf. There were lectures on a number of topics that had interested me, in part historical, in part reporting recent progress. The spirit was very lighthearted compared to ordinary conferences, and the conference dinner was an occasion of great warmth and no sentimentality.

A photograph was taken after one of the sessions, containing some 150 faces (not all the participants were present), and later the organisers had trouble identifying the people in the photograph, particularly those of early vintage. I sat down with the photo, and was gratified to find that I could recognize all but a few of them. The exceptions were either temporary visitors to Oxford, who had joined the meeting, or people who had acquired beards or a similar disguise since I had last seen them. Eventually the gaps were filled and the published photograph now has a complete set of names attached.

I felt sure that the department would continue to prosper under its new head, Roger Elliott, and so it did. One knows that time seems to pass more quickly as one gets older—probably because one's internal clock is slowing down—but it takes an effort to realise that by now he has been running the department for almost as long as I did! Oxford has an unwritten law that on retiring you do not stay in the same department. The thought behind this rule is evidently that you should not get in your successor's hair. My relations with Elliott were such that my continued presence in the department probably would not have caused any embarrassment, and he indeed invited me to stay, but I felt that this was a sensible rule and worth observing. I was invited to join the Nuclear Physics Laboratory, in which by now I feel quite at home. It is now next door to Theoretical Physics, so that I can remain on speaking terms with the theoreticians.

I also remain a member of New College, which elected me an honorary fellow. I still have all the privileges I had before, except I no longer have a seat on the governing body or on college committees. This is hardly a deprivation—few people like to sit on committees, and they should never be allowed to! The college has the tradition that every retiring fellow has his portrait drawn, unless he is distinguished enough to be painted in oil. When I was asked to choose the artist, I enquired if a cartoon was acceptable, and hearing that it was, I approached "Marc", the well-known journalist and cartoonist Mark Boxer, whose work I greatly admire. He accepted the commission, and an amusing caricature now hangs among the other portraits and adorns the cover of the report of the retirement symposium. We also wanted to say good-bye to many other people with whom we had been associated in the university, the college, and otherwise, and we arranged a party in New College for some of them. The invitations called it our "Coming-out Party", which some found frivolous.

I knew I would miss two things after retiring: one was the contact with students, the other was having the services of a secretary. The latter has been mitigated by my receiving, as Genia's present for my seventy-fifth birthday, a word processor, on which in fact I am writing this book. I find this is equivalent to about half a secretary, but, alas, it does not do the filing. These deprivations, however, are balanced by the absence of regular duties, and therefore the freedom to travel when and where we choose, or when and where we are invited. We were now free to satisfy our desire to travel.

Footloose. One Foot in Seattle

A good way for me to implement the Oxford injunction to keep out of my successor's hair was to disappear from Oxford for the following academic year. The University of Washington offered me a part-time professorship, for six months in the year. I could hold this position for three years, until I reached their retiring age, which is 70.

I also was invited to spend three months at the University of Sydney, where my former student, Stuart Butler, was professor of theoretical physics. At the termination of my Oxford professorship (to be honest, two weeks before—it was vacation), we set out for Australia. We decided we could stop in four places on the way, and after much thought settled on Isfahan, Bangkok, Hong Kong, and Bali. Isfahan is a most beautiful city, which today would be rather difficult to visit. We thought we would simply be tourists there. But it turned out there was a new university, and one of the lecturers was an Englishman who had gone there for a year's exchange, had married a local girl, and stayed. He acted as a guide for us, and I ended up giving a lecture at the university. Although this was some time before the revolution in Iran, we were already aware of the tensions. One could feel the hatred of the mullahs and of the traders in the bazaar for everything foreign, particularly for the many Americans with scantily clad women and men in shorts. One heard many rumours about corruption in high places and in the shah's family. But the universities were generously supported, and there were plans to start an Open University on the British model.

In Bangkok we were just tourists, since my friend Franz Jacobsohn, who lived there, had retired some years before. In Hong Kong I had some academic connections, and I lectured both in the University of Hong Kong and in the Chinese University, and we were lavishly entertained by both. Bali was enchanting and still relatively unspoilt. We liked Balinese music, which is very different from Western music but fairly easy to understand, or at least to enjoy. With its beautiful landscape, the cheerful and colourful people, and the intricate carvings on the temples, houses, and even on the signposts, Bali was the highlight of our journey.

The Theoretical Physics Department of the University of Sydney had a lively and friendly atmosphere. It was somewhat under strength, as several excellent members had recently left. Stuart Butler was much involved in university administration. The physics school was the creation of Harry Messel, an energetic physicist with a talent for publicity and for raising funds. We did not see much of him, as he spent much time in the tropical north where he and his group were fitting radio transmitters to crocodiles to track their movements. We rented the porter's lodge of the university's Catholic college (most colleges are denominational) and became friendly with the rector, a great connoisseur of opera and Australian wines, which we found surprisingly good.

I gave some lectures at Canberra, a city populated almost entirely by civil servants and academics. We also made an excursion to Melbourne, where Butler's pupil Bruce McKellar had built up an impressive research group, and to Adelaide.

In Adelaide we had the pleasure of spending a weekend with Oliphant, who was then governor of South Australia. The post of governor is usually held by retired generals or admirals, who are experienced in administration but often tend to be somewhat pompous. It apparently was a welcome change to have a scientist in this job, particularly one who, like Oliphant, was very direct and outspoken. He was very popular with his fellow countrymen, who dislike pomposity. In life at his residence, Government House, strict protocol was of course unavoidable. Each day a duplicated sheet would carry the day's programme, explaining who was to be where and in what attire. When one evening we were asked to be downstairs at 6 o'clock and we were on our way down the stairs at 5:58, we met an aide coming up to make sure we remembered. Genia and I had a joint sitting-room; Genia had a bedroom, bathroom, and dressing room, whereas I had only a bedroom and bathroom. Lest I felt deprived by this, the brass plate on the door stated that Prince Philip had stayed there recently.

Our excursion to the Great Barrier Reef was not motivated by any physics. We were fortunate in being there during a full moon, and during the season when the turtles were laying eggs, so we could watch them at night time—an exciting experience. From Sydney, we went on to Seattle with stops in Tahiti and Hawaii, where we just missed an eruption of the big volcano.

Six months in Seattle, in the by now familiar surroundings and among many friends, were followed by three weeks in Mexico City, where our friends, the Mondragóns, were our hosts. Since our last visit the University of Mexico had grown, but the exciting architecture of the original buildings had become diluted by cheaper unimaginative additions. The city had also grown, and problems of pollution and traffic congestion were worse than ever. But it was still an exciting place with its continuous tradition from the ancient to the modern. The university's Physics Department contained many theoreticians working on diverse interesting problems, and I had profitable discussions with many of them, including Gastón García, who had recently completed the Oxford D.Phil. under my supervision. We wrote a joint paper on his thesis subject.

The following academic year, I went to Leiden for four months as Lorentz Professor, a visiting professorship named after the great theoretician H. A. Lorentz. The Kamerlingh Onnes Laboratory in Leiden is an old and famous centre for low-temperature physics, and the associated Institute for Theoretical Physics has a distinguished tradition. It is now led by Peter Mazur, a Belgian whose work is in statistical mechanics, and with whom I found much common ground.

However, our stay in Leiden had its distressing side. C. J. Gorter, an outstanding experimental physicist who had also contributed to notable theoretical work, was suffering from Alzheimer's disease, the progressive loss of memory. During our time in Leiden we watched his condition deteriorate; initially he appeared to enjoy our company, but at the end he was embarrassed when he could not remember what was expected of him when a dish of food was put before him. Genia tried to help his wife, who went through an incredibly hard time, with compassion and advice. He became very miserable and soon had to be taken to a mental home; we could feel only relief when some years later we heard of his death.

Dutch academic life is very pleasant but has its share of red tape. My appointment as Lorentz Professor needed the approval of the Queen of the Netherlands. I took up my duties on 1 October, and the Queen's letter approving my appointment was signed on 15 October, which seems reasonable. It was received by the university in mid-November and was considered by the relevant committee, which had to fix my stipend, in mid-December. Because by this time it was vacation, the news was not published until mid-January. This confused our friends, who knew I was expected to leave at the end of January, and thought this was a new appointment. (But I did receive my salary during this time.) Another amusing aspect of their procedures arose through my contributions to the state pension fund. I was expected to get my contributions back when I left, but this turned out to be impossible because I had been over pensionable age when I served; instead, I was entitled to a pension, though a very modest one, based on my four months of service. I now receive it regularly, but each month I must prove that I am still alive. I do this once each month by cutting the masthead off a local newspaper which has the date printed on it, putting my signature on it, and mailing it to the Netherlands. One other former Lorentz Professor enjoys the same treatment, but now the regulations have been changed.

After Leiden we made another brief visit to Mexico City, and then went back to Seattle. Ron Geballe had been promoted to higher duties in the university administration, and was succeeded as chairman by Ernest Henley, a distinguished theoretician. He and his wife became our close friends, and by now he, too, has moved up to become a dean. As a regular member of the faculty, I participated in the discussions about the choice of the next chairman, David Bodansky, a nuclear experimentalist.

That year there was an innovation in my teaching. Besides giving graduate lectures on a technical subject, namely solid-state theory, I conducted a seminar on problems of disarmament, based largely on my experience of the Pugwash conferences. The attendance was not large (as is usual with courses that do not directly contribute to the students' professional qualifications) but the students were keen, and it was an interesting and satisfying experience.

For the first three months of 1977 I was a visiting professor at U.C.L.A, the Los Angeles campus of the University of California, where we were looked after hospitably by our old friend Nina Byers, who is a professor there. I gave a course of lectures to graduate students and generally tried to make myself useful. During our stay there, we made a trip to Cornell University in Ithaca, New York, where a series of lectures in honour of Hans Bethe had been instituted, and I was to give the first set of Bethe lectures, in the Bethe Auditorium, with Hans Bethe sitting in the front row. This was a time of record frost and blizzards in the eastern half of the United States; all the waterfalls around Ithaca were frozen solid. Coming from the balmy California weather, this was a traumatic experience and it was a miracle that our planes got us there without a hitch.

For the last few weeks of our stay in Los Angeles we were joined by Genia's sister, Nina. She had visited us in England several times because it was becoming easier, at least for pensioners, to obtain passports for foreign travel, if they had an invitation from relatives. (Sometimes the British visa took more time and more trouble than the Soviet passport.) After Gaby and Ronnie had shown her the sights of the New York area, she flew to Los Angeles, and we later drove together up the Pacific Coast to Seattle.

Here I repeated the disarmament seminar, and also started a new kind of lecture course. I called it "Surprises in Theoretical Physics". It contained examples where an apparently obvious conclusion turned out to be invalid, or an approximation that seemed unreasonable was in fact justified, and other similar surprises. I repeated these lectures later in other places, and as they were popular with the audiences, turned them into a book (*Surprises in Theoretical Physics*, Princeton University Press, 1979).

That summer we had a remarkable escape from a potential disaster. Returning from an outing into the mountains, we were driving along a reasonably fast road, with only one lane each way, when going round a bend I was confronted by two cars abreast. My reaction was rather slow; I braked with all my force (though I was not aware of doing so) but did nothing else. The offending car pulled over to the verge on my right and, with sand and gravel flying, got past without touching us. The whole incident was over before we had time to become afraid, but I realised afterwards that it was my slow reaction that had saved us. If I had been faster I would have pulled on to the verge myself and there would have been a head-on collision, with each car doing 50 m.p.h.

Bird of Passage Again

In 1977 I reached the retiring age for the University of Washington, and acquired the title of Emeritus Professor. I already held that title in Oxford, but in Seattle it brings a real benefit: I am now allowed to park a car anywhere on the university campus free of charge. This second retirement ended the regular long visits to Seattle, and our nomadic life became even more erratic. It would be tedious to recount all these journeys in order, and a selection will have to do.

We spent two long periods in Orsay, the science faculty of one of the many universities of Paris, and in Saclay, the French atomic energy laboratory. Ever since my school days I felt incapable of speaking French properly, though I could understand and write it reasonably well. Now, after some prolonged stays in France, I began to lose my inhibition, and occasionally managed to address audiences in French. In Orsay I was attached to the Nuclear Physics Institute, whose theoretical department was chaired by Nicole Vinh Mau, who as Mlle. Gilbert had been one of our students in Birmingham. Later her husband, a former Vietnamese, succeeded her as chairman. In Saclay, too, we were among old friends, including Cyrano De Dominicis, another Birmingham Ph.D. Although it belonged to the atomic energy organization, the department to which I was attached was concerned entirely with academic research, and in fact was outside the fence surrounding the secret work. We had to show our passes to a guard only to get to the canteen for lunch. As one might expect in France, the quality of the food was enough to make up for the slightly inconvenient access and the rather crowded and noisy conditions in the mess hall. Our second visit to Saclay/Orsay coincided with another visit from Nina, and we were happy to be able to take her with us and show here something of France.

We visited Pisa several times, where our host was our friend Luigi Radicati. We had been there earlier, in the days when one stayed and ate, as well as worked, in the beautiful old building of the Scuola Normale. Breakfast was served in bed by an old-style butler, and the professors took their meals in a small and elegant dining room. Italian food and drink being what it is, there was on most days at least one professor who asked only for rice, and by way of explanation said "fegato", his liver was giving trouble. Now the school has grown and all the space is needed for academic purposes, and visitors stay in a modern hostel and eat in a canteen by the school. Like the French Ecole Normale, the school was founded by Napoleon, and it selects the ablest students of the country, with their maintenance and other expenses taken care of. Enrico Fermi was a student there, and the staff always has hopes of finding a second Fermi among the students.

During one of these visits we were invited to the wedding of Radicati's son, Luca, in Palermo, and we decided to go, as he was one of our "grandsons by proxy", born when his parents were in Birmingham. We attended the wedding in a chapel in the old city, which was surrounded by streets with traffic so dense that the service had to be delayed while the minister extricated himself from a traffic jam. The reception, held in the large and beautiful flat of the bride's parents, all decorated in the style of Art Nouveau (dating from a time when it was really new), was a memorable experience.

Several trips to Copenhagen were nostalgic returns to a place with many memories. The head of the institute was now Aage Bohr, the son of Niels, whose contributions to the theory of the nucleus, together with his colleague Ben Mottelson, have been deservedly recognised by a Nobel Prize. I wonder what his father would say about this example of inheritance of genius? I was invited to edit the nuclear physics volume of Niels Bohr's collected works, and my later visits were devoted entirely to this task. It was a great opportunity to study his writings and correspondence. I was already familiar with the great care he devoted to each step in his arguments, and to marshalling the experimental data in support of his pictures, but it was interesting to trace all this in his notes and letters as well as in his published works. Translating his Danish letters into understandable English while preserving his personal style was a difficult task for me, and I needed much help from the series editor, Erik Rüdinger, and others.

In 1980 we were incensed to hear that a film, "A Man Called Intrepid", was to be shown in Copenhagen. This was based on a rather unreliable book about intelligence during the Second World War, and sensationalised a story that was treated more briefly in the book about Niels Bohr and atomic energy. In the film Bohr is an absent-minded scientist who does not know what goes on in the world, and does not appreciate the significance of his own research. He is shown working, during the war, in a laboratory in Norway that is guarded by German military police. In fact, of course, he had not been to Norway during the war and had kept aloof from the Germans during the occupation; he had thought more deeply than anyone about the future effects of nuclear weapons on international relations. The appearance of this film in Copenhagen, of all places, was an outrage.

In Danish law the defamation of a dead person can be treated as libel, but for some reason nothing was being done, except that the more intellectual newspapers denounced the film. Genia and I, in the company of a well-known Danish scientist, called on the cinema manager and suggested he might display a notice explaining that this film was for entertainment only, and not a documentary; but, after considering the suggestion, he refused. So for three days Genia stood outside the cinema with a placard protesting against the film. Many passers-by stopped to discuss the matter. Some said it did not matter, everyone knew that the facts were wrong, but Genia pointed out that the young people would not know, and that some of the allegations would stick. Some young people said, "Thank you. Now, when we see something is wrong, we shall do something about it." Her stand attracted a good deal of publicity, including full second-page coverage of the most popular tabloid. I later had occasion to see what effect this kind of film can have. After it was shown on TV in England I talked to an historian, who happened to have seen it. When I mentioned Bohr, he said, "Oh yes, the man who worked for the Germans"; he refused to believe my explanation of the facts.

Our three-month stay in Brazil in 1980 was memorable. It was our first acquaintance with South America and with the lively atmosphere in the Physics Institute of the University of São Paulo headed by H. M. Nussenzveig, another former visitor to Birmingham. But it was also during this time that Genia became seriously ill. Our friend Guido Beck was about to go on a long journey, and wanted to show us Rio, so we spent three stiflingly hot days there, and we saw as much of Rio as most visitors see in a much longer time. At the end Genia felt unwell, and it turned out she had a periodic virus infection, which would recur every Monday for six weeks. She had all the complications imaginable. She did not see as much of Brazil as she had wanted, but she got a good view of their well-organised medical services.

Brazilian doctors still make house calls, unlike their colleagues in the United States. When Genia fell ill in Rio, a doctor appeared in twenty minutes. Tests are done in private laboratories, and a nurse or technician sent by them will keep the appointment to the minute. All this has to be paid for, and the doctors are often called the "White Mafia". Poor patients depend on voluntary hospitals or on the local pharmacist, who is a most useful person: if you are not in hospital, he will come to give you injections prescribed by the doctor. He has a vast stock of medicines from all countries, and will sell them all, including the ones marked "By prescription only". Genia spent a few days in hospital, and so did I, since a close relative of the patient is expected to stay there as well—a custom originating from Portugal. Genia had time to read books and newspapers to get an understanding of Brazilian culture and politics. She recovered in time for us to spend a week seeing some of the attractive old towns, and she was left with no permanent disability, except for some loss of balance.

In 1981 I was invited to spend three weeks in Japan, and we made this part of a trip around the world. In March of that year was the date of our golden wedding anniversary, and we timed our itinerary so as to be in Los Angeles at that date, where the March weather would be least likely to interfere with the arrival and departure of planes. We invited our children and grandchildren, so there was a family gathering of sixteen people. It was easy to provide for all this travel: I had recently been awarded the Enrico Fermi Medal, a prestigious award by the U.S. Department of Energy for work related to atomic energy, which, besides the honour, carries a substantial amount of money. Nina Byers had made all the reservations for us, and the anniversary was celebrated in her garden; she was made an honorary member of the family for the occasion.

The invitation to Japan came from the Nishina Memorial Foundation, set up in the memory of Y. Nishina, a great theoretical physicist with close associations with Copenhagen. The president of the foundation was Ryogo Kubo, whom we had met before, and who is an eminent authority on statistical mechanics. The secretary was Mrs. Sumi Yokoyama, a friend of a friend of ours, who looked after us most hospitably; we spent a weekend in her country house and met one of Nishina's sons and his family. After Nishina's death Sumi had looked after his two sons, practically adopting them. I lectured in a number of universities, and the itinerary extended from Hiroshima in the south to Sendai in the north. We moved north with the cherry blossom, traditionally a time for merrymaking. Only in Sendai we were too early for the blossom.

We expected that after the tightly scheduled journey through Japan we would be very tired, and had arranged to make a stop on the way back home. A convenient point on the route was Delhi, but as it would be too hot there at the time, we decided to spend a few days in Nepal and Kashmir. As it turned out, the arrangements in Japan had been so smooth that we were not in the least tired, but we kept to our plan. Nepal was unexpectedly exciting. Kathmandu and its surroundings are full of the most intricate and delicate carvings; any old house, any palace, and any of the many Hindu and Buddhist temples is a delight to see. There was so much to see that after four days we were exhausted and thankful for the restful stay on a houseboat in Srinagar that followed.

A journey to Australia in 1982 was exceptional in that it was not motivated by either physics or Pugwash. On our previous visit we had made the acquaintance of a very interesting couple, Myer Rosenblum, a solicitor, and his wife, Lyla. Rosey, as he is called by everyone, had been an athlete in his youth, and was a discus thrower in the Olympics; he still coaches the sport. He also played rugby and still plays tennis at an age of over 70. In addition, he is very musical: he plays the piano and the bassoon at a professional standard, and he knows details of practically every opera. For some years he ran an agency that brought distinguished musicians to Australia. He has read widely, and his shelves contain much of the world's literature—Genia found that he had even read the most obscure Russian writers, albeit in translation. Though he had no scientific education, he is very interested in the sciences and scientists and always has interesting questions for me. Lyla is also an excellent musician and an outstanding cook. On their walls are plates decorated by Picasso, acquired before Picasso's fame made such items prohibitively expensive. Rosey is indeed a modern Renaissance man.

The Rosenblums visited Oxford a few times, and on one of these occasions invited us to come and stay with them in Sydney—hence, our 1982 trip to Australia. Their house is in a wonderful location by the Sydney "harbour", which is really not a port but a large and winding bay of great beauty. I did call at the university to see old friends, and even gave a talk, but this was not the object of the trip. We also spent an evening with Stuart Butler, now the Director of the Australian Atomic Energy Research Laboratory, and his wife. He died unexpectedly shortly afterwards.

In Sydney we had a fascinating encounter. We met an elderly lady,

Mrs. Ilse Rosenthal-Schneider, who had been a student in Berlin, starting before the First World War. She had studied under Einstein, Planck, and Lise Meitner, her subjects being physics and philosophy. It turned out that, if the thesis was in part philosophical, one could not get a Ph.D. without having passed in Greek. She had never studied Greek, and it supposedly took three years to learn it. Einstein's advice was to submit the thesis to another university, but she persisted and passed the exam in Greek in six months. Her thesis examiner was Max von Laue, and she kept in correspondence with Einstein. She has recently published a book about this correspondence (*Reality and Scientific Truth*, Wayne State University Press, 1980). She now lives alone, and is occasionally visited by her grandchildren. Her recollections of her studies are as clear as if they had taken place yesterday.

In 1982 I spent a month in Munich in the Physics Department of the Technical University. This was the first time since the war that I went back to Germany for more than a few days. It had taken me a long time to get over the trauma of the Nazi period in my attitude to Germany and Germans. I understood all along, of course, that there were many decent people in Germany, and that most of the people I met later had not yet been born or were children at the time of Hitler. When Germans visited England, I always assumed they were decent people unless there was some reason to think otherwise. But emotionally the thought of going to Germany remained uncomfortable for a long time. I did go back for some short visits. The first was in 1963 to receive the Max Planck Medal, an award given to theoretical physicists. It was given to several émigrés, and although I like to think that the award was based mainly on merit, it is probable that the wish to make amends for the past was also present. The presentation ceremony took place at a conference in Hamburg. The speaker was Heisenberg, and in his citation he summarised my research work, including in it one paper by my son, Ronnie. I was amused and pleased by this slip.

I went to Göttingen in 1966 for Hund's seventieth birthday, as I already mentioned, and to a panel discussion about the future of physics in Bonn in 1976, where I encountered Hund again. By now I was quite relaxed about present-day Germany and intrigued by returning to Munich after more than fifty years.

Genia had expected to accompany me, but Nina had, once again, been able to accept our invitation to come to Oxford. She had been ailing for some time. When she arrived she had lost much weight and was very depressed. Genia gave her all possible care, but the doctors could not do much, and the recovery progress was very slow. Eventually her depression lifted, and she seemed better, but her physical condition deteriorated, and she had to be taken to hospital. I left for Munich with a heavy heart. Five days later Nina died. She was a remarkable person, with a phenomenal knowledge and memory, and always willing to go to trouble for others. She had a hard life, and it was some slight consolation that her last days were spent in the comfort of an English hospital, and without much suffering.

I came back for a few days. I now regretted having committed myself to be in Munich—perhaps I should have cancelled the visit even then. By some strange form of inertia I find it very difficult to go back on a promise to do something, or to go somewhere, even if the circumstances have changed.

These events marred my stay in Munich, but I found the research group congenial and made new friends. The city had of course changed greatly, but the historic buildings and the museums had survived or had been restored. The house in which I had been a lodger in 1927 had disappeared, but the street was recognisable. The general appearance of most streets had become more international, and the very efficient modern transport system looked the same as anywhere else. The baker even sold rolls of a shape known in my time only in Berlin, and they were known by their Berlin-dialect name. But the local patriotism, by which people think of themselves first as Bavarians and less directly as Germans, has persisted.

In 1983 Los Alamos celebrated its fortieth anniversary with a reunion. This was, like a school reunion, a wonderful occasion to meet old friends, to marvel at the number who were still alive, and to note that others had aged so much more than yourself (while they, no doubt, made the same observation in reverse). Appreciating the age level of those present, the organisers had given us name badges with half-inch high lettering. A number of people were in wheelchairs or on crutches, but in almost all cases this was due not to age but to recent accidents. The conference programme was concerned with current advances in science, and the role of the laboratory in the development of nuclear weapons did not figure on the programme. However, the participants were reminded of it in a brilliant address by Rabi entitled "We Meant So Well", and in an after-dinner speech by Viki Weisskopf on the same theme. Both got standing ovations.

I also attended a number of Pugwash conferences, including a large quinquennial one in Warsaw in 1982, at the time of martial law in Poland. Some people felt that under the circumstances the conference should not be held, but it was decided to go on with it, provided the normal functioning of the conference was not interfered with. To cancel it would have endangered the neutrality that is a very essential ingredient of Pugwash. The functioning of the conference was indeed not affected by the situation in Poland. Mr. Rakowsky, the deputy prime minister, not only gave an address of welcome at the opening session, but returned for a meeting of several hours to answer questions. We—the participants from the West—were not convinced by his explanations, but people were free to ask any questions, however critical, and the debate was on a civilised level.

For some time Genia and I had realised that at our age we could not foresee how long we would be able to drive. Without a car, life in our house on Boar's Hill would be very inconvenient, and if we waited until we could no longer drive, our children and our friends would have to move us. In 1981 we saw a flat in Oxford that we liked, and we decided to do the sensible thing and move ourselves. We are now within walking distance of the laboratories and the shops, and while we still enjoy the use of a car, we can contemplate with equanimity the possibility of having to give it up.

Epilogue

According to a story circulating in the thirties, Niels Bohr once dictated a passage to Dirac, and at one point said, "Now I don't know how to finish this sentence." Dirac, according to the story, put his pen down and said, "I was taught at school that you should never start a sentence without knowing its end." I freely admit that I started this book without knowing clearly how I would end it. The proper epilogue of a biography is an epitaph, but in the case of an autobiography this does not seem feasible. Some authors end their memoirs by giving the reader the benefit of the wisdom distilled from their long experience, their moral precepts, and their view of the future.

I have lived through times containing so many surprises that most predictions were proved wrong. I see no reason why the future should not be like that. According to one of my favourite definitions, an optimist is a person who believes the future is uncertain, and in that sense I am a firm optimist. (An alternative Russian definition seems to me less appropriate: an optimist is one who says things are so bad now, they could not possibly get any worse.)

As to moral precepts, I do not believe I could validly express the lessons of my experience in a few simple rules. If there are any lessons to be learned, the reader will have to pick them up from my narrative.

One lesson I learned is that in life, as in research, the hardest thing is to ask the right questions, rather than finding the right answers. Any opportunities I missed—and I had my share of these—resulted from failure to see the questions to ask.

There is a useful categorisation of people, which Genia devised originally for children, but which is applicable generally. She distinguishes "golfers" and "tennis players". The golfer drives his ball without depending on any external stimulus. The tennis player's game is to respond to the ball that comes at him; without capable opponents his game will suffer. In these terms I am, as a physicist, a typical tennis player. Some of my best work was provoked by other people's attempts that seemed to me wrong or misleading. Outside of physics I am also better in reacting to situations than creating them. I am not apt to start revolutions in physics or elsewhere, but I am quite prepared to work hard to support a revolution if it seems to me necessary, or to counter it if I think it wrong.

340

I find any problem within my competence with which I am confronted challenging and enjoy the effort of solving it. It must be a problem I can recognise as useful, but not necessarily one I would have selected spontaneously. On the whole this makes life pleasant. I do not hanker after the unattainable, and the reader of my story will know that I do not carry any chips on my shoulder.

In a long life, already well beyond the biblical ration of three-score years and ten, I have seen many changes in life and in the world. Our fathers' generation took it for granted that changes would all be improvements, that progress must lead to a better quality of life. We have learnt to question this; we believe today that progress provides opportunities for improvement, but also opportunities for disaster and for new kinds of cruelty and suffering. The world will not become a better place unless we try hard to make it so. I hope I have not only added a few small bricks to the growing edifice of science, but also contributed a little to the fight against its misuse.

Brief Chronology

1907   Author born in Oberschöneweide, near Berlin
1916-25 Gymnasium (Hindenburg-Schule, later Humboldt-Schule, Oberschöneweide)
1925-26 Berlin University
1926-28 Munich University
1928-29 Leipzig University
1929-32 Eidgenössische Technische Hochschule (E.T.H.), Zurich
1929   Dr.phil. (Leipzig)
1930   Odessa Conference
1931   Visiting Lecturer, Leningrad; marriage
1932-33 Rockefeller Travelling Fellowship, Rome and Cambridge
1933-35 Grant at Manchester University
1935-37 Research at Mond Laboratory, Cambridge University
1937-63 Professor at Birmingham University
1940   Frisch-Peierls Memorandum
1940-43 Atomic-energy work for M.A.U.D. Committee and Tube Alloys
1943-45 Work for Manhattan District, New York and Los Alamos
1952   Term at Institute for Advanced Study, Princeton, New Jersey
1959   Semester at Columbia University
1960   First attendance at Pugwash Conference
1963-74 Wykeham Professor, Oxford University; Fellow of New College
1967   Battelle Professor, University of Washington, Seattle
1974   Retirement
1975-77 Half-time professor at University of Washington

Index

Library of Congress Cataloging in Publication Data

Peierls, Rudolf Ernst, Sir, 1907-
Bird of passage.

Includes index.
1. Peierls, Rudolf Ernst, Sir, 1907- .
2. Physicists—Great Britain—Biography. I. Title.
QC16.P375A32 1985   530'.092'4 [B]   85-42697
ISBN 0-691-08390-8